"WE TALKED MOSTLY IN THE EARLY HOURS OF THE MORNING. JOHNSON SLEPT POORLY THESE DAYS, WAKING UP AT 5:30. TERRIFIED AT LYING ALONE IN THE DARK, HE CAME INTO MY ROOM TO TALK. GRADUALLY, A CURIOUS RITUAL DEVELOPED. I WOULD WAKEN AT FIVE AND GET DRESSED. HALF AN HOUR LATER JOHNSON WOULD KNOCK AT MY DOOR, DRESSED IN HIS ROBE AND PAJAMAS. AS I SAT IN A CHAIR BY THE WINDOW, HE CLIMBED INTO THE BED, PULLING THE SHEETS UP TO HIS NECK, LOOKING LIKE A COLD AND FRIGHTENED CHILD. IN THOSE DAWN TALKS, I SAW HIM AS PERHAPS FEW OTHERS, EXCEPT HIS WIFE AND CLOSE FRIENDS, HAD SEEN HIM: CRUMPLED, RAGGED AND DEFENSELESS. . . ."

—from *Lyndon Johnson &
The American Dream*

For a sampling of the extraordinary praise this remarkable book has received from reviewers across the nation, please turn the page.

"BRILLIANT . . . FASCINATING . . .
Kearns has made Lyndon Johnson so whole,
so understandable that the impact of the book
is difficult to describe. It might have been
called 'The Tragedy of Lyndon Johnson,'
for he comes to seem nothing so much as a
figure out of Greek tragedy."
—HOUSTON CHRONICLE

"A FINE AND SHREWD BOOK . . .
EXTRAORDINARY . . . POIGNANT . . .
THE BEST WE HAVE TO DATE!"
—THE BOSTON GLOBE

*An extraordinary portrait of a generous,
devious, complex, and profoundly manipulative
man . . . Kearns became the custodian not
only of LBJ's political lore but of his
memories, hopes, and nightmares. . . . We
have it all laid out for us in this wrenchingly
intimate analysis of a man whose virtues,
like his faults, were on a giant scale.*
—COSMOPOLITAN

"A REMARKABLE BOOK . . .
ILLUMINATING . . . RARE . . .
FASCINATING . . . A BRAVURA
PORTRAIT OF LBJ!"
—SAN FRANCISCO EXAMINER

"SUPERB!"—KINGS FEATURES SYNDICATE

"COMPELLING!"
—THE NATIONAL OBSERVER

"A FASCINATING, IMPORTANT AND UNPRECEDENTED ACCOUNT OF A PRESIDENCY!"—THE MILWAUKEE JOURNAL

"Johnson's every word and deed is measured in an attempt to understand one of the most powerful yet tragic of American Presidents."
—CHICAGO TRIBUNE

"A GRAND AND FASCINATING PORTRAIT OF A MOST COMPLICATED, HAUNTED, AND HERE APPEALING MAN."—THE VILLAGE VOICE

"AN EXCEPTIONALLY VALUABLE NEW BOOK . . . remarkable insights . . . without question the finest study available on Lyndon Johnson, the man and the politician."—THE COLUMBIA STATE

"BRILLIANT AND ENGROSSING . . . Doris Kearns has written a book which everyone should want to read."
—LOUISVILLE COURIER-JOURNAL & TIMES

"Huge both in scope and size . . . a sensitive rich portrait of LBJ. . . . She pulled no punches!"—ARIZONA REPUBLIC

"TOPNOTCH!"—THE HARTFORD COURANT

Big Bestsellers from SIGNET

☐ **THIS IS THE HOUSE by Deborah Hill.**
(#J7610—$1.95)

☐ **THE DEMON by Hubert Selby, Jr.**
(#J7611—$1.95)

☐ **LORD RIVINGTON'S LADY by Eileen Jackson.**
(#W7612—$1.50)

☐ **ROGUE'S MISTRESS by Constance Gluyas.**
(#J7533—$1.95)

☐ **SAVAGE EDEN by Constance Gluyas.**
(#J7171—$1.95)

☐ **LOVE SONG by Adam Kennedy.**
(#E7535—$1.75)

☐ **THE DREAM'S ON ME by Dotson Rader.**
(#E7536—$1.75)

☐ **BLACK WORK by Macdowell Fredericks.**
(#E7538—$1.75)

☐ **SINATRA by Earl Wilson.** (#E7487—$2.25)

☐ **SUMMER STATION by Maud Lang.**
(#E7489—$1.75)

☐ **THE WATSONS by Jane Austen and John Coates.**
(#J7522—$1.95)

☐ **SANDITON by Jane Austen and Another Lady.**
(#J6945—$1.95)

☐ **THE FIRES OF GLENLOCHY by Constance Heaven.**
(#E7452—$1.75)

☐ **A PLACE OF STONES by Constance Heaven.**
(#W7046—$1.50)

☐ **KINFLICKS by Lisa Alther.** (#E7390—$2.25)

☐ **THE KILLING GIFT by Bari Wood.**
(#J7350—$1.95)

THE NEW AMERICAN LIBRARY, INC.,
P.O. Box 999, Bergenfield, New Jersey 07621

Please send me the SIGNET BOOKS I have checked above.
I am enclosing $_____(check or money order—no
currency or C.O.D.'s). Please include the list price plus 35¢ a
copy to cover handling and mailing costs. (Prices and numbers
are subject to change without notice.)

Name_____

Address_____

City_____ State_____ Zip Code_____
Allow at least 4 weeks for delivery

Lyndon Johnson and the American Dream

★ ★ ★ ★ ★

Doris Kearns

A SIGNET BOOK

NEW AMERICAN LIBRARY

TIMES MIRROR

Portions of this book originally appeared in
Atlantic Monthly and *McCall's*.

Copyright © 1976 by Doris Kearns

All rights reserved. No part of this book may be used or reproduced
in any manner whatsoever without written permission except in the case
of brief quotations embodied in critical articles and reviews.
For information address Harper & Row, Publishers, Inc.,
10 East 53rd Street, New York, N.Y. 10022.

Library of Congress Catalog Card Number: 75-42831

This is an authorized reprint of a hardcover edition published by
Harper & Row, Publishers, Inc. The hardcover edition was published
simultaneously in Canada by Fitzhenry & Whiteside Limited, Toronto.

SIGNET TRADEMARK REG. U.S. PAT. OFF. AND FOREIGN COUNTRIES
REGISTERED TRADEMARK—MARCA REGISTRADA
HECHO EN CHICAGO, U.S.A.

SIGNET, SIGNET CLASSICS, MENTOR, PLUME AND MERIDIAN BOOKS
are published by The New American Library, Inc.,
1301 Avenue of the Americas, New York, New York 10019

First Signet Printing, August, 1977

1 2 3 4 5 6 7 8 9

PRINTED IN THE UNITED STATES OF AMERICA

To the memory of
my mother and father
and to
Richard and Bert Neustadt

Contents

Preface

Lyndon Johnson's life took him through a succession of public institutions: the House of Representatives, the Senate, the Vice-Presidency, and the Presidency. He first came to Washington when Herbert Hoover was still President; his public career spanned the depression, the New Deal, World War II, Korea, postwar economic expansion, the cold war, the Eisenhower years, the New Frontier, the Great Society and Vietnam. He was a candidate for office from a fairly liberal congressional district with a populist tradition, then from a conservative state dominated by powerful economic interests, and, finally, his constituency was the entire nation.

This staggering diversity of historical circumstances and public institutions, which constituted the changing environments of Lyndon Johnson's public life, provides an unusual opportunity for understanding the interplay between personality and institutions in America. Lyndon Johnson's character, his favorite methods of acquiring power and of using that power, his personal strengths and weaknesses, can all be viewed in different contexts, thus providing an invaluable look at both the changeless dynamics of power and the changing structure of the American political system in the past forty years.

On a still larger canvas, Lyndon Johnson's story provides a panoramic view of the changing nature of American life in the twentieth century. The world in which Johnson grew up was a different world from the one he came to lead. He grew up in an America where almost every household contained the text and the message of Horatio Alger—the triumph of character, determination, and will over all adversity. Success or failure was determined entirely by the individual himself; structural barriers simply did not exist. In weekly college newspaper editorials on getting ahead, playing the game, and striving to succeed, Johnson preached that with industry, temperance, promptness, and generosity the persistent man would inevitably triumph. All his life Johnson retained the belief that any problem could be solved by personal force. He believed he could make a friend of anyone—Nikita Khrushchev, Ho Chi Minh, Charles de Gaulle—if only he could sit alone with him in a room and talk. Indeed, there were few who could resist the influence of his personal presence. He possessed a wholly intuitive and profound capacity to see into other men's natures. His greatest gift of leadership was the ability to understand, persuade, and subdue; that gift was an indispensable attribute of his success in college in the 1920s, in the National Youth Administration in the 1930s, and in the Congress in the 1940s and '50s.

And Johnson believed that, when success came, it must be used to benefit others. Whether it was Lyndon the college student producing accomplishments for his mother, the husband and father producing wealth and security for his family, the Majority Leader producing legislation and electoral victory for his party, or the President of his country producing a Great Society for his people and what he believed to be progress for Southeast Asia—the desire to benefit others was ever the prime motive for his quest for power. The power he gained made good works possible, and good works, he believed, brought love and gratitude.

Yet this man of such intensely personal gifts, who received understanding and transmitted influence through other men's eyes, was destined as President to deal with an enemy abroad and power groups at home (blacks, students, the peace movement) who were unsusceptible to personal persuasion and ungrateful for his "gifts," was compelled to reach out to a constituency of two hundred million citizens while sitting alone in his office staring into the lens of a camera, and was required to sit at the head of a gargantuan bureaucracy largely managed by people he could neither know nor observe. The war in Vietnam and the rising domestic unrest challenged the traditional American faith in the capacity of the American government to do good for others at home and abroad. The course of events in the 1960s seemed to show that paternalism—the wish to reform, reshape, and control—was inextricably bound to American generosity, and that American benevolence was often tyrannical.

It was, however, impossible for Johnson to understand the tumult in the streets, the continuing capacity of the North Vietnamese to resist his will, or his own steadily deteriorating popularity. After all, he believed, he had given more laws, more houses, more medical services, more loans, and more promises to more people than any other President in history. Surely he had earned the love and gratitude of the American people. Yet as he looked around him in 1967 and 1968 he saw only paralyzing bitterness and hatred. Uncomprehending and deeply hurt as he was, it was natural that he would seek the cause of his decline in the personal animosity and motives of individual enemies—the press, the Eastern intellectuals, and the Kennedys—and even more natural, though surprising at first glance, that he would decide to withdraw from the world of politics and go back to the place where he was born, where, at least, as his father had told him years before, "The people know when you're sick and care when you die."

The Prologue to this book attempts to establish the circumstances under which I had access to some of the personal material and conversations from which I formed many of my judgments about Johnson's childhood and crucial aspects of his psychic structure. Johnson talked to me in the last five years of his life; moving backward in time from his stormy Presidency, to his years as Majority Leader of the Senate, to his early years in the Congress, and finally, as death chipped away at the defenses of a lifetime, to his memories of childhood. It is, as Erik Erikson has pointed out, important to know not only what a man says about his life but under what conditions and at what stage in his life he speaks. Therefore the description of the nature of my relationship with Johnson is intended to help establish the psychological relevance of my evidence.

Following this description, I discuss Johnson's childhood and the years of his early youth. Here, as elsewhere throughout the book, I wish the reader to know Lyndon Johnson emotionally, to be able to experience vicariously the feelings that he experienced, to understand why he behaved as he did. And through his various experiences within his family and his cultural setting, I observe the formation of certain patterns of behavior, which stayed with him through the rest of his life.

Having examined Johnson's characteristic ways of dealing with the world, my study turns to an examination of each of the successive institutions Johnson encountered from the time in 1931 when he became secretary to Congressman Richard

Kleberg to his dramatic withdrawal from politics in 1968. In portraying Johnson's career, I do not attempt to give a balanced treatment to every stage, nor to analyze in equal depth the many policies and measures he sponsored. In each chapter, I have chosen those events and policies which, in my judgment, best enable us to understand the private man beneath the public figure and best reveal the interplay of influence between leadership, institutional structure, and historical conditions. Taken as a whole, these chapters will, I believe, help us to understand why it was possible for Johnson to be hugely successful in some settings and not in others, and, beyond that, to recognize that the very patterns of behavior and belief responsible for his greatest successes contained within them the seeds of his ultimate failure.

This analytical narrative is followed by an Epilogue describing Johnson's final years of life on the ranch. Up to this point we shall have witnessed Johnson only as a man of power—acquiring power, exercising it, or, when young, hopeful of obtaining it. Here, by looking at that one time when both the reality and the hope of power were gone, we shall see how powerful and fixed were those qualities which drove him into politics and public life, how well he understood, just below the surface of consciousness, the necessities of his own survival, and how formidably American he was.

Doris Kearns

Prologue

In the spring of 1967, I was nominated for the White House Fellows program. The program was designed to allow young people to work as special assistants to the President and members of his Cabinet. At a conference house in Virginia, a committee of Cabinet members, government officials, and journalists interviewed the finalists. At the time, I was a candidate for a Harvard Ph.D. in Government preparing for an academic career and wanted some opportunity for actual experience in government. And yet, at best, my desire to join the Johnson administration was equivocal. So during the interviews I made no effort to conceal my antiwar activities and made it clear I could not work on anything to do with the war, but believed strongly in the domestic programs of the Great Society, particularly in the area of civil rights. These admissions did not seem to perturb the committee, many of whom, like John Oakes, editorial page editor of the *New York Times*, and John Gardner, Secretary of the Department of Health, Education, and Welfare, were themselves opposed to the war.

My selection was to be announced in a White House ceremony the first week of May. A month before, I had coauthored an article for the *New Republic*. This essay, "How to Remove LBJ in 1968"—the *New Republic* chose the title—argued for a new political party to be formed from an alliance of blacks, poor, the lower middle class, and women—a party that might give a voice to the presently unrepresented and, at the very least, bring about "the removal of Johnson, Rusk and Rostow from power in the American government" by splitting the normal Democratic vote and ensuring victory for a Republican Party which, we assumed, "scenting victory, will avoid their urge to nominate Nixon or Reagan."[1]* The

*Notes begin on page 427.

1

reasoning is a clear demonstration that purity of intention is no substitute for political knowledge.

A week before the article was to appear, on May 7, 1967, I went to the White House for the ceremony and the dance that would follow. There, I first met Lyndon Johnson. He was already in the ballroom when I entered. His appearance startled me. The picture in my mind had been a caricature: the sly televised politician, his features locked into virtual immobility, eyes squinting, ears that seemed to dangle like thick pendants affixed to the sides of his head. Now I saw a ruddy giant of a man with a strong mobile face, and a presence whose manifest energy dominated an entire room filled with Senators, Representatives, Cabinet officials, White House staff members, and reporters. Beginning each dance with a different woman, he moved gracefully across the floor.

My turn to dance with the President came in the middle of the evening. He walked up to me and began to talk. "Do your men ever dance at Harvard?" he teased. "Of course they do," I said. "Bull," he responded. "I know what goes on up there. And I bet they can't dance like I'm dancing right now." With that, he started to move me in wide circles around the floor. "I have one question," he asked suddenly. "Do you have a lot of energy? It's important for me to know." "Well," I replied, surprised at how easy it seemed to make small talk with him, "I hear you need only five hours of sleep, but I need only four so it stands to reason that I've got even more energy than you. In fact," I continued, even more surprised to find myself confiding in him, "I hate going to bed at night and I love waking up in the morning."[2]

Abruptly, Johnson interrupted to say that at my age he had also hated to sleep, but now his burdens with the war were such that sleep represented a welcome escape.

The dance ended, but as Johnson moved away, he said in a loud whisper that he had already decided that I should be the White House Fellow assigned to work for him on the White House staff.

It was not to be that simple. The next week the issue of the *New Republic* containing my article appeared in Washington. There was a flurry in the press, which was evidently amused at the idea that Lyndon Johnson had tried to waltz the New Left and had been spurned. A commentator on the 6 P.M. news even speculated that I might be an agent from the New Left who had been infiltrated into the Fellows program to get close to the President in order to change his mind about the war. The articles were light in tone, but I found the publicity embarrassing. The media were trying to turn me into a heroine of the peace movement, while, in fact, I was going to work in an administration against which my friends and colleagues were protesting and beginning to organize. My sense of guilt at going to work in Washington returned, intensified by the fact that the publicity threatened to make trouble for the entire staff of the White House Fellows program who had helped select me; who were dedicated people, sincere believers in the value of their work, and whom I had come to like and respect. I had heard of the President's reaction to earlier, more trivial public embarrassments. I could easily imagine his punishing, or even canceling, the entire White House Fellows program for its error in selecting me. He had already abolished the annual Medal of Freedom award because he did not approve of some who had been selected to receive it, among them critics of his Vietnam policies. I considered, and discussed with friends, the advisability of resigning. But then, a few days later, I received a phone call from Postmaster General Larry O'Brien, who told me that, despite the rumors, the President still wanted me to come to Washington and participate in the program. There was no further talk of my working for the President directly.

I was assigned to the Labor Department, where, to my great satisfaction, I was put to work on skill-training and education projects for young city blacks. Shortly after the Fellows assembled in the fall, we were invited to an informal discussion with the President, which became—as did so many of his meetings in that last year and a half—a monologue on the importance of our war effort in Vietnam. After finishing, he said he had time for only one question, swiveled abruptly, and pointed directly at me. "You," he commanded. Startled, mentally immobilized by my surprise, I found my lips forming the words I had been thinking the moment before: "Don't you understand—how can you possibly not understand—how deep and serious the country's opposition to the war in Vietnam is?" Neither I nor my colleagues could hear his mumbled reply, but his veiled look of anger was unmistakable. The session was closed. Once again I left the White House, for what was surely the last time, shaken by the unintended encounter.

Through my work in the Labor Department, I began to

feel that some steps, however gradual, were being taken to improve the lives of black Americans. But on April 4, 1968, four days after Johnson's withdrawal from the presidential race, civil rights leader Martin Luther King was shot and killed and all progress came to a halt as large-scale riots broke out in more than twelve major cities.

The next morning I was at work in the Labor Department when we were told that Johnson was planning a major speech to a joint session of Congress. He had asked Secretary of Labor Willard Wirtz—who had written speeches for Adlai Stevenson—to help prepare a draft. For three days, while entire blocks of Washington were aflame, a small group of us, designated by Secretary Wirtz, worked late into the night, driving home exhausted through uncanny, deserted streets, halted periodically at barricades where armed soldiers looked inside the car. Finally, we finished a draft that called for a "massive effort" to improve ghetto life, to be paid for by transferring money from the defense budget and Highway Trust Fund, and by raising taxes on the more affluent. We had convinced ourselves that King's martyrdom had created a moment of opportunity equal to that of his march on Selma, that the President could speak now as he had spoken then, and that Congress and the country would respond—this time to the denial of economic justice—as they had then to the denial of legal equality. We were undoubtedly wrong. Too much had changed since 1965—for Johnson and, even more, for the country. At the last minute Johnson canceled plans for the speech. A canvass of opinion in Congress had convinced him that the riots had destroyed whatever sense of injustice, compassion, or guilt King's death had produced; that the country was in no mood for progressive words on race.

His decision depressed me, and I was still disturbed when, a few weeks later, I met the President at a White House dinner. Shaking my hand, he politely asked how I was, and what I'd been doing. To my surprise, I found myself not simply responding, but launching into a speech of my own about the speech he should have given. He started to reply, but was interrupted by a photographer, who hurried him off to pose with ice-skating star Peggy Flemming. We didn't talk again that evening.

The next day, however, the President's appointments secretary called to say that President Johnson wanted to see me at the White House at 5 P.M. When I walked into the Oval Office, the President was in the midst of signing documents and his back was turned. I stood there silently, looking across the great office at the figure intently bent over his desk, the man suddenly appearing like a symbol out of one of my high school textbooks. I cleared my throat to let him know I was there.

He swiveled in his chair and, without a greeting, in strong, almost accusing tones, said, "First you say I should be dumped from the ticket. Then you criticize me for not making a speech. I've got nine months left in office without another election. I want to use those months to do and say all the things that should be done and said simply because they're right. And you can help me. You should be happy now that you've had your way, and now that I've removed myself from the race, it is time for you to remove yourself from the Department of Labor and come to work for me until I have to leave. Anyway," he added, "I've decided to do some teaching when I leave office. I've always liked teaching. I should have been a teacher, and I want to practice on you. I want to do everything I can," he concluded, "to make the young people of America, especially you Harvards, understand what this political system is all about."[8]

So I became a member of the White House staff, my office door two doors away from that of the President. Through my windows as well as his appeared the swiftly intensifying beauties of Washington's half-Southern spring. His last there. Most of my work in the White House concerned itself with the development of manpower projects—my specialty from the Department of Labor—and I worked with Joe Califano and Larry Levinson, the chief staff members for domestic affairs, rather than with the President. With Johnson himself, my main role was to listen as he talked. At around 9 or 10 P.M., one or two evenings a week, I sat for an hour or two in the little sitting room next to the Oval Office while Johnson recounted his activities of the day, reading to me from the stack of memos and letters on his desk. As I sat and listened to Johnson describe the details of his day, what he had done and how he had felt, the scene struck me as bewilderingly familiar. I could only think of my own childhood memory of my mother patiently listening to me, perched on a high stool in our kitchen, tell her in excruciating detail everything I had done that day at school.

My perceptions of him during those last nine months in the White House were as complicated and contradictory as he was himself. At one moment, he could be the statesman, grappling with the full range of responsibilities and executing his office with skill and intelligence. And since Lyndon Johnson's White House completely resonated with his personal moods and activities, it seemed to me at such times that I was at the center of government and power, of history itself. Moments later, the ambience could tilt toward absurdity when personal idiosyncrasy sent the very staff that had just been hard at work on matters of high policy off on a desperate search for huge quantities of a specific brand of peanut brittle which Lyndon Johnson needed within half an hour.

As President, Johnson could command detailed reports from any of his agencies and departments on almost any difficult question of state, and receive them within hours. But he also extended these prerogatives, and with the same urgency, to the most trivial of his personal desires. If he expressed a preference for a felt-tipped pen or a particular style of shirt, the manufacturer would be called upon to deliver three dozen within the hour. When he told his staff that he liked to read his reports in three-ring binders, 180 loose-leaf notebooks appeared almost immediately. The White House seemed to be a colossal warehouse, open twenty-four hours a day to accommodate the ever-shifting tastes of Lyndon Johnson.

Typically, when one morning he announced a new campaign to lose ten pounds, by late afternoon the White House was stocked with 150 pounds of cottage cheese, 275 containers of yoghurt, 40 loaves of diet bread, 15 boxes of Melba toast, and 10 pounds of his favorite diet candy, flown in by courier plane from his favorite store in San Antonio, Texas. The night the diet came to an end, gallons of ice cream and platters of homemade cookies suddenly found their way into the gleaming white refrigerators and stainless-steel kitchens. Aware that the slightest mishap could send Johnson into a fury, the domestic staff spent hours anticipating his most trifling whims. Informed of his preference for low-calorie drinks, the staff installed a special tap for Fresca in the cubbyhole immediately outside the Oval Office. Lyndon Johnson had only to push a button on the arm of his chair and within seconds a glass of Fresca would appear.

The contradictions extended into everything. As Commander in Chief, there was no doubt that he had to be able to be in immediate contact with the Pentagon, congressional leaders, foreign diplomats, and others in case an emergency should arise. But Johnson had embraced the possibilities offered by his presidential communications network with the unqualified excitement of an eleven-year-old who'd been given the world's biggest walkie-talkie. He had push-button phones installed in every place he might conceivably be—in his bathroom, in his bedroom, in his sitting room, in his dining room, in his theater, in his cars, on his motorboats, and on his planes. The pool at the White House and the pool at the ranch were both equipped with a special raft for a floating phone. The short-wave communications system enabled Johnson to reach any guest who was in a Lyndon B. Johnson car within twenty miles of his ranch house. His voice could be heard simultaneously on all of the thirteen loudspeakers installed around his Texas property. Buzzers buzzing, lights flashing, beepers whining—Johnson delighted in receiving and sending signals testifying to his existence at the center of the nation.

Television and radio were his constant companions. Hugging a transistor radio to his ear as he walked through the fields of his ranch or around the grounds of the White House, Johnson was a presidential teenager, listening not for music but for news. The transistor gave Johnson an exclusive beat, allowing him to play newscaster, dispensing bits and pieces of the latest news to his staff and guests. Since he liked to watch the evening news on all three networks at once, Johnson had the famous three-screen console built into the cabinet beside his desk in the Oval Office, and a duplicate installed in his bedroom. He had it equipped with an automatic control so he could tune in the sound of whichever network was, at that particular moment, commenting on him or his activities. To the left of the console stood the wire tickers—AP, UP, and Reuters—the keys steadily imprinting the bulletins across the unrolling paper. "Those tickers," Johnson later said, "were like friends tapping at my door for attention. I loved having them around. They kept me in touch with the outside world. They made me feel that I was truly in the center of things. I could stand beside the tickers for hours on end and never get lonely."[4]

Many dread loneliness, but "loneliness" for Johnson was not a state of mind. He could not bear to be by himself, not for an evening or for an hour. Always there were people, in his office, at his house, in the swimming pool, even in the bathroom. At the Senate, as in the rooming house he first occupied when, at twenty-three, he came to Washington, he would roam the corridors looking for people to talk to, persuade, and learn from. But in the Oval Office there were moments when privacy was necessary; thus the news tickers were installed to create a continuing presence.

Not only companions, the tickers were an additional source of control—or a sense of control—over events. Immediately after reading an inaccurate or displeasing story on the AP ticker, Johnson would call newspaper editors, present them with his version of the facts, and insist upon a corrected story in the late city edition. Similarly, by carefully watching the coverage of a political event on the 6 P.M. news, Johnson could get the news director on the phone, and demand a correction before the same story reappeared on the 11 P.M. news.

Johnson's often baffling and contradictory but always dazzling display of energy extended to every aspect of his life. It seemed that, except when he slept, he was in constant motion. When he got hungry, he often invited whoever was with him at the time, whether it was the Secretary of the Treasury discussing the balance of payments or his personal secretary taking dictation, to join him at the family table. At night, after dinner, he would gather guests, staff, and family around. Then he sat and talked about anything he pleased until one or two in the morning. For long periods, conversation would lapse into monologue. To leave was unthinkable.

If Johnson was in high spirits, then an unmistakable air of life and vitality characterized his entire staff. Conversations were easy and pleasurable, luncheons stretched out, relations were cordial. Johnson, relaxed, was a superb storyteller. He could meet with any group and pick up something from the topic of conversation that reminded him of a story, which he would then proceed to tell in great detail, accompanied by mimicry and gestures and uproarious laughter. Johnson filled his anecdotes with inflated words and feelings. He could, to great effect, convincingly appear to recreate the look and the feel of any person in almost any situation, whether he himself had been there or not. But most of the stories had a point— one simple idea. Ribbing and teasing—usually associated with the details of another person's private personal life—were central to all Johnson's stories. By directing his ridicule toward someone outside the assembled group, he created an atmosphere of intimacy inside, a feeling of camaraderie. And when Johnson told a story, he expected enthusiastic listeners, seeing his humor as a gift to his audiences. The ritual telling demanded a ritual response even if, as often happened, the same story had been heard a dozen times before.

Visitors were sometimes surprised to find out later that narrative details, even entire stories, were untrue; a revelation which, when communicated to others, added to Johnson's reputation for duplicity. Admittedly, Johnson was often duplicitous, both in private and in public. But in these simple and intimate gatherings he usually had no practical purpose or motive for deception. He was simply a highly skilled practitioner of a very old Texas tradition. "The tall tale spread West," Marcus Cunliffe writes in his history of American literature, "to reach inspired heights of mendacity. It required a narrator and an audience—fittingly among a people who liked nothing better than to be lectured at. . . . Political oratory was a variant of the tall tale. Was it true? The question had little meaning. What mattered was the story itself."[5]

I was told that Johnson had always been a generous and demanding giver, but before his White House days he had never been able to distribute so dazzling an assortment of presents. Every White House budget includes an allocation for gifts. Numberless trinkets—ranging from booklets, bracelets, and bowls to charms and certificates—are distributed in the name of the President. At no time before, however, had the budget been as large or as personally managed as it was under Lyndon Johnson. For most Presidents, the distribution of gifts is a routine function handled mechanically by the staff. For Johnson, the giving of gifts was a personal task, "a great opportunity," he said, "for engraving my spirit on the minds and hearts of my people." In the first year of his Presidency, the stock of presidential gifts more than tripled. To the traditional bowls, lighters, tie clasps, and cufflinks he added electric toothbrushes, engraved with the presidential seal; waterproof watches, inscribed with the initials of Lyndon B. Johnson and the Biblical injunction: "Do unto others as you would have others do unto you"; and orange and yellow scarves with a special border design—a chain of initials: 526 LBJ's.

There was a hierarchy of gifts, beginning with certificates delivered to all those who came within the presidential presence. Each time a person flew on "Air Force One" or on a presidential helicopter, he received a certificate attesting to that fact. If he flew with President Johnson eleven times in the course of a year, he received eleven certificates. Every person attending a White House dinner received two mementos—a place card lettered by a White House calligrapher and a printed menu, with the presidential seal in gold at the top, describing the food and the wines, the occasion and the date. To the members of his staff, Johnson personally delivered "CARE" boxes filled with all the foods he loved the most— 10 slabs of peanut brittle, 30 ounces of fudge cake, 6 pounds of chocolate. And, of course, the countless pictures of the man himself. In the distribution of these photos, Johnson's enthusiasm seemed strangely disproportionate; he treated pictures of himself with unabashed pride, the way a grandfather treats pictures of his grandchildren.

There was often a ritual connected with the giving of the gifts. Johnson often gave the same person the same gift again and again; the giver decided what he wanted to give, not what the recipient wanted to receive. "I give these toothbrushes to friends," Johnson explained to me, "for then I know that from now until the end of their days they will think of me the first thing in the morning and the last at night." In the last month of Johnson's Presidency, I received my first electric toothbrush. "Open it," Johnson said to me as I awkwardly held the gift unopened in my hands, "open it and tell me, have you ever seen anything like that in your entire life? Tell me now, what do you think?" I didn't tell him what I thought, for, in truth, I didn't know what to think. But I had to thank him, so I did. Several weeks later he handed me another package, still another toothbrush. When he noticed that I was perplexed, he glowered and said: "Why the hell should I give anything to anyone who is not grateful for my gift?"[6] There was, as Johnson saw it, an ethic to the charitable act, an expectation of gratefulness, a ritual that demanded the proper completion. So it happened that over time I was given, and with a measure of good grace accepted, no less than twelve electric toothbrushes!

Johnson's generosity was real. But I did not see then that it offered an insight into an important part of his nature. The giving and receiving meant something more than a simple token of feeling or gratitude; it was as if the exchange somehow created a magic bond that linked the recipient to the giver, a bond compounded, in Johnson's mind, of dependence, interest, even love; as if, somehow, those clashing states were aspects of a single condition, one state of mind. It reflected attitudes which, as we shall see, influenced his use of office and power throughout a long political career. "How is it possible," Johnson asked me, angrily, "that all these people [meaning the American people] could be so ungrateful to me after I had given them so much?"

More than anger was involved here; Johnson was deeply hurt—almost desperate—at the recognition that his generosity had not been appreciated. Of course, I was seeing him at a time of failure. We shall examine other times, when things were going well and the public was on his side. Then Lyndon Johnson was ebullient and could accept occasional displays of what he thought was ingratitude with relatively good humor. In addition, the experience of a long political career had confirmed him in the belief that there were no differences that could not be settled by upping the ante. That conviction was part of his character, and had shaped his mode of conduct throughout a long and successful political career. Now it seemed no longer to work, and he could not understand it.

A month before Johnson left office he asked me to go back to Texas with him to work full-time on his memoirs and the establishment of his presidential library and the Lyndon B. Johnson School of Public Affairs at the University of Texas in Austin. One evening he insisted on an answer. "Now I want to know," Johnson began, sitting up in his chair, "why you fidget and weave whenever I talk about your coming with me to Texas when we're done. I just don't understand it. Ten times, maybe more, I've taken you with me. I've tried my best to make you love it. And I've outlined again and again all the work that has to be done on the memoirs, the library, and the school. Still, you won't say yes. What are your objections?"

"I want to get back to teaching," I replied. "I just started before coming to Washington, and it's important to me."

"It's done," Johnson interrupted. "I've got you a position at the University of Texas. You can teach all you want. Hell, you teach about the Presidency, don't you? Well, I am a President. You can teach me, and I can teach you. Now what could be better than that?"

Without answering directly, I explained that I had also

made plans to work part-time on a manpower project in the black Roxbury section of Boston. "Oh, hell," Johnson said, leaning closer, "I can get you all the poor people you want. I can get them from Austin and San Antonio. If you go to Roxbury with no money and lots of goodwill, you'll accomplish absolutely nothing . . . so if you really want to help poor people, you'd better come to Texas.

"Now, what's your next objection?"

Losing ground by the moment, I said that all my liberal beliefs had been shaken by my experience of working in Washington, that I needed time to myself to re-examine my ideas, to study and think.

"Think!" he interjected. "Don't you worry. I'll get you a little cabin on the lake, Lake LBJ. It'll be perfect for thinking. I'll get you a blue sky and some rippling water and some old trees, all the things you thinkers need to produce big thoughts. And you can go there whenever you want, except when you're working with me. Now what else could you possibly need?"

"All the people I care about are in Washington or Cambridge," I replied, beginning to feel, as had so many who had preceded me in this office, a little overwhelmed.

"No problem," Johnson replied. "I'll invite a millionaire to the ranch every weekend, and I'll buy you pretty clothes, and I'll put you on a diet and give you a fabulous salary so you can look beautiful all the time. And I'll take you on trips with me—to Russia, where you've always wanted to go" (I had studied the Russian language for three years), "and to Africa and South America. And then you'll have lots of interesting stories to tell your handsome young millionaires.

"Now," Johnson summarized, "what girl in her right mind wouldn't come and work with the President of the United States under these conditions?"

I felt hopeless. But, as he talked, I suddenly saw myself wearing a Lyndon B. Johnson outfit, sitting by the Lyndon B. Johnson Lake, making conversation with a Lyndon B. Johnson millionaire. Nothing would be mine, perhaps not even myself. "I wouldn't be comfortable," I managed to say. "It's not possible. I don't belong there. It's your home and I know you love it . . . but I need to be with my friends." Then, hopefully, in search of extrication: "Maybe we can work something out on a part-time basis."

"No," Johnson said, moving back. "Either you come or

you don't. And I'll tell you, you're dead wrong if you think that money and travel and nice clothes don't matter. They do matter, to you and every other American."[7]

The subject had not come up again. Then on Sunday afternoon, January 19—the President's last full day in office—Johnson called me at home and asked me to come to the White House immediately and talk about my plans. A light snow, almost rain, was falling; the walk from my apartment in southwest Washington to the White House took nearly an hour. By the time I reached the gate I was prepared for my talk with the President, but not for what I saw when I entered. Overnight, everything had been dismantled. Empty chairs and desks stood in the middle of vacant offices, surrounded by rolled-up rugs and stacked-up pictures. The elevator was out of operation; canvas and ladders littered the stairs; dozens of painters and other workmen were moving through the corridors. The next day's transition was being prepared.

The President was sitting by himself in the Oval Office. It alone remained untouched; painters and furniture movers would not enter until the President had departed. I thought of a hundred repetitious news items, the sentimental classic of every urban-renewal project: the aging man who held out and refused to be relocated, staying on as long as he could while the neighborhood was being demolished around him.

As I entered, Johnson looked up at me across the mahogany vastness of the presidential desk. "I need help," he said gently, the voice barely audible above the steady clicking of the news tickers, "part-time as you wish, on weekends, during vacations, whatever you can give. As soon as I get settled at home, I'm going to write my memoirs. Those memoirs are the last chance I've got with the history books, and I've got to do it right. I've got to get my story out from beginning to end. We've got to go through my papers, and diaries, and ask hard questions to jog my memory. I want you all to be like vultures with me, picking out my eyes and my ears, tearing the memories and experience out of my guts, putting all my insides into your sacks so you can help me write my story. Then I'll go over your drafts again and again until I remember everything I want to say. Will you do it? Will you help me?"

He stopped. This time he made no fancy promises. "Of course I will," I said. There was a long pause and then:

"Thanks. Thanks a lot. Now you take care of yourself up there at Harvard. Don't let them get at you, for God's sake, don't let their hatred for Lyndon Johnson poison your feelings about me."

I turned to go, but he called me back to say one more thing. "It's not so easy to get the help you need when you're no longer on top of the world. I know that and I won't forget what you're doing for me."[8] Even at this moment of helplessness, his ambitions shattered, reduced to asking the help of a twenty-five-year-old girl, the greatest political bargainer of them all had not wholly lost his touch.

And probably I had wanted to do it all along—to understand the man who had so influenced national life, how President and Presidency shaped each other and influenced the nation. Seeing Johnson vulnerable, without the armor of his office, might have made me aware that I would now have an opportunity to learn these things. But, of course, Johnson couldn't have known that—or could he?

So for the next four years, while teaching at Harvard, I spent long weekends, parts of summer vacations, and winter holidays with the President and his wife at the ranch. The work on the memoirs was fascinating but difficult. There was no shortage of material—there were 31 million papers in storage in Austin and a dedicated staff engaged in the process of sorting them out so we could use what we needed for the memoirs. Harry Middleton and Bob Hardesty, two former speechwriters, were in charge of the project. I was assigned to cover the chapters on civil rights, economics, and the Congress, but we all worked together reading through hundreds of files, memos, and transcripts, preparing questions for the President.

The publishers had recommended a trilogy: the presidential years first, the Senate years second, the boyhood years third. The order seemed to make economic sense; the volume on the Presidency would create a momentum for the other two. But it failed to account for the anxiety Johnson experienced in reliving the frustrations of those painful presidential years. Indeed, it soon became clear that he would rather be doing anything else than working on his memoirs. The moment a formal interview began, he stiffened; the moment it was over, he relaxed, had Lady Bird join him, and expanded colorfully on the subject he had just discussed with dull rhetoric. Yet, if ever we tried to incorporate our notes from these informal sessions into the draft, he took them out, insisting that this was a presidential memoir and had to be written in a stately fashion. So the man who talked for the memoirs was the man Lyndon Johnson thought he should be—the statesman above the fray, a soft-spoken observer of events whose opinions were offered with uncharacteristic deference and humility. Whereas Lyndon Johnson was filled with powerful emotions, with anger, rage, and sympathy, the image he projected was that of a calm, almost cold man, a sober fellow, with pinched energy; humble, earnest, and crashingly dull.

Once in the course of working on the memoirs, I told Johnson of an incident described in a new book by reporter Hugh Sidey. Sidey had written that when Johnson was talking to the troops in Korea in 1966, he falsely claimed that his great-great-grandfather had died at the Alamo. Sidey interpreted Johnson's statement to mean that the President wanted to have some blood connection to these dead heroes, so he simply voiced his desire as fact.[9] Before I finished retelling the story, Johnson interrupted: "God damn it, why must all those journalists be such sticklers for detail? Why, they'd hold you to an accurate description of the first time you ever made love, expecting you to remember the color of the room and the shape of the windows. That's exactly what happened here. The fact is that my great-great-grandfather died at the Battle of San Jacinto, not the Alamo. When I said the Alamo, it was just a slip of the tongue. Anyway, the point is that the Battle of San Jacinto was far more important to Texas history than the Alamo. Why, the men who fought there were as brave as any men who have walked the face of the earth."[10]

He went on to describe the battle for another fifteen minutes. By the end of our conversation, I had heard not only that San Jacinto was the most important event in the history of Texas but that his great-great-grandfather had been the hero of that great and courageous moment. Later, I learned that Johnson's great-great-grandfather had not died at San Jacinto, or even been there, just as he had not been at the Alamo. He was a real estate trader and he died at home, in bed.

Johnson was never to write a Volume Two on the Senate or a Volume Three on the boyhood years. Though he talked with me about helping him on the Senate book, it was clear that he wanted nothing more to do with any formal writing about his life. Moreover, his physical condition was deteriorating. In the early spring of 1970, I flew to the Army's Brooke General Hospital in San Antonio, where Johnson had suddenly been hospitalized for chest pains. This attack was not serious, but from then on he would suffer continual pain, and from then on he seemed increasingly anxious to talk about his past. More and more he asked me to accompany him as he went about his daily errands—his staff meetings with the field hands in the morning, his work in his office, endless rides over his property to check up on things undone, afternoon walks to the birthhouse—and all the time he talked, recounting stories from his past.

No longer anxious to explain the policies of his Presidency or expand on the mistakes and misdeeds of his opponents, he spoke, rather, of his motives, of why he wanted what he did; beginning slowly, ever so tentatively, to reveal glimpses of the personal anxieties which underlay his political decisions. Moving backward from his stormy Presidency, he found comfort in recreating earlier days: the Senate leadership, his beginning years in Congress and as Texas Director of the National Youth Administration. He would get up from his chair, stride around the room, his mind accelerating to that familiar agility, voice and gestures shifting, taking on all the varied roles of the master storyteller. Those were good years, exciting; years of ambition continually renewed by a steady upward rise, of desires fulfilled through mastery and control over the men and events that concerned him. Increasingly, as he came to dwell within these more pleasant memories, Johnson's compulsion to run every detail of the ranch lessened. He began to settle into his retirement, enjoying the time with his wife, his daughters, and his grandchildren, seemingly content with long, half-idle, unplanned days.

Nevertheless, his physical strength was gradually ebbing away. His hair whitened; wrinkles appeared in his skin; hollows deepened beneath his eyes; the backs of his hands became flecked with spots of brown. His intestinal system was in continuous turmoil. The chest pains returned; it was often difficult to breathe. "I feel a bad pain in my angina these days," he said to me one summer afternoon, interrupting himself in the middle of a story about his first race for Congress. "I went to a doctor in Mexico, and he said my

blood pressure was perfect, and he wished it would shoot up
so he could get me worried. But I have an instinct something
is wrong. Last night's drink was the first in ten days. I've lost
ten pounds and been exercising each day. But I'm still worried. I've got an instinct."[11] More than two and a half years
remained. But he was beginning to die, and he knew it.

It was then that he began to talk more and more about his
childhood. Though my visits were shorter and less frequent in
the last two years, his conversations became more focused
and more intense, covering in one day or one afternoon
material that had previously stretched over weeks of rambling
talk. Encroaching, unmastered death chipped away at the defenses of a lifetime, and, bit by bit, a story I had never heard
before began to unfold—a painful story of an unhappy boy
trapped in a divided home, relentlessly tumbled among the
impossible demands of an unyielding mother, love offered
and then denied in seeming punishment; contempt for a father who had failed, admiration for a father who was a
model for a Texas manhood; commanded to be what he
could not be, forced to become what he was not. How different from his earlier public descriptions—the rags-to-riches
rise from a happy childhood, guided by an adoring mother
and the example of a manly, principled father. Sometimes he
said more than he could accept and, after recounting some
terribly revealing story, the old defenses re-emerged and he
would disclaim the obvious meaning of what had just been
said. But something seemed to drive him on as far as his
reach and memory would permit.

We talked mostly in the early hours of the morning.
Johnson slept poorly these days, waking up at 5:30. Terrified
at lying alone in the dark, he came into my room to talk.
Gradually, a curious ritual developed. I would awaken at five
and get dressed. Half an hour later Johnson would knock on
my door, dressed in his robe and pajamas. As I sat in a chair
by the window, he climbed into the bed, pulling the sheets up
to his neck, looking like a cold and frightened child.

In those dawn talks, I saw him as perhaps few others, except his wife and close friends, had seen him: crumpled,
ragged, and defenseless. He spoke of the beginnings and ends
of things, of dreams and fantasies. His words seemed to flow
from some deep well of sadness, nostalgia, and longing. It is,
of course, impossible for me to sort out dream or memory
from fantasy. After all, I was listening to a man who had al-

ways had a peculiar relationship with words. If there were in-consistencies with facts—his grandfather at the Alamo—how much more treacherous were memories and dreams and yet how much more revealing. For what a man like Johnson chose to remember may be even more important to under-stand than what really happened.

Other biographers and members of the family, with the benefit of additional information, will help us to understand whether, for example, Johnson's family relationships were as he described them to me. At an earlier stage in his own life, Johnson portrayed these relationships quite differently. What I can offer here is simply my account and my interpretation of what Johnson told me in the last stage of his life.

As I listened to him speak, I often wondered why I was his audience, why he permitted and apparently trusted me to hear all this. One day, a year and a half before he died, he took me on a long car ride. He wanted to tell me, he said, that all along he'd been hiding from me the fact that I re-minded him of his dead mother. In talking with me, he had come to imagine he was also talking with her, unraveling the story of his life.

Perhaps this was so, but it is more likely that he talked to me simply because I was there, present, as he moved, know-ingly, terrified, toward death.

I often took notes as we talked, and Johnson rarely object-ed. A few times he interrupted a story to admonish: "Now I don't want you to tell this to anyone in the world, not even to your great-grandchildren." None of these passages has been recorded here. But he never asked me to stop taking down his words. More often he would look over, see that I was simply listening, and demand, "Hey, why aren't you writing all this down? Someday, someone may want to read it."[12] I was never asked to be an official biographer, but Johnson knew I was thinking of writing a book about him. Indeed, that may have been among his purposes. No Texan, he believed, no crude frontier leader, no President who was not a Kennedy, could intrude upon the literary province of the intellectual Northeast, which condemned and despised him. But I was a teacher at Harvard, already a member of that inner group which wrote the books and which, he firmly believed, shaped the final verdict of history. Perhaps, even at the end, Lyndon Johnson was looking, planning, for some chance to achieve that place in history which meant so much to him.

I listened through long hours of recollection to this immense and brilliant personality, who had overcome so much, victor in a thousand conquests, now defeated, dying, but still exerting his incredible will in order to master, no longer the action, but some understanding of what had happened to his life and of who he was.

Chapter 1

Growing Up

On the north bank of the Pedernales River in Stonewall, Blanco County, Texas, a mile of dirt road connects the ranch house where Lyndon Johnson died to the small farmhouse in which he was born. During his last years, Johnson often ambled the stretch of grassy river bottom, checking on his grazing Herefords, talking the entire way past the shack that once was his grandfather's house, past the low stone wall bordering the family cemetery, to the meticulously restored museum, his birthplace.

There, his talk sometimes turned to his childhood, stories attached to this room or that furnishing. Once, standing at the entrance to his parents' bedroom, where Lyndon slept when his father was away, Johnson described to me a long-remembered ritual: "First my mother washed my hands and face with water, then tucked me in between the cool, white sheets. She crossed then to that old marble dresser on the far side of the room and seated herself on the straw chair in front of the mirror. I watched her take out the long brown pins from her hair. Then she shook her head from side to side, brushing her hair. I used to count, fifty strokes with one arm, fifty with the other. Always the same. Then she emptied a pitcher of water into the washbowl and, with a small yellow cloth, she scrubbed her face, throat, and arms. Then she came back to the bed, said her prayers, and climbed in beside me. Propped against two pillows, she read to me from books she had read with her father long ago ... Browning, Milton, Dickens. I liked it better when she talked about when she was a young girl."[1]

The world Rebekah described, as Johnson remembered it, was very different from the shabby life she was then leading with her husband and children on the bank of the Pedernales. Her parents had money, position, respectability. They lived in a two-story house surrounded by trees, terraced flower gardens, and a white picket fence. Her people—unlike their poor and ignorant neighbors along the Pedernales—were a proper, civilized breed of educators and preachers of European culture. She projected herself to her son as a dreamy young girl who had spent her afternoons reading poetry under the shade of the big trees in those gardens, her evenings discussing literature with her father, Joseph Wilson Baines.

Baines, a lawyer, educator, and lay preacher in the Baptist church in Blanco, Texas, was seen by his devoted daughter as the paradigm of religious ideals, moral thought, and civic duty.[2] In the late 1870s he had served Texas as Secretary of State and afterward as a member of the state legislature, where, as Rebekah told her son, "he thrilled the chambers with eloquent speeches on the rights and duties of mankind, the evil of liquor, the importance of cleanliness in thought and deed, and the iniquity of speculation."[3] With his encouragement, Rebekah had attended Baylor University—she was one of a small number of Texas women in college at that time —where she majored in literature and planned to write a novel about the old South before the Civil War.

"I'm certain she could have been a great novelist," Johnson told me. "But then her daddy died and it all came apart. All his life he had spoken out against the speculators. He was as righteous as they come. Then in 1904, while my mother was in college, he lost all his money on one disastrous deal. It killed him. He became very depressed and his health got worse until he died.[4]

"My mother said it was the end for her, too. In early 1907 she moved with her mother to a smaller house in Fredericksburg, Texas. She taught elocution and corresponded for the local paper. She still wanted to do something big, to go places and write, but she said that after her father's death she lost her confidence in everything. By the time my father came into the picture she'd given up. She'd met him the year before, after he'd won his first victory in the state legislature. Her father thought he was the most promising young politician in Blanco County and wanted her to interview him for the family newspaper. He was tall. Six feet four."[5]

Sam Johnson was a small-time farmer and trader in real estate and cattle. A great storyteller, his language crude and often vulgar, he was apparently a new kind of man for Rebekah, the opposite of her father. Eight months after her

father's death, she married him and moved to the little farm
on the Pedernales.

The anecdote Johnson told me of his mother's life does not
cohere. If she had possessed the talents of a great novelist, it
is hardly likely that her writing would have been completely
stopped by her father's death. And her only published work,
a history of the Johnson clan, is a highly mannered and sentimental rhapsody. "Now the light came in from the east," she
wrote of Lyndon's birth, "bringing a deep stillness, a stillness
so profound and so pervasive that it seemed as if the earth itself were listening. And then there came a sharp, compelling
cry—the most awesome, happiest sound known to human
ears—the cry of a newborn baby; the first child of Sam Ealy
and Rebekah Johnson was 'discovering America.' "[6] And her
splendid image of Joseph Baines, a man who insisted on morals in politics and inveighed against speculators and drinkers,
must be reconciled with the man who lost all his money on
one speculative deal and introduced his only daughter to the
hard-drinking, practical Sam Johnson.

However concocted, Rebekah's family portrait, the types
and conceptions she delineated, nonetheless affected Lyndon
Johnson for the rest of his life, forcing divisions between
intellect, morality, and action, shaping ideals of the proper
politician and the good life. By contrasting the idyll of her cul-
tured youth with the grimness of her marriage, Rebekah left
her son forever ashamed of his roots on the Pedernales.

There is a sense in which Rebekah's story resembles that of
many other educated women in the West, who found themselves trapped in a land and a life that they loathed, and yet
whose only choice seemed self-denial. The "good woman"
never complained in public; she considered it her duty to
repress any awareness of the disparities between the civilization she had left behind and the one in which she had now
placed herself.[7]

In her ancestral history, Rebekah writes only: "I was determined to overcome circumstances instead of letting them
overwhelm me. At last I realized that life is real and earnest
and not the charming fairytale of which I had so long
dreamed." A life devoid of all she reverenced—reading and
long conversation—a tedious life of feeding chickens, scrub-
bing wash, sewing clothes, growing vegetables, became simply
the problem of "adjustment to a completely opposite person-

ality ... to a strange and new way of life, a way far removed from that I had known in Blanco and Fredericksburg."8

To her son, however, Rebekah voiced her profound discontent, describing in anguishing detail the ordeal of her life on the Pedernales with Sam Johnson. "My mother," Johnson said, "soon discovered that my daddy was not a man to discuss higher things. To her mind his life was vulgar and ignorant. His idea of pleasure was to sit up half the night with his friends, drinking beer, telling stories, and playing dominoes. She felt very much alone. The first year of her marriage was the worst year of her life. Then I came along and suddenly everything was all right again. I could do all the things she never did."9

"How children dance," Rainer Maria Rilke wrote, "to the unlived lives of their parents," suggesting in poetic language much of the analysis that follows. In the course of this analysis psychiatric knowledge will be used as a means of understanding the formation of Johnson's behavior. This body of knowledge, however, is and perhaps always will be incomplete. There are mysteries of the human mind that no analytic technique can penetrate—mysteries which, over time, even the greatest psychiatrists, poets, dramatists, and novelists have been unable to explain. There is, for example, no psychiatric principle that can explain Johnson's immense talents, his extraordinary ability to harness his personal needs and direct his strength—tirelessly and with practical intelligence—toward the highest public achievements, or his capacity to sustain a private life whose intimate stability was rare, even among those not subject to the disintegrative pressures of a public career. Indeed, to know fully the disabling conditions of Johnson's youth can only increase admiration for the inexplicable power of his will.

Remembering his early years, Johnson spoke almost exclusively of his mother. When he mentioned his father, it was to enumerate his liabilities as a husband and explain what he did to Rebekah.

"One of the first things I remember about my daddy," Johnson said, "was the time he cut my hair. When I was four or five, I had long curls. He hated them. 'He's a boy,' he'd say to my mother, 'and you're making a sissy of him. You've got to cut those curls.' My mother refused. Then, one Sunday morning when she went off to church, he took the big scissors and cut off all my hair. When my mother came home, she refused to speak to him for a week."[10]

Contention between Sam and Rebekah was not restricted to the nurture of their son. There were constant disputes over how the household should be managed, whether it would be a home or a hostelry. "I remember one Thanksgiving," he said. "Holidays always seem to mean a lot to women and they certainly did to my mother. She had gotten out the wedding china and roasted a huge turkey. Everything was set just right. She sat at the head of the table with her fancy lace dress and big wide sleeves. She was saying the prayers when a knock came on the door. My daddy answered and found a Mexican family with five children.

"They lived nearby. My father had done a lot to help them over the years. Now they were returning his favor. They had brought him a green cake, the biggest cake I'd ever seen. Well, the minute he saw them out there, cold and hungry, he invited them to dinner. He was always doing things like that. The dinner was loud. There was a lot of laughing and yelling. I liked it. But then I looked at my mother. Her face was bent toward her plate and she said nothing. I had a feeling that something was wrong, but I was having such a good time I didn't pay attention. After the meal, she stood up and went to her room. I followed a little behind her and heard her crying in there. I guess she was really counting on it being a private occasion. I looked at her sad face and I felt guilty. I went in and tried to make her feel better."[11]

Yet these discords were mild, Johnson remembered, in comparison to the fights provoked by his father's drinking. In the Baines' family code, sobriety was essential; it ensured the cardinal quality, self-control. Sobriety was a promise of industry and reliability. Nor was Rebekah alone in her dismay; at that time, women throughout the West regarded liquor as the most threatening rival for their husband's acceptability, devotion, and income. Their anxiety sustained the Prohibition movement, which enlisted the support of thousands, among them Rebekah Baines Johnson. This war between good and evil was manifest in the two main symbols of the small Western towns—the church, with its steeple pointing upward to heaven, and the low saloon, with its swinging doors leading straight down to hell. There was no room in Rebekah's Protestant ethic for uncontrolled and frivolous behavior. Economic and social ruin awaited the drunkard. Temperance was both the sign of morality and the key to economic success.[12]

According to her son, Rebekah saw this conviction painfully vindicated in her own husband's intemperance. "There was nothing Mother hated more than seeing my daddy drink. When he had too much to drink, he'd lose control of himself. He used bad language. He squandered the little money we had on the cotton and real estate markets. Sometimes he'd be lucky and make a lot of money. But more often he lost out. One year we'd all be riding high in Pedernales terms, so high in fact that on a scale of A to F, we'd be right up there with the A's. Then two years later, he'd lose it all. The cotton he had bought for forty-four cents a bale had dropped to six cents a bale, and with it the Johnsons had dropped to the bottom of the heap. These ups and downs were hard on my mother. She wanted things to be nice for us, but she could never count on a stable income. When she got upset, she blamed our money problems on my father's drinking. And then she cried a lot. Especially when he stayed out all night. I remember one bad night. I woke up and heard her in the parlor crying her eyes out. I knew she needed me. With me there, she seemed less afraid. She stopped crying and told me over and over how important it was that I never lose control of myself and disappoint her that way. I promised that I would be there to protect her always. Finally she calmed down and we both fell asleep."[13]

The image of Rebekah Baines Johnson that emerges in these stories is that of a drastically unhappy woman, cut off from all the things that had once given her pleasure in life, stranded in a cabin on a muddy stream with a man she considered vulgar and brutish, a frustrated woman with a host of throttled ambitions, trying, through her first-born son, to find a substitute for a dead father, an unsuccessful marriage, and a failed career. She seemed under a compulsion to renew on her son's behalf all the plans and projects she had given up for herself. The son would fulfill the wishful dreams she had never carried out, he would become the important person she had failed to be.[14]

"She never wanted me to be alone," Lyndon later recalled: "She kept me constantly amused. I remember playing games with her that only the two of us could play. And she always let me win even if to do so we had to change the rules. I knew how much she needed me, that she needed me to take

care of her. I liked that. It made me feel big and important.
It made me believe I could do anything in the whole world."[15]

From his position of primacy in his mother's home,
Johnson seemed to develop what Freud has called "the
feeling of a conqueror, that confidence of success that often
induces real success."[16] The early privilege of his mother's intense love was a source of great energy and power. He
learned the alphabet before he was two, learned to read and
spell before he was four, and at three could recite long passages of poetry from Longfellow and Tennyson. "I'll never
forget how much my mother loved me when I recited those
poems. The minute I finished she'd take me in her arms and
hug me so hard I sometimes thought I'd be strangled to
death."[17]

But as strong as Rebekah's feelings undoubtedly were, one
gets the impression Lyndon never experienced her love as a
steady or reliable force, but as a conditional reward, alternately given and taken away. When he failed to satisfy her
desires—as he did when he refused to complete the violin and
dancing lessons she set up for him when he was seven and
eight—he experienced not simply criticism but a complete
withdrawl of affection. "For days after I quit those lessons
she walked around the house pretending I was dead. And
then to make it worse, I had to watch her being especially
warm and nice to my father and sisters."[18] The same experience was repeated later when Johnson refused to go to college and Rebekah closed him out for weeks, refusing to speak
or even to look at him.

One cannot prove the existence of a pattern on the basis of
three or four remembered incidents. But there does seem to
be a connecting link between the syndrome implicit in
Johnson's childhood memories—of love alternately given and
taken away—and the pattern observed in nearly all his adult
relationships. With friends, colleagues, and members of his
staff, Johnson was capable of unusual closeness; he enveloped
people, one by one, in the warmth of his affection and
concern. If the hospital bill of a friend needed payment, he
paid it. If an employee's child needed a new coat, he bought
it. If a secretary's house needed renovation, he supervised.
But in return he demanded a measure of gratitude and loyalty so high that disappointment was inevitable. And when
the disappointment came, Johnson tended to withdraw his affection and concern—the "Johnson freeze-out" it was

called—hurting others in much the same way his mother had hurt him years before.

So predictable was his tendency to spoil the relationships he most cared about that it suggests in him the presence of a powerful fear attached to the experience of intimacy: a fear reminiscent perhaps of that he must have felt years before as a consequence of the unique role he'd been asked to play in his mother's life. For though the young boy took obvious pleasure from certain aspects of his special role—"I loved it when my mother needed me and when she told me all her secrets"[19]—he is certain to have feared, at least subconsciously, that his father might one day cease tolerating his presumption and take revenge. Johnson does remember the "absolute terror" he experienced one night when he was wakened from sleep in his mother's bed by the sudden opening of the bedroom door, only to find a younger sister standing there, in her nightgown, crying out for her mother. And from the fears of the boy would develop in the man a continuing sense that, in the end, his power to command love and affection was illegitimate, momentarily wielded but easily overthrown.[20]

While admitting the pain and confusion he felt as a child, Johnson refused to recognize his mother as a possible source. But it is a commonplace of psychiatric observation that too much devotion and tenderness can lead to great trouble when the child has to step from the tiny kingdom of his mother's home.[21] When Johnson first went to school, he stood next to his teacher all day long, refusing to let go of her skirt. As the teacher, Katie Dietrich, told the story many years later, she could hardly understand him the first two weeks. He had a peculiar way of rolling his *r*'s and his own way of talking. If she asked him to read the lesson, he would simply stand there, unmoving and mute. Finally, she called "Miss Rebekah," who suggested that perhaps things would progress if Lyndon were allowed to sit on the teacher's lap whenever she asked him to read. She tried and the tactic succeeded.[22] Still, Johnson wanted to be home, and in three months got his wish. He contracted whooping cough, the first of a series of illnesses that strangely abetted his desires, and had to be kept at home for the remainder of the school year.

So close was the boy to his mother, as Johnson recalled, that one imagines him as an only child when in fact he had four siblings: Rebekah, born when he was two, Josepha when he was four, Sam when he was six, and Lucia when he was eight. Of his relations with his siblings Johnson said very little. There is one vivid scene, however, which he described as a memory but which may, instead, have been a dream or even an aggressive fantasy against both his mother and the unborn child she was then carrying: "I was throwing a baseball to my oldest sister, Rebekah. We were playing in the yard in front of our house. Mother was watching. My younger sister, Josepha, was sitting in her crib behind us, crying. I threw the ball straight and fast, but just as it left my hands Mother moved toward Josepha and stepped right in the path of the ball. She was very pregnant with Sam then. The ball hit her hard, right in the middle of her stomach, and she lost her balance and fell down. I was terrified at the thought of what I'd done. I was certain that her belly would pop just like a balloon. Later, I found out that she had been even more frightened than me. She was, she told me much later, certain that the baby had been damaged. But at the time she said nothing of her fear; she immediately gathered me up into her arms and held me until I finally stopped crying."[28]

It is difficult to imagine that a boy of five could throw a ball with sufficient force to knock an adult woman to the ground. It is also difficult, though not impossible, to accept the certainty of Rebekah's belief that in her fall she had damaged her unborn child. The interesting detail is Johnson's memory that his mother stepped right into the path of the moving ball, permitting the argument that she and not he was responsible.

"But that wasn't all," Johnson continued. "Later that day, I left home to walk to my grandfather's house, which was a half-mile up the road. Mother, always afraid that I would fall into the river, had told me never to leave the dirt path. But the day was hot and the road was dry and dusty and I wanted to cool my hands and feet. I left the road and ran down to the river bank. I was skipping along until I fell on the roots of a dead tree, and hit my head. I tried to get up. My head hurt. I fell back and lay still. I thought I would be left there forever. It was my punishment. Then, suddenly, my parents were there. Together they picked me up and carried me home. They put me to bed, blew out the light, and sat down at the end of the bed waiting for me to fall asleep. All the time they kept talking in a low voice. They sounded good together. Mother's voice was not as cold as it usually was when she talked with Father. His voice was warm, too. I remember thinking that being hurt and frightened was worth it so long as it ended this way. I thought that I would have been willing to go through the experience a hundred times to be sure of finding at the end a thing so nice and friendly as my parents were then."[24]

The boy's willingness to exchange physical pain for mental peace provides an interior window on the constant tensions that must have shaped his childhood days. Further evidence of these tensions is suggested in Johnson's memory of his grandfather's house just down the road as "the perfect escape from all my problems at home."[25] Years later Johnson told how much he loved to visit with his grandfather late in the day, when the two of them could talk undisturbed for two hours or more. "I sat beside the rocker on the floor of the porch, thinking all the while how lucky I was to have as a granddaddy this big man with the white beard who had lived the most exciting life imaginable."[26]

The elder Sam Ealy Johnson had spent his working life as a cowboy, driving herds of cattle from Fredericksburg, Texas, across twelve hundred miles of dangerous country to Abilene, Kansas. Three years before the beginning of the Civil War, he and his brother Tom, both men in their twenties, had come to the East Texas valley where the slim Pedernales River cut through harsh caliche soil. Their cattle-raising enterprise was interrupted when both brothers entered the Confederate Army. Returning after Appomattox, the brothers worked long days, constructed a rock barn for protection against Indian attacks, seeded pasture, bought cattle on credit during the spring and sold them in the fall. During the late sixties rising cattle prices brought increased prosperity, and in the boom year of 1870 Sam drove over seven thousand head of cattle to Kansas, returning with over $100,000.[27]

The old man had endless stories to tell of these days on the trail, and a renowned narrative gift, only to be matched and exceeded by his grandson, who, sixty years later, could recreate these conversations as if they had occurred the day before, adding, one always suspected, a few embellishments of his own. "Eleven cowboys," as Johnson remembered it, "made an average crew for a trail herd of fifteen hundred cows. Gathered and branded in Texas, the cattle were driven up the Chisholm Trail until they reached Abilene, Kansas, where they were slaughtered and sent East by railroad. When the rivers that crossed the trails were cold, the cattle would often balk partway across, circling and jumping on top of one another instead of moving in a straight line. Then the lead cowboy would have to ride out in front of the herd and get the cattle moving."[28]

The young boy would never forget his grandfather's image of men and cattle circling aimlessly in the cold, treacherous currents, their continued progress dependent on the daring and skill of the lead cowboy. In later years he was to describe the arena of national affairs as a huge swampland in which the participants often wandered, mired and confused, in circles of endless debate until the appearance of strong leadership. It is an irony he would not have appreciated that later commentators would accuse him of bringing the nation into just such a swampland—Vietnam—through the exercise of these very qualities of leadership and will.

But subduing a stampede was the most dangerous adventure of all. As he remembered his grandfather's version of it, "There was no foretelling what might start a stampede. It might be a clap of thunder, a lightning flash, a strange smell, or the rattle of a single snake in the middle of the night." Or, Lyndon always insisted his grandfather said—but it was more likely his own retrospective parable—"It might be started by one or two troublemaker cows that went around hooking the sleeping cattle."[29] One steer stood up, then another, and more and more until the whole herd was on its feet. To soothe the cattle down, lullabies were sung. That failing, all you could do was to outrun the wild herd, trying to swing its leaders around into its tail end, so as to turn the mass into a circle that would wind down like a spent top. You had to ride at a dead run in the dark of the night, knowing there were prairie dog holes all around and knowing that if the horse stepped into one of these holes, you could be crushed to death by the oncoming stampede.[30]

His grandfather talked, Johnson said, until the sun set. Even then, the boy did not want him to stop. But the talk always came to an end when Sam Ealy Johnson stood up. "You better go along now, son, your mama is waiting." Then, seeing the boy's disappointment, he invited Lyndon into the study, where there was a roll-top desk opened by a large gold key. Grandfather Johnson took the key from his pocket and unlocked the bottom drawer, filled with sticks of candy in all the colors of the rainbow. Every day the boy chose a different color, his grandfather locked the drawer, returned the key to his right pocket, and suddenly, from his other pocket, pulled another present—a big red apple. "I remember how I thought that deep pockets were wonderful things to have."[31] Lyndon remembered hurrying down the road, mounting the steps of his house in haste, anxious to avoid his mother's displeasure.

Johnson's image of the intrepid cowboy stayed with him the rest of his life, although he never experienced the working day of the cowboy, nor the long and lonely nights on the plain, for by the time he was born in 1908 the world of the cattle drives had collapsed. In the 1880s and '90s as the railroads penetrated the West, the long drives to market became increasingly unnecessary. Frightened cattle farmers, realizing the precariousness of their situation, began to fence in land which, until then, had been open. The stringing of barbed wire and the building of fences brought the cattle drives to an end. Indeed, the decline of the Western farmer had been going on for decades. Between 1860 and 1890 commodity prices declined persistently while the price of manufactured goods, protected by tariff barriers and monopolies, continued to rise. The economic life of the many in the West became increasingly dependent on the decisions of the few in the East—the monopolists who kept prices up, the middlemen who handled commodities on the exchanges, the railroads that levied heavy rates, the money powers that determined rates of currency, the political elite that supported a tax structure which bore disproportionately on land.

During this period of economic distress Johnson's grandfather had joined the newly found Populist Party, often traveling hundreds of miles to attend the large political camp meetings that so resembled evangelistic revivals, reading and circulating a prodigious number of crudely printed pamphlets from the Populist press, spreading the word of new hope for the common man. And in 1892 the Populist Party had supported its own candidate for President on a platform calling for government regulation of railroads, telegraph, and telephone, a graduated income tax, reform of the currency system, and a series of political reforms, including the secret ballot, the initiative and referendum, and direct election of Senators.[32]

But the Populist Party was also dead by the time Lyndon Johnson was born—killed through a combination of Republican McKinley's overwhelming victory over Populist-Democrat Bryan in 1896 and the Spanish-American War in 1898—and the reformist impulse had fallen into the hands of the Progressives, who shared a narrower vision of social change. This narrowed vision and the closing of the frontier meant a closing in of horizons for Sam Johnson, as for many of his generation. Accustomed to continual movement, the old man spent the last decades of his life in his small farmhouse on the Pedernales. And the more the past receded, the more idealized it became.

In the picture the old man created for the young boy, the dangers of the frontier were romanticized, its tedium forgotten. Fantasy mixed with memory, gradually lifting ordinary events to the level of heroic legend. Extravagant claims were made for the courage and daring of the cowboy: the tall, strong he-man, ready for action in any situation.[33] And with the idealized man came an idealized female: the strong, courageous pioneer woman, called upon to protect her home and family from the ravages of nature and the attacks of Indians. The stories Johnson heard about his grandmother, Eliza Johnson, fit this image. Over and over, his grandfather described the day when his wife, alone in the house with an infant child, hid beneath a trap door, her handkerchief stuffed in the baby's mouth, while Indians ransacked the house above.

"I always felt a little uneasy hearing those stories about my grandmother," Johnson later said. "For I knew that as we sat there and talked on the porch, she was inside the house, lying flat on her back, paralyzed with a stroke which she'd had when I was three or four. But so long as we stayed outside on the porch I felt happy and safe."[34]

The porch in front of the house was happy and safe; so, too, was Johnson's relationship with his grandfather—the adult who seemed to provide the boy with the pleasure of love without the constraints he experienced in his own house.

When Johnson was five, his family left the cabin on the river and moved to a frame house in Johnson City. His father had found some real estate business in Austin and wanted to be nearby. The new house was larger and more pleasant than the old one, and the move gave Rebekah an escape from her isolation. Though Johnson City was hardly more than a village, it had a high school, in which she soon taught debating, a newspaper, for which she wrote a weekly column, and an opera house, in which local plays, directed by Rebekah, were performed. Rebekah organized a Browning Society. She gave private lessons in elocution and she taught a class in "Old Bible." She joined a temperance society.

Johnson was not as happy as his mother about moving into town. The excitement of the new house was spoiled for the boy by the feeling that he had left behind his closest friend—his grandfather. Now he saw his grandfather only when the whole family went back to visit the farm, and he hated these visits since he had to sit in the parlor and listen to the adults talk. Even worse, he then had to see his paralyzed grandmother. Always before, she had remained in the bedroom, but now, when his whole family came to visit, they brought her to a chair and he would have to confront her sitting next to him: "Her skin was brown and wrinkled. Her body was twisted. I was afraid that I was meant to kiss her. I tried to imagine her as the strong pioneer woman she had once been. I remembered the amazing stories I had heard about her staggering courage in the face of Indian attacks. But age and illness had taken all life out of her face. She never said a word. She sat perfectly still. And I was terrified to sit beside her."[35]

It was in this period, Johnson later said, that he began having, night after night, a terrifying dream, in which he would see himself sitting absolutely still, in a big, straight chair. In the dream, the chair stood in the middle of the great, open plains. A stampede of cattle was coming toward him. He tried to move, but he could not. He cried out again and again for his mother, but no one came.

In later conversation, Johnson suggested a relationship between the chair in the dream and the chair where his paralyzed grandmother used to sit. As a child, he had, as he remembered it, a persistent fear of becoming paralyzed and sitting forever, like his grandmother.[36] But recurrent dreams are generally a statement of profound psychic dilemmas, suggesting unresolved problems far beyond the reach of daily events. Seen in this light, the boy's paralysis presents one solution, albeit painful, to the fear of acting out the forbidden Oedipal wish to eliminate the father and take the mother. Termed in psychiatric literature a "castration" or "punishment" dream, the paralysis would restrain what in young Johnson's case seems to have been a particularly powerful combination of desire, fear, and guilt.[37]

The Pedernales was not Thebes, however, and the importance of the dream lay more in its particular meaning than in its archetypal form. The cattle drive was the domain of the male in the world of fantasy and fact created for Johnson by his grandfather; controlling a stampede of cattle by one's own intense motion was the supreme test of a man's courage and skill. Pitted against this practical, active life was Rebekah's world of books and beauty and morality, a feminized world of dreamy thinkers whose idealism led inevitably to ruin and collapse. Both worlds rigidly defined—the one the object of aspiration, the other the object of scorn. Boys were supposed to be active, to run, shout, and get dirty; they were never to cry and never to play with dolls. Girls were supposed to read and sit still, dress pretty and stay clean, cry a lot and play with dolls. Yet Lyndon's mother always kept him clean and she read to him at the end of the day. She brushed his hair in long, yellow curls, dressed him like little Lord Fauntleroy, bought him a violin, and enrolled him in dancing class. He knew that his friends were laughing at him for taking time with these feminine things. He loved his mother and loved being close to her, but he feared he was becoming a sissy.

The equation of femininity, intellectuality, and paralysis—and the corresponding compulsions to move, keep control, stay in charge—becomes even clearer in later versions of the same dream which Johnson claimed he dreamt repeatedly for several months after his heart attack in 1955 and then again after North Vietnam's Tet offensive in 1968. In these dreams, which we will discuss later in more detail, Johnson had become Woodrow Wilson, the President he once characterized as "too intellectual" and "too idealist" for the people's good. In the dream, he was lying in a bed in the Red Room. His head was still his, but from the neck down his body was dead, victim of that paralysis which had held both Wilson and his grandmother in their final years. In the next room, he could hear all his assistants squabbling over who would get what parts of his power. He could neither talk nor walk and not a single aide tried to protect him.

Not long after the move into town, Johnson's grandfather died. He was seventy-seven years old. Johnson did not remember seeing the body. The experience that did stand out in his memory was a cool, dark moment in a corner of the family cemetery. He described that moment to me nearly sixty years later as we stood on the shaded plot, a hundred yards from the birthhouse, which still serves as the family cemetery, and where he, too, is now buried. Canopied by oaks beside the Pedernales, it is a lovely, restful place. Johnson, however, was agitated as he walked among the low stone markers and read them aloud one by one: Sam Ealy Johnson (1913); Sam Johnson (1937); Rebekah Johnson (1958). He pointed to a giant climbing oak and said he remembered standing by that tree at the ceremony for his grandfather, watching the coffin as it was lowered into the ground. A light rain had then started to fall. He remembered thinking at the time how happy the rain would make his grandfather. He recalled that during the ceremony he caught sight of his father's tearful eyes and the big red splotches on his cheeks. This was the first time he had seen his father cry. He had often seen his mother in tears, but she was a girl. It frightened him. When the small crowd began dispersing, Johnson ran up to his father and they walked together down the dirt road. He knew from the tone of his father's voice that a terrible thing had happened. As they walked away, he looked back at the tree against which he had been standing and felt, he said, that something within him had banged shut.[38]

Johnson remembered turning to his father after his grandfather died. The two had grown closer with the move into town, but now, with Grandpa Johnson dead, a feverish eagerness to resemble his father took possession of him. He listened to his father talk and, rejecting his mother's elocution lessons, adopted his father's crude, colorful, and alive way of talking. Yet unlike Sam's crudity, Lyndon's would always be controlled; with the son, the use of swearwords and obscenity usually had a point.

Imitating his father's friendliness, Lyndon struck up conversations with everyone he met. He became a favorite of all the older people in town, asking them how things were going, how they were feeling and what they thought about the latest political happenings. This capacity to charm his elders produced advantages with his peers: as one of his childhood friends later said, "Lyndon could talk my parents into anything, letting us do anything or go anywhere."[39]

In school, Johnson became something of a troublemaker.

He wanted to be outside with his father. His chronic restlessness earned him extra tasks as punishment, such as bringing in the firewood and cleaning the blackboards. He often failed to complete his lessons. But Rebekah refused to give up. Every morning at breakfast, holding his lesson book in her hand, she would read aloud to Sam the lesson of Lyndon's that was due that day. Forced to listen, Johnson would learn. If it took longer to read the lesson than to eat breakfast, Rebekah would walk him to school, reciting from the primer all the way. Still, Johnson never came to like reading for its own sake. He could sit still only if the stories were real histories and real biographies, that is, if they spoke mostly of the actions of other men. "Is it true?" he repeatedly asked. "Did it actually happen, Mama?"[40]

In the evenings, Sam liked to sit in the brown rocker on the porch, swapping tales and jokes with three or four of his political friends. Something in the laughing voices of these men excited Johnson's imagination. The boy stood in the half-darkness by the doorway, straining to hear these stories filled with colorful details about the comings and goings of the political figures of the day and the great historical figures of the past. He heard a lot of discussion about James Ferguson, the champion of the tenant farmer, elected Governor of Texas in 1914 on a liberal platform calling for a law fixing farm-rental prices. Re-elected in 1916, Ferguson ran into difficulties with the state legislators that led to his impeachment in 1917. Lyndon's father admired Ferguson greatly, and his uncle, Clarence Martin, serving as chief counsel for Ferguson's defense, argued that the charges against him were based solely on conservative opposition to his liberal stance. He also heard talk of Teddy Roosevelt and Woodrow Wilson. His father supported Wilson's New Freedom, but the defeated Bull Mooser, Teddy Roosevelt, remained the local hero. "Whenever I pictured Teddy Roosevelt," Johnson later said, "I saw him running or riding, always moving, his fists clenched, his eyes glaring, speaking out against the interests on behalf of the people."[41] There was also much talk of local county figures and endless calculations on how different families would vote in the next election.

"Mother found little of interest in those nightly sessions; to her, such politics were low and dull, and so were Daddy's friends. What attracted her wasn't personality, not detail—she saw that as gossip—but great issues and great ideas. She had

the Southerner's passion for rhetoric. To her the greatest politicians were the greatest orators—Daniel Webster, John
Calhoun, William Jennings Bryan."[42] Rebekah tried to interest
Lyndon in debate; she even coached his debating team at
school, but, for a long while, Lyndon simply mumbled too
much.[43]

"Mother was interested in national politics, not local. I
think she was hoping that someday my father would run for
national office—in particular for the same congressional seat
her father had tried and failed to get decades before. I'm not
sure when it was he ran for that seat, but Mother said the
problem was that he was too eloquent for the people's tastes.
He was more concerned about saying the right things than
about winning and he lost to a lesser man who sold himself
to the people door to door. But my father had no desire for
national office; he had no desire to leave his home."[44]

Sam had courted Rebekah during his first stint in the state
legislature (1904–1908). In those years, marked on the national level by Teddy Roosevelt's Square Deal, Sam earned
the reputation of a loyal progressive, supporting bills to tax
insurance, telephone, and sleeping car companies; to regulate
rates charged by public utility companies (water, gas, electric
power); to enact a franchise tax on corporations; to establish
the eight-hour workday; and to regulate lobbying. When his
two terms were up, however, he stayed out of politics for
nearly a decade and devoted his attention to his real estate
business.[45]

Though Sam failed to secure a stable income for his family
during those years, he kept up his ties with the legislature and
remained an important figure in the local power elite. After
the war in 1918, when Lyndon was ten, Sam began another
stint in the legislature, which lasted until 1924. The war had
bred an ugly intolerance in the country, and Texas was no
exception. In the spring of 1918, under the sway of strong
anti-German sentiment, a loyalty bill was passed in the legislature which specified that any person using disloyal language
at any time or place in the presence of another would be subject to imprisonment. "My father stood right up against that
situation," Johnson later said. "He got up on the floor of the
House of Representatives and made a wonderful speech
pleading for tolerance and common sense. He was a great
civil libertarian. He threw himself into the battle against the
provision that would have granted the power of arrest to ev-

ery Texas citizen, and that provision was defeated even
though the bill succeeded. He will always be a hero to the
German-Americans in our area for that. At the same time, he
fought the Ku Klux Klan and defended civil liberties on all
levels.

"I loved going with my father to the legislature. I would sit
in the gallery for hours watching all the activity on the floor
and then would wander around the halls trying to figure out
what was going on. The only thing I loved more was going
with him on the trail during his campaigns for re-election.
We drove in the Model T Ford from farm to farm, up and
down the valley, stopping at every door. My father would do
most of the talking. He would bring the neighbors up to date
on local gossip, talk about the crops and about the bills he'd
introduced in the legislature, and always he'd bring along an
enormous crust of homemade bread and a large jar of
homemade jam. When we got tired or hungry, we'd stop by
the side of the road. He sliced the bread, smeared it with
jam, and split the slices with me. I'd never seen him happier.
Families all along the way opened up their homes to us. If it
was hot outside, we were invited in for big servings of
homemade ice cream. If it was cold, we were given hot tea.
Christ, sometimes I wished it could go on forever."[46]

This growing identification with his father produced both
strain and pleasure. By comparison with most citizens of
Johnson City, Sam Johnson had a certain dash and style—
even if his dash and style were sometimes employed to glide
over his failures as head of the family. Sam Johnson never
did rise in the political world. He remained for life what he
was the day Rebekah married him—a small-time farmer and
trader who enjoyed local politics. If only the boy could have
felt as proud of him openly as he loved him privately. As it
was, Lyndon remained forever uneasy about having become,
in so much of his mind and his spirit, Sam Johnson's son.

Some of the tension came in the form of competition between father and son. Lyndon's younger brother, Sam Houston, describes one such episode. When he was three and
Lyndon was nine, the two brothers slept together in a small
room right next to their father's bedroom. At about midnight,
as he was snuggled warmly against his brother, he would hear
his father call: "Sam Houston, come in here and get me
warm." The boy crawled out of Lyndon's bed and went to his

father, holding himself perfectly still until his father fell asleep. Then he would hear Lyndon's call: "Sam Houston, come on back, I'm getting cold." Back he went, moving away from his father, quiet as a burglar, so that again he would snuggle up to his big brother.[47]

Aside from the slavish position of Sam in this peculiar game of power and convoluted sexuality, this episode reveals again Lyndon's uncommon presumption—the belief that he was somehow entitled to the same rights and privileges as his father. The younger brother's compliance with his older brother's wishes, even in the face of his father's contrary command, suggests the powerful position Lyndon held in his family structure. And when his father was away, this position was strengthened: Lyndon was left in charge of the household, responsible for taking care of his mother and delegating the daily chores to his sisters and brother.

The more serious tension between father and son reveals itself in a story Johnson later told about his first experience killing an animal. "In the fall and the spring, I spent every moment when I wasn't in school out in the open. With the other boys, I went hunting squirrels and rabbits. I carried a gun and every now and then I pointed it at the animals but I never wanted to kill any of them. I wanted only to know that I could kill if I had to. Then one day my daddy asked me how did it happen that I was the only boy in the neighborhood who had never shot an animal. Was I a coward? The next day I went back into the hills and killed a rabbit. It jumped out at me from behind a bush and I shot it in between the eyes. Then I went to the bathroom and threw up."[48]

The lessons in manhood continued. When he was fifteen, Johnson smashed up his father's car. He had borrowed the car to meet a new girl at a church gathering. On meeting Johnson, the girl realized that she was three years older and very quickly took off with someone else. Feeling sorry for himself, Johnson gathered a few of his friends and they went off together for a couple of drinks. Then they all piled into the car to go home. On the way, the car hit a bridge and turned upside down. The boys were not hurt, but the car was totally wrecked. Johnson was, as he remembered it, too frightened to know what to do. "I knew only that I could not face my father. I had four dollars in my pocket, so I hopped the bus to New Braunfels, where my uncle lived. I thought I could hide out there for a few days. The second day, Daddy tracked me down on the phone. I walked to the phone, feeling like I was going to the guillotine. I tried to keep my legs and my voice from shaking. My uncle looked at me in silence and I felt the blood rising to my face.

"My daddy said: 'Lyndon, I traded in that old car of ours this morning for a brand-new one and it's in the store right now needing someone to pick it up. I can't get away from here and I was wondering if you could come back, pick it up, and drive it home for me. And there's one other thing I want you to do for me. I want you to drive it around the courthouse square, five times, ten times, fifty times, nice and slow. You see there's some talk around town this morning that my son's a coward, that he couldn't face up to what he'd done, and that he ran away from home. Now I don't want anyone thinking I produced a yellow son. So I want you to show up here in that car and show everyone how much courage you've really got. Do you hear me?'

"'Yes sir,' I replied. I hung up the phone, shook hands with my uncle, and left right away."[49]

In telling the story, Johnson saw this as a lesson in manly courage. By returning home he was asserting the masculine virtue of "sticking it out." But as Johnson himself discloses, Sam had already informed him that the damage had been undone, or had led to benefit in the form of a brand-new car. Slipping away from responsibility had proved a sheer gain. He had avoided a confrontation with a perhaps irate father, delaying his return until the potential punisher became an actual accomplice. We shall encounter this aversion to confrontation many times again in Johnson's later life; so fearful was he of any remote appearance of weakness or loss of face, and so rigid was his definition of courage, that often he would shun situations where he was unable to assert his mastery.

In telling the story, Johnson also emphasized his father's generosity in deciding not to punish his son for wrecking the car. And, indeed, there was a certain generosity in Sam Johnson's handling of the accident. For all that, one need only picture Lyndon driving around the courthouse square fifty times to suggest the shame he must have felt in being forced to make his private accident the public property of Johnson City.

In this tale, as in the tale of the rabbit, the evidence suggests that, despite Johnson's conclusions, the boy was deeply humiliated by his father's tests of manliness. And, as before, Lyndon refused to admit anger toward his father, endeavoring rather to admire his father's manner of raising a son. "Oftentimes my father would talk to me through my mother. She'd be standing over the stove where she spent her life and he'd come in saying, 'Rebekah, you know that son of ours has the most foolish judgment of anyone I know ... why, he ...' and before you knew it, I was mending my ways."[50] But Lyndon's resentments would not remain unburied; self-esteem wounded by humiliation became vindictive.

The more powerful he became, the more Johnson forced people around him to submit to *his* tests of manhood.[51] Visitors to the LBJ Ranch were handed rifles and expected to shoot an antelope or a deer in the presence of the Majority Leader; politicians and bureaucrats were called upon to swim naked with the President in the White House pool; members of the Cabinet and the White House staff were compelled to accompany their boss into the bathroom and continue their conversation. From the boy's fear of being tested came the man's determination that *he* would be the one giving instead of taking the tests.

Just the same, Johnson seemed to endure his father's testing far better than his mother's gloomy silence. As Johnson remembered it, Rebekah said nothing to him about the smashup. Indeed, she had refrained for months from commenting about his mediocre performance in school or his frequent evenings on the town with his friends. She had her own way of showing her displeasure—not to yell or even to scold, but to greet her son at all times with an impassive stare. She made no secret of the fact that his drinking, fast driving, and generally aggressive behavior displeased her; nor did she conceal the repugnance she felt at the reputation he had established in school as a sluggish student who treated everything as a joke. Johnson knew by his mother's withdrawal that he had not lived up to the splendid vision she had held of him as a boy.

When Johnson graduated from high school in May, 1924, Rebekah allowed her quarrel with her son to surface at last. When she spoke, daily taking him to task for his slovenly manner, she had, as Johnson later described it, "a terrible knifelike voice."[52] She inquired scrupulously into his plans for the future and, eliciting no assurance that he was even willing to entertain the notion of college, she closed him out completely. During supper she would direct her remarks to her husband and her younger children, never so much as confirming Lyndon's existence. Directly after supper, she went to bed.

"We'd been such close companions, and, boom, she'd abandoned me. I wanted to please her, but something told me I'd go to pieces if I went to college. I'd just finished ten years of sitting inside a school; the prospect of another four years was awful. It would make me a sissy again and I would lose my daddy's respect."[53]

In this stormy period, Johnson suffered a recurrent dream that he was sitting alone in a small cage. The cage was completely bare, he said, except for a stone bench and a pile of dark, heavy books. As he bent down to pick up the books, an old lady with a mirror in her hand walked in front of the cage. He caught a glimpse of himself in the mirror and to his horror he found that the boy of fifteen had suddenly become a twisted old man with long, tangled hair and speckled, brown skin. He pleaded with the old woman to let him out, but she turned her head and walked away. At this point in the dream, as he remembered it, he woke up, his hands and his forehead damp and dripping with sweat. He sat up in the bed and then, not fully knowing what he meant by it but believing in it faithfully, he said half aloud: "I must get away. I must get away."[54]

The dream is almost too good, too easy to fit into the pattern of his other dreams. It is without jagged edges, the false doors, blank spaces, and swerves that usually complicate our memories of dreams. I wondered as Johnson described it to me whether he was telling it in part for my sake. Perhaps the obvious interest I had shown in his earlier dream provoked him to construct an additional one. Perhaps he said to himself: "You intellectuals, you like dreams? I'll give you all you like." There is no way of knowing.

But whether it was truly a remembered dream or simply a yarn spun for the sake of the conversation, the image of the jail and the old woman suggests again a hostility toward his mother. He has done the duty his mother has asked of him. He has voluntarily caged himself in another educational prison. But the price of recovering his mother's love is nothing less than his own manhood. Yet here, as always, the bad feelings toward her had to be deflected, as if an acknowledgment of her failings would be treasonous. She was ever the "great lady," the "perfect woman," "brilliant," "sexy," "beautiful," and "endlessly enchanting." Over time, however, while unfailing in his expressions of love for his mother, Johnson adopted those patterns of behavior she most despised: he wheeled and dealed behind closed doors; spoke crudely; interrupted family occasions with unexpected guests; turned to alcohol for relaxation and solace; and expressed a lasting distrust and fear of ideas, intellectuals, debates, books, and eloquence.[55]

Actually, he believed, it was the intellectuals who hated him: "The men of ideas think little of me, they despise me."[56] And that, too, reflected his unconscious perceptions of his mother's feelings. That there was some truth to this—given the prejudices of the literary and publishing world toward the boisterous style of the Texan—made it all the more useful for overlooking his own feelings of hatred toward the type of people whom his mother so admired. It was not he who wanted to injure them; it was they who wanted to injure him and were responsible for his failure. In retirement, Johnson sincerely believed that he would have been the greatest President in his country's history had it not been for the intellectuals and the columnists—the men of ideas and the men of words.

From time to time, Johnson's antagonism toward these men of culture assumed the crude shape of simple exhibitionism. His penchants for talking to visitors while on the toilet, for using crude and scatological language, and for exhibiting his sexual organs were especially pronounced when he dealt with "gentlemen of culture." In renouncing his civility he stripped them of theirs; he reduced them to his own ignominy, in which he celebrated a triumph over his mother's voice within him.

In this antagonism toward the men of ideas, however, Johnson's attitudes were shared by many others, an aspect of an indigenous anti-intellectualism. For years in America, intellect had been pitted against active work and practicality since theory was held to be the opposite of practice; frequently it had even been pitted against democracy since affairs of the mind were associated with aristocracies.[57]

The sad and poignant thing for Johnson, however, was not his anti-intellectualism in itself but his need to be accepted by the very people he scorned. For the boy's hidden feelings toward his mother were succeeded by the man's feelings

toward Culture: subdued awe and blatant bitterness, a sense
that he, unlike the Eastern intellectuals, had none of those ridiculous and precious tokens, an Ivy League degree and a
facility for words. "They" came into the world fully clothed;
he remained essentially naked no matter how much power he
acquired. "My daddy always told me," Johnson once remarked, "that if I brushed up against the grindstone of life,
I'd come away with far more polish than I could ever get at
Harvard or Yale. I wanted to believe him, but somehow I
never could."[58]

In drifting back and forth between these feelings of awe
and bitterness, Lyndon Johnson's behavior is reminiscent of
an important strain in the American struggle for national
identity. The country was born in repudiation of Europe, yet
many Americans were forever turning to Europe for approval
and justification of the way of life they had created—especially in matters of culture, art, and intellect. For generations, Europe contrived to haunt and heckle the American
imagination; Europe's greater genius would be denied one
day, enhanced the next. This ambivalence often took the
form, as did Lyndon Johnson's own ambivalence, of a conflict over the comparative value of will, on the one hand, and
intellect on the other.

Yet our concern here is not simply with the conflicts from
which Lyndon Johnson suffered, but with how he surmounted
or utilized these conflicts, adapting them to the realities of his
life. And here the interesting biographical fact is that Johnson
knew enough at the age of fifteen to know that he simply had
to get away.

That summer—the summer of 1924—the opportunity arrived. A group of Johnson's friends had decided to leave
home and go to California. For each of the boys the trip no
doubt meant something different—adventure, the hope of
work. There was a report, one of the boys later recollected,
that money out there grew on trees and that a person had but
to reach up and get it. Lyndon, youngest of the group, listened in as they made their plans; he watched as they fixed
up the old Model T that would carry them West. He wanted
desperately to go along, but he knew that his parents would
never allow him to leave. "Going was one hell of a problem,"
he said. "I decided I'd just say to my mother and father that
I was going West with the boys. I knew it would be an emotional scene, but one night I decided to look them straight in

the eye and reveal my plans. But when I reached the front door of my house, I began to shiver uncontrollably. At last, I went in. They sat opposite one another at the kitchen table. My sisters and brother were there. I tried to speak, but I couldn't say a goddamn word. I lost my nerve."[59]

One week later, before the sun came up on a Monday morning, the boys took off in their Model T. At the last minute, Johnson decided, without asking or telling anyone, to go with them. He jumped into the car. "Here I am," he said. "Let's hurry along and be on our way."

During the entire trip Johnson walked around carrying his suitcase as though it were incredibly heavy and had within it enough clothes to last a family of twenty for fifteen years. His companions could not imagine why Johnson took so much along and yet wore the same clothes day after day. Then one afternoon the baling wire that Johnson had used to tie up the suitcase came loose and it opened on the street. Out rolled the sum of Johnson's worldly possessions—a straw hat!

Johnson saw the trip, when he talked about it later, in cartoon imagery. He recounted brushes with gruff poker players, scenes of burying money in underground holes, and fancies of reliving his grandfather's life on the frontier.[60]

But the old frontier had promised economic and spiritual independence, and in California, in 1924, that independence was not easy to secure. Indeed, Johnson was barely able to survive on the grapes he picked, the dishes he washed, and the cars he fixed. Just the same, he remembered living happily for a time in different places. Free of both his mother and his father, he found he had an immense curiosity about the different kinds of people with whom he worked—the field hands in the Imperial Valley, the cooks in the all-night cafés, the garage mechanics in the big cities. He found himself constantly entertaining his fellow workers with stories and jokes. People seemed to like him; they admired his quickness.

Johnson lived the vagabond life for nearly a year; then, when his money dried up completely, he took a job in Los Angeles as a clerk to a criminal lawyer. The job was no accident. The lawyer was a cousin of Rebekah's. There Lyndon stayed for another year, until one August day in 1926 when, suddenly, faced with an offer of a ride to Texas, he decided that after two years' absence he was ready to return.

Johnson would long remember this trip back home; he

later theatrically designated it *the* moment when he found his
vocation of politics. On the trip, as Johnson recounted it, he
thought a great deal about his parents. "I still believed my
mother the most beautiful, sexy, intelligent woman I'd ever
met and I was determined to recapture her wonderful love,
but not at the price of my daddy's respect. Finally, I saw it
all before me. I would become a political figure. Daddy
would like that. He would consider it a manly thing to be.
But that would be just the beginning. I was going to reach beyond my father. I would finish college; I would build great
power and gain high office. Mother would like that. I would
succeed where her own father had failed; I would go to the
Capitol and talk about big ideas. She would never be disap-
pointed in me again."[61]

Johnson reached his boyhood home on a Sunday afternoon. When he walked inside the door, he carried with him
an air of pride and self-respect. At supper that night, there
was, as he remembered it, much conversation. Later, left in
his room, he knew that somehow things were different. He
was ready to embark on his future career.

Perhaps the trip was, as Johnson believed, a turning point,
marking the transition from childhood to adulthood. The separation from home obviously helped to distance Lyndon in a
positive way from his mother's ceaseless pressure. And the
resolve he felt the night he returned certainly showed up in
the rapid successes he achieved once he entered college. But
turning points are rarely as dramatic as we remember them
to be. Despite his resolution, Lyndon stayed away from the
study of books for another six months, taking, instead, a job
with a road gang. Finally, one hot afternoon in February,
1927, he went to his mother and said: "All right, I'm sick of
working just with my hands and I'm ready to try and make it
with my brain."[62]

The next day Rebekah phoned San Marcos College, where
her mother had found work as a house mother after her father died. Primarily a teachers college, San Marcos was *the*
college in Southwest Texas; it was inexpensive, familiar, and
close to home. One week later, Lyndon was admitted as a
provisional student, pending the completion of a series of
entrance exams. "I'll never forget," Johnson later said, "how
my mother helped me out on those exams. She came to San
Marcos and stayed up with me the entire night before the
math exam, drilling me over and over until it finally got into

my head."[63] From the breakfast table in Johnson City to a student room at San Marcos College, she was always his coach. But this time necessity limited Rebekah's aid; San Marcos was thirty miles from Johnson City and Rebekah still had four younger children at home. So after the exam, she went home, leaving Lyndon on his own in an environment that provided numerous outlets for his abilities and talents, allowing him for the first time to employ all those resources he had developed as a child as a protection against the unremitting tensions at home: negotiation, charm, manipulation, avoidance, and control.

Released from the constant dilemma of his parents' conflicting demands, Johnson's prodigious energies turned from an inner world of turmoil, undependable love, and need to the external environment. From the world of work and the conquest of ever-widening circles of men, Johnson hoped to obtain the steady love he had lacked as a child. The problem was that each successful performance led only to the need for more. There was no place to rest so long as love and the self-esteem based on love depended upon another's approbation. So Johnson plunged into ceaseless activity, always searching for the one thing external success could never provide: the reassurance of being loved for who he was rather than for what he was doing.[64]

Chapter 2

Education and the Dream of Success

"What you accomplish in life," Lyndon Johnson wrote in the college paper during his freshman year, "depends almost completely upon what you make yourself do . . . perfect concentration and a great desire will bring a person success in any field of work he chooses. The very first thing one should do is to train the mind to concentrate upon the essentials and discard the frivolous and unimportant. This will ensure real accomplishment and ultimate success."[1]

One is tempted to dismiss these words as the recitation of an acquired credo, and yet Johnson's college years reflect an incredibly precocious understanding of the requisites for achievement. In the first month he studied the structure of the college as he had, less consciously, come to understand the treacherous currents of his family home, and later would strive to master the relationship of men and position that constituted the Congress, the Senate, and the executive branch of government. Nearly all of the seven hundred students came from small towns and rural areas within a hundred miles of San Marcos—from the German settlements of Fredericksburg and New Braunfels, the prairie communities of Lockhart and Gonzales, the hill-country towns of Blanco and Johnson City. There were ten buildings on the campus, plus laboratories, shops, gymnasiums, and athletic fields. The faculty numbered fifty-six; some departments had only one or two members.[2]

Freshman Johnson wanted to know precisely how things worked, who made them work, what activities to join, what courses to take, which professors to seek out—all with a view to recognition, achievement, and a maximum of control over this new environment. There were, in his ability to comprehend the dynamics of San Marcos—its pulse points, sources of energy and command—a prescience and a discipline rare in anybody; extraordinary, almost shocking, in a boy of eighteen—so extraordinary, indeed, that one's credulity would

49

be strained by Johnson's account were his portrait not corrob-
orated by classmates who recall his ambition, his overwhelming, often overbearing personality, and especially his incessant
motion: half-racing through the campus with long, loping
strides; talking with both arms flailing; sitting at his desk
while restless fingers drummed the surface. He did not, as
they remember, work like most other people; the energy
never seemed to wear down.[3]

From the beginning Johnson set out to win the friendship
and respect of those people who would assist his rise within
the community which composed San Marcos. Most obvious
was the president of the college, Cecil Evans, whose favor
would have a multiplier effect with the faculty and student
body. But Johnson was not alone in the desire to have a
special relationship with Evans. "I knew," Johnson later said,
"there was only one way to get to know Evans and that was
to work for him directly."[4] Without that daily contact, given
the demands on any college president and the natural distance between the administration and students, Johnson figured that at best he could become one of the thirty or forty
students whom the college president could identify by name.
And that, clearly, was not enough.

It was the policy of the college to give students—especially
scholarship students—part-time employment, in the library,
cafeteria, bookstore, and in the construction and janitorial
crews—wherever it was possible to dispense with regular employees. Johnson's first job was on the college clean-up crew
picking up papers, rocks, and trash. Most of the students considered this unpleasant work, worthy of the minimum effort
necessary to avoid being fired. But Johnson brought to it the
same zeal he now brought to everything else. He imagined
himself in a race to determine who could clean up the most
trash in the least amount of time. The reality, of course, was
that Johnson raced only against himself since he alone cared,
yet his eagerness left its mark: when he applied for a better
job, he received it at once, assistant to the janitor of the
science building. At this post he again labored with extravagant enthusiasm, and again his efforts were rewarded: the
next job he got was the one he had coveted all along—special
assistant to the president's personal secretary.[5]

In this post Johnson's assigned job was simply to carry
messages from the president to the department heads and, occasionally, to other faculty members. Johnson saw that the

rather limited function of messenger had possibilities of expansion; for example, encouraging recipients of the messages to transmit their own communications through him. He occupied a desk in the president's outer office, where he took it upon himself to announce the arrival of visitors. These added services evolved from a helpful convenience into an aspect of the normal process of presidential business. The messenger had become an appointments secretary, and, in time, faculty members came to think of Johnson as a funnel to the president. Using a technique that was later to serve him in achieving mastery over the Congress, Johnson turned a rather insubstantial service into a process through which power was exercised. By redefining the process, he had given power to himself.

Evans eventually broadened Johnson's responsibilities to include handling his political correspondence and preparing his reports for the state agencies with jurisdiction over the college and its appropriations. After all, as the student was quick to explain, his father had been a member of the state legislature and Lyndon had often accompanied him to Austin, where he had gained some familiarity with the workings of the legislature and the personalities of its leaders. This claim might have seemed almost ludicrous had it not come from someone who already must have seemed an inordinately political creature. Soon Johnson was accompanying Evans on his trips to the State Capitol in Austin, and, before long, Evans came to rely upon his young apprentice for political counsel. For Johnson was clearly at home in the state legislature; whether sitting in a committee room during hearings or standing on the floor talking with representatives, he could, in later reports to Evans, capture the mood of individual legislators and the legislative body with entertaining accuracy. The older man on whose favor Johnson depended now relied on him or, at least, found him useful.

Another man wooed by Johnson was Professor Harry Greene of the government department, one of the most popular and highly respected members of the faculty and the coach of the debating team. Johnson thought him a teacher possessing special flair and integrity, a fearless expectation of popularity, and a contempt for petty obstacles. Here was a man sufficiently confident to say: "I know that this is right and that is wrong." Greene believed that history and culture should be useful. He liked poetry that could be recited, songs that could be sung, paintings that told a story. With these opinions Johnson wholeheartedly agreed. His only problem was to find time with the master. During and after class Lyndon bombarded Greene with questions, comments, and criticisms. At the end of the day, he aggressively sought Greene out, engaging him in still more conversation. The more Johnson talked, the more Greene responded. Eventually, these talks at the end of the day became a ritual desired by both teacher and student. Again, at least in Johnson's mind, the roles of apprentice and master seemed easily reversible.

Johnson had not been at San Marcos very long before discovering that a small group dominated nearly all activities of the student body: the student council, college newspaper, class offices, literary magazine, etc. Most members of this governing elite were athletes. Their organization, founded as an exclusive social fraternity a decade before, was called the Black Stars. Johnson was not an athlete, and when his name came up for consideration by the Black Stars, it was rejected. One can only speculate as to the effect of this rebuff, but rejection was always a powerful source of dread and energy in Johnson's life, compelling him either to withdraw from danger—as he fell ill or contemplated quitting before nearly every election contest—or to find some way to nullify its consequences. Whatever the psychic implication of this particular exclusion, the practical consequence was to make Johnson the leader of a mini-revolution in campus politics that was to end the power of the Black Stars.

Johnson swiftly formed his own secret organization—the White Stars—whose purpose was to wrest political control from the Black Stars. The initial problem was to keep their identity secret until a long-range strategy had been developed and they had built up enough strength for a direct challenge. "We had a rule," Johnson said, "that no more than two of us could be seen together on the campus. If a third member came along, we had special code signals as to which one was expected to leave."[6] So compelling was Johnson's insistence upon secrecy that decades later one of the White Stars, describing the group for the Johnson Library's Oral History Project, felt constrained to say: "LBJ and a few other campus leaders felt . . . that everybody needed competition. So there was a group composed of some eight or nine that organized another secret fraternity and in order that I don't violate some vows I took some forty years ago, there are portions of it that I will not discuss."[7] The elaborate nature of the concealment suggests, more than practical safeguards of conspiracy, a powerful inner inclination toward secrecy in the acquisition and use of power, which was to manifest itself decades later on a far larger stage.

Each of the six original members of the White Stars was responsible for learning about the participants in different student groups: the YMCA group, the townies, the debating society, the music and art group. Several nights a week the secret cabal met to pool their information. From these discussions Johnson became aware of a widespread, if concealed, resentment against the Black Stars. Although 90 percent of the students were nonathletes, the athletes received all the privileges: they went to the head of the cafeteria line, they registered first during enrollment, they were excused from regular chapel, they were feted at special banquets.

Still, these injustices were trivial, Johnson believed, alongside the tremendously inequitable distribution of the student activities fund. On admission to San Marcos, each student paid a fee of $17, a considerable sum for most. The money, totaling nearly $12,000, was turned over to the student council, which had the power to decide how it should be spent. Over the years the student council, dominated by the Black Stars, had allocated most of the fund to athletic activities. Johnson discovered the extent of this preference by examining the budget in the president's office. Eighty percent of the funds went into campus sports, the remainder being divided among the debating team, the drama society, the glee club, special speakers, and other campus activities.

Johnson later claimed that the moment he saw these figures he knew that redistribution of the funds would become the issue to muster the White Stars. Nevertheless, he moved cautiously, assigning each White Star the responsibility of finding out from the members of each campus group the answer to two questions. First: what are the things which you, as a member of the debating team (or the glee club or the drama society), want to do but cannot do because of insufficient funds? Second: do you realize that if your organization received even one-fifth as much as the athletic groups, you could do all these things and more? On this foundation of discontent, the White Stars mounted their campaign. Johnson's technique was that of the entrepreneur who aimed not simply at satisfying present needs but at developing new and expansive ones.

Within one year, their membership expanded to twenty, the White Stars ran an insurgent slate of candidates for student offices against the traditional slate of Black Stars. Johnson's strategy worked. Five of his slate were elected to the student council: three, including Lyndon Johnson, to the college newspaper, and two to the literary magazine. With this early victory, however, Johnson would not be content: "Ambition," he wrote at the time, "is an uncomfortable companion many times. He creates a discontent with present surroundings and achievements; he is never satisfied but always pressing forward to better things in the future."[8]

The key to Johnson's strategy for increasing the power of the White Stars turned on his ability to render political things that previously had not been—that is, to make new matters negotiable. He prodded the new members of the *College Star* and the *Pedagog* to use their positions to publicize the activities and accomplishments of nonathletes. Recognizing the power of patronage, he asked the secretary to the president if he could share some of the administrative burden involved in distributing student jobs. Before long, students could recognize White Star supporters by one look at the roster of jobs. The inside jobs in the library, in the cafeteria, in the bookstore, and in the administrative offices were held by White Stars; all the outside jobs in construction, maintenance, and painting were allotted to the Black Stars.

By the time Johnson reached his senior year the White Stars had gained considerable power in the college. The one office that had eluded them was the presidency of the senior class. Knowing—or perhaps fearing—that he himself had made too many enemies, Johnson selected Bill Deason, his best friend, as the group's candidate. It would be an uphill fight; the Black Stars had nominated Dick Speer, perhaps the most popular boy in the school. Into this campaign Johnson poured all his youthful passion. Day and night he caucused the White Stars, determining which blocs were leaning what way. The final count taken on the night before the election showed Deason behind by the substantial margin of twenty votes. "We were very discouraged," said Bill Deason, recalling that evening, "and we gave up and quit; that is, all except LBJ. There was our group, there was the athletes' group, and then there were folks who belonged to neither group . . . and

there was a third group which we called the YMCA group
. . . and they had been against us because Dick Speer was
also a member of the YMCA and a fine outstanding student.
So there wasn't any reason why they shouldn't support him.
But LBJ in his inimitable way said to himself, 'Well, if I can
change that group, we might win it. The rest of you may go
to bed, but I'm not.' "9

Throughout the night Johnson tramped from boardinghouse to boardinghouse, courting votes. Looking back,
Johnson recalled a dreadful evening, cold and drizzly. He
was exhausted, but he felt that he had to keep going until the
last possible moment.

At San Marcos politics meant talking with individuals, often very sleepy individuals. That night, student after student,
strongly wishing to silence Johnson when he began to talk,
ended up transfixed. Johnson possessed an uncanny instinct
for knowing which of his own qualities would produce the
greatest impact on each person. Ebullience, fits of rage, logical argument, patriotic exhortation, flattery: this acute and
indefatigable young man could alter his language and his
tone to solicit the desired effect.

Here, as would be the case in the future, reliance on the
forcefulness of his persuasive power was central to Johnson's
success. "His greatest forte," Deason said, "is to look a man
in the eye and do a convincing job of selling him his viewpoint; he could do it then and he can still do it today."10 The
next day, when the votes were counted, Deason had won by
eight votes; and thereby the White Stars gained complete control of campus politics. That year a basic redistribution of the
student activities fund took place in the direction of intellectual and cultural pursuits.

In addition to his central role in campus politics, Johnson
became the editor of the *College Star*, a prize-winning de-
bater, and an honors student. The world of San Marcos had
accommodated his gifts. If some found him tiresome, and
even his friends admitted that he was difficult, they were nonetheless bedazzled by his vitality, guile, and endurance, his
powers of divination and ability to appeal to the core interests of other people. And his gifts were more concentrated
than those of others in a student body typically torn by conflicting aspirations and divided desires. Ambition so united
every element of his personality that in the course of three

years he had made himself the absolute center of the small world of San Marcos.

Even in college, Johnson did not regard, or at least did not portray, success as an end in itself. The drive for power was justified by the belief that in controlling others he was acting in their best interests, giving them things they could not provide for themselves. His mother had taught him, Johnson explained to me, that power had value only when used to benefit people. And his editorials in the college paper reflect an emerging self-portrait which corresponds faithfully to his mother's ideal. "There is a selfishness," he wrote in 1929, "which is more sordid than that which comes of the love of money alone. It is the selfishness which restrains one from the doing of goodly deeds. . . . Glorious as is genius, it is of little value unless it is wisely and practically applied for the comfort and welfare of mankind. Great and desirable as is talent, failure to use it in the interest of humanity only adds to the responsibility of him who has it. Powerful and useful as is wealth, it places added responsibility on him who is its possessor."[11]

Nor were these sentiments confined to Johnson's public editorials; they appeared as well in his frequent letters to Johnson City. "My dear mother," Johnson wrote,

> The end of another busy day brought me a letter from you. Your letters always give me more strength, renewed courage and that bulldog tenacity so essential to the success of any man. There is no force that exerts the power over me that your letters do. I have learned to look forward to them so long and now when one is delayed a spell of sadness and disappointment is cast over me.
>
> I have been thinking of you all afternoon. As I passed through town on my way home to supper I could see the mothers doing their Xmas shopping. It made me wish for my mother so much. I thought of the hard times that you always have in seeing that every child is supplied with a gift from mother. I hope the years to come will place me in a position where I can relieve you of the hardships that it has fallen your lot to suffer—and I'm going to begin on a small scale right now. The enclosed is very small but you can make it go a long way. I don't

guess daddy has found me a job—so I may not get home for the holidays. I'll be thinking of all of you every minute. I love you so much,

Your son . . .[12]

Whether it was the college student promising gifts to his mother or the President of the United States producing houses and jobs for the American people, Johnson always associated the delivery of "good works" with the attainment of power and position. After he left the White House, Johnson would contrast his outlook with the conduct of his successor and others. "Some men want power simply to strut around the world and to hear the tune of 'Hail to the Chief.' Others want it simply to build prestige, to collect antiques, and to buy pretty things. Well, I wanted power to give things to people—all sorts of things to all sorts of people, especially the poor and the blacks."[13]

Lyndon Johnson was never the anonymous donor. Rather, his was a most visible benevolence which reminded recipients at every turn of how much he had done for them. Giving was a necessary part of a mission to reform, reshape, and thereby redeem. Paternalism was inextricably bound to such generosity. The cost to the recipient of the goods Johnson delivered seemed fair enough to him—gratitude, affection, a trust manifested by the willingness to let him decide what was best for them. In time, there was no mistaking his gifts: they had "LBJ"—and later "USA"—stamped all over them.

Already apparent during his college days was the pious preacher in his pulpit, an image he worked so hard to project. Nearly all his editorials begin and end with a moral injunction. The student who courted votes door to door in the middle of the night, tempering his appeal to the sensed desire of every individual, wrote:

The world today is looking for men who are not for sale;
Men who are masters of themselves and their tempers;
Men who place principle above all else;
Men who are honest and true;
Men who love work and the contentment it brings;
Men who are willing to lose sight of self, ease and
    pleasure in the effort to serve others.[14]

"Duty," Johnson editorialized that same year, "drives its devotees with a relentless hand through trials that seem in-

tolerable. No labor is too arduous for Duty to exact, no sacrifice too great for her to demand, no service beyond her command."[15] Duty's gender is feminine. Rebekah had insisted
that, in politics, the true gentleman always proceeded from
the most splendid of motives in pursuit of the highest ideals;
good works evidenced divine sponsorship; every action should
reflect fealty to the social good and public benevolence demonstrating a Christian spirit. The protagonist in Rebekah's ro-
mance of the godly politician, so alien to the brutal realities
of political life that her husband relished, had been her own
father. Her description of the public-spirited man left no
room for the continual striving, deceptions, and bruising com-
petitions, the elements of seduction and compulsion, which
are the stuff of political life, and the means by which public
power is secured and maintained even for the most beneficent of ends. It is not simply that she thought power should
be exercised for public good. That, after all, is a conviction
shared by many more participants in public life than fashionable cynicism allows. But it contained the prescription that
motives and means should be equally pure. It invoked "the
servant of the people," a long and partly mythic tradition
running through Benjamin Franklin, Thomas Jefferson, and
Andrew Carnegie—the tradition of the gentleman of rank
who sets aside his own concerns and dons the robe of public
service and benevolence as an expression of democratic
equality and duty.[16]

The characterization of public life contained in Johnson's
college writings had a counterpart in the nature of father-
hood. "When troubles beset the family," he wrote in his very
first editorial, the mother can find comfort in "tears and con-
fidences," but the father "must square his shoulders, reso-
lutely grit his teeth, suppress his emotions and with renewed
courage meet the issue." The father, Johnson explained, was
"the producer, the provider and the protector."[17] These were,
of course, the very capacities which Rebekah felt her own
husband lacked. And her son had been burdened from his
earliest years with the tales of Sam's weakness and failure,
along with the sense that he, Lyndon, must compensate for
his father's deficiencies and assume the role that Sam had abdicated—a responsibility with unbearable and inadmissible
overtones. "At the center of my mother's philosophy," Johnson explained to me, "was the belief that the strong must
care for the weak. From the early days when she knew that I

was to be the strongest of the five—with the most ambition and self-discipline and the most successful—she made me feel responsible for the weaker ones in the family, who used to get into trouble by drinking and cavorting around. On weekends they would run off to the city and rack up enormous bills. Mother would ask me to fix things up. I resented it every time, but I always did what she asked. For she would tell me over and over that the strong *must* care for the weak."[18]

The day would come when this older brother/father, responding to the needs of blacks, would offer the civil rights bill; as panacea to the nation's need, offer the Great Society; and, amid the final crisis of his career, use Rebekah's lessons—almost her words—to justify America's involvement in Vietnam: "There is," he told the country, "a great responsibility on the strong. The oldest member of the family has got to look after the smaller ones and protect them when the wolf comes to the door. The boy of the household has got to look after his sisters. Now it's not true that we've got to police all of the world ... but the good Lord has smiled kindly upon us and we have an obligation as fellow human beings to help protect our neighbors against a bunch of desperadoes."[19]

If Johnson's college writings have the qualities of baccalaureate sermons, one must remember that he was voicing the accepted pieties of his day and place—the small-town Texas where success was a reward for virtuous effort, ambition was an admired good, and there was little room for cynicism. If running through Johnson's life there is a duality of word and deed, as if the spoken word were vapor, it would be a mistake to assume that Johnson was simply a young Machiavellian who understood that it is well for a leader or an aspirant to power *to seem* religious, sincere, faithful, and humane. Conceptions of sacrifice, duty, and benevolence were as inseparable from and as deeply rooted in his character as his political skills and his pursuit of power.

San Marcos was also the setting for Lyndon Johnson's first serious love, twenty-year-old Carol Davis. She was, he recalled, "very beautiful, tall and blond with dark blue eyes. Her skin was pale and very soft. She was very clever and everyone admired her. I fell in love with her the first moment we met. She seemed so much more alive than all the other girls I knew, interested in everything; she played the violin and wrote poetry but also liked politics and loved the out-of-doors. I still remember the summer evenings we spent together, lying next to the river in a waist-high mass of weeds, talking about our future. I had never been happier. After a while we began to talk about marriage.

"We decided that Carol's parents had a right to know that we were as serious as we were. The Davises were one of the oldest and best families in Kerrville [a town about fifty miles from Johnson City]. Mr. Davis was a wealthy banker, an extreme conservative in politics, and a member of the Ku Klux Klan. I knew it would be a difficult relationship, but I believed that I could win them over. So one evening in June, Carol arranged for me to be invited to her home for a family dinner. The dinner began with a couple of glasses of wine, which made me more talkative than usual. I talked about my experiences in California and my activities in college. But the atmosphere, which was cold to begin with, just got colder and colder as I talked. I realized there was nothing I could do or say that night that would be considered right. Carol's father hated everything about me."[20]

Each sensed rebuff compelled him into further monologues as he searched with increasing urgency for some key to the father's approval. The capacities which had already become his most reliable armor and weapon were now failing him in what must have seemed one of the most important quests of his life. It was always difficult for Lyndon Johnson to understand that there were some passions and ideas which could not be subdued or overwhelmed by any appeal of which he was capable.

"I won't let you, I won't have my daughter marrying into that no-account Johnson family," Davis is reported to have told his daughter. "I've known that bunch all my life, one generation after another of shiftless dirt farmers and grubby politicians. Always sticking together and leeching onto one another so the minute one starts to make it, the others drag him down. None of them will ever amount to a damn."[21] In Lyndon's presence that night, Davis was no less direct. As Johnson remembered it, before that evening was over Davis had assailed his father's politics and then disparaged his grandfather, saying that everyone in Blanco County knew that Sam Ealy Johnson had been "nothing but an old cattle rustler." "No criticism could have hurt more," Johnson explained to me. As far as he was concerned, that was it. " 'To hell with the whole family,' I said to myself. 'I'll never marry

Carol or anyone in the whole damn family. Davis is right about the Johnsons sticking together; they always have and they always will and they don't need to mix with the likes of the Davises to get along. We'll make it on our own.' I left the Davis home that night determined never to see Carol again. For a long time after I got back to my room, I sat in a chair without moving. I felt numb and angry.

"The next morning Carol came into my room. Her face was red from crying, she looked as if she hadn't slept at all. She told me that until this moment she'd loved her father more than any other man and that to go against him on a matter as important as this would bring terrible pain to her for the rest of her life. But she'd decided that she had to do it. She loved me and she wanted to marry me. All the while she was talking I thought of the many nights we had dreamed of our future together. But all this had to be put in the past, forgotten. It could never work for us. I told her that, I was very firm, and after a long moment of silence, she went away. Long afterward, I still felt the pain of losing her; I missed her, and I missed the nights along the water terribly. I was lonely as I had never been before. But this did not change the way I felt."

After that morning Johnson did not see Carol Davis again until seven years later when she attended his opening speech for his first congressional campaign in February, 1937. Mr. Davis, Johnson recounted, was leading the Blanco County opposition to his candidacy, and had personally authored and spread a claim that, if elected, the first act of this young radical would be to fight for public confiscation of all the power companies (which, in fact, Johnson claimed, is precisely what he wanted to do). Johnson remembered beginning his speech with a blunt denunciation of Davis and his friends as enemies of the people, and, as he spoke, being startled by the unexpected glimpse of Carol Davis leaning against the back wall of the auditorium.

"She was wearing a white dress. Her face was pale and sad. I sensed the agony she was experiencing in listening to me attack her father. As soon as I saw her, I stopped in midstream and softened my speech, suggesting that perhaps there were two sides to all these questions and that it was important to recognize that all these men were honorable men, no matter how much we disagreed with them. Six weeks later, I saw her one last time. It was the day after I won the election.

I was in the hospital at the time, having come down with appendicitis three days before. When I awoke, I saw her standing in the doorway. She was wearing a flowered yellow dress. We were both married by then. I'd married first, then Carol. Carol's match had pleased everyone in her family. She'd married a young banker who became a partner in her father's savings bank. But here she was, looking more beautiful than I'd remembered. She said that she had just come to tell me how happy she was for me and that, even though her father had led the opposition, she had defied his wish and voted for Lyndon Johnson. I knew then that she was still in love with me. The vote proved it. But there was nothing left to be done about it."

Much of Johnson's account of his relationship with Carol Davis cannot be verified. Nevertheless, there is no reason to challenge the description of his youthful desires and intentions, the hostility of Mr. Davis, and the sudden rupture of his relationship with Carol. These elements of the story are given credibility from other sources and by the assumption—based on the evidence of his entire life—that it would be grotesquely out of character for Lyndon Johnson to contrive a fictional humiliation and defeat. As for the rest of the melodrama—the more interesting part—we cannot know how much is actual event and how much fantasy or flawed memory. We can suspect that his description of the young man compelled to sacrifice his great love in defense of his family's honor, only to find even greater happiness while Carol still suffered the consequences of her father's brutal scorn, represents the refraction of an intense but remote episode through the wishful ego. But such inevitable distortions are less significant than the way in which Johnson remembered. He did not, for example, see anything disproportionate in his reaction to Mr. Davis' condescension and hostility; nor, seemingly, any cruelty in his abandonment of the young woman who loved him and was willing to defy her own family to go ahead with marriage. Moreover, Johnson's account contains the unvoiced assumption that personal honor and family duty left a man of principles no other choice. His story indicates no awareness that he was requiring sacrifice as well as making it, inflicting pain as well as bearing it; that the moral issues might be ambiguous. Ordinarily, Johnson was alert to every nuance in his stories and anticipated all possible reactions in order to guide them. Yet in the narration of this episode, those intuitive faculties have been suspended. Personal rejection was so unbearable to Johnson, so mortally threatening, that withdrawal was necessary. An emotional imperative surfaced as the inevitable behavior of a rational and principled man.

A self-preserving action disguised as honor and principle upheld—this pattern is illustrated with remarkable consistency throughout Johnson's life. Episodes of rejection, actual or apprehended, seem to cripple Johnson's faculties and even, at times, interrupt his normal state of physical health and vitality. In the above recollection of Carol Davis, for example, their last meeting occurred in the hospital room to which the stricken candidate had been rushed just two days before the congressional election. His appendicitis had been authentic. Yet he was also seriously ill shortly before an astonishing proportion of his elections.

By the time Carol visited, the doctors had performed successful surgery and the people had made their favorable decision. And how did Johnson know that she still loved him? Why, she had voted for him: "The vote proved it." And undoubtedly she—along with many others—would vote for him again.

Lyndon Johnson's college days spanned the latter part of the 1920s, that curious decade in which the world—or what we now call the Western world—was adjusting to a new reality that it had not yet perceived. In retrospect it can now be understood that World War I was a great watershed, the beginning of a period of dissolution in which established landmarks of thought, values, and the social order would be displaced.[22] Young Americans emerged from the war, Fitzgerald wrote, "to find all gods dead, all wars fought, all faith in man shaken." He wrote, of course, for himself and for a relatively small group of artists and intellectuals. To them the pointless carnage of the war, the sensed shattering of an older order, demonstrated the corrosive futility of national loyalties, efforts at social change, the expansive ideals and material striving which coalesced in what was called the "American dream." "All was nada y pues nada," mused a character in a story by the young Hemingway, in the supreme expression of the nihilism toward which the mostly expatriate artists and the resident intellectuals who made up the "lost generation" were attracted. But they were expatriates for a reason. For most

Americans the vaguely sensed passage from familiar certainties opened onto new horizons of opportunity along traditional American lines—material prosperity, personal success, innovation; the natural reaction of a nation for whom change was both expected and desired. The hero of the day was not the Great Gatsby—that would come only decades later—but Charles Lindbergh. The authentic voice of Blanco County in 1925 was the editorial page of the *Record Courier:*

> When you hear an old timer sigh for the days of his fore-fathers, smile to yourself and think of this ... there has never been a time when life bettered itself so rapidly and consistently ... socialism and its more radical brother, communism, in its wildest imaginations has never contemplated the distribution of wealth in the manner and by the means by which it is now being distributed ... by dividing and selling vast corporations in small pieces to the man on the street, the wage earner and the house-maid.[23]

These sentiments were far truer to the shared orthodoxy of the time than the creative outpouring which drew strength from its opposition to the dominant faith and from the fear that most Americans were right to anticipate a future of limitless and totally absorbing material accumulation. If Sinclair Lewis saw the life of George Babbitt as a nightmare, the voters nonetheless sent Warren G. Harding and Calvin Coolidge to the White House. It was to take the depression, with its demonstration of unexpected and dangerous flaws in the material order, to bring the "lost generation" home.

But in Johnson City or San Marcos the dominant concern in the 1920s was not how to achieve "the good life," and certainly not a "great society," but how to make a living. Most of the three hundred residents of Johnson City made a meager living raising goats, cattle, and sheep on small plots of land. The "city" had no paved roads, no electricity, no gas, no trains, a few telephones and a few automobiles. There was one local bar, an eating place, a courthouse that showed movies, a church, a barbershop, and a drugstore. The hours of work were long; the moments of leisure were scarce; and there were few decisions about consumption to be made. Advertisements for clothes and household goods stressed not fashion, but durability and price. Shoes were sold for "more

days of wear in every pair." The families of Johnson City
were compelled to save their money for basic material possessions; they had little or nothing left to squander on the
luxuries, the trappings of affluence, which could be seen in
popular magazines and in films. Johnson's neighbors had no
big-city taste for lipstick, rouge, or breath freshener; scarcely
more than a dozen ads for such cosmetics appeared in local
papers during the entire decade. The *Record Courier* and the
Blanco *News* were full to the brim, however, with news of
worm eradicators, reports of miracle cure-alls, and notices detailing the days of the year when the circuit dentist or doctor
would be in town for his biannual visit.[24]

Among these Americans, the prosperity of others—even
the most outrageous luxuries of the very wealthy—did not inspire envy or thoughts of revolution. They were a spur to
their own progress. They saw not the dusty, shabby homes in
which they were presently living, but the shiny new homes
they would build when their labor was rewarded with
economic success. Through an almost magical compound of
persevering ambition and rewarded hope, big wealth was pro-
tectively linked to the average man. Optimism led to quietism, even celebration, as citizens tried to fit every event into
a pattern of inevitable progress. Though the economic hard-
ships which Johnson experienced and saw during those early
years made him aware that a wealthy few controlled much of
the land and the labor of the people, he did not seem to
resent, but desired, the possession of economic power. In the
1920s Johnson's picture of society was of a hard-working,
continually striving community. No one disagreed with what
was to be sought. The only question was how to get more of
the good.

And the "good" often meant "more." In young Johnson's
environment respect for quantity was unquestioned. The
farmer rejoiced in a big crop and the rancher in a large herd.
Anything that promised to increase the quantity of anything
being produced was self-evidently desirable. A thing became
a hundred times as important if it was a hundred times as
big. People counted and calculated, they figured and reckoned, measuring quality by numbers.

Inconceivable was the notion that one might find sadness
or sterility at the top of the ladder of success. Like most
young men, Lyndon Johnson saw the success of the self-made
man as a dramatic vindication of the American way of life.

Horatio Alger was the classic invitation to identification and emulation. "Do and dare," "be brave and bold," "strive and succeed"—these were the recurrent themes in Johnson's college editorials. In weekly editorial sermons on "getting ahead," on "sincerity," on "thrift," and on "playing the game," Johnson preached that with industry, temperance, promptness, and generosity, the persistent man would inevitably triumph, that where there was a will, there was a way. Cultivate Poor Richard's virtues and failure is impossible; fail to cultivate them and success will elude you forever. It was never clear in Johnson's writings whether all these virtues were necessary or any one was sufficient, for promptness was rewarded as handsomely as charity, idleness punished as severely as theft. But to Johnson's mind, it was the total result and not the particular means that counted; "It is," the young editor wrote in 1929, "ambition that makes of a creature a real man."[25]

The Johnson of the 1920s considered ambition and self-mastery the mainsprings of American activity, the driving wheel of cultural, social, and economic progress. What better proof could there be than the extraordinary feat of Charles Lindbergh in crossing the Atlantic? For Johnson, Lindbergh's flight in 1927 represented the triumph of the individual on his own. It served to reaffirm what he had known all along. "Lucky Lindbergh is the hero of the hour," the young editor wrote,

> yet the adjective which most characteristically describes Lindbergh is not lucky, but plucky. . . . A sketch of his life reveals the grit and determination that have been outstanding traits of his. . . . He is a simple, straightforward, plucky lad whose first lesson learned was self-mastery. He did not give up when hardship and trials beset him. . . . His pluck carried him through to success and fame. . . . It is a wonderful thing to make the first transocean flight and achieve spiritual independence. Still more wonderful is the fact that this feat lies within the grasp of all of us. Students, the choice lies with you. Do not sigh for Lindbergh's wonderful luck, but determine to emulate Lindy's glorious pluck.[26]

The curious thing in Johnson's interpretation is his concentration on only one-half of Lindbergh's message—the triumph of the individual. By singling out the fact that Lindbergh rode alone, by talking of him as though he were the reborn pioneer of the frontier, Johnson projected his sense that the source of America's strength lay somewhere in the past. But side by side with this nostalgia there was also the more ominous fact that Lindbergh's exploit was a window to the future: a victory for the machine, a triumph for the plane as well as for the man.[27]

Lindbergh's flight quickly came to embody and represent qualities that Americans prized but were afraid of losing. For many, something had gone out of American life after the war, some simplicity, some innocence, some confidence in the autonomous powers of the individual. It was the loss of an American myth. But it was not Johnson's loss. "We must not forget," he wrote in 1927,

> the things for which it [the war] was fought. It was a war fought to make the world safe for democracy. . . . Let us strive to carry on as best we can in the struggle for world democracy. . . . By honoring our heroes, by upholding democracy, by reverencing our laws and by promoting peace, we in a measure show ourselves striving to become worthy of the supreme sacrifices the war exacted. . . . Ours is the duty, the privilege, the God-given task to bear onward the lighted torch. Let us fail not, for to break faith with those who sleep in Flanders field would indeed be the deed of a craven and ignoble soul— carry on.[28]

Lyndon Johnson never questioned that this was the best of all countries. This assumption of superiority imposed a moral obligation to share the American way with the world. And it was accompanied by a sense of justified outrage at the slightest criticism of America. Lack of faith in America or in its heroes was considered treason. Johnson's was a society where the problem always lay with the critic, not the country. "Down with the debunking biographer," he wrote in 1929. "It now seems to be quite a thing to pull down the mighty from their seats and roll them in the mire. This practice deserves pronounced condemnation. Hero worship is a tremendous force in uplifting and strengthening. Humanity, let us have our heroes. Let us continue to believe that some have been truly great."[29]

In his defense of the hero, Johnson spoke for all the values that were under attack by artists and many intellectuals. "Not the cynics," Johnson wrote in 1927,

> but the men of faith are responsible for the progress of humanity.... For example, in the great struggle of the Revolution ... two matchless leaders were Thomas Paine and Benjamin Franklin. Paine was only a revolutionist and a destroyer. He had no faith to sustain him. He passed from the scene of action reviling the great Washington, preferring libertinism to liberty, and predicting the final downfall of the new nation.... Franklin was upheld by a great faith. He had something to replace the discarded government. He was a great constructor, a builder, a man of vision and faith.... Faith builds, but cynicism destroys.[30]

Faith builds, cynicism destroys; do and dare, strive and succeed: by the time Johnson graduated from college in August, 1930, these tenets were central to everything he did. His achievements in college had confirmed his faith in individual will. A crude and excessive young man in the eyes of many, yet he contained the motley strains that had long been shaping a native American psychology. Child of the passing frontier, he revealed it in its strengths and in its weaknesses. His Americanism was the reflection of an America that is no longer ours. Energy, goodwill, resourcefulness, enterprise, optimism, inventiveness, and exaggerated faith in self—these were the qualities Johnson brought in abundance to his brief career in teaching and his lifelong career in politics.

In his March, 1965, speech proposing the voting rights bill, President Johnson explained that his convictions on this issue were rooted in his experience as a teacher of Mexican-American children in Cotulla, Texas. "My students were poor," he told the joint session of Congress, "and they often came to class without breakfast, hungry. They knew even in their youth the pain of injustice. They never seemed to know why people disliked them, but they knew it was so, because I saw it in their eyes. I often walked home late in the afternoon, after the classes were finished, wishing there was more I could do."[31]

It is unlikely, however, that any of the three thousand

residents who made up the population of Cotulla in 1928 felt that Lyndon Johnson should be doing more. It is more probable that they were overwhelmed and slightly baffled by the frenetic torrent of activities, attention, and projects that accompanied the arrival of the young new principal of the Welhausen Ward Elementary School. The job had been secured for Johnson by his patron, President Evans of San Marcos, so that the promising college sophomore could earn enough money to complete his education. Indeed, during his nine months at Cotulla, Johnson earned twelve credits in special extension courses, enabling him to complete his degree requirements little more than a year after his return to San Marcos.

There is no indication that Johnson approached his new duties with the tentative caution that would seem appropriate to one entering a different and rather alien environment. The cultural gap between Cotulla and Johnson City was far greater than the two hundred miles of Texas that separated them. About 75 percent of Cotulla's three thousand inhabitants were Mexican-Americans, most of whom spoke only Spanish. Bounded by the sun-baked fields, Cotulla was a small cluster of streets and buildings. Few of Cotulla's residents had journeyed as far as the neighboring town. Although to those who could read English the Cotulla *Record* brought weekly reports of major national and Texas events, most of the families of Johnson's pupils lived in dirt hovels, engaged in a continual struggle to wring a bare subsistence from the dry and treeless land. They were too preoccupied with survival to think much about success.[32]

For Johnson, the qualities and circumstances of the local life were handicaps that obstructed his determination to improve the prospects of his pupils and open the way to fulfillment of those desires for success which he believed were universally shared. He assumed that his Mexican-American pupils possessed these desires, albeit stifled and denied expression by the impoverishing conditions of their lots. "I was determined," Johnson said later, to improve the lives of "those poor little kids. I saw hunger in their eyes and pain in their bodies. Those little brown bodies had so little and needed so much. I was determined to spark something inside them, to fill their souls with ambition and interest and belief in the future. I was determined to give them what they needed to make it in this world, to help them finish their education. Then the rest would take care of itself."[33]

And in the nine months he was there, before leaving on his own quest to "make it in this world," Johnson applied himself to the task. The ability to compete could only be acquired through activities that were wholly lacking on his arrival. Within three months, therefore, he had introduced a spectacular array of contests—spelldowns, public speaking tournaments, volleyball games, baseball games, track events, field events. Since Cotulla had no money for equipment of any kind, Johnson invested half of his first month's salary to buy softball bats and gloves, volleyballs, and basketballs. In addition to his administrative duties and his teaching, Johnson became the debating coach, the softball coach, the volleyball coach, the song leader, and, in his spare time, he later claimed, the assistant janitor. At first, Johnson had the children practice and compete with each other; after a while, he invited their parents to watch, and finally, he arranged field days with a dozen other neighboring schools in the region. Since Cotulla had no buses to take the children to and from these trips, Johnson worked to persuade those few parents who owned cars to participate in the activities at the school. That the parents showed so little interest proved a continual disappointment, but so long as he remained principal the contests continued. The year he left, they ended.

Johnson refused to accept the fact that many of his students had never learned English. Convinced that without English their future opportunities would be severely limited, he made a rule that no Spanish could be spoken on school property, including the playground. Pupils caught speaking Spanish were brought to his office and punished. It was true, of course, that knowledge of English would be necessary to break out of the confinements of Cotulla poverty. But his approach contained no awareness that his pupils' own cultural traditions and language might constitute an independent source of strength and fulfillment. Indeed, in teaching American politics, Johnson appeared at times to forget his students completely. Children whose parents were denied the right to vote were told that if they worked hard and studied well, they could one day become the President of the United States.

There is no reason to doubt that Johnson's enterprising days in Cotulla were motivated by sincere compassion and intense feelings, nor that the impact of his activities was largely constructive. Yet there is more than a hint of something compulsive, an unremitting drive to organize and prescribe conduct in accordance with the configurations of his own beneficent will. But Johnson never seemed aware, in Cotulla and afterward, that the benefactor might destroy his recipient's capacity to grow and find expression on his own.

Among Johnson's fondest memories was his childhood friendship with a Mexican-American boy named Huisso, who was his closest playmate when the Johnsons still lived on the farm. The two boys learned to ride together, Johnson recalled, in the big field that separated his home and Huisso's family's cabin. "The problem was that Huisso could barely keep up with me, and I always wanted to race. His horse was thinner and weaker than mine; it hadn't received the kind of food or care that mine had. One day I got an idea. Every morning I would go to the bins behind our house, take some oats and give them to Huisso, and Huisso would feed his horse double the amount he usually got until he got as fat and strong as mine. This went on for some while, and Huisso's horse got fatter and fatter. His stomach stood out more and more. Finally, I decided the time had come for the big race. Together we marked the starting point and the finishing point. Off we went, but almost immediately Huisso fell way behind, and I won easily. We tried a second race, but I won again, this time by even more distance. So we tried one more time, and Huisso pushed his horse as hard as he had ever pushed anything. This time the horse seemed to be moving much faster, but in the middle of the race it simply slipped out from under him. It had collapsed. It was dead. It was too much, I guess, too much running, too much food, too much care. It just didn't seem fair after all we had done. We cried and cried and cried until I thought we would never stop."[84]

After his year at Cotulla, Johnson returned to San Marcos to complete his degree. Back on campus, he resumed his leadership role. Yet even as he consolidated his dominant position in the affairs of San Marcos, he was searching out a more expansive arena for his capacities and ambitions. "I thought originally I'd be a teacher," he told me, "but the head of Teachers College counseled me against it. Dr. Evans told me there wouldn't be enough competition in the classroom to satisfy me. He thought I was a competitive animal. My ambi-

tion, he said, was laudable—to be either a teacher or a
preacher or a politician. Teachers can see the fruits of their
work in the performance of their students, preachers in the
morality of their parishioners, and public servants in the
people's progress. But he thought that being a public servant
would be best because I'd have to meet the challenges of the
time at the very moment they were happening."[35]

Undoubtedly Johnson liked teaching. For fifteen happy
months after his graduation from college he taught high
school in Houston. Teaching was on the list of future career
possibilities. He considered its advantages and satisfactions,
contemplated alternatives, and consulted with older men. But,
in retrospect, it seems clear that there was never really any
choice; his course had been fixed from the time when the
spellbound young child had listened to his father discussing
the latest political news of Blanco County. His childhood experience and the inner need to both emulate and surpass his
father combined with his natural capacities to draw him
toward that political vocation to which he was so perfectly
suited. "I wouldn't want to be building great towers or big
dams as an engineer, or big banks as a banker, or big insurance companies as a businessman," he explained. "All those
things are essential, but the thing that gives me the greatest
satisfaction is dealing with human beings and watching the
development of those human beings."[36] To "deal" with others,
to help them, to direct their actions and desires, to achieve
mastery in the society of men, would provide not only the
greatest satisfaction but the most effective protection against
inward dangers and the most ample scope for Johnson's
restless energies and unique skills. If teaching was a profession, politics was his calling.

In June of 1928 the Democratic National Convention was
in Houston preparing to nominate Al Smith. Ignoring the college rules against automobile trips outside the San Marcos
area, Lyndon Johnson persuaded a friend to drive him there.
With a bundle of editorials from the *College Star* for credentials, he talked convention officials into admitting him as a
member of the press. After the excited leader of the White
Stars watched Franklin Roosevelt deliver the nominating
speech, he returned to the San Marcos campus and was
promptly summoned by Dean Alfred Nolle to explain his absence. Years later Nolle remembered that Johnson gave such
an animated and colorful account of his experiences at the

convention that the original purpose of the meeting—to take some disciplinary action—was completely forgotten.[37] And soon afterward Lyndon Johnson, then a college senior, was to give his own speech on behalf of another man's candidacy, initiating the events that were to bring him to Washington.

Near San Marcos was the village of Henley, where in mid-July of each election year candidates for state and local office traditionally journeyed to attend an all-day political picnic. Amid wild oak trees and milling picnickers, the candidates were called one by one to the platform for speechmaking. According to Johnson, this was considered one of the most important political events in south-central Texas. He had come to the picnic with his father every year from the time he was ten. He loved being there, he said, listening to the funny old master of ceremonies as he shouted out the names of the candidates, and watching the different ways speakers responded to the call. Some, he recollected, walked sedately to the platform, a country wagon with its tailgate let down, and delivered a straight and serious speech. Others skipped and hopped all over the platform, yelling incomprehensibly for ten minutes. He recalled that the older he got, the more he wanted to be up front instead of down below. In 1930 he got his wish.

The master of ceremonies called out the name of Pat Neff. Neff, a former governor, had been appointed State Railroad Commissioner and was now up for election in his own right. Three months before, Neff had given Sam Johnson a job as railway inspector. Neff's name was called once, twice, and three times, but no one responded. His turn to speak was about to go by default when a young man was seen running through the crowd, his arms waving, calling out, "By God, I'll make the speech for Neff." Introduced simply as Sam Johnson's boy, the young man proceeded to explain why Neff was a good man and why he should be elected. He talked earnestly and with great spirit, walking up and down. As he went on, the already excited young man's voice rose to a shout and his arms flew out. When he finished, the crowd responded with great applause.[38]

This impromptu performance impressed Willy Hopkins, a rising young politician running for the state senate from a district that included San Marcos. Hopkins sought Johnson out after the speech, talked with him for ten minutes, and then invited him to manage his campaign for the legislature.

Johnson accepted at once and, while finishing up in college, he managed Hopkins to victory.

The following year, Hopkins returned the favor by suggesting young Lyndon's name to Richard Kleberg, heir to the legendary King Ranch, who had been elected to Congress in a special election that had been called to fill a vacancy in the 14th Congressional District. On Hopkins' advice, Kleberg called Johnson at Sam Houston High, where he had just started his second year of teaching, and asked if he would come to Corpus Christi to discuss the possibility of an appointment on his Washington staff. A member of the history faculty who was in the office when Johnson received the call reported later that he was so excited that he didn't seem to know what to say. That night the young teacher left for Corpus Christi, and the following afternoon Kleberg announced to the press that Lyndon Johnson had been appointed his legislative secretary. Two weeks later, after receiving a leave of absence from Sam Houston High, Johnson left for Washington.

Johnson recalled that the eastbound train left Houston at four in the afternoon. "All that day I'd gone about feeling excited, nervous, and sad. I was about to leave home to meet the adventure of my future. I felt grown-up, but my mind kept ranging backward in time. I saw myself as a boy skipping down the road to my granddaddy's house. I remembered the many nights I had stood in the doorway listening to my father's political talks. I remembered the evenings with my mother when my daddy was away. Now all that was behind me. On the platform more than two dozen people, relatives and friends, waited about to say goodbye. I tried to say something important to my mother, but I couldn't think of anything to say. When the train came, I felt relieved. I kissed my parents and climbed aboard."[39]

Johnson remembered that even before the station was out of sight, he had turned to look along the chain of cars leading to a black engine spouting large circles of brownish smoke and never saw Rebekah and Sam leave for the Pedernales farm. Whenever Rebekah had sent a letter to San Marcos she had written across the back of the envelope, "Mizpah," which means, "The Lord watch between me and thee, when we are absent one from another." But Johnson had never really left before; indeed, his mother's letters often contained revisions of the college themes and editorials that he had sent for her correction and approval. But he was really going now. Nevertheless, the bond between them, between all three, did not require divine watchfulness. Rebekah and Sam, in ways they could not have conceived, were also being carried with gathering momentum toward an unimaginable future.

For two days the train moved through the states of the Old Confederacy toward the city where Lyndon Johnson would, with one short hiatus, spend the next thirty-seven years; a city whose intricacies and half-secret movements he would master, and, for a while, dominate as completely as he had dominated the small campus at San Marcos.

One can only try to imagine the confused multitude of plans and intentions that tumbled through the mind of this restless, ambitious young man as he alternately sat and roamed through the cars until, as the train began to slow, he looked impatiently through the grimy window of the exit door, rushed down steps still vibrating from their arrested motion, and strode across the vaulted caverns of Union Station, from whose entrance one can see the familiar dome of the American Capitol. Lyndon Johnson had left home, but he had come to where he belonged.

Chapter 3

The Making of a Politician

Upon his arrival in Washington it was both natural and expectable that Johnson would want to learn how things worked in the nation's capital—the relationships and sources of power—just as he had at Johnson City, San Marcos, and Cotulla. The task, of course, was more formidable. Many a small-town giant had been swallowed up by a city whose concerns were as varied as the affairs and populace of the nation. Nevertheless, to Johnson the activating principles were much the same. If he had more to learn than ever before, that meant only that there was no time to waste. The day after his arrival he moved into the Dodge Hotel, where he would be assured of natural and informal contact with the seventy-five other congressional secretaries resident in the same building.

Before Johnson had even finished unpacking his suitcase, he was walking up and down the hall, knocking on doors, shaking hands, and telling each person his life history and future plans. One bathroom at the end of the corridor served all the tenants on the long floor. That first night, as Johnson later described it, he went in and out four times and took four separate showers so that he could talk with as many people as possible. The next morning, beginning at 7 A.M., he went into the bathroom five different times at ten-minute intervals to wash his face and brush his teeth. Within a week, Johnson had chosen five young men who he had decided were the most clever, the most experienced, and the most informed to be his "teachers." He possessed, Johnson liked to claim years afterward, a sensitive mechanism which allowed him immediately to evaluate the intelligence of a person and the worth and validity of his information.[1]

With the help of his new acquaintances, Johnson wanted to take apart the clock of the congressional world in order to discover what made it tick and how each of the many tiny pieces fit together. He had already learned to concentrate on events behind the scenes, but he needed guidance in working his way through the informal channels of power. At the same time, he wanted to understand the pros and cons of the major policy struggles that would be confronting the Congress in the months ahead. So desperately did Johnson crave this knowledge that his every conversation, whether over meals or during strolls around the Monument, became a planned interview in which he probed, questioned, and directed the discussion to his ends. At lunch, he deliberately pushed himself to the head of the cafeteria line so that he could finish eating before the others sat down, and be free to concentrate on the questions he wanted to ask. If the answer seemed unclear or incomplete, he would demand clarification. If he was still not satisfied, he would turn to someone else and ask for a counteropinion. "The astonishing thing was," a fellow resident later said, "that Lyndon made us feel as if we were the pupils and he were the teacher and we wanted to be sure to perform as well as we could."[2] Living in the Dodge, another resident, Arthur Perry, observed, "was like living in a permanent debating society, with Lyndon as the focal point."[3]

If people were the main source of Johnson's education, he also read the three daily newspapers in the Washington of 1931, as well as the *New York Times*, the *Wall Street Journal*, and the local Texas papers. Every evening he assembled a packet of night reading, including the daily *Congressional Record*, copies of pending bills, pamphlets, booklets, newsletters of various organizations, official publications, and committee reports; he relaxed in bed with a sheaf of government documents as others relax with a good mystery. Congressional secretary Arthur Perry, who observed the education of Lyndon Johnson in the ways of government, concluded, "This skinny boy was as green as anybody could be, but within a few months he knew how to operate in Washington better than some who had been here twenty years."[4]

As Johnson was learning his way on Capitol Hill, the administration, led by Herbert Hoover, was fighting for its survival and that of the national economy. Johnson arrived in Washington in the winter of 1931, as the nation entered its third year of depression. Twenty-eight thousand businesses had failed that year, farm income had dropped three billion dollars, and eight million people—one worker in every seven—were unemployed. Belief that the decline was a temporary misfortune was being displaced by the apprehension that the sources of collapse might be fundamental and resistant to known remedies. Still, Washington was not entirely a gloomy, stagnant city that winter. Having controlled the administration of national government for more than seven decades—interrupted only by the administrations of Grover Cleveland and Woodrow Wilson—the Republican Party was now on the defensive. In ways yet undefined, the old order was changing. And amid such enormous distress there was an inevitable intensity, a sense of excitement mingled with hope, in the mounting prospect of new leaders and new policies. Washington shared this anticipation with the country, but Washington also had more personal and specific concerns. It was a town with only one business—national politics and government—and the old management was on the run. One could already foresee new opportunities for the talented and ambitious, dangers for the long-established. And there would be plenty of talk in what Henry James had called the City of Conversation.

It was, to the extent that James' characterization was fair, a city marvelously adapted to the talents of Lyndon Johnson. Conversation for him was always a medium through which he sought to impose his will, as well as a source of information that helped him direct his energies toward desired goals. By analyzing the composition of San Marcos College and inquiring into the wishes of diverse student groups, he had been able to consolidate and activate the powerful coalition of nonathletes that had helped topple the Black Stars. In the late 1950s, as Senate Majority Leader, he would utilize a decade of investigation into the political imperatives and personal qualities of individual Senators to devise civil rights legislation that members could support for different, often contradictory, reasons. His intuitive grasp of the ways in which men and institutions might be moved to action was always grounded in an extensive accumulation of detailed knowledge, deliberately and laboriously acquired. Information was power, or, at least, a primary instrument of power. It strengthened, made more effective, his drive for control over successively larger environments until the arena became so vast it could not be comprehended in the same fashion by even the most tireless and encompassing mind. And such information would serve his compelling inward need to neutralize the possibility of surprise; a possibility which he perceived as a danger, and a danger which would be increased by uncertainty or ignorance about the motives, capacities, and intentions of others. In the process of self-education, as in so many of Johnson's modes of operation, the imperatives of psychic structure coalesced with the pragmatic requirements for achievement in the political world.

Richard Kleberg took little interest in his duties as a Congressman, devoting his time, energy, and interest to the Washington social scene. As a result, Lyndon Johnson had almost complete responsibility for the office. Within a week's time, Johnson recognized that he needed help. Characteristically, he turned to old friends, persuading Gene Latimer and Luther Jones, two star debaters from San Marcos, to join the staff. The three young men worked eighteen hours a day, seven days a week, managing to create a fully functioning office in less than three weeks' time. But not without tension. The story is told and retold of a Saturday evening when Johnson came back to the office after dinner to find both Gene and Luther gone. On Luther's desk was a note saying that they had gone to an early movie and would be back at nine. Feeling betrayed, Johnson began angrily sorting through a pile of mail; on the bottom was a postcard from a constituent demanding to know why his letter, sent a week before, had not yet been answered. Grabbing the card, Johnson ran to the local theater, searched through the darkness until he found Gene and Luther, and led them outside, where, standing in the street, he delivered a five-minute monologue on responsibility, public service, and democracy. "Can I see the card, Lyndon?" asked Gene. Johnson gave it to him. "Why, Lyndon, that's Charlie Davis, the fellow with all those complications over at the Department of Agriculture. And, Lyndon, don't you remember, that's your case." Anxious to smooth things over, Johnson invited his associates to a local restaurant, where five minutes after the first drink arrived, he jumped up. "Okay, we've been relaxing long enough, now let's get back to work, there's still three more good working hours until we fold."[5]

Johnson did not permit the demands of Kleberg's office to keep him from pursuing his education in the operation of Congress. He accepted an extra job as doorkeeper on the Democratic side. This entailed bringing onto the House floor cards from visitors who wanted a Congressman to come to the lobby for a talk, a relatively menial task previously assigned to some teenage relative of a Congressman. It allowed

Johnson to observe, from the perspective of the House floor, the give and take, the speeches and whispered conversations, and the application of rules and precedents that play so fundamental a role in the legislative process. Enabled to follow his natural inclination to learn more from observation than from study, Johnson worked to master the complex, formal procedures that governed the House, and fathom the unwritten, equally inviolable code of authority and privilege that determined the actual power of House members and decisively shaped the legislative product.

Few secretaries to a Congressman would want to be a messenger boy; the same time could be spent writing speeches, preparing for hearings, or in the unending exchange of views and gossip with colleagues. Johnson was not simply an eager young man anxious to assume any task that might come his way. His choice derived from a comprehension of how he might advance his purposes and ambitions. Racing across the San Marcos campus with messages from the president, he was preparing his claim to other benefits that Mr. Evans could confer, and, more significantly, to partake in that authority which he seemed so anxious to serve. As a Senate leader, despite his responsibilities for high matters of national and party policy, he would assume the "burden" of assigning office space understanding that the prospect of spacious accommodations might prove more persuasive than the most powerful argument in debate.

The job of congressional messenger helped Johnson to acquire data that would enhance his effectiveness as a Congressman's assistant. More significant in Johnson's rise, it facilitated contact with older men and the opportunity to solicit their approval. Throughout his life, Johnson's ambitions were assisted by powerful and successful patrons. His capacity to establish such relationships was one of his most extraordinary attributes, one that we shall examine more fully in the context of his Senate years.

Necessarily, the first step was to bring himself to the attention of those whose help or approval he sought. Johnson's access to the House chamber gave him the chance to meet dozens of Representatives. In conversations on the floor he cultivated his relationship with Sam Rayburn and Wright Patman, both of whom had served in the Texas legislature with his father. As he walked with House members to the lobby where visitors were waiting, Johnson talked so rapidly and with such vigor that Congressmen could not help but pay attention and remember.

Johnson knew, however, that political power could not be based solely on the capacity to gain notice from and win the respect of other individuals, or even to dominate their actions. The necessary foundation for achievement in Congress was an elected base in the congressional district or state. History had demonstrated that even the most august Senate leader, deferred to by his colleagues and by Presidents, could be eliminated from public life because he had failed to give adequate attention to the needs and vanities of his constituents back home. So Johnson, in his management of the Kleberg office, gave first priority to constituent requests. Through prompt and helpful answers to the several hundred people who wrote in each month for help or information, word of Kleberg's zeal on behalf of his constituents would begin to spread across the district. Since many of these requests—especially those from the most substantial citizens—involved personal contact, Johnson was also beginning to make a reputation for himself among the solid citizens of Texas as a helpful man, one who got things done. And since most of this "case work" involved problems with one bureaucracy or another (a pension not paid, a request not granted, a contract not fulfilled), Johnson had to spend hours each day penetrating the bureaucratic maze. He sought the knowledge—not easily accessible—of who had the power of decision over the particular matter in question, and, the source of authority identified, by what means influence could be exerted. This often required innumerable telephone calls. But in the end persistence usually paid off.

At the time Johnson began work for Congressman Kleberg, the legislative secretaries belonged to a discussion group called the Little Congress.[6] If less formally structured on the basis of seniority than its parent body, the Little Congress had become a kind of old-timers' club, led by the most senior staff members, and with agendas that avoided controversial speakers and topics. More and more, newcomers to the Hill were declining to join what had once been a prestigious and influential group. Lyndon Johnson decided before his first meeting was over that he wanted to be Speaker. It would be a struggle because of the seniority rule, but he thought he could win. The best way to wage a fight, he perceived, was to increase the membership of the organization by promising something new and different—an extension of the technique used at San Marcos.

Johnson began his campaign by caucusing five of his friends and getting their support. Soon, by patrolling the House corridors, they had talked with every legislative assistant on the Hill. They sought to persuade all of them to attend the next session of the Little Congress, where they could help revitalize the organization.

This intensive canvassing by Johnson and his friends brought about two hundred people to the organizational meeting. The meeting room, which had been half empty for years, was filled to capacity. The Old Guard placed their senior member in nomination. One of Johnson's lieutenants placed in nomination the name of Lyndon Johnson. The senior member delivered a routine account of the past activities of the organization. Then Johnson stood up and promised that if he was elected Speaker, he would change the character of the Little Congress; he would bring in celebrated speakers, sponsor important debates, arrange votes on pending issues. Under his leadership, it would become not only an educational forum but also a significant force on the Hill. At twenty-three, Lyndon Johnson became the youngest Speaker in the history of the Little Congress.

Johnson never relaxed in his information-gathering and in his efforts to familiarize himself with the political process. Accompanying colleagues to a baseball game, he would insist on talking politics between the innings and even between pitches. At a swimming pool, he would paddle around for a few minutes, then wait for the others to join him in conversation. He rarely went to movies or plays because he disliked sitting quietly in a dark theater for three hours. Parties were bearable since he could invariably find someone ready to talk politics. At the Texas Society Ball, he danced with the wives of Congressmen rather than with single girls and discussed the latest news in that evening's paper.[7]

Increasingly, the hours away from his office or the House lobby became a continuation of the compulsive political quest. Sleeping four or five hours a night, he began to cultivate an unusual capacity to nap for a few minutes at idle moments—while riding in the back of a car or sitting at his desk—to recharge his energies for the hours to come. Almost all his associates were engaged in some governmental work—

Congressmen, staff members, and bureaucrats. He came to evaluate their conduct and opinions in terms of political significance: what it told him about the motives and intentions of others, how current controversies were likely to be resolved, which demands or claims were likely to be met and which refused. Increasingly, he came to view all relationships as continually shifting political combinations based largely on shared self-interest. And to a considerable extent he was accurate, for politicians generally form alliances and not friendships. Individuals and institutions achieve their ends through continual barter. But deals are not bonds. Indeed, intense emotional involvement with anything—with issues, ideology, a woman, even a family—can be a handicap, not only consuming valuable time, but, more importantly, reducing flexibility and the capacity for detached calculation needed to take maximum advantage of continually changing circumstances.

Certainly, most participants in public life are not as intensely "political" as Lyndon Johnson was. His obsessive single-mindedness was an aspect of his nature that had evolved from the inner need to protect himself from the perplexing hazards of his childhood. Whatever its sourse, this quality was an invaluable asset in his public career. Through a relentless scrutiny of people and events based on the assumption that human activity was essentially "political," a system of exchange, he was able to achieve an extraordinary degree of mastery and success within his environments; whether dealing with the intense politics of family, small town, or college or the machinations of Washington, he was uncommonly equipped for the process of mastery. Each successive victory vindicated his outlook and fortified the qualities that had brought him success. Before long he had become a consummate political animal. This may help explain the frenzied quality of Johnson's enterprising activity, his scrupulous avoidance of tranquillity. More and more, he depended upon his skills in politics to stave off the consequences of inner conflicts, and provide him a surrogate for love and acceptance.

The picture which emerges from the above description is that of a man for whom all human contacts had a purpose. He wanted to be liked by everyone he met, but defined friendship in terms of a willingness to accommodate his ends. "I was always very lonely," Johnson told me toward the end of his life.

Johnson was on a short trip to Austin when he met Claudia Taylor—or "Lady Bird," as she had been called since she was a child—just as she was graduating from the University of Texas with a degree in journalism. He was immediately drawn to this shy and sensitive young woman. Later he said that he knew at once that Lady Bird was a woman of great common sense and reasonableness. Her opinions were remarkably shrewd. And beyond all this, beyond her gift of intelligent judgment, she had an even more precious quality—absolute dependability. To his credit and good fortune, Lyndon Johnson determined not to let this woman go.[8]

Within two hours of the meeting, Johnson arranged to see Lady Bird at 8 A.M. the following day. After breakfast, he suggested a drive in the country. "He told me all sorts of things that I thought were extraordinarily direct for a first conversation," Lady Bird later said, "about how many years he had been teaching, his salary as a secretary to a Congressman, his ambitions, even about all the members of his family, and how much insurance he carried. It was as if he wanted to give me a complete picture of his life and of his capabilities."[9] During this first conversation, Johnson also told her about Rebekah and said that he would like it if the two of them could meet sometime. Lady Bird casually responded that it would be nice to meet Johnson's mother, whereupon Johnson changed direction and headed for Johnson City. And for the rest of his few days in Texas Johnson resolved "to keep her mind completely on me until the moment I had to leave for Washington four days later. I invited her to come with me to Kleberg's ranch in Corpus Christi. I had business there, but I knew she'd be impressed by seeing me walk so comfortably around this famous ranch."[10]

"Everything was so big at that ranch," Lady Bird recalled, "the rooms, the fields, the beds, the chairs, that I felt a little like Alice in Wonderland coming into a kingdom of giants. Somehow I knew, though I wasn't sure why, that this was a trip I would never forget." Yet when they drove away, she later admitted, she found herself curiously anxious to get home. There was something so consuming about the man with whom she had now spent the last three days that she had an impulse to run back to her own life.[11] But Johnson recognized this impulse: If she wanted to go home, why that was fine with him—he would go with her. She had met his mother, now he would meet her father. So Lyndon and Lady

Bird set off together for Karnack, Texas, and the large, white house, known locally as the Brick House, where Lady Bird had grown up and her father, Thomas Taylor, still lived.

Mr. Taylor had grown up in Evergreen, Alabama. His parents were poor dirt farmers. There were a number of plantations nearby, the largest of which belonged to the Patillo family. Minnie Patillo, the same age as Thomas Taylor, rode her new horse beyond their plantation one summer day and found herself on unfamiliar terrain. Turning the horse around, she stumbled on a log and fell. Taylor found her lying on the ground, bandaged her leg, gave her some water, and brought her to the Patillo home. For months afterward Minnie Patillo and Taylor met secretly. After a year of such meetings, Tommy asked Minnie's father for her hand in marriage. Old Man Patillo laughed at the presumptuous boy and told him to leave, at which point Tommy is reputed to have answered: "You'll see, I'm going away to make a lot of money and I'll be back. And when I come, you'll beg me to marry your daughter." Tommy left Alabama for Karnack, Texas. There he built and stocked a grocery store. Within six years Taylor had become a successful businessman and had accumulated enough money to buy the largest house in Karnack and to change Mr. Pattillo's mind. He went to Alabama and returned to Karnack with Minnie Patillo as his bride.

Lady Bird had only the vaguest recollections of the mother who was to die when she was five. The descriptions of friends and relatives suggest a dreamy woman who spent a lot of time by herself, walking in the woods, reading novels and reciting poetry. Minnie's health was never good; her three pregnancies, two boys and a girl, spent her strength. A fourth pregnancy, when Lady Bird was five years old, ended in death for both the child and the mother. When Minnie died, her unmarried sister, Effie, came to live at the Taylor home. "I was very lucky," Lady Bird later said. "No one could have been a better second mother to me than Aunt Effie. I loved her very much." Relatives remembered Lady Bird as a well-behaved child whose calm demeanor suggested an unusually strict control over her feelings.[12]

She was a diligent student and graduated at the top of her class in both high school and college. To all those who knew her at the time, she seemed a very capable and remarkably disciplined young woman.

Lady Bird's father had waited six years for his bride; the

young man she was now bringing to her home from Austin was equally determined, if far less patient. They reached the Taylor family home in time for dinner with Captain Taylor, as Lady Bird's father was called. Lady Bird recalls that after dinner, taking her aside, Mr. Taylor remarked: "Daughter, you've been bringing home a lot of boys. But this time you've brought a man." The morning after this meeting, so unlike his humiliation at Mr. Davis' table, Johnson returned to Washington. When he had gone, Lady Bird felt what she later described as an unaccustomed loneliness. "I had never before considered myself a lonely person," she said. "I had spent so much of my life by myself that I had gotten used to being alone. But then Lyndon came into my life and in one week's time he had become so much a part of me that when he left, I felt his absence terribly. It was embarrassing to admit that so much could happen in such a short time. Here was this man I barely knew talking about marriage and I was seriously considering the idea."[13]

Daily, Johnson wrote or telephoned Lady Bird from Washington. When he returned to Texas seven weeks later, his first stop was at the Taylor home, where he urged: "Let's get married. Not next year, after you've done over the house, but about two weeks from now, or right away. If you say no, it just proves that you don't love me enough to dare to marry me. We either do it now, or we never will."[14] The following week, on November 17, 1934, Lyndon married Lady Bird, a match which provided that totally secure and loyal center to his private life which alone could have sustained him through the exigencies of his public career, and its four-year aftermath.

Two weeks after the marriage, the newlyweds received these sincere and shrewd congratulations:

> My precious children:
>   Thinking of you, loving you, dreaming of a radiant future for you, I someway find it difficult to express the depth and tenderness of my feelings. Often I have felt the utter futility of words, never more than now when I would wish my boy and his bride the highest and truest happiness together.
>   My dear Bird, I earnestly hope that you will love me as I do you. Lyndon has always held a very special place in my heart. Will you not share that place with him,

dear child? It would make me very happy to have you for my very own, to have you turn to me in love and confidence, to let me mother you as I do my precious boy.

I hope and hope you know is composed of desire and expectation, that Lyndon will prove to be as true, as loyal, as loving and as faithful a husband as he has been a son.

My dear boy, I have always desired the best in life for you. Now that you have the love and companionship of the one and only girl I am sure you will go far. You are fortunate in finding and winning the girl you love and I am sure your love for each other will be an incentive to you to do all the great things of which you are capable. Sweet son, I am loving you and counting on you as never before.

My dearest love to you both,
Mamma[15]

Here extended to Lady Bird in these disarming and prayerful sentiments is a full share in the franchise of her son, of which she will remain chief proprietor. Her closing—"counting on you as never before"—is ambiguous and somehow ominous. Counting on him for what? His loyalty to his wife? His continuing success in the public world? Continuing loyalty to his mother? That Rebekah remained the signal woman and influence in Lyndon's life there can be no doubt. It is a testament to her love for him and to the power of her own thwarted aspirations. That Lady Bird would become not her adversary but the chief lieutenant of her surrogate's rise is a testament to her shrewdness.

To both mother and wife Lyndon Johnson would always ascribe a scarcely credible perfection. But it is evident that they were crucially different women. The mother's inordinate passion for her son had been employed to spur achievements which she herself had determined. The wife endeavored to sustain and better organize the terrible energy Rebekah had been instrumental in setting loose. Where Rebekah withdrew into a stony anger over Sam's spontaneous Thanksgiving Day invitation, Lady Bird gracefully hosted unexpected throngs, welcoming the political friends Lyndon perpetually invited to their house. Where the mother confided her severest disappointments to her son, Lady Bird complained to no one. Amid the most complicated intrigues and struggles of her husband's career she remained outwardly composed and reasonable. If his incessant demands and orders (he instructed her to avoid full skirts and low shoes, often picked out her clothes, depended on her not only to manage the house but to lay out his clothes in the morning, fill his pens and his lighter, put the correct pocket items in place, pay his bills—in short, to manage him) or his occasional abuse in front of company became too much for her to bear, she possessed, or soon developed, a strange ability to take psychic leave.

Such phrases as "Her spirit took flight to some remote place" or "Her soul was elsewhere," if much out of fashion, suggest the nature of the phenomenon that was to be Lady Bird's saving grace with so devouring a man. "Bird," Johnson would call out at such moments, "are you with me?" And straight off, her accustomed alertness and competence reappeared.[16] Without such devotion and forbearance, without a love steadily given and never withdrawn, the course of Lyndon Johnson's continuing ascent in the world of politics becomes inconceivable.

During the final year of his life, he told me that he had come to understand that. She was his support, a helper in and necessary condition to his great enterprise—a figure central to his life.

In June of 1935, President Roosevelt created, by Executive Order, the National Youth Administration, to provide jobs for hundreds of thousands of young people forced out of work or school by the Great Depression. Roosevelt signed the order on a Tuesday morning; that same afternoon Johnson was on the phone with Sam Rayburn, Alvin Wirtz, Maury Maverick, and Tom Connally, proposing himself as the perfect candidate for Director of the Texas NYA.

It was characteristic of Johnson to react with celerity when he saw something he wanted and thought he could attain. (Yet, as we shall see, he could be equally hesitant if the object of his ambition seemed more uncertain.) His quickness gave him an immediate advantage over potential competitors. It was to assist him at many turning points, from his first congressional nomination to his selection for a leadership post in the Senate. In this instance Johnson's opportunism in lining up support resulted in his appointment—within a month of the Executive Order—as the youngest NYA Director in the country.

So Johnson left Washington, but for a while only, knowing that power of the kind he desired was accessible only to those elected to office. He had used his time in Kleberg's office to impress and befriend several wealthy and influential Texans. But in order to attain elected office he would also need to create a much broader political base. He saw in the NYA an ideal vehicle for building the constituency from which he could return to Washington on his own. And the job itself was admirably suited to Johnson's personal talents. The program's purpose—providing constructive labor for young people—had virtually complete public acceptance. Thus it was unnecessary to fight for support from public platforms. His task was to enlist individuals and institutions, public and private, as "sponsors" of work projects. It was the type of face-to-face persuasion at which he excelled.

With his characteristic and decisive energy, Johnson canvassed the state—by car, phone, and plane—talking with officials in the road departments, schools, hospitals, universities, libraries, conservation bureaus, and recreational facilities—swiftly signing up 350 sponsors who agreed to provide the materials, housing, and supervision for their particular project. Within six months, eighteen thousand young Texans were at work building parks, constructing buildings, painting murals, planting grass, repairing school buses, sewing clothes, surveying land, and laying bricks. Johnson worked at his office or on the road from seven in the morning until eleven at night. From 11 P.M. to 1 A.M. or later, he read the volumes of regulations and orders that flowed continuously from the national NYA, and prepared field reports to Washington which detailed how many youths were at work, for how many hours, and what they were doing. He was totally immersed in his work. "You'd ask him about the weather," a friend recalled, "and he'd start talking about the projects." Once again, Johnson's single-minded labors brought rewards. Aubrey Williams, the national NYA Director, spoke of Lyndon Johnson as the best administrator he had. When Eleanor Roosevelt visited Texas in 1936, she called on the NYA headquarters in Austin, telling reporters she wanted to meet this brilliant young man about whom she had heard such high praise.[17]

The NYA job not only helped Johnson to move closer to his political goals, but also influenced his approach to public problems. It gave him direct acquaintance with the implementation of public policy, challenging him to develop new resources and new skills. In other ways, it constricted Johnson's vision: the NYA experience confirmed his belief that in order to meet public goals it was necessary only to pass a good bill and put a good man in charge. This reinforcement of his assumption that all Americans wanted essentially the same thing would make it increasingly difficult for him to understand and deal with the conflicts of a later time when the country was divided over goals themselves.

As NYA Director, Johnson was responsible for conducting visitors from other states through his operation in Texas. He would remember one of these visitors—the Director of the Kansas NYA—for the rest of his life. As Johnson described it, he was staying in a seedy hotel in Houston on the Saturday when the woman arrived. While they were walking through a park he saw a copy of the Houston *Post* lying open on a bench. The headline caught his eye: "Congressman James P. Buchanan of Brenham Dies." The moment he saw that, he later said, his mind began churning with the possibilities and hazards of this windfall. "I just couldn't keep my mind on [my visitor]. I kept thinking that this was my district and this was my chance. The day seemed endless. [She] never stopped talking. And I had to pretend total interest in everything we were seeing and doing. There were times when I thought I'd explode from all the excitement bottled up inside. The worst thing was that I couldn't say a word about it. Finally, finally, the tour ended and I went home.

"As soon as I got home," Johnson continued, "I talked with Bird and then I called Senator Wirtz—the biggest single influence of my life [an honor variously applied to his mother, his father, his wife, and several friends]. 'Bad idea!' Wirtz responded. 'Why, you've only been here twelve months. You don't even know the mayor. You're young, enthusiastic, and ambitious and all that, but that's not enough.' 'Well, that's what I was thinking,' I said. 'Wait a minute now,' Wirtz replied. 'Now I don't mean to say there's *no* chance. Why don't I come over and let's talk it out.'

"So Wirtz came over and he and Lady Bird went on a half-mile walk. Bird just wanted to know if it was idiotic or not. She was going to call her daddy for money if we went ahead. We had $3,900 in baby bonds, but we needed much more. Finally Wirtz said go ahead. Bird called her daddy. I was on the other end of the phone, my heart pumping the whole time. She told him what we were thinking, that if we did go we would need $10,000 of the money her mother had left her. 'Ten thousand dollars,' her father asked. 'Isn't that a great deal? What about five thousand or three thousand?' 'No,' Bird said, 'we've been told it must be ten.' Then he decided right just as he always did where I was concerned and said: 'All right, ten thousand will be transferred to Lyndon's bank by tomorrow morning.' And I was at the bank at 9 A.M. the next morning and there it was."[18]

Several days after Buchanan's funeral, almost all of the four hundred residents of Johnson City gathered to hear Sam Johnson's boy announce his candidacy for the United States Congress. Once again, his swiftness to act proved critical. Buchanan's widow had been planning to announce her own candidacy within the week. Had she been the first to announce, it would have been difficult for others to challenge the bereaved widow. Moreover, widespread recognition of her name would have been an important advantage since the special election was to be held in only six weeks. Once Johnson announced, seven others followed his lead. Mrs. Buchanan decided not to run.

Johnson read his statement from the porch of the white house in Johnson City where as a boy he had spent so many hours listening to his father talk politics. Twelve months before, Sam had suffered a serious heart attack and was forced into retirement. But after his son announced his candidacy, he struggled to his feet. "My father became a young man again," Johnson said, describing the scene. "He looked out into all those faces he knew so well and then he looked at me and I saw tears in his eyes as he told the crowd how terribly proud he was of me and how much hope he had for his country if only his son could be up there in the nation's capital with Roosevelt and Rayburn and all those good Democrats. There was something in his voice and in his face that day that completely captured the emotions of the crowd. When he finally sat down, they began applauding and they kept applauding for almost ten minutes. I looked over at my mother and saw that she, too, was clapping and smiling. It was a proud moment for the Johnson family."[19]

As manager of Johnson's campaign, Wirtz decided that his first and most difficult problem was to differentiate his candidate from the others. Johnson himself was never adept at separating himself from political opponents on the basis of

substantive convictions. Indeed, he was always to shy away
from direct confrontation on controversial issues. His strength
as a political campaigner was not in public combat, but in the
ability to organize, assemble greater resources, and run faster
and longer than anyone else. Yet, at this stage, he was a political unknown compelled to find some way of persuading
voters to select him over seven opponents, all of whom were
Democrats and strong supporters of Roosevelt. Wirtz saw his
opportunity in Roosevelt's recent proposal to enlarge the Supreme Court to fifteen members in order to ensure a pro-New
Deal majority. None of the candidates for the Buchanan seat
had yet been willing to endorse the already controversial
"court-packing" plan. Wirtz suggested that Johnson state his
complete agreement and then denounce his opponents as enemies of the plan and, therefore, of FDR. Johnson agreed. "I
didn't have to hang back," Johnson told his audiences, "like a
steer on the way to the dripping vat. I'm for the President.
When he calls on me for help, I'll be where I can give him a
quick lift, not out in the woodshed practicing a quick way to
duck."[20] In the course of the race, three of Johnson's opponents stated that they, too, were supporting the plan, but
by then it was too late. The impression that Johnson stood
alone against all the others had already been created.

Johnson poured massive energy into those forty-two days
of campaigning—a torrential, seemingly tireless flow of personal activity and labor which no other candidate could
match. He visited every village in the district, walked countless streets, shook hands with everyone he met. If he saw
someone working in a field as he drove by, he would stop the
car so he could talk with the farmer as he did his plowing.
The experience of this campaign vindicated his belief that
politics was essentially personal relations. In a twenty-minute
appearance, he limited his speeches to five minutes so that he
could spend the remaining fifteen minutes "touching" his audience. "A five-minute speech," he later said, "with fifteen
minutes spent afterward is much more effective than a fifteen-
minute speech, no matter how inspiring, that leaves only five
minutes for handshaking."[21] When he did speak, he promised
to help President Roosevelt, talked of his intention to bring
electricity to the farm—milking machines to ease the farmer's
labor, washing machines to reduce his wife's drudgery, light
for the family home. His slogan, less commonplace than it
would be now: "Lyndon is a man who gets things done."

In the week before the election, Johnson developed stomach pains. Barely able to speak, he refused to slow down until two days before the election. The pains had become so sharp that he had to be rushed to an Austin hospital. An emergency operation removed his appendix.

From his hospital bed he learned that he had received twice as many votes as his nearest rival. At the age of twenty-nine, he had been elected to the Congress of the United States. And there was another victory—the exultance of his mother: "My dear Lyndon," Rebekah wrote,

> To me your election not alone gratifies my pride as a mother in a splendid and satisfying son and delights me with the realization of the joy you must feel in your success, but in a measure it compensates for the heartache and disappointment I experienced as a child when my dear father lost the race you have just won. The confidence in the good judgment of the people was sadly shattered then by their choice of another man. Today my faith is restored. How happy it would have made my precious noble father to know that the first-born of his first-born would achieve the position he desired. It makes me happy to have you carry on the ideals and principles so cherished by that great and good man. I gave you his name. I commend you to his example. You have always justified my expectations, my hopes, my dreams. How dear to me you are you cannot know my darling boy, my devoted son, my strength and comfort.... Always remember that I love you and am behind you in all that comes to you....[22]

Upon his release from the hospital, the new Congressman spent only two days at home before leaving for Washington. His father accompanied him to the train station. Johnson later described the complicated feelings he experienced that day. As he waited for the train, he recalled the scene at the same station six years earlier when he was leaving for his first trip to Washington to become Kleberg's legislative secretary. Then his father had been strong and healthy; now Lyndon had to bend over to kiss the old man whose frame was bent by sickness. But years later, Johnson still recounted his father's parting words: "Now you get up there, support FDR all the way, never shimmy and give 'em hell."[23]

During the summer Sam Johnson suffered another major heart attack. He was put in the hospital and kept in an oxygen tent for months. When Lyndon returned to Texas on his father's sixtieth birthday, Sam pleaded with his son to take him out of the lonely hospital and back to his home where he could be with friends and family. At first Lyndon resisted. The doctors said that Sam needed an oxygen tent, and none was available in Stonewall. But Sam Johnson would not listen to logical objections. "Lyndon," his son recalled him saying, "I'm going back to that little house in the hills where the people know when you're sick and care when you die. You have to help me."

Finally, Johnson agreed. "I realized," Johnson said later, "how dangerous it was to let my father go home. But I also believed that a man had a right to live and to die in his own way, in his own time. God knows that hospital depressed me something terrible and I was only visiting. No matter how sweet the nurses and the doctors are, they're not your family. They don't really know anything about you, they don't know anything about all the things that are going on in your head. In fact, they won't even talk to you about the fact that you're going to die because they're so busy running around pretending that you're absolutely fine. So there you are, facing the most frightening event you'll ever face, and you're all alone. Yes, I understood why my daddy wanted to leave and I respected his wish. I brought him his clothes, I helped him dress, and I carried him home."[24]

In his own room in the Johnson City house, Sam briefly seemed to improve. Then only two weeks later, on October 23, 1937, he died. The funeral was held the next day and Sam's body was laid to rest beside that of his father in the small family graveyard.

Shortly after his election to the House, Johnson was invited to meet President Roosevelt, who was then on a cruise in the Gulf of Mexico. The new Congressman was asked to join the President when the presidential yacht came into Galveston. There have been many colorful descriptions of that first encounter between Johnson and the man who was to be his patron, exemplar, and finally the yardstick by which he would measure his achievement. It has been reported that Johnson attempted to create an instant intimacy with Roosevelt.[25] He used a warm, familiar tone as if the two were old friends and equals. He asked personal questions about Roosevelt's family and his fishing luck. Instead of dismissing this brash young man for his impertinence, the President evidently enjoyed the conversation. Yes, the fishing was good: he had caught two tarpon, one of which weighed ninety pounds and was almost five feet long. Yes, he felt relaxed on the boat and liked the open air. He invited Johnson to join him at the dockside ceremonies and ride next to him in the open car on the way to the railroad station. During their ride, Johnson, remembering that the President was especially interested in the Navy, talked of his own interest in warships and of his concern for American naval power. If there is considerable question about the depth of Johnson's knowledge and interest in naval affairs, there can be none about his capacity to deal with persons of authority by appealing to their preferences. At the close of the trip, Roosevelt handed Johnson a slip of paper, saying, "I can always use a good man to help out with naval matters in Congress. Here's a telephone number. When you get to Washington, call it and ask for Tom. Tell him what we've talked about." Tom turned out to be Thomas Corcoran, an influential member of Roosevelt's staff. The slip of paper meant a coveted seat on the House Committee on Naval Affairs.

Johnson used his newly won access to the White House to make good on some of the promises he had made to his constituents during the campaign. Later he explained that his first goal was to become a major influence on the lives of the people in the 10th District. To that end, he brought about the construction of a housing project for the slums of Austin, secured two important WPA projects in his district, and, most importantly, successfully labored to persuade the Rural Electrification Administration to bring electric power to the people of the hill country.[26] Any town in his district that wanted a new post office or a government project found an effective advocate in Lyndon Johnson. Once again, he built a base of power by supplying goods and services to as many people as he could.

"When I thought about the kind of Congressman I wanted to be," Johnson said much later in life, "I thought about my Populist grandfather and promised myself that I'd always be the people's Congressman, representing all the people, not just the ones with money and power.

"My grandfather taught me early in life that neither misery

nor squalor is inevitable so long as the government and the people are one . . . so long as the government assumes the positive role of eliminating the special interests that cause most of our problems in America—particularly the moneylenders largely confined to New York, and those who had the money supply and knowledge and possessions in New York, Chicago, and Boston. They'd always been paid proportionately a far higher percentage of the total end product than they deserved. They lived off our sweat, and even before air conditioning they didn't know what sweat was. They just clipped coupons and wrote down debentures we couldn't spell and stole our pants out from under us."

The anger in Johnson's voice rose steadily: "And because of them [the moneylenders] the guy who produces that tall piece of maize over there"—pointing to a field hand—"never gets what he deserves. They're leeches, cancerous, and they'd be unnecessary evils if we had the right kind of money management. And they control our banking and money system. If we ever have a revolution and throw out our system for Communism or fascism, they'll be the prime reason for it and the first victim. I believed it as a child, and I believe it still."[27]

The class antagonisms Johnson expressed here seemed close to the gut of a man whose entire childhood had been spent among struggling farmers. Yet throughout his public life Johnson prudently suppressed these radical sentiments, yielding to the more dominant trend of American thought: the belief that America is a classless society, that any man willing to work can rise to the top, that, in the end, cooperation and conciliation yield better results than provocation and division.

"I never wanted to demagogue against business, Wall Street, or the power companies," he told me. "I wanted a minimum of rhetoric that would inflame or incite against either business, management, or labor. Whenever I talked with businessmen, I never engaged in personal infighting. I thought FDR was wrong [when he labeled businessmen economic royalists]; he didn't realize you can appeal to the pride of businessmen—make them know their grandchildren will be looking to see how their money was spent, and if they want to lie comfortable in their grave, they better make sure some of it went to public activities."[28]

But Johnson's critique of the demagogue—in Roosevelt and others—was complicated by a curious mixture of envy,

fear, and awe. "When I first came to the Congress with Kleberg, I was simply entranced by Huey Long, so much so that
I made a special deal with the doorkeeper to let me know
when Long was about to speak on the Senate floor. For leading the masses and illustrating your point humanly, Huey
Long couldn't be beat."[29]

Yet if Johnson envied the demagogue his ability to rouse
large audiences, he was ultimately frightened by emotionally
charged language and its latent prospects of conflict. Beneath
his expressed belief that politics required reasonable discussions, not rhetorical speeches, lay a deep characterological
fear of direct and open conflict, a lifelong tendency to withdraw from confrontation. And this personal need to avoid
conflict at any cost was reinforced by years of service in a
legislative process deliberately designed to translate potentially disruptive situations into practical problems resolvable
by bargaining and negotiation.

Most professions and professional institutions impose a
way of living, a mode of behavior, upon the individual, reinforcing some characteristics, changing others. When Johnson
entered the Congress, he had already spent three years in
studying and absorbing the traditions, folkways, and precedents of the House of Representatives. He already understood that a freshman Congressman should proceed with
caution, defer participation in important public controversies,
and refrain from any attempt to establish independent stature,
until he has consolidated his position and gained the confidence of his colleagues. Power in the House is based on
seniority. Rewards are in the hands of the leadership, and cooperation with the leadership is requisite for any member who
wants to be effective. Johnson understood this, and as a member of the House displayed a self-deprecating modesty and
a capacity for hard work that helped him win the approval of
the two men whose acceptance he most needed: Carl Vinson,
chairman of the Committee on Naval Affairs, and Sam Rayburn, respected and powerful member and, in 1940, Speaker
of the House.

In the past, Johnson's initial subordination to his more powerful elders had been a means of acquiring authority. In an institutionalized body, governed by seniority, however, this
process was very slow. The House was no institution for a
young man in a hurry. Within three years Johnson had be-

come, in his words, "terribly restless and unhappy." When the first opportunity came, he decided to run for the United States Senate.

Once again, a death provided his opening. On April 9, 1941, Senator Morris Sheppard died of a brain hemorrhage and a special election was called. Johnson again called upon Alvin Wirtz to manage his campaign and looked to President Roosevelt for special support. And, as before, he worked harder, spent more money, made more speeches, and met more people than his opposition. But this time Johnson was up against far more formidable competition in the candidacy of Pappy (Wilbert L.) O'Daniel, the incumbent Governor of Texas. And in 1941, unlike 1937, the young politician's relationship with Roosevelt would prove a liability in an increasingly conservative Texas. First returns showed that Johnson was the victor by a narrow margin of 5,000 votes. On the second day, delayed returns and some last-minute recounts put O'Daniel ahead by 1,311 votes. Despite several reports of fraud on the part of O'Daniel's forces, Johnson decided not to contest the election. The reason for this willingness to accept the dubious results is not entirely clear, though colleagues at the time suggest that his decision to hold back was made in the context of an awareness that on his side there were violations of the laws regulating campaign contributions and expenditures.

Looking back on his defeat, Johnson described the months that followed as "the most miserable in my life. I felt terribly rejected, and I began to think about leaving politics and going home to make money. In the end, I just couldn't bear to leave Washington, where at least I still had my seat in the House. Besides, with all those war clouds hanging over Europe, I felt that someone with all my training and preparedness was bound to be an important figure."[30]

As war approached, we can begin to discern in Johnson's fragmentary references to foreign problems his lifelong tendency to impose his conception of relations within American society onto relations between discordant nations. Consequently, tangible divisions and real clashes of interest were considered disagreements that men of goodwill could resolve to the mutual benefit of all the parties. Johnson ascribed war to a few evil men overriding the preferences of "the people," who were basically good and who sought a tranquil prosperity. "I am persuaded that the people of the world have no grievances, one against the other. The hopes and desires of a man who tills the soil are about the same whether he lives on the banks of the Colorado or on the banks of the Danube."[31] The danger of conflict arose only when the popular will was displaced by the authoritarian will of a self-aggrandizing few. With men like these, reason, the common ground of discussion, was gone. Stopping such men was possible only if the democratic countries were prepared to meet force with force—a course which Johnson urged on his colleagues in the period preceding Pearl Harbor. "Nothing," he proclaimed on the House floor, "so challenges the American spirit as tackling the biggest job on earth. That is what this is. Americans are stimulated by the big job—the Panama Canal, Boulder Dam, Grand Coulee, Lower Colorado River developments, the tallest building in the world, the mightiest battleship. So fortification of the greatest democracy makes all other projects seem trival."[32]

Five months after his return to the House, the Japanese attacked Pearl Harbor. The next day Lyndon Johnson, the first Congressman to enlist in the armed forces, entered the Navy. Twelve months later, President Roosevelt issued a special order that returned all Senators and Congressmen to Capitol Hill. Nevertheless, Johnson's memory of this brief service never faded. He considered General MacArthur's awarding him the Silver Star for participation in an overseas inspection mission in the Australian area as among the high moments of his life. Details of this mission are ambiguous. Depending on his mood and on the nature of the audience, Johnson told the story different ways. On some occasions, he tended to deprecate his own role in the mission, insisting that he was not really the one who should have received the Silver Star. Yet, on other occasions, he described, in detail, his courageous behavior when his plane was surrounded by enemies and almost shot down. One fact is clear: Johnson wore the battle ribbon of his Silver Star in the lapel of his jacket for the rest of his life.

The experience of World War II would make a far-reaching and decisive impression on Lyndon Johnson. For him, as for most others of his generation, it would be the event that resonated in their minds whenever they thought about international affairs: the decisive lesson. "From the experience of World War II," he later claimed, "I learned that war comes about by two things—by a lust for power on the part of a few evil leaders and by a weakness on the part of the people whose love for peace too often displays a lack of courage that serves as an open invitation to all the aggressors of the world."[33] Throughout the late forties he described the lessons of World War II in language strikingly parallel to his explanation of the reasons that led him into his own war in Asia.

"One thing is clear," Johnson said in the House in 1947. "Whether communist or fascist or simply a pistol-packing racketeer, the one thing a bully understands is force and the one thing he fears is courage. . . . I want peace. But human experience teaches me that if I let a bully of my community make me travel the back streets to avoid a fight, I merely postpone the evil day. Soon he will chase me out of my house."[34] "Indeed," Johnson continued in conversation, "if you let a bully come into your front yard, the next day he'll be up on your porch, and the day after that he'll rape your wife in your own bed. But if you say to him at the start, 'Now, just hold on, wait a minute,' then he'll know he's dealing with a man of courage, someone who will stand up to him. And only then can you get along and find some peace again."[35]

Only if the American people were brave enough to overcome the temptation to flee responsibility could the bully be stopped. "We have fought two world wars," Johnson argued in 1947, "because of our failure to take a position in time. When the first war began, Germany did not believe we would fight. Well-meaning pacifists sincerely desired peace. The Great Commoner [William Jennings Bryan] resigned from the highest position in the Cabinet because he thought Wilson's foreign policy too aggressive. Thus the Kaiser was led to believe we were complacent and lacked courage. Unrestricted submarine warfare began and we went to war. During earlier stages of World War II, Roosevelt enunciated the doctrine of quarantining aggressors. But there were protests . . . the America Firsters led by Colonel Lindbergh exploited the hesitancy of many of our citizens to prepare for adequate national defense. The tactics of these ostriches and their fellow travelers encouraged indeed if they did not induce Hitler to ignore us and the Japs to attack us."[36]

The way to prevent conflict was to stop aggressors at the start—the lesson of Munich. In every war, Johnson believed, the enemy is an alien force that "invades" the allies' house.

Such a view does not facilitate an understanding of civil war. And from the fact of America's initial indifference to European politics, Johnson concluded that the indifference that kept us from taking an early and firm position was the cause of both world wars. America alone, our attitudes and behavior, were the key to war and peace. Nor was this mode of thought unique to Lyndon Johnson. On the contrary, it was deeply rooted in the American experience, as Louis Hartz has argued: "Americans seem to oscillate between fleeing from the rest of the world and embracing it with too ardent a passion. An absolute national morality is inspired either to withdraw from 'alien' things or to transform them: it cannot live in comfort constantly by their side."[37]

In the 1940s truth seemed simple, even if the task seemed hard. Johnson shared the nation's faith that America's problems, and those of the world, could be resolved if our will was steadfast and we applied enough power at the right time. So Americans accepted the mantle of leadership with the enormous confidence that comes from the conviction that the ends of action are never in doubt, and that the achievement of those ends is always within the power of the brave and skillful. The unquestioned belief in the American mission—the seed of both terrible evil and tremendous good—was the fountainhead of both the man's and his country's postwar enterprise and benevolence.

"We in America are the fortunate children of fate," Johnson said in 1946. "From almost any viewpoint ours is the greatest nation; the greatest in material wealth, in goods and produce, in abundance of the things that make life easier and more pleasant . . . nearly every other people are prostrate and helpless. They look to us for help—for that inherent courageous leadership. . . . If we have excuse for being, that excuse is that through our efforts the world will be better when we depart than when we entered."[38]

This was the spirit that persuaded America to tackle the problem of European recovery. "If this foreign aid bill becomes a law," Johnson argued in 1947 in support of the Marshall Plan, "for the first time in the history of the world a great Nation will attempt to urge peace. We can discard the dismay and cynicism of the past and assume a new posture of statesmanship, we can prepare to fight the peace. By sending food, by sending financial aid, by sending both abroad, we

contest with evil in a battle for peace. If despair is replaced
by faith, if desolation is replaced by construction, if hunger is
answered by food—if those things are done, we shall be vic-
tors in the battle."³⁹

There was in this statement another assumption characteristic of America: that war itself could be eliminated by eliminating the poverty that left "the people" vulnerable to the
tactics and seductions of evil leaders. What self-determination
was to Woodrow Wilson, a healthy Gross National Product
was to Lyndon Johnson—the assurance of peace with justice.
"Only when we root out the very causes of war," Johnson
later suggested, "the poverty of man's body, the privation of
his spirit, the imprisonment of his liberties, will there be a final surrender of violence itself."⁴⁰ In Europe, events in the
wake of World War II seemed to justify this faith. Wealth,
invincible optimism, and the military protection of the North
Atlantic Treaty Organization proved a powerful combination
for the restoration of Western Europe. America's enthusiasm
and sense of boundless possibility were further augmented
when the aftermath of war was accompanied neither by re-
version to economic disarray nor by political isolationism. "It
was a wonderful time," Johnson recalled later. "We were the
strongest nation in the world, perhaps even in history, confident, alive, and victorious."⁴¹

During the years right after World War II, the tendency to
equate America's way of life with the goals of civilization itself was so widespread that it had become nothing less than a
national assumption. American ethnocentricity deepened, and
as the cold war began, a new adversary arose. "As we Americans debate these issues," Johnson warned in 1948, "the great
Russian bear, a bear who walks like a man, is stalking across
Europe; and to every citizen of that unhappy continent, a
bear on the back doorstep is much more persuasive than an
eagle across an ocean. . . . Where the great bear's shadow
touches, all else is blotted out. If Italy is lost, Greece will be
cut off and Turkey isolated. The bell has tolled for Rumania,
Yugoslavia, Czechoslovakia. It is tolling for Finland, Norway,
Sweden. Each toll of the bell brings closer the day when it
could toll for you and for me."⁴²

"I pray," Johnson said in a spirit reminiscent of Theodore
Roosevelt's concern with America's manly virtues, "we are
still a young and courageous Nation, that we have not grown
so old and so fat and so prosperous so that all we can think

about is to sit back with our arms around our money bags. If we choose to do that I have no doubt that the smoldering fires will burst into flame and consume us—dollars and all."[43]

In the hour of new crisis, Johnson believed, the American nation must summon its greatest resource—national unity. "These are days when we must put country above party; national interest above self-interest. . . . Over Berlin hangs the cloud of World War III. In meeting that crisis we do not ask whether our foreign policy follows the Republican line or the Democratic line. We ask only that it follow the American line."[44] This was the spirit of bipartisanship from which the policy of containment was born.

Yet a way of interpreting actions rooted in old traditions that have been successfully applied in the past may result in error and failure when applied to new conditions. What seemed the wisest solution for Western Europe in the 1940s surely was not the solution for Asia in the 1960s, when drawing lines across political borders to mark the limits of permissible Communist advance was perceived as aggressive action by those who now characterized Communism as a house divided, administered from different centers, with conflicting goals and interests.

It was during this period that Johnson laid the financial base which eventually made him a millionaire. Johnson kept the doors to his financial history tightly closed, assuming, even in his most unguarded moments, the posture of an Horatio Alger figure who rose from rags to riches by hard work, determination, pluck, and luck. The story, as I heard Johnson tell it, began in 1943 when he came home from the Navy to discover that an Austin radio station—KTBC—was up for sale.

"The station was bankrupt when we took it over for $17,500—the price of its debts. A series of bad managers had simply let it go, never really pushing for expansion. It was a risky buy, but I had the feeling that with Lady Bird's energy and talent we could make it go. And we did, we took that little station out of the red. In the first year we made a profit of eighteen dollars. I still remember the big celebration we had. And once we had it in the black, we made sure to keep it there."[45]

Beneath this account seems to be a more interesting story—pieced together by investigative reporters—of the connections between Johnson's public service and his successful private enterprise.[46] The evidence is largely inferential; there is no demonstration of any specific illegal or even unethical act. And there may well have been no transgression. The laws by which government regulates business afford ample scope for conferring immense benefits on a favored enterprise without overstepping the limits of statutes or established procedure.

The rising fortunes of KTBC in Texas paralleled Johnson's rising political career in Washington. As Louis Kohlmeier wrote in his Pulitzer Prize-winning series in the *Wall Street Journal:* "Like two young oaks springing up side by side, the LBJ careers in government and business grew mightily—their trunks rising parallel and branches intertwining."[47] From the first year's profit of eighteen dollars, the assets of KTBC rose to nearly two million dollars in ten years, and to seven million within twenty years. By 1964 the net earnings—with profits accruing to the Johnson family—exceeded $500,000 annually.

A broadcasting enterprise can exist and expand only with government approval. The success of KTBC was vitally dependent upon a long string of favorable decisions handed down by the FCC: permission to increase its transmitting power to 1,000 watts; permission to broadcast twenty-four hours a day; protection against competitive invasion; permission to affiliate with network stations; approval of requests for television permits. And if the FCC was important to KTBC, Lyndon Johnson was important to the FCC. As a member of the Senate Commerce Committee, which is the overseer of the FCC, Johnson was inevitably involved in all the major decisions concerning the status and personnel of the FCC.

The picture that emerges, however, is more subtle than these facts might suggest. Senators who served with Johnson on the Commerce Committee insist that he assiduously refrained from using his committee post or Senate leadership position to influence broadcasting legislation; on the contrary, he stayed in the background on most issues related to the FCC. Nor did Johnson ever involve himself formally with KTBC. In all his business ventures, Johnson followed the pattern he had established in college when he secured the presidency of the student government for the White Stars by putting his loyal friend Bill Deason out front while he remained behind the scenes. Over the years, a succession of Johnson loyalists manned the business offices at KTBC: Lady Bird, Jake Pickle, John Connally, Jesse C. Kellam, and even Bill Deason himself.

Naturally, it was impossible to keep Johnson's influence— the presence of Johnson's power—from being felt in both the FCC and the management of KTBC. And how could it be otherwise when television regulation, like most business regulation, is built upon informal alliances and nonpublic agreements between members of Congress, members of interest groups, and members of the federal bureaucracy?

KTBC was only the foundation of Johnson's accumulation of wealth. He used the station's profits to make highly profitable investments in land and in bank securities.[48] Here again, the nature and scope of Johnson's operations are obscure. When asked about his land holdings at a press conference on April 16, 1964, Johnson was technically correct when he replied: "I own a little ranch land, something in excess of two thousand acres."[49] But this technical answer ignored the many thousands of acres held under Johnson's total or partial control in the names of other men. The exact figures are unknown, but it is indisputable that from the base of one radio station acquired in 1943 Johnson accumulated several millions of dollars in the course of his public life.

Still, all these public and private activities were not adequate to Johnson's energies and ambitions. His work in the House became routine; so, too, his money-making. At the age of forty he felt, as he later described it, that "something was missing from [his] life." Finally, in 1948, the other Senate seat in Texas opened up. But this would not be a special election. He could run for only one office, and if he lost the Senate fight, then his House seat would also be gone. "At first," Johnson said, "I just could not bear the thought of losing everything."[50] He had waited seven years for this chance; now that it had finally come, he fell into severe despondency. Friends and relatives urged him on, but he could not make the move. Finally, one morning a group of frustrated friends and associates came to Johnson and suggested that since he was not running, he might help them to persuade young John Connally to take his place. That afternoon Lyndon Johnson announced his candidacy for the United States Senate.

The campaign followed a familiar pattern. In this one-party state personality mattered, not issues. Johnson was able to equivocate on every question; after all, his opponent—Coke Stevenson—was doing the same. This time Johnson deliberately chose to downplay his liberal ties. He rarely mentioned the Roosevelt years and almost never spoke of President Truman. Instead, he continually invoked those three classic and bland political assets: peace, prosperity, and progress. Traveling by private helicopter, he visited twenty towns a day, maneuvering the craft onto pastures, baseball fields, and building tops.

Three weeks before the election an exhausted Johnson was hospitalized for kidney stones. He was unwilling to undergo an operation to remove them, and insisted that no one should know he was in the hospital. Convinced that he could pass the stones himself, Johnson was determined to avoid the necessity for a postoperative recuperation as well as any public disclosure of his illness. But after three days in the hospital with no change in his condition, John Connally, Johnson's campaign manager, told the press where his candidate was. When Johnson found out what Connally had done, in defiance of his orders, he immediately drafted a statement withdrawing from the race. In essence, he reasoned: "If I can't control my own campaign, I certainly can't control the Senate, and if I'm not in control, I'm much better off in Johnson City where no one can hurt me." Fortunately for Johnson, the aide who was assigned to release the statement disregarded this order, too. On Lady Bird's advice, the aide decided to wait until morning. During the night, Johnson passed the kidney stones, and in the morning he acted as if absolutely nothing had happened the night before.

The campaign resumed the following day, and on November 3, 1948, by a margin of 87 votes out of 900,000 cast, Johnson was proclaimed the victor. Stevenson immediately charged Johnson with illegal ballot-stuffing. The fight carried all the way to the Supreme Court. There Johnson's lawyer, Abe Fortas, persuaded the Court that it had no jurisdiction to review the counting of ballots in a Texas Senate election. With the refusal of the judiciary to intervene, Johnson won his Senate seat. But the closeness of the victory left Johnson with the jeering nickname "Landslide Lyndon." Although he secured the office he had wanted so long, the legitimacy of his power was left in question.

Chapter 4

Rise To Power in the Senate

The freshman Senate class of 1948 was an exceptional group. It included Hubert Humphrey, the crusading former Mayor of Minneapolis, whose eloquent advocacy for a strong civil rights plank in the Democratic platform had helped drive several Southern delegations from the party; Paul Douglas, the liberal intellectual, professor of economics at the University of Chicago; Estes Kefauver, symbol of the South's new progressivism, the insurgent who had defied and defeated Boss Crump of Memphis; Clinton Anderson, Secretary of Agriculture in President Truman's first administration; Robert Kerr, millionaire, former Governor of Oklahoma; Russell Long, son of the Kingfish, Huey Long. Rarely had so many men come to the Senate with already established reputations. Indeed, Lyndon Johnson was among the least known of this most publicized freshman class.[1]

Yet three years later it was Johnson, not Douglas or Humphrey or Long or Kefauver, who was elected party whip, and who two years after that became the leader of the Democratic Party in the Senate. Chance played a role, but, in retrospect, one can see that the institution of the Senate—its size, modes of function, and the relationships and process through which influence was exercised—was almost ideally adapted to the most formidable of his personal qualities.

Power in the Senate had been exercised since 1937 by an informal coalition of conservative Republicans and Southern Democrats, in which, during the Truman years, the conservative Republicans agreed to vote with the South against civil rights legislation if the Southern Democrats voted against Truman's social and economic legislation. Born in the struggle to defeat FDR's court-packing plan, this coalition had enhanced its power over the years by the steady accumulation of key committee chairmanships, the mastery of parliamentary procedure, and the concerted skill of its leaders—

Richard Russell of Georgia, Allen Ellender of Louisiana, Walter George of Georgia, Tom Connally of Texas, and Kenneth McKellar of Tennessee.

The power of this inner club was evident at once to the entering freshman. Its members ate lunch at a special table, where, others believed, they discussed and determined how and when various issues would come to the Senate floor. Always before, in every institution, Johnson had sought to attach himself to the sources of power. Now, in the Senate, he could see at once what was required—deference to the elders, hard work, a low profile, specialization, and an acquiescence to inner-club priorities.

From the beginning Johnson recognized that the influence of Richard Russell would be decisive to his hopes for leadership.[2] The undisputed leader of the Senate's inner club, Russell commanded the respect of almost every member. His judgment of Johnson would influence the judgment of all the rest. But the Senate did not lack for ambitious men, many of them shrewd enough to recognize Russell's unique position in the Senate hierarchy. And Russell had many responsibilities, many supplicants—few of whom could be completely ignored or slighted if Russell did not want to risk weakening his own position. And finally there were only so many hours in a day. Johnson could impress Russell with his qualities only if he could establish regular working contact. The Senate offered more formal opportunities than those offered by a desk outside the college president's office at San Marcos or a message carried into the chamber by a legislative secretary. "I knew there was only one way to see Russell every day," Johnson explained, "and that was to get a seat on his committee. Without that we'd most likely be passing acquaintances and nothing more. So I put in a request for the Armed Services Committee—and fortunately, because of all my work on defense preparedness in the House, my request was granted."[3]

Having established an access to Russell which would not appear as the imposition of a flagrant ambition, since it arose naturally from their common responsibilities, Johnson was in a position to make use of one of his most powerful faculties—the ability to judge the qualities, needs, and values of other men. From this understanding he could then adapt his conduct to that course most likely to attain his end: in this case, the trust and approving respect of Georgia's Senior Senator. In temperament and personality the two men were radically dissimilar. The older man was quiet, courtly, aloof; the younger, flamboyant, discourteous, and intimate. Senator Russell shunned publicity and led a monastic life. He dressed like a conservative small-town banker and worked in an austere office, devoid of any token of power or wealth. Johnson, on the other hand, continually pursued public self-promotion and indulged a developing taste for expensive, fashionable clothes and elaborately plush surroundings. Russell had spent his youth in a small farm town in Georgia, where he had absorbed the unshakable conviction that separation of the races was the most desirable and beneficial condition for both Negroes and whites. But Johnson, raised in a town where there were no Negroes, received no such indoctrination. Indeed, his father had been a publicly proclaimed enemy of the Ku Klux Klan and his grandfather a member of the Populist Party.

However, Johnson had a goal whose achievement required that differences—superficial or profound—be submerged. Accordingly, he adapted to Russell's habits and character so skillfully that the two soon came to seem much alike. Courting Russell, Johnson toned down his appearance and took on a more civilized demeanor.

"Johnson learned to observe amenities with Senator Russell," said Bill Jorden, long-time assistant to the Georgia Senator. "With other Senators he would just walk right into their offices, wouldn't even say how d'ya do. He would just barge in single-mindedly. Amenities were not part of his relationships. But Russell was totally incapable of responding to that. He had an Old World courtliness. He was not the type whom you could put your arm around. So Johnson learned. He always referred to him as 'Senator Russell' and always sent in a note from the outer office to say he would like to come in."[4]

"Under magnificent self-control," two commentators observed, "the Lyndon Johnson of the early Senate years was a subdued fellow not seen before and not to be seen again until his painful vice-presidential period."[5] "His manner," it was said by *Newsweek* in 1951, "is quiet and gentle, and everything he does, he does with great deliberation and care."[6] Directing his attention to his committee work, Johnson became a specialist in the subject matter and legislative problems related to his assigned responsibilities. He shied away from speaking to the galleries or the press in favor of quiet accommodation within the sanctum of the Senate.

A shift toward more conservative politics accompanied

Johnson's tempered style, helping him to gain acceptance to the inner club, whose members were generally conservative. Yet he was also, and perhaps more strongly, motivated by the changing nature of his constituency.[7] He now represented the state of Texas, which was far more conservative as a whole than the 10th District, which had sent him to Congress. Johnson's rightward drift culminated in 1949, 1950, and 1951, when he supported the oil and gas industry, fought Truman's nomination of liberal Leland Olds to a third term on the Federal Power Commission, and defended the Taft-Hartley Act.

Although Johnson's new style was contrived and his "new politics" expedient, he did share with Russell a genuine and consuming devotion to the Senate. A lifelong bachelor with few intimate friends and virtually no social life, Russell cared for the Senate with an intense fidelity that young Lyndon honestly respected and understood. Yet, at the same time, Johnson also saw in these same feelings a potential source of advantage. "Richard Russell," Johnson explained, "found in the Senate what for him was a home. With no one to cook for him at home, he would arrive early enough in the morning to eat breakfast at the Capitol and stay late enough at night to eat dinner across the street. And in these early mornings and late evenings I made sure that there was always one companion, one Senator, who worked as hard and as long as he, and that was me, Lyndon Johnson. On Sundays the House and Senate were empty, quiet and still, the streets outside were bare. It's a tough day for a politician, especially if, like Russell, he's all alone. I knew how he felt for I, too, counted the hours till Monday would come again, and knowing that, I made sure to invite Russell over for breakfast, lunch, brunch or just to read the Sunday papers. He was my mentor and I wanted to take care of him."[8]

Johnson drew from his fellow addict and mentor, Russell, a knowledge of Senate function that could be acquired only by sifting daily political events to ascertain where power had been lost and where gained. And yet because Johnson's ambition extended beyond the interests of the Southern bloc and the inner club, it became necessary for him, even while courting Russell, to maintain a distance that others would recognize. He chose the issue of civil rights on which to demonstrate that his loyalty did not entail complete subordination. He did not want to be inextricably linked to what he recognized as a losing or regional cause. Yet he wanted to forfeit neither Russell's friendship nor his enabling power. And so Johnson's first step was to placate Russell: he decided to deliver his maiden speech in support of the filibuster. In January, 1949, the liberals in the Senate, supported by President Truman, were trying to break cloture in order to secure enactment of a Fair Employment Practices Commission. Johnson's speech—a structural defense rather than an ideological assertion—was, according to his mentor, "one of the ablest I have ever heard on the subject."

Having openly and effectively allied himself with the Southern position, Johnson then felt free to decline Russell's invitation to join the Southern caucus, twenty-two Southern Senators who met each week, knowing that membership would indelibly brand him a conservative. Johnson refused, then voted faithfully along the lines of caucus members. Johnson always found ways to serve those he needed, and to conform to their standards and values, but he never submitted his will, never became the devoted and unquestioning subordinate. This autonomy was a source of strength, preventing him from losing sight of his own goals or his capacity for independent action when new opportunity arose. It helped create the kind of impression that, however loyal, he was his own man, which made it possible for others to take seriously his ambitions for positions of leadership and independent authority. After protecting himself from future recriminations born of false expectation, Johnson remained Russell's friend, loyal associate, active supporter, and effective ally in the effort to achieve a large majority of the legislative action that Russell desired.[9]

Still, Johnson recalled that after three years in the Senate he had felt an "increasing restlessness." The major leadership positions in the Senate, a half-dozen important committee chairmanships, were awarded on the basis of seniority. Senator Scott Lucas of Illinois seemed entrenched as party leader; as was Party Whip Senator Francis Myers of Pennsylvania. Then, in the elections of 1950, both Lucas and Myers were defeated. Johnson's swift reaction to the defeats well illustrates Machiavelli's dictum: "Fortune is the ruler of half our actions . . . she allows the other half or thereabouts to be governed by us." Examining the lives and deeds of the great princes, Machiavelli concluded: "It will be seen that they owed nothing to fortune but the opportunity which gave them matter to be shaped into what form they thought fit; and without that opportunity their powers would have been wasted, and without their powers the opportunity would have come in vain."[10]

Johnson knew that the party caucus would merely ratify the leadership choices previously made by the inner club. Most Senators had mixed feelings about the desirability of becoming party leader or whip. The responsibilities of these positions often trapped one in Washington, reducing contact with constituents. Furthermore, during those years the elected leaders were only front men for the actual leaders of the club. Johnson knew all this, but these were the only available possibilities for changing his status in the Senate, and consistent with his ambition, any change was preferable to a situation that seemed to provide long-time stasis. And perhaps he recognized a potential that others did not see. He told Russell that a leadership position was one of the most urgently desired goals of his life. Once more, the ability to put himself forward paid off.[11] The caucus elected Johnson party whip, the youngest in history. In that role Johnson was expected to keep in touch with all the members of the party. These contacts enabled him to learn even more about the Senate and its individual members and enlarged his opportunity to gain the respect of others—resources that would sustain him through the decade. His new title had not changed his subordination to Russell, but it assisted him in beginning to gather the means with which he would advance from apprentice to a full partnership.

Then, in November, 1952, another opportunity opened, when young Barry Goldwater, department store owner from Phoenix, defeated the Democratic Minority Leader, Ernest McFarland. Once again Johnson moved swiftly and with careful calculation, and again circumstances favored him. If either Richard Russell or Lister Hill, of Alabama, had shown the slightest interest, the office would have been his. But Johnson knew they had no such interest. So the day after McFarland's defeat, Johnson launched his campaign for the leadership, making a series of phone calls to Democratic Senators across the country to inform them that he had decided to run. He persuaded three important Senators—Richard Russell, Earle Clements of Kentucky, and J. Allen Frear of Delaware—to openly promote him for leader while he remained silently at his Texas ranch.

James Rowe, a long-time friend of Johnson, remembers a

luncheon meeting during this period at Drew Pearson's house, where a group of liberal Senators had gathered to develop a plan for blocking Johnson. After several hours of debating, they concluded that the only hope of success was to support Lister Hill. But when they telephoned Hill at his home in Alabama, they discovered that only a few minutes earlier Hill had pledged his support to another caller—Lyndon Johnson. Within two more days Johnson had received thirty endorsements. And on January 3, 1953, Lyndon Johnson was formally elected Minority Leader.

Why Lyndon Johnson—who was, after all, among the most junior members of the Senate? There are several answers. First of all, he chose his goal and then focused his entire energies toward its achievement, resisting other roles that a Senator might strive to fulfill; spokesman for his region or state, lobbyist for particular interest groups, advocate for causes, specialist on foreign affairs, education, or defense. Among the group of stellar newcomers, Johnson alone had deliberately chosen to pursue the role of party leader. Douglas and Humphrey had elected to become spokesmen for their liberal allies across the nation, seeming not to worry about their influence inside the Senate. Kefauver had decided to seek a national arena by exploiting the Senate's investigative resources to expose what he saw as serious and dangerous flaws in national life. Robert Kerr had opted, instead, to represent sectional, even personal, interests. And although he was to become one of the most powerful men in the Senate—at times even regarded as the unofficial "leader"—it was this choice which finally kept him from the formal office and, eventually, the content of party leadership. In each instance, the chosen role not only suited the personality and natural inclinations of the man but enhanced his strength among his constituency.

A Senator's most important decision is what to make of a job whose function is ill-defined and whose possibilities are many—what to do with his time, how to allocate his resources, and where to concentrate his energy.[12] However much he may desire it, no Senator can satisfy the expectations and demands of everyone. Nor is it necessary. He must strive rather for respect in those social and political circles he regards as significant. Sociologists call such circles the "relevant others," the persons with whom the political leader establishes or feels the closest identification and on whom he builds his following. Almost inevitably, this identification starts a process by which, over time, he comes to apprehend the part as though it were the entirety of his function. Yet he must choose because resources—money, time, energy, staff, information, and goodwill—are limited. What is used for one role and one purpose cannot be used for another. Each role has its cost: choosing to be a spokesman for outside groups may reduce leverage inside; choosing to become a party leader inside may reduce linkage to the outside. And, of course, the choice may—and often does—reflect the politician's own inclinations, values, and sense of what matters.

Since a Senator's initial choice of audience depends largely on the character of the organization and constituency from which he drew most of his support, his subsequent behavior will respond to the expectations of those people (although changing political circumstances may oblige him to reach out for new sources of support in order to increase his strength or to compensate for disaffections). Moreover, a constituency large enough to elect a Senator will inevitably contain many whose goals and desired performances are contradictory, thereby providing room for a considerable range of action.

Johnson's decision to strive for leadership within the party appears to have been taken almost immediately upon coming to the Senate. James Rowe recalls a conversation with the new Senator in which he tried to persuade Johnson that, unlike the House, the Senate was a national forum, which could provide Johnson with the opportunity to free himself of dependence on insiders such as Speaker Sam Rayburn and Armed Services Committee Chairman Carl Vinson, who had, in Rowe's view, increasingly constrained Johnson during his later years in the House. Rowe urged him to speak bluntly about a wide variety of national problems, in the tradition of a Borah or a Norris or a Wheeler. "That's not the way I see it," Johnson responded. "It may have been possible years ago, but today you have to get along in the Senate if you want to get anything done."[13] For Johnson, effectiveness was defined almost solely in institutional terms. Simply to raise issues in order to generate discussion was—and would remain—for Johnson nothing more than "rambling talk."[14] He wanted to be on the inside, "where the decisions took place, where things really happened."[15]

In the end, Johnson was one of the very few Senators willing to accept the combination of political risk and little real authority attendant on party leadership in the 1950s. He alone saw the equation differently. What appeared as unacceptable costs to others were to Johnson a regular and expected price of the apprenticeship, the often menial tasks, which he had accepted and built on many times before. And here, as before, Johnson proved able to conduct his office with a mixture of subordination and independence that secured his acceptance along with a recognition of his abilities. He had used these qualities and methods before to build from an unpromising base. And he would do it now as Minority Leader. (In the Senate in 1953 there were forty-eight Democrats, forty-seven Republicans and one Independent, Wayne Morse, who had left the Republican Party during the 1952 elections but had agreed to vote with the Republicans on the question of running the Senate. This produced a 48–48 tie, which was broken by Vice President Richard Nixon, to give Republican Taft the majority leadership and leave Johnson with the minority post. Two years later, in 1955, Morse switched his position; the Democrats gained control of the Senate and Lyndon Johnson became Majority Leader.)

By the middle of the decade the powerful "Senate men" who had raised Johnson to the position of titular leader found themselves reduced to lieutenants in a system directed, in fact as well as in name, by the party leader—Lyndon Johnson. Johnson, in a manner without precedent, had made himself the absolute center of the Democratic Party in the Senate. This transformation would have seemed unimaginable in 1953 when he assumed the then titular and insubstantial post of Minority Leader. The party machinery that he inherited had been rendered impotent by an inner club determined to eliminate any force capable of challenging their power. Moreover, even the formal authority of the Minority Leader was unimpressive. He was not an officer of the national party. Unlike the Speaker in the House of Representatives, he was not even a formal official in the Senate. His only formally established authority was his chairmanship of the steering committee that controlled the appointment of members of standing committees. In the Congress of the nineteenth century that power of appointment had been significant. A good committee assignment was critical, both to build prestige and influence within the Senate and to acquire the capacity to serve constituents. By Johnson's day, however, the increased sway of the seniority system had greatly diminished the leader's freedom to grant or deny such assignments.

However, Johnson had become Minority Leader without the slightest illusion about the relationship between his formal position and the actual authority—both the process and the men—that governed the conduct of the Senate. After all, he was, as we have seen, a man who believed that success in any institution depended upon the most detailed possible knowledge of the way things worked—how and why some objectives were achieved and others defeated, which individuals exercised the greatest authority, and what were the sources and limits of that authority. In the Senate as elsewhere, he pursued such knowledge with unremitting, almost obsessed persistence—through his own observation and from the experienced and powerful men to whom he gained access. This information was synthesized by a mind gifted with an almost shocking capacity to comprehend the structure of an institution, to become aware of the process through which it operated, and to sense the vulnerabilities of that process. Many knew the Senate as well as, or better than, Lyndon Johnson. However, he saw not only the present realities of his new position but the exciting possibilities that might be latent in hitherto insignificant functions and forms of control.

He began his seemingly quixotic effort to transform the post of party leader—not only because he sensed concealed possibilities, but also because it soon became clear to him, as he later explained, that he "could no longer bear to be an apprentice to the elders, simply sitting back and taking their orders."[16] He brought to the position of Minority Leader a combination of determination and skill that produced dramatically far-reaching changes in an environment whose forms had remained constant for many years. The functions of a Minority Leader offered little to build upon, but Johnson had often found ways to stretch meager resources. And almost certainly one of the sources of this ability was the popular faith that was part of his heritage. The point of a Baptist sermon popular during his youth was to persuade listeners that acres of diamonds were within reach of those willing to search and endure long and difficult labor. The early settlers of his native Southwest found harsh soil, which seemed sterile but which later proved, after sustained and exacting effort, to yield an abundance of food and flowers.

Johnson's challenge was to increase his resources without

seeming to threaten those with established power who would, if aroused, defeat his efforts; and, at the same time, to emancipate himself from bondage to the inner club. In this process he understood the critical importance of developing foundations on which new authority might be constructed but which others did not perceive as potential sources of power. From the moment of awakening he thought about ways in which he might enhance his authority. Other men about him were too tired at night to think; still others preferred to relax after hours. None used their limited energies and time to reflect upon the implications of Johnson's action. But for Johnson the evening hours were an opportunity to "review the day's activities" and to "figure out how to do better tomorrow." "I knew from the start," Johnson later recalled, that "all relations of power rest on one thing, a contract between the leader and the followers such that the followers believe it is in their interest to follow the leader. No man can compel another—except at knifepoint—to do what he does not want to do."[17]

Johnson reassured himself that open coercion was not a practical possibility in the quest for Senate leadership; his instrument would be the power of persuasion. By providing others with services and desired resources, he would establish superiority over them; by providing benefits that would serve the political and personal interests of others, he would attain power. Yet the line between persuasion and coercion is thin and ambiguously drawn; the receipt of regular rewards from a benefactor who will also be the source of future benefits can create a dependency close to coercive power, because the ability to bestow also implies the authority to discontinue or refuse as a sign of disapproval or as a punishment. It was with this understanding that Johnson introduced his reform of the seniority system.

Johnson knew there is nothing more difficult than to initiate a new order of things, understanding, in his own terms, the principle which Machiavelli had explained—that "the reformer has enemies in all those who profit by the old order, and only lukewarm defenders in all those who would profit by the new order ... who do not truly believe in anything new until they have had actual experience of it."[18] And the committee system was not just another aspect of the legislative process; it was the foundation of power and the principal determinant of the conduct of Senate business. Thus Johnson dissembled his aim in such a way that his request for change seemed like a trivial departure which did not threaten the governing mores of the Senate.[19]

First he visited the Senate elders—beginning with Richard Russell—to seek their views on a proposal to guarantee each new Senator at least one good committee assignment, arguing that the present system deprived some of the most important activities of the Senate of the benefits of young and vigorous talent. But the new rule could be implemented only if the senior Senators were willing to act as statesmen devoted to the well-being of the Senate as an institution by relinquishing one of their three major assignments in order to make room for the freshmen. And Johnson knew that even those who agreed that the proposal would have beneficial results might find it difficult to sacrifice personal prerogatives for a general ideal. So he coupled his plan for a voluntary surrender of committee seats with a suggestion that the committee system be reorganized; that twelve members be subtracted from each of the minor committees and added to the major ones, thus adding to the total number of good assignments. Here again Johnson reflected the classic American tendency, and his own preference of personality, to reduce the possibility for conflict by increasing the supply of resources. He was also trying to demonstrate that one could act the statesman without that cost to political advantage which persuaded most men to restrain their noblest impulses.

Russell was sympathetic to Johnson's proposed reforms in the committee system. Once Russell appeared to agree, thus preventing a disciplined and insuperable opposition, Johnson arranged to make the change immediately so that all the bitterness of those adversely affected could be expressed and allowed to fade in a short time, after which he could begin to reap the benefits of the change little by little over a long period. And the benefits to Johnson were considerable. He had acquired for himself a substantial power of appointment, and gained the favor of the freshmen Senators, who would most benefit from the change.

The significance of this new power—its potential for influence—was considerably strengthened by the typical freshmen's unfamiliarity with the Senate. Uncertain what committees to apply for, they would naturally consult Johnson, who would convey his own assessment of which committee assignments would be of benefit to them. By guiding and influencing their judgments, he was often able to make certain that, when they applied, choices could be granted. Henry Jackson went to Interior, Stuart Symington to Armed Services, Mike Mansfield to Foreign Relations, and on and on. In this way Johnson became the patron of the freshmen; from their first week in the chamber he was able to persuade them that he was the source of significant rewards and favors.[20]

"I want," freshman Senator Gale McGee wrote to Johnson,

> to take time to convey to you my deep personal appreciation for the committee assignments. Because of these appointments we freshmen have no alibis if by the end of this session we have failed to produce—in other days I suspect freshmen Senators have been able to excuse their early actions by the heavy hand of the old seniority system—but not now. Your action has given to us both individually and collectively both the responsibility and opportunity to write a constructive record.[21]

Thus Johnson imposed his command over resources that did not seem especially valuable and became the principal benefactor and support of colleagues who had little influence. He accomplished this almost without conflict or opposition precisely because authority and influence of this kind had been of no significance to the exercise of Senate power and were not perceived as a potential threat to those who ruled. It did not occur to his powerful associates—respectfully consulted in every move—that from such insubstantial resources Lyndon Johnson was shaping the instruments that would make him arbiter and, eventually, the master of the United States Senate.

The process of acquiring resources and extending their value went on in many ways. By party rule, the leader is also chairman of the Democratic Policy Committee, whose establishment was originally proposed during the hearings on the Legislative Reorganization Act of 1946. It was intended to formulate overall legislative policy that would be consistent with the party platform so as to increase the agreement between the expressed goals of the party in Congress and the pledges it had made to the electorate. As soon as the proposal had emerged from committee, it was opposed by Sam Rayburn, who insisted that it would reduce "flexibility"—in other words, the power of the congressional establishment to formulate its own policy without advice or harassment from outside. Consigned to limbo in the House, the proposal was adopted by the Senate and funds for staff and operation were appropriated in late 1946. So when Johnson took office, he inherited a committee that had links to the national platform and the Democratic National Committee, and—at least in theory—was accountable to the party as a whole. Clearly, the arrangement was a restraint on the authority of his leadership position. Yet simply to abolish the committee—if that were possible—was certain to produce serious conflict within the Democratic Party and with some Senators. So Johnson embraced the committee, but in a manner calculated to make it his instrument and not his guardian. And he accomplished this by so limiting its functions that it became a part of the Senate structure.[22]

Under his chairmanship, the Policy Committee did not determine overall legislative priorities and goals. It was confined largely to the task of scheduling legislation on the floor, and providing a forum for announcements, briefings, and discussions among the members of the leadership structure. But decisions of schedule were also significant decisions of substance. Whenever a Senator wished either to expedite or to delay a bill, he would have to request Johnson's assistance. Every day the leader's office would receive a half-dozen such requests:

> Dear Lyndon:
> I would consider it a great favor if you could help me to achieve postponement of the textile bill. As it is now written, it poses enormous problems for the textile industry in my state and I have promised them that I will obtain a delay until at least next month so they can study it further.

> Dear Lyndon:
> I would be eternally grateful if you would help me to obtain early consideration of the Bank Holding bill. It is a bill that matters a great deal to me and the timing is of the utmost importance.

> Dear Lyndon:
> I respectfully request your assistance in scheduling S. 2345, a bill that I consider of grave importance to me and to my constituents.[23]

Johnson would bring all these requests to the weekly meeting of the seventeen-member Policy Committee—carefully chosen to represent centers of power—and the juggling would begin. The decisions not only could determine the time of debate but would influence its outcome. For, as Johnson recognized, "Timing can make or break a bill. The first weeks provide the best opportunity to fight off a filibuster, the last weeks to avoid a conference committee, and the middle weeks to explore the issue. Sometimes the best tactic is delay—allowing time for support to build up and plunge—moving immediately to take advantage of momentum. Still other times the best timing inside the Senate depends on what's going on outside the Senate, such as primaries or elections or marches or something."[24]

But, Johnson affirmed, he imposed limits upon the use of the classic maneuver of indefinite delay: "I made sure to carry it off in my own way—the Senate Policy Committee was *not* the House Rules Committee. I would never let it bottle up legislation indefinitely. I can remember countless times when Russell would say: 'I don't like this bill one bit, but let's get it out.' "[25] In the end, however, the decisions of the Policy Committee were the will of Lyndon Johnson, so much so that he began to refer to it as "my cabinet."

If the Policy Committee became Johnson's instrument, so did the caucus of Democratic Senators, originally designed as the governing body of the party in the Senate. Johnson convened the caucus only once at the beginning of each Congress, and limited even this meeting to ratification of the leader's tenure in office and the election of lesser officials. Johnson would open these meetings with long, platitudinous statements and fill the rest of the time with announcements and briefings; after an hour, when the call for adjournment came, absolutely nothing had passed but sixty minutes. To a man whose leadership depended on presenting different faces on each issue to each of the different Senators, it was indispensable to avoid group discussions of the same issues. Beyond this, Johnson recognized that so long as there were alternative sources for services and decisions—for committee assignments, information, evaluation of the prospects for particular legislation—the individual Senators would be less dependent on him.[26]

Once again, the key to Johnson's strategy lay in his ability to give political significance to functions previously excluded—to make new matters negotiable. According to the Senate rules, for example, the duty of assigning office space in the Capitol fell to the Senate Committee on Rules and Administration, where it was to be carried out "in strict accordance with precedence and seniority." Johnson found a loophole in the rules which allowed him to transfer the "burden" of the assignment process to the party leader's office, which would, he explained, "make matters simpler." Once in control of this new "duty," he then relaxed the seniority requirement and turned office assignment into a new tool of influence. After a while, insiders could recognize Johnson's allies by one look at the roster of office suites—the larger suites in the New Senate Building were reserved for friends, the smaller suites in the Old Building were allotted to "the troublesome ones."[27]

Control of the Senate Democratic Campaign Committee provided Johnson with additional leverage. The committee was intended to provide money and support to Senators involved in close races. Johnson magnified the committee's importance by concentrating its limited resources in smaller states, where they could make the most difference. In a state like Wyoming or Nevada or Idaho, a grant of $10,000 could have an enormous impact, not only on an election but on a winning recipient's attitude toward the Majority Leader. The limited resources were distributed in accordance with a system designed to promote a sense of significant gratitude and obligation in as many Senators as possible.[28]

The steady increase in Johnson's power enhanced both his energy and his ego. "I began to feel that I was growing in size as well as importance. . . . I took great pleasure in the position I was building."[29]

In these years in the Senate, more than in college and far more than in the House, Johnson managed to recreate the earliest world he had ever known, his world with Rebekah, run by his clock, centered on his person, allowing him once more to perform the role he enjoyed the most—the role of the exuberant child with an endless supply, indeed almost a monopoly, of things to barter. Only now his hegemony did not depend on somebody else, not even on a loving mother; it was Lyndon himself who had made it so and would keep it that way. What Rebekah had bestowed on her young son, she in part withdrew as he grew older. Now, at last, Johnson seemed safe from any repetition of that betrayal.

While building these tangible bases for the enhancement of his authority, Johnson was also developing an incomparable system of intelligence, through which he sought to learn the wants, the needs, and the desires of each of the Senators. "It requires great fortune as well as great industry to retain [dominions]," Machiavelli once wrote, and "one of the best and most certain means of doing so would be for the new ruler to take up his residence there. . . . Being on the spot, disorders can be seen as they arise and can quickly be remedied, but living at a distance, they are only heard of when they get beyond remedy."[30] Johnson went one step further: he not only took up residence in a physical sense—in the unequaled hours spent on the job—but he took up residence in a psychological sense as well. He incorporated the Senate into his own psychic processes, became inwardly absorbed by its mores, events, and members, and took his obsession with him wherever he went. For him, there was no time off from work, since the interior landscape of his mind was perpetually concerned with legislative issues, personalities, and procedures.

Johnson's search for information was ceaseless, a quest that was characteristic of his mind and not a method of conduct that could be suspended. Each encounter, whatever its purpose, was also a "planned interview," in which Johnson probed, questioned, and directed the conversation according to *his* ends. Whether in the office or in the cloakroom, over lunch or over drinks, Johnson somehow made others feel that every conversation was a test in which they were expected not only to come up with the answers but to score 100 percent, resulting in a tension that often brought forth additional information.

The style of the questioning naturally varied. Indeed, on some occasions—such as the frequent lunches he held for freshmen Senators and their legislative aides—everything would take care of itself. Eager to please the powerful man, the invited guests would compete with one another to see who could provide the leader with the most interesting tidbits. On other occasions, Johnson would call someone in because "I need your advice, and I can only confide my problems in you." By the end of the conversation, however, the other Senator was confiding far more than Johnson had disclosed to him. Johnson would invite small groups of Senators to intimate dinner parties at his house, followed by long hours of discussion in the parlor, where the drinks and the warmth conspired to encourage unguarded talk. Political purpose pervaded the beginning, the middle, and the end of these dinners, and if others failed to perceive this, that was further testimony to their success.

In all his work, Johnson relied heavily on his staff—particularly Robert Baker, secretary to the Senate Democrats—to extend his presence and power. Bobby Baker had come to the Senate in the 1940s as a teenage page and had stayed year after year. When Johnson became Minority Leader, he promoted Baker, then twenty-five, to become assistant secretary to the leader. Having spent more than a decade of his life in the Senate cloakroom, Baker knew as much about the workings of the Senate and the habits of individual Senators as any staffman twice his age. Johnson valued this quality in Baker, and, over time, Baker became a confidential assistant.[31]

The essence of Baker's technique was reciprocity. In return for the information he received about a particular Senator's attitude toward a bill or another Senator's plans for an investigation, he provided information about the content of legislation and on the Senate schedule being planned by the leadership. As one member described it: "Baker's information was essential in planning your schedule. As soon as he told you it would be safe for you to go home this Wednesday, you could pack up and go, knowing full well that your bill on wildlife would not be brought to the floor that day. Or he might say, 'You are interested in labor matters, aren't you? Well, you'd better stick around.' "[32]

In the end, however, Johnson sought far more than fragments of information about a particular Senator's attitude toward a bill or an issue. From facts, gossip, observation—a multitude of disparate elements—he shaped a composite mental portrait of every Senator: his strengths and his weaknesses; his place in the political spectrum; his aspirations in the Senate, and perhaps beyond the Senate; how far he could be pushed in what direction, and by what means; how he liked his liquor; how he felt about his wife and his family, and, most important, how he felt about himself. For Johnson understood that the most important decision each Senator made, often obscurely, was what kind of Senator he wanted to be: whether he wanted to be a national leader in education, a regional leader in civil rights, a social magnate in Washington, an agent of the oil industry, a wheel horse of the party, a President of the United States. It was also taken for granted that each Senator desired to secure and strengthen the support of his constituency and that few other matters could ever be strong enough to persuade him to seriously risk a loss of election support. Johnson, however, also perceived that such support could be perfected and enhanced in many ways, that in a complex society each Senator had latitude in deciding just whom he would represent.

As Johnson's mental portraits of his colleagues became more complete, his political touch became finer. The party leader makes a host of assignments: the senatorial delegation to the NATO Parliamentary Conference in Paris, a trip to Ireland for the unveiling of a statue, a journey to Europe for the dedication of American military cemeteries in England, France, and Italy, the congressional delegation to the Parliamentary Association in India, appointment to the FDR Memorial Commission or the Civil War Centennial Commission, membership on the National Forest Reservation Commission, and on and on.[33] For Johnson, each one of these assignments contained a potential opportunity for bargaining, for creating obligations, provided that he knew his fellow Senators well enough to determine which invitations would matter the most to whom. If he knew that the wife of the Senator from Idaho had been dreaming of a trip to Paris for ten years, or that the advisers to another Senator had warned him about his slipping popularity with Italian voters, Johnson could increase the potential usefulness of assignments to the Parliamentary Conference in Paris or to the dedication of the cemeteries in Italy. If he recognized that the Senator from Oregon could use an official trip to India as a way of shoring up his reputation for expertise in foreign affairs, while the Senator from Massachusetts considered himself a lay historian, then the assignments for the parliamentary meeting in India and the Civil War Centennial Commission would fall into place.

Moreover, Johnson understood that the fewer the wants and needs of an individual, the less dependent he is on others. So his entrepreneurial spirit encompassed not simply the satisfaction of present needs but the development of new and expanding ones. He would, for instance, explain to a Senator that "although five other Senators are clamoring for this one remaining seat on the congressional delegation to Tokyo, I just might be able to swing it for you since I know how much you really want it. . . . It'll be tough but let me see what I can do."[34] The joys of visiting Tokyo may never have occurred to the Senator, but he was unlikely to deny Johnson's description of his desire—after all, it might be interesting, a relaxing change, even fun; and perhaps some of the businesses in his state had expressed concern about Japanese competition. By creating consumer needs in this fashion, and by then defining the terms of their realization, Johnson was able to expand the base of benefits upon which power could be built.

These calculations about the most important concerns of each Senator became even more important when Johnson distributed the assignments for standing committees. Working from two tally sheets—the first listing the principal, second, and third choices of each member, and the second listing past assignments—Johnson managed to keep an exact count of the chips in his bank—which Senators owed him how much and which were due for new investment.[35]

Although continually calculating advantage, Johnson did not overlook the strength of affection. Indeed, he built his network of allies, not only through the use of his varied authorities, but through his careful and deliberate use of the most important resource of all in a continuing body like the Senate—personal attention. No courtesies were too small or too difficult for the leader to dispense.

Recognizing that the older men in the Senate were often troubled by a half-conscious sense that their performance was deteriorating with age, Johnson made a special point of helping them with their committee work, briefing them on the issues, and assisting them on the floor. These were men who had once been at the center of things, who had experienced the power to control events. "Now," as Johnson put it, "they feared humiliation, they craved attention. And when they found it, it was like a spring in the desert; their gratitude couldn't adequately express itself with anything less than total support and dependence on me. And besides, I always liked to spend time with older people. When I was a boy, I would talk for hours with the mothers of my friends, telling them what I had done during the day, asking what they had done, requesting advice. Soon they began to feel as if I, too, was their son and that meant that whenever we all wanted to do something, it was okay by the parents so long as I was there."[36]

Aware of the fact that a limited number of difficult mo-

ments, such as failure in work, sickness, or death, are likely
to be sensed as "tests" of friendship, Johnson was a faithful
presence in personal crisis. For example, he forced himself to
attend the funerals of Senator Byrd's favorite niece and Senator Russell's mother, even though he hated all funerals;
indeed, he was apt to become physically ill in the presence of
death. Yet he believed that the fact he had come at a moment of profound personal meaning would be remembered
and—someday, in some interwoven way—would have com-
pensations. About that, as well as about the responses to
hundreds of cards and flowers dispatched on special occasions, he was right. He was right, too, about the effects of
praising fellow Senators in person, and of dispatching telegrams to birthday gatherings, on wedding anniversaries, and
to family reunions.

Nor did Johnson limit his demonstrations of affection to
Senators and their assistants. During the Christmas and
Easter seasons, the leader's office was stacked with hundreds
of boxes of candy for delivery to all those men and women
who worked for the Senate—the telephone operators, the jan-
itors, the Capitol Hill policemen, the waiters in the Senate
dining room, the elevator boys, the help in the mimeo room.
These tokens were Johnson's way of saying: "I see you; I
care about you; you, too, are a part of this great institution."
The warmth of their response to this act of recognition was
manifest as he walked through the halls with his colleagues,
to whom he could say: "They care about me, too"—meaning
also, but only implied by his manner: "They are a part of
me, and so are you."

Johnson's capacities for control and domination found
their consummate manifestation during his private meetings
with individual Senators. Face to face, behind office doors,
Johnson could show a different face, a different form of behavior and argument. He would try to make each Senator
feel that his support in some particular matter was the critical
element affecting the well-being of the nation, the Senate, and
the party leader; and he would also seek to demonstrate that
faithfulness to the highest obligations of public service by an
act certain to be honored—given the nature of the particular
matter at hand—would also serve the practical and political
interests of the Senator.

"A lot of people," Johnson would later say, "have written a
lot of nonsense about my private meetings with Senators;

that's because most of the writing is done by the intellectuals, who can never imagine me, a graduate from poor little San Marcos, engaged in an actual debate with words and with arguments, yet debating is what those sessions were all about.

"But the Harvards, they picture it, instead, as a back-alley job with me holding the guy by the collar, twisting his arm behind his back, dangling a carrot in front of his nose, and holding a club over his head. It's a pretty amazing sight when you think about it. I'd have to be some sort of acrobatic genius to carry it off, and the Senator in question, well, he'd have to be pretty weak and pretty meek to be simply standing there like a paralyzed idiot.

"But you see they [the intellectuals] never take the time to think about what really goes on in these one-to-one sessions because they've never been involved in persuading anyone to do anything. They're just like a pack of nuns who've convinced themselves that sex is dirty and ugly and low-down and forced because *they* can never have it. And because they can never have it, they see it all as rape instead of seduction and they miss the elaborate preparation that goes on before the act is finally done."[37]

The arrangements that preceded a private meeting were elaborate indeed.[38] First, there was a general head count to determine who stood where and why. This was followed by a more detailed inquiry to help determine which Senators were the key to the outcome of an issue—which Senators, for example, could serve as "umbrellas,"[39] whose support would make it possible for four or five others to vote the right way; which Senators were undecided or whose positions were not firmly supported by convictions or political necessity. Then Johnson reviewed the data on each Senator in question—a political breakdown of the power groups in his state, an analysis of his supporters, an evaluation of his voting record. To this material, Johnson would add his personal understanding of the Senator and the people around him. Finally, Johnson would practice his intended approach, often in the presence of one of his aides. He sorted out in rambling fashion the possible arguments pro and con, experimented with a variety of responses, and fashioned a detailed mental script from which he would speak—in a manner designed to seem wholly spontaneous—when the meeting took place. And the meeting itself might seem like an accidental encounter in a Senate corridor; but Johnson was not a man who roamed through halls in aimless fashion: when he began to wander, he knew who it was he would find.

After the coincidental encounter and casual greeting, Johnson would remember that he had something he would like to talk about. The two men would walk down the corridor, ride the elevator, and enter an office where they would begin their conversation with small talk over Scotch. As the conversation progressed, Johnson would display an overwhelming combination of praise, scorn, rage, and friendship. His voice would rise and fall, moving from the thunder of an orator to the whisper reminiscent of a lover inviting physical touch. Transitions were abrupt. He responded to hostility with a disconcerting glance of indignation; the next minute he would evoke a smile by the warmth of his expression and a playful brush of his hand. Variations in pitch, stress, and gesture reflected the importance he attached to certain words. His appeal would abound with illustrations, anecdotes, and hyperbole. He knew how to make his listeners *see* things he was describing, make them tangible to the senses. And he knew how to sustain a sense of uninterrupted flow by the use of parallel structure and a stream of conjunctions.

From his own insistent energy, Johnson would create an illusion that the outcome, and thus the responsibility, rested on the decision of this one Senator; refusing to permit any implication of the reality they both knew—but which in this office began to seem increasingly more uncertain—that the decisions of many other Senators would also decide the results. Johnson's argument invoked country and party, loyalty to the leadership, reminders of past services and hints of future satisfactions—but always in a form that disavowed any intention that there was a debt to be paid or trade being offered. There was the welfare of the Senate to be considered and a casual mention of certain powerful interests. All of these mingled arguments were set forth as if they constituted a unitary motive for action, and this was all presented as if Johnson's object were not persuasion, but to "reason together" in hopes of clarifying the considerations that would help a man to make his own informed decision. Nor did Johnson neglect the substantive content of the matter being discussed. Few appreciated the extent to which he studied and mastered the provisions of particular legislation, and in these sessions he would debate the substantive merits, not only to explain or convince, but to provide the Senator with arguments he might later use to explain his action to his constituency—to tell them how he saved the taxpayer money, or prevented the adoption of an even more foolish and wasteful law.

Whatever the issue, however, the particular format remained the same: Johnson would state his case and prove it, refuting objections in advance and concluding with a review of what had been said and what had to be done. But logic, reasons, explanation, and appeals to motive do not alone explain Johnson's success at influencing others. They were reinforced at all times with a powerful demonstration of passionate belief. In Johnson, as we have already seen, calculation and conviction were easily confounded. "What convinces is conviction," he would say later. "You simply *have* to believe in the argument you are advancing; if you don't, you're as good as dead. The other person will sense that something isn't there, and no chain of reasoning, no matter how logical or elegant or brilliant, will win your case for you."[40]

What gave the most effect to these individual sessions was the wondrously exact fit of the appeal to the man at whom it was directed. Johnson had studied his man carefully and used that knowledge to supplement his powers of intuitive judgment. Thus he could often sense what his listener must be thinking and feeling, enabling him to shape his language and modulate his tone in such a way that what he wanted the Senator to do was made to seem the same as that which the Senator himself had wanted all along. As Johnson later described it: "When you're dealing with all those Senators—the good ones and the crazies, the hard workers and the lazies, the smart ones and the mediocres—you've got to know two things right away. You've got to understand the beliefs and values common to all of them as politicians, the desire for fame and the thirst for honor, and then you've got to understand *the* emotion most controlling that particular Senator when he thinks about this particular issue."[41] Thus Johnson could choose the arguments, words, and rhythms that persuaded each listener best—solemn words and cadenced speech for noble matters, casual words and clipped phrasing for less exalted and more pressing ones.

Johnson was also that rather rare American man who felt free to display intimacy with another man, through expressions of feeling and also in physical closeness. In an empty room he would stand or sit next to a man as if all that were available was a three-foot space. He could flatter men with sentiments of love and touch their bodies with gestures of affection. The intimacy was all the more excusable because it seemed genuine and without menace. Yet it was also the product of meticulous calculation. And it worked. Faced with the ardor and the bearing of this extraordinary man, the ordinary Senator would generally succumb.

Johnson's performance was not without cost. Toward the end of June, 1955, he began to feel continuously tired, so tired in fact that he agreed to take a vacation over the July Fourth weekend at the estate of George and Herman Brown near Middleburg, Virginia. He left his office late in the day on Saturday, July 2, for the two-hour drive. On the way down, he felt faint and experienced trouble drawing breath. By the time he reached Middleburg he felt nauseous. Certain, however, that it was only indigestion, Johnson refused to let the Browns call a doctor until another guest, Senator Clinton Anderson, warned him that all of Johnson's symptoms pointed to one thing—a heart attack.[42]

The doctor was called and Johnson was rushed to the hospital, where he went into severe shock. For several days he remained in critical condition. His illness was diagnosed as myocardial infarction, necessitating a hospital stay of six weeks followed by three months of complete rest at home.

During his months of convalescence Johnson was haunted by his childhood fear of paralysis. The nightmares returned, and with increased intensity. "They got worse after my heart attack," he said. "For I knew then how awful it was to lose command of myself, to be dependent on others. I couldn't stand it. But at least I was home with my family and friends. These were people I could trust."[43] During this period Johnson's temperament was more mercurial than ever before. Responsive to affection one day, he would fall into a rage the next. Recurrent talk of resigning from politics was followed by furious bursts of activity, countless visitors, and constant phone calls. Submission to the most inconvenient orders of mother and wife was followed by refusal to obey their gentlest suggestions.

Gradually, Johnson's strength returned, due in large part to his family's constant care, and in late September he signaled his return to the political scene with a public statement expressing his pride in the performance of the Eighty-fourth Congress. Comparing its first session with that of the previous Congress, he enumerated statistics to prove that this Senate and, therefore, its Majority Leader were larger in achievement and, therefore, in stature. "This session," he announced, "passed about 30% more bills in about 30% less time; it left fewer measures hanging on the calendar and fewer measures lost in committee files; it confirmed nearly 40,000 presidential nominations as compared to 23,500 during the first session of the 83rd Congress."[44]

On the opening day of the second session of the Eighty-fourth Congress, January 2, 1956, Johnson was back in the Majority Leader's place. Within a matter of days, it seemed as if he had never been away.

The fact that most interactions in the Senate were face to face was essential to Johnson's ability to persuade his colleagues, and to do so in a manner which permitted them to believe that their actions were in accord with what they had always wanted and thought. Johnson's effectiveness in persuasion depended on his ability to keep others from perceiving that they were yielding to a stronger will. Trades and deals, even threats, could be understood and accepted, but not psychic submission. Awareness that this was an attribute of his leadership would precipitate his overthrow. Reliance on intimacy was the key to the Majority Leader's success in the Senate, and that success would continue so long as he was able to conduct his job through a series of one-to-one encounters. This was possible only in an institution like the Senate, where the limited number of relevant participants permitted Johnson to develop as many different political selves as there were individuals about whose opinions he was concerned. In the secrecy of his office, he could show a different side of himself to each one of the different Senators who entered. Demure with Richard Russell, he could swagger and swear with Robert Kerr. A populist with liberals, he could be a gas and oil man with the conservatives. It was the essence of Johnson's leadership to play a distinct role specifically adapted to the qualities of the person with whom he interacted. And this, in turn, required control over access to information. He could not let the members of his audience exchange and compare information, often contradictory, about the situation he was defining differently for each of them. His secrets had to be kept.

"Structures differ," Robert Merton argues, "as to whether they allow insulation and concealment or not."[45] In contrast to the Presidency of the 1960s, the Senate of the 1950s protected Johnson remarkably well from having his activities become known to his colleagues or to the general public. Both the nature of the Senate—with its heritage of the cloakroom—and the structure of the senatorial press—with its tradition of inside reporting—operated to insulate Johnson's activities from the public spotlight.

"When," Erving Goffman writes, "the members of a team go backstage where the audience cannot see or hear them they regularly derogate the audience in a way that is inconsistent with the face-to-face treatment. Customers treated respectfully during the performance at the sales counter are often ridiculed, even caricatured, when the salesmen are backstage."[46] Johnson's backstage was the cloakroom. There, in the company of his Southern friends, where no one else could see or hear him, Johnson would imitate the speech, tone, and manner of the liberals, calling them the "ultra hots" or the "fancy boys," casting doubts on their virility. Of course, when speaking with liberal Senators, he showed nothing but convincing respect. And it worked—so long as the whole was separated into compartments, so long as each of his several roles was seen by different persons, so long as no Senator stumbled upon a show that was not meant uniquely for him.

Johnson was often able to use the same behavior with the press as he did with his colleagues, dividing it into separate components, and carving out a special relationship with each of the reporters. Especially important in this regard was the fact that William S. White, a fellow Texan and friend of Johnson since the NYA, just happened, during Johnson's stewardship, to be covering the Senate for the *New York Times*. "I knew that White admired subtlety," Johnson said, "and that if I played it right, I'd come out looking very subtle myself."

But Johnson did not apply his skill in one-to-one relations only to White. "You learn," he said, "that Stewart Alsop cares a lot about appearing to be an intellectual and a historian—he strives to match his brother's intellectual attainments—so whenever you talk to him, play down the gold cufflinks which you play up with *Time* magazine, and to him, emphasize your relationship with FDR and your roots in Texas, so much so that even when it doesn't fit the conversation you make sure to bring in maxims from your father and stories from the Old West. You learn that Evans and Novak love to traffic in backroom politics and political intrigue, so that when you're with them you make sure to bring in lots of details and colorful description of personality. You learn that Mary McGrory likes dominant personalities and Doris Fleeson cares only about issues, so that when you're with McGrory you come on strong and with Fleeson you make yourself sound like some impractical red-hot liberal."[47]

Yet the press had its own demands and traditions, which were different from those of the Senators. What worked with individual members of the press proved a failure when large numbers of reporters assembled for a press conference in the Majority Leader's office. What had been expansive in private appeared arrogant in public. What had seemed witty was now dull. As his audience increased in size, Johnson could no longer rely on the almost physical intensity that he could focus on another individual. Away from the security of bilateral sessions, where he was at his best, his mind seemed untuned, and his voice dropped to a monotonous muttering, audible only to those who sat close to him. In such situations he was at his worst. Even for those who could make out the words, his metaphors did not seem to fit, his adjectives were bland. Large audiences alarmed Johnson. In public gatherings the presence of even one enemy whom he could not disarm with the instruments of his personal faculties could deprive him of control of his language and manner, tend to unstabilize him. And in spite of, or perhaps because of, his mother's attempts to teach him elocution, Johnson remained tense with written texts or formal questions and answers. At his press conferences, he would proceed, in slow, belabored phrases, cluttered with pauses, repeating again and again the litany of the Senate's accomplishments. And in the end, when the reporters tried to parse just what it was that he had said, they found out that in fact he had said nothing at all.

If Sam Johnson's boy created the private style, Rebekah's son could not accept the public image. Always he came back with the same theme: "People don't understand one thing about me, that is, the one thing I want to do is my job. . . . Some are always writing that I'm a backroom operator. They say I'm insensitive. How would you like your little daughter (or your mother) to read that you are a backroom operator, a wire puller, or a clever man?"[48] Johnson could not choose between arguments: that the world, including his severest critics, lived by the grace of backrooms; or that there was no such thing as "backroom rule," that "persuasion in private discussion mirrored public debate." At different times, and sometimes at the same time, he made both arguments. And in the end, he was fatally vulnerable to the sound instincts of public opinion, which, if offered success as the sole justification for the means by which power is exercised, can admire the process while it works but assail it when things go wrong.

In the Senate, however, press conferences were not the source of information for the important reporters. They depended on the face-to-face conversations with the Majority Leader in which Johnson excelled. Here he could play the role he liked the best: the benefactor distributing needed services—information, details, plans—in return for favorable coverage.[49] Because there were few alternative sources from whom Senate reporters could obtain the information they needed, they remained dependent on Lyndon Johnson. Later, we will see how badly this worked under the very different operational conditions of the Presidency.

Of the many arenas in which he moved throughout his long career, none was more congenial to his spirit and faculties than the Senate of the United States.

That institution—with its style of gentlemanly behavior and its substance of realistic maneuver—provided Johnson with an opportunity to accommodate, for the time being, the split between his public and his private self; he was at ease with both the genteel world of the Southern committee chairmen and the hard-dealing world of Western gas and oil men. For Johnson, the polite, polished conduct on which the Senate prided itself had a familiar ring; these were the forms cherished by Rebekah Baines and her father. And if the facts of life in the Senate belied the fiction, so they had in his home. Not only was Johnson able to accept and work with both the fiction and the fact, as does every successful Senator; he relished their coexistence, which was both reminiscent of the trials of childhood and annulled them: now he was in control—his was the authority to bestow and withdraw—and he was receiving more than he had to give.

Undoubtedly, institutional conditions—face-to-face relations, the limited number of actors, insulation, and monopoly—helped Johnson to cope effectively with many different types of situations. However, to overemphasize the fit between the individual and the nature of the Senate institution can also be misleading, giving the impression of a wholly static relationship, as if Johnson's qualities and modes of behavior just happened to conform to the Senate's firmly established style of decision-making. In fact, the relationship was dynamic and complex; the Senate's conception of itself was at least to some extent represented—or enhanced—by the party leader. Johnson increased his power by using possibilities inherent in the established structure and traditions of the Senate, but he also used this authority to modify the conduct of the Senate to conform more closely with his methods of leadership. For example, Johnson evolved a system for handling procedural questions that was a natural extension of his personality. Because he himself felt uncomfortable in larger groups and formal debate, he gradually shifted senatorial and public attention away from the floor to the places where he felt most at home—the cloakroom, the office, the hallways. He established a rule that, wherever feasible, the Senate leadership would negotiate unanimous-consent agreements limiting debate to a specified number of hours for each side. Indeed, debate beyond a sparse allotment of time became a favor which a Senator had to request from the Majority Leader.

On the floor itself, Johnson was in perpetual motion. Visibly impatient at any delay, he would frequently leap ahead of a page boy to rush a Senator's amendment to the clerk's desk. The moment one amendment was disposed of he would be on his feet reminding another Senator that he was scheduled to offer the next amendment. Over time, Johnson developed a set of signals to the Senate clerks. If things were moving well, and the votes were in place, he would twirl his finger rapidly in a circular motion, and the roll call would proceed at a fast clip. If his aides were still out looking for a Senator whose vote was essential, Johnson would push the palm of his hand gently downward, and the names would be called at a slow pace.

Johnson was extremely successful in manipulating attendance on the floor, somewhat as a musician manipulates an accordion—expanding or contracting it at will. He could muster a respectable vote for a Senator's bill that was bound to lose—an act which could be a substantial boon to the man who wanted his constituents to take him seriously. When Johnson favored a bill, he could organize a group to applaud a Senator as he spoke on its behalf. Alternatively, when a "troublesome" Senator was due to speak, he could let others know that attendance on the floor would be closely watched and subsequently punished. He would exploit the right of the leader to be recognized first, in order to control and determine when legislative fights would be initiated and the terms of conflict. The stories of his legerdemain are legion: On one occasion Johnson wanted the Senator from Arkansas to be absent from a vote scheduled for two o'clock, so he arranged a special lunch in honor of the Senator to be held at the other end of the city. On another occasion, Johnson was positive that an important bill would pass if an undecided Southern Senator could be made to support it. In the middle of the floor debate, Johnson walked over to the Senator, told him that he had to leave the chamber for an hour or so, and asked the potential dissenter to take over as floor manager. The Senator hesitated, agreed, and voted for the bill.[50]

One should not overlook that one of Johnson's most important resources in building his base of power was what one observer called "the biggest, the most efficient, the most ruthlessly overworked and the most loyal personal staff in the history of the Senate."[51] Those who made up that stuff found that working for Johnson subjected them to unpredictable expressions of feeling. "One minute," a member of Johnson's Senate staff remarked, "he would give an aide a tremendous tongue-lashing, and then he would turn right around, give him an expensive gift, and say to him, 'You know you are my right arm.' "[52]

"You never want to give a man a present when he's feeling good," Johnson explained. "You want to do it when he's down!" Similarly, Johnson justified his violent swings in feelings and conduct by the need to keep his staff continually off guard in order to ensure that they would not relax their efforts. Everything—from staff meetings to rides in his car— was by invitation only, allowing Johnson to arbitrarily freeze out or bring in anyone at any time.

Yet if one of his staff decided to leave, Johnson would become desperate, begging him to stay, attempting to bribe him with material objects, fulsome praise, and reassurance of his love; to pressure him by claiming that he could not possibly get along without his services. It generally worked. "He told me," one of the staff recalled, "that if I stayed I'd be his right-hand man, I'd be his chief of staff, I'd be with him every minute of the day. And as I looked at him, I realized that while he handled the pettiest things in the pettiest way imaginable, he handled the big things in a big way, such that whenever I really needed him he was there."[53] So the aide who thought of leaving remained, perhaps because he felt he had now acquired the intimacy that Johnson had hitherto denied him. And with this, the play would start all over again. Johnson would return to his typical pattern, the aide would find it increasingly difficult to stay with him, and again threaten to leave, whereupon Johnson would once again shower him with love and praise: he would stay to begin another cycle.

But Johnson's aides were not the only ones whom he treated as manipulable instruments, clay in the potter's hand. There were also a half-dozen or more colleagues who became, through a tangled web of affection, resentment, and dependency, the objects of his domination. Hubert Humphrey is one example, perhaps the most interesting one.[54] While he was reform mayor of Minneapolis and a candidate for the Senate, Humphrey had become a national hero. Then in 1948, he suddenly took the floor at the 1948 Democratic Convention to deliver an impassioned plea for a strong civil rights plank in the party platform. A strong plank was adopted—too strong for many Southern delegates, who walked out of the convention to form their own party. Humphrey's dramatic and successful performance undoubtedly helped him to win election to the Senate. But his term of glory did not last long. As soon as he entered the Senate, he found himself the target of the inner club—not only for his performance at the convention, but also for his compulsion to talk too fast, too much, and on too many issues. Then Humphrey chose to speak out against Harry Byrd, the Senator from Virginia, the mild-mannered aging priest of the Democratic Caucus. Outraged by this already disliked freshman Senator's attack on a very senior member, the Senate establishment retorted with a withering denunciation of Humphrey from both sides of the aisle.

Within a matter of days, Humphrey had become anathema to everyone—except to Lyndon Johnson, who seemed to foresee that someday Humphrey might be useful to him just as he now needed help from Johnson.

So Johnson took Humphrey under his wing, tutoring him on the unwritten rules, urging him to become a "liberal doer" and not just a "liberal talker." "Johnson sought me out," Humphrey later recalled, "and would visit me from time to time. He always had a good sense of humor. He would say to me that he wanted to cross-breed me with Byrd. If he could get two pints of Byrd's blood in me to cool me off and a little of Russell's restraint, I'd be great. Johnson didn't enjoy talking with the liberals. He didn't think they had a sense of humor. He thought that most liberals were never so unhappy as when happy, or so happy as when unhappy. So he wanted someone in the liberal ranks for information and help. Perhaps he came to the conclusion I could be had. I never felt I was. I felt I was getting more than giving."[55]

The grateful Humphrey learned his lessons well: he mastered parliamentary skills, he settled down to the work of his committees, and he became, over time, the principal envoy from the camp of the liberals to Lyndon Johnson's court—and, thus, a central figure in the Senate's inner club.

But Humphrey paid a price for his reclamation. As the relationship grew, Humphrey's independent will, while not shattered, was softened, bent, and guided. Johnson's power did not tyrannize; it exerted a diminishing compression, a process that would be repeated, with more devastating impact, in the 1960s, when Humphrey became Johnson's Vice President. "When I picture Hubert in my mind," Johnson later said, "I picture him with tears in his eyes; he was always able to cry at the sight of something sad, whether it be a widow with her child or an old crippled-up man. And that part, it's just fine; it shows he can be touched.

"The trouble is," he continued, "that he's never learned to put feelings and strength together; all too often he sways in the wind like a big old reed, pushed around by the pressures of staff and friends and colleagues."[56] In these words, Johnson seemed almost sad, as if he wished that the very men who had submitted to his will had fought a little harder against him.

Yet Johnson never lost his deep respect for Humphrey's brilliance, talent, and ability. On another occasion he said of Humphrey: "He has the greatest coordination of mind and tongue of anybody I know. He's genuine, he has a depth of sincerity and real compassion. He doesn't have a lazy bone in his body and not a dishonest bone. He is truly a happy warrior. Maybe he doesn't have enough reserve because he feels very deeply about human problems. People from Minnesota have a propensity for talking. When I was Vice President, I disagreed with Kennedy on three or four basic things, but never publicly. Hubert Humphrey also disagreed with me, but there is a difference between disagreement and disloyalty. I told the Cabinet I considered myself a B Vice President but Humphrey was an A or A plus."[57]

Lyndon Johnson tried to be everything to everybody in the Senate—and, in defiance of the cliché, he succeeded. His power did not evaporate, as power often does with most men the longer they exercise it; instead, the use and even the abuse of his power seemed only to increase it. His personality did not fade and become indistinct, as personality often does in most men who must continually adapt to others; instead, even though it bent enough to seduce and reshape other wills, Johnson's own will became stronger. Yet Johnson often seemed as discontent in conquest as he was eager in pursuit. Perhaps he always needed some new challenge to his powers of domination and control; perhaps this man who so feared paralysis in himself dreaded equally the sight of a man "melting" under him, even as he sought it.

But was the process of conquest and control his sole purpose? Or was there more, alongside his father's demand—to make himself great among the men whose company he shared? Was there also his mother's dream—to do good for others?

Chapter 5

The Senate Leader

During the Senate years, few questioned Lyndon Johnson's skill in attaining power; that was an undeniable reality, continually on display. But as he rose in prominence and began to exhibit an impressive mastery over the Senate unequaled in modern political history, there was increasing criticism. One group of critics argued that Johnson had subverted the safeguards of representative democracy: by taking the process of decision into his own hands, he had deprived individual Senators of independent judgment. Other critics complained about the purpose to which Johnson's power was put. Some argued that in the end his awesome system yielded little but legislative trivia, affecting the lives of the American people in marginal ways at best. Worse still, they said, Johnson conceded too much to the Eisenhower White House, forfeiting the chance to raise the issues that might provide a strong platform for his party and a progressive alternative for the nation.[1]

The argument that Johnson's conduct in some way violated and endangered principles of democratic government became a matter of public controversy. Johnson, however, disdainfully rejected any argument that his conduct might do any such thing. This was evident in the controversy that erupted when Senator William Proxmire of Wisconsin argued in 1958, directly challenging Johnson on the floor of the Senate,

> to end one man rule in the Senate, to win dignity and full representation for all Democratic Senators . . . to win democracy. . . .
>
> There has never been a time when power has been as sharply concentrated as it is today in the Senate. In January 1958, the Senators assembled in the Democratic caucus and listened to the Majority Leader read a speech which he had previously prepared—there was not

a single matter of party business discussed. There wasn't even a mention of party program . . . the next meeting of the Senate caucus was a full year later. The only business of the entire caucus had taken less than two and a half minutes. And Senators had to surrender for another year their right and duty to determine the Democratic party's policies and programs.[2]

Proxmire's expression of concern with procedure reflected the themes of the American Political Science Association in its celebrated 1950 report, "Toward a More Responsible Two-Party System." That report had called for more frequent party caucuses, more concretely programmatic platforms, and more direct accountability to the public. Paul Douglas echoed Proxmire's concern, arguing that "Under Johnson, the Senate functions like a Greek tragedy: all the action takes place off-stage, before the play begins. Nothing is left to open and spontaneous debate, nothing is left for the participants but the enactment of their prescribed roles."[3]

Johnson believed, however, that, as he later put it, the debate was not a reflection of a genuine difference of conviction, that all this "fuss about democracy and procedure had nothing to do with my leadership and everything to do with the liberals' need to criticize. First they tell me they want a strong leader in the Senate so they can get results. So I give them leadership and I get results. Then they change their tune, and say that what they really want is democracy, and participation, and decentralized leadership. Then, in the same breath, they contradict themselves by crying out for hundreds of caucus meetings where they can go around binding everyone else to their positions, while refusing, on their part, to be bound to anything but their own conscience. It just doesn't hold water. The only link is in their endless need to cut me up. No matter what I do, it'll never be good enough for them. This one-man-rule stuff is a myth. The theory that one man is able to tell sixty-four other Senators how they shall vote is nonsense. I do not know how one can force a Senator to do anything. I have never tried to do so."[4]

To the extent Johnson's response was not only an attack on the motives of his critics but an answering argument, the essence of his argument was that, given the character of the Senate, no single man could possibly hope to dominate decisions over a wide range of issues. Because there were numerous bases for political influence—expertise, geography, the possession of committee positions, and a member's right to vote, that might be useful to his objectives on other matters, and the like—each Senator could make himself heard at some crucial stage in the process of decision. Issues were resolved through bargaining between individuals and groups, in a variety of forums and discussions, which, because they were separate, permitted agreement to be based on a large diversity of terms and understandings. Debates, either in the caucus or on the floor, could only hamper, even cripple, this process, which was, Johnson argued, the only way in which important issues could be resolved. Legislation was the product of private negotiation, not public debate. The proper function of public debate—indeed, its only useful function—was to ratify and increase general acceptance of a decision that had already been made. Public words, Johnson felt, were stumbling blocks to effective action; and the less ambiguous, the more harmful. Public expressions tended to freeze men into positions, making it more difficult for them to accept later compromises or modifications, and thus reducing or limiting the capacity for bargaining that was the source of effective legislative action. "The process itself," Johnson said, "requires a certain amount of deception. There's no getting around it. If the full implications of any bill were known before its enactment, it would never get passed."[5] This observation implied that if those full implications were described in public debate, many potential supporters would be forced into opposition.

Johnson was incapable of sympathetic understanding for Senators who were concerned with process instead of results. He had no patience or respect for those who challenged desirable results on the basis of concepts and ideas; he seemed almost to perceive them as individuals who had succumbed to fantasy. Tending to view reliance on the dictates of conscience to justify conduct as a sign of cowardice, Johnson saw preoccupation with principle and procedure as a sign of impotence. Such men were "troublemakers," more concerned with appearing forceful than in exercising the real strengths that led to tangible achievement. Even worse, the press tended to echo their critique. "Every so often," Johnson suggested, "the writers get hard up and begin writing about a liberal revolt against Johnson. Well, every couple of years we have a caucus and there has never been a single vote against me. Now what kind of revolt is that?"[6]

In fact, most of the Democratic Senators did not complain about Johnson's leadership, nor were they anxious for procedural reforms that might threaten the familiar political context within which they preferred, and were accustomed, to operate. Since they wanted to appear independent to their constituents, they preferred the discreet dominance of Johnson to the open discipline of a party caucus with genuine power to bind them to the freely and collectively determined choice of a majority of their colleagues. In their relationship with the Republicans, the objective was different. They wanted to appear united. Thus productive unity or agreement on measures that might be inadequate or of little significance was far preferable to the paralyzing divisions that great issues would create. And Johnson seemed almost uniquely capable of providing this kind of unity while somehow preventing the potential sources of great division from ever emerging. Thus the general atmosphere, as the publication *The Washington Window* described it, was one of contentment with the way things were:

> During the past weeks the Senate has been the scene of a David and Goliath drama that isn't quite working out the way the Bible has it. The David role was played by Senator Proxmire . . . Goliath by Lyndon Johnson. Contrary to the Bible story, when the dust had settled, it appeared that instead of Goliath being slain, it was David who was slain . . . after Proxmire spoke, only a few daring Senators came to his support and in the end his crusade was a one man battle that ended in apparent failure.[7]

In short, the Democratic majority accepted Johnson's direction because they believed it was best for the Senate and for themselves. Leader and followers were bound in a relationship that served their common interest. And even though the belief was generally sincere, Johnson, as we have seen, had also created some tangible motives to support and accept his leadership. He had been able to acquire great power and from that power to construct a brilliant and complicated system of governing, which his subjects would accept, even welcome, because it also satisfied their own needs.

Widespread support and praise for his leadership did not lessen—perhaps it strengthened—Johnson's intransigent refusal, perhaps his inability, to pay any attention to the complaints of a minority: that he had extinguished debate in a chamber that had long prided itself on providing a forum for public debate without imposed limits and often of high quality; that although it was not a requirement of senatorial democracy that every member take part in every decision at every stage, it was essential, at least, that members be provided with access to the determinative legislative negotiations at some stage. Nor could Johnson see any difference of basic principle between a process that depended on one man to produce consensus through individual agreements and one that provided a procedure for collective discussion and consideration. To Johnson debate could involve issues of principle—to assist the blacks or restrain the unions—but not the method used to achieve results. That was a practical question—one of effectiveness and of comparative utility. Nevertheless, problems of process and procedure were to become important issues during the 1960s when the demand for participation spread and grew in intensity, influencing and reflecting movements for change far beyond both the Senate and the party system. But during the 1950s there was no possibility of a basic change in the decision-making structure. The essential condition for change—widespread dissatisfaction with current procedures—simply did not exist.[8]

Johnson's critics, who eventually included Senator Joseph Clark and Senator Patrick McNamara, Democratic National Chairman Paul Butler and ADA Chairman Joseph Rauh, fared little better in their second goal—to reshape the party so that it would "raise all the great issues, confront the Executive and educate the general public." This conflict also reflected basically different conceptions: in this case, the nature of the relationship between executive and legislature, along with the preferences and expectations of the American public.

In Johnson's view—which many shared—the Presidency was the only institution in the American system capable of consistently initiating major legislation. It was up to the President to identify problems, first bring them to public attention, and to draft bills designed to solve them. The executive must provide the agenda for congressional action and set forth the subject matter and priorities for debate and decision. Congress itself was not, in his view, equipped with the expertise, the time, or the type of coherent organizational structure needed to formulate and initiate programs of action on a regular and systematically related basis. "Whenever my critics in the Congress talked to me about the responsibility of creating issues, I came back to the question of where in the hell they expected the issues to come from—from our heads? If an issue is not included in the presidential agenda, it is almost impossible—short of crisis—to get the Congress to focus on it. That's the way our system works; but these fellows never understood that. They didn't understand—with all their calls for Congress to have all sorts of expertise and classified information, in order to act in foreign affairs—that the congressional role in national security is not to act but to respond to the executive."[9]

Johnson was annoyed and upset when, in 1958, the Democratic National Committee created an Advisory Committee "to coordinate and advance efforts in behalf of Democratic programs and principles." He was convinced that the Advisory Committee, chaired by Paul Butler, would hamper his continual effort to construct ad hoc majorities for particular legislation—majorities which, in many cases, must necessarily be composed of both Republicans and Democrats. The Advisory Committee's stamp of approval would be "a kiss of death" with many Republicans who might normally have been willing to support a bill but would find it difficult, often impossible, to help enact that same legislation once it had been labeled a "Democratic priority." Moreover, the liberal cast of the Advisory Committee made it likely that its recommendations would arouse the suspicion of conservative Democrats. Though "completely powerless to produce any votes," the Advisory Committee would be "completely capable of deepening divisions within the Democratic Party," and of polarizing Senate members along party lines, making the Majority Leader's task infinitely more difficult.

Undoubtedly, Johnson also apprehended that the committee might become a threat to his own power since it was presuming to participate in decisions that had been largely within his authority; trying to exercise from the outside those functions that he had not allowed the Senate's own Democratic Policy Committee to perform. Moreover, as Johnson would later suggest: "The idea that the congressional Democrats have a responsibility for taking the national Democratic platform and program and trying to push it through the Congress is simply crazy. A political party at a national

convention draws up a program to present to the voters. The
voters can either accept it by giving the party full power, reject it by taking the party completely out of power, or give it
qualified approval by giving one party the Congress and the
other party the Presidency. And when we in the Congress
have been given a qualified mandate, as we were in 1956, it
means that we have a solemn responsibility to cooperate with
the President and produce a program that is neither his blueprint nor our blueprint but a combination of the two. It is the
politician's task to pass legislation, not to sit around saying
principled things."[10]

Johnson's general view that there was a natural division of
functions and prerogatives between President and Congress
was applied with special insistency to the area of foreign policy and national security. In 1958 Senator Joseph Clark suggested legislation requiring the President to submit to the
Congress an annual report on the state of national security.
"The Congress and the public," Clark argued, "cannot make
intelligent decisions without authoritative information, yet
public information on military matters consists mainly of
leaks from the Pentagon and piecemeal bits of information
put out in press releases or submitted to Congressional committees."[11] Johnson was swift to reject the Clark proposal.
Conforming to the gentlemanly customs of Senate debate, his
language was gentle, the terms a bit equivocal, but those
familiar with the code of Senate debate understood that he
was taking a firm and unappealable position. "I would be
somewhat inclined against such a new report," he told the
Senate, "since the subject matter involves at all times a substantial quantity of classified data. . . . I would be a little fearful that we might be inviting through this the establishment
of a custom through which the President might feel compelled to present to the public a rosier picture than the facts
would warrant. It is my judgment that the basic information
necessary for an appraisal of the nation's security is available
to the Members of Congress through existing channels in just
about the best fashion, even though it has its imperfections."[12]

Nor did Johnson restrict his insistence on his concept of
the proper relations between President and Congress to in-
fringements proposed by liberal Democrats. In 1955 the conservative Republicans sponsored a resolution that would put
the Senate on record against President Eisenhower's participation in the Big Four summit meeting unless he first ob-

tained a commitment from the Soviets to include the status of
the Eastern European satellites as part of the agenda. "This
resolution," Johnson argued on the floor, "would make
Congress the controlling factor instead of a partner in the
field of foreign affairs. It would place a loaded gun at the
President's temple. . . . In our dealings with other nations,
only one man can speak for our country. He cannot speak
clearly if his words must be strained through a Congressional
gag. When he sits down to negotiate with the chiefs of foreign states, I want them to know he is backed to the hilt by
every loyal American."[13]

Johnson believed that the prevalent mood of the American
people about questions of foreign policy was one of "indifference and passivity." He perceived the public as "not only
peaceful, but apathetic," concerned primarily with domestic
prosperity and with the private values of family, home, and
work. Yet he was also convinced that beneath this tranquillity
was concealed the possibility of "a mass stampede, a violent
overreaction to fear, an explosion of panic" such as, he
thought, had occurred in the heyday of Joseph McCarthy.[14]

Johnson, like most of his colleagues in Washington at the
time, believed McCarthyism was a mass movement, a reaction by great numbers of people to the loss of China and to
the stalemate in Korea. Though later studies have suggested
that McCarthy's support lay more in the political needs of
different groups in Washington than in the fears of the
masses, the perception that McCarthy had enormous popular
influence restrained the men in Congress from moving against
him.[15] So McCarthy was able to continue his ravaging assaults
until, undone by his own extravagant excesses, perhaps intox-
icated by his enormous success and deluded by a growing
conviction of his invulnerability, he chose to direct his accusations at the institution of the military. The inevitable
showdown came in the Army-McCarthy hearings, where his
performance was viewed by nationwide television audiences.
The result was to virtually destroy the perception that
McCarthy was a believing crusader and to create a widespread criticism and dislike of his personal qualities. The
hearings themselves—with their revelation of how little support there was for McCarthy's accusations—along with their
impact on public opinion, opened the way for a select committee and then the Senate itself to censure McCarthy's conduct. As a result, his effectiveness diminished rapidly and

soon disappeared entirely. And, not long thereafter, McCarthy died.

But long after McCarthy's death, Johnson continued to fear that a demagogue might rise to power by unscrupulously exploiting and intensifying popular fears and suspicions of Communism and the aggressive intentions of Communist power. That fear, seemingly justified by the McCarthy precedent, helped to provide Johnson and many others with a reason and rationalization for cooperation between Democrats and Republicans in the conduct of foreign policy. Bipartisanship was one means of keeping control in responsible hands, and permitting a reasonable and solidly designed foreign policy. "The more the two parties could agree," Johnson argued, "the smaller the area of conflict shown to the American public and the less I worried about the public's tendency to go off on a jag, paralyzing itself in the endless debate or stampeding us in panic."[16] "We've junked the old Taft practice," Johnson said in 1953, "that the duty of the opposition is to oppose. As a result some people say I've been petticoatin' around with Eisenhower. Well, that's not true . . . but I want to make absolutely sure that the Communists don't play one branch of the government against the other, or one party against the other as happened in the Korean War. I've read the Constitution. I know where the basic responsibility for foreign policy lies . . . the real danger is that the other side is going to underestimate us. It's happened before. The danger is they'll think we're fat and fifty and fighting among ourselves about free enterprise and socialism and all that. We might mislead them so they'll think these Americans are just the country club crowd. That's a mistake our enemies have made before. If you're in an airplane, and you're flying somewhere, you don't run up to the cockpit and attack the pilot. Mr. Eisenhower is the only President we've got."[17]

There is implied in this statement an excessive reliance on expert knowledge and experience, along with an equally implicit belief that the possession of presidential authority included possession of unequaled information, understanding, and skill. This assumption was to guide Johnson during his own Presidency and contribute to the rise of popular opposition and the erosion of his own leadership. Johnson's statement excludes a possibility on which many would finally insist—the possibility that the passengers might be entitled to consult with, even instruct, the pilot about where they wanted to go. But in the 1950s, to Lyndon Johnson, the concept that the people or even the Congress should be permitted to determine the basic direction of foreign policy seemed "just plain wrong."

None of this is meant to suggest that as Majority Leader Johnson simply rubber-stamped the actions of the President. On the contrary, he evolved a clever balancing act: support for Eisenhower on some bills and opposition on others; a stern anti-Communist line, but not so hard or rigid that he was joined in common cause with the Republican conservatives; help for Eisenhower's programs, but not enough help to anger the more partisan Democrats; occasional attacks on Eisenhower's foreign policy, but not the frequent and fundamental attacks that could open him to an accusation that he had abandoned bipartisanship.[18] Having taken the "hard line" by adamantly opposing the admission of Communist China to the United Nations in 1953, Johnson took the "soft line" during the Indochina crisis of 1954, and argued against Dulles' proposal that America provide air support for the French at Dienbienphu. Quick to support Eisenhower against charges by conservatives that inviting Khrushchev to visit the United States was an act of appeasement, Johnson consistently questioned the adequacy of our military preparedness. Although these alternations of support and opposition undoubtedly evince careful political calculation, Johnson's choice of issues and positions also reflects a consistency of outlook that he later described as his basic position in international relations: "the belief in holding your hand out while keeping your guard up, opening your lines of communication while keeping your powder dry."[19]

Nor does Johnson's insistence that Congress could not take the lead on many matters mean that he believed Congress could never lead. On the contrary, he asserted that there were many circumstances—especially when an administration fails to act during conditions of crisis—under which Congress could and should take the initiative, exercising what one scholar has called its "reserve capacity" for leadership.[20] This is precisely how the Congress of the late 1950s behaved in the areas of civil rights and space exploration under Johnson's leadership. The development and conduct of national policy toward issues of civil rights and space technology had been neglected, virtually immobilized, by presidential inaction and by division within the administration. Then dramatic and momentous events—the Supreme Court's decision in *Brown* v. *Board of Education* and the Soviet Union's launching of Sputnik—created a vastly enlarged public awareness and a new sense of urgency. It became clear that action was necessary. Yet the same events had severely weakened the natural impulse to rely on presidential leadership by helping to illuminate past inadequacies, while the feeble ambiguity of the administration's response further undermined public confidence in the administration's intentions and capacities. Thus the way was open for Congress to take the initiative, and the legislative branch assumed the task of determining national policy and action. And when the process was complete, the major credit for the results—the National Aeronautics and Space Administration, and the Civil Rights Act of 1957—was given to Lyndon Johnson.

On the night of October 4, 1957, as Johnson later described it, he was at his ranch when the news of Sputnik came across the television. He remembered taking "a walk ... with eyes lifted skyward, straining to catch a glimpse of that alien object which had been thrust into the outer reaches of our world"; he remembered "the profound shock of realizing that it might be possible for another nation to achieve technological superiority over this great country of ours"; and in response, he decided that very night that somehow something had to be done.[21]

The Subcommittee on Preparedness immediately launched a series of investigations into the American space effort which was to result in the establishment of NASA the following year, and lead to the Apollo program and man's landing on the moon in the next decade. Johnson knew that no large and long-term public enterprise could be sustained without popular support. From the start, he felt it was necessary to make the American people realize the importance of the struggle for space. The first step involved the preparation and delivery of a series of public statements such as the one he presented to the Democratic Caucus in 1958. "Control of space," Johnson argued, "means control of the world. . . . From space the masters of infinity would have the power to control the earth's weather, to cause drought and flood, to change the tides and raise the levels of the sea, to divert the gulf stream and change temperature climates to frigid. . . . There is something more important than the ultimate weapon. That is the ultimate position—the position of total control over earth that lies somewhere in outer space ... and if there is this ultimate position, then our national goal and the goal of all free men *must* be to win and hold that position."[22]

Johnson knew that his Senate hearings could also be used to dramatize the issue. Yet there was also a danger that if his hearings conducted an overly aggressive and accusatorial effort to assign blame for the Soviet Union's dramatic triumph, or magnified the significance and danger of the Soviet accomplishment, the result might be to provoke panic or fear, leading to an angry and self-destructive search for scapegoats or conspirators. The middle course was to arouse both the public and the President by coupling shame with possibility for the restoration of pride. He would conduct the hearings so as to persuade them that with Sputnik we had suffered a defeat as serious as Pearl Harbor, but, at the same time, prevent a kind of resigned desperation with reassuring evidence that the struggle could still be won if we had the will and endurance to fight it all the way. Just as the young college editor told his fellow students that Lindbergh's success was due not to luck but to pluck, so now the Majority Leader told his fellow Americans that the Soviet success was due not to magic or superior resources but to determination—a determination we could match and surpass. "Our people are slow to start," Johnson later said in analyzing why America had originally lagged in the space effort, "but once they start they are hard to stop."[23]

Johnson's display of leadership in the creation of a national effort to acquire a superiority in all the varied possibilities of space exploration was surpassed only by his role in the passage of the 1957 Civil Rights Act.[24] In the 1940s and the early 1950s, six different civil rights bills were defeated on the floor of the House and the Senate. The structure of power in the Congress, where Southerners and conservatives had disproportionate authority, coupled with a mood of public complacency, had created a situation where legislative action seemed very unlikely if not wholly impossible. However, between 1954 and 1957 three events dramatically altered the context within which the issue of civil rights would be considered: first, the Supreme Court's decision in *Brown* v. *Board of Education*, which provided constitutional sanction for some black claims and which catalyzed the nascent civil rights movement; second, the defiant and often violent refusal of the South to comply with *Brown*, which generated mounting support in other parts of the country for some form of protective legislation; and third, the elections of 1954 and 1956, which made it clear to Republicans and Democrats alike that increasing numbers of blacks were willing to desert candidates of the Democratic Party for Republicans who seemed likely to better serve their interests. Without these events, it is hard to imagine any action by Lyndon Johnson, or anyone else, that could have reversed the regular pattern of congressional defeat.

In 1956, in response to mounting political pressures, Attorney General Herbert Brownell convinced Eisenhower that a civil rights bill should be submitted to the Congress. The administration bill included three provisions: the creation of a Civil Rights Division within the Justice Department; authority for the Justice Department to intervene on behalf of individuals whose civil rights were being violated—in housing, education, voting, or law enforcement; and the appointment of a Civil Rights Commission to recommend further legislation.

Just as external events modified the situation within the administration, the actions of the administration changed the situation within the Senate. The administration's civil rights bill failed to pass that first year, but this failure prepared the way for success a year later. For the position of the administration had joined the issue, opened it to public debate. The issue of civil rights could no longer be quietly shelved. There was no longer any way for members to evade public and personal responsibility for choice. By 1957, Johnson later observed, "One thing had become absolutely certain: the Senate simply had to act, the Democratic Party simply had to act, and I simply had to act; the issue could wait no longer."[25] As leader of the Senate, Johnson was concerned that a continuing stalemate would seriously damage the Senate's prestige in the nation. As a leader of the Democratic Party, Johnson felt that the failure of a Democratic Congress to approve a civil rights bill proposed by a Republican administration would erode Negro support for the Democratic Party. As a man with presidential dreams, Johnson recognized that it would be almost impossible for him to escape all responsibility for the failure of the Senate to act, that failure on this issue at this time would brand him forever as sectional and therefore unpresidential.

In these circumstances, it is possible to imagine persons of quite different temperaments deciding, as Lyndon Johnson did, that "something had to be done." But the situation was so complicated and the chances for success so small that the course of events might well have been different if the Majority Leader's capacity had been more typical or less extraordinary. "Although," Riesman and Glazer wrote, "different kinds of characters can be used for the same work within an institution, a 'price' is paid by the character types that fit badly as against the release of energy provided by the congruence of character and task."[26]

What elements of this problem made for congruence? Most important was the fact that the civil rights issue intensified and brought to focus Johnson's recurrent fear that "the whole thing"—his leadership, the Senate, the world—would fall apart if he lost control even for a moment, thus permitting the forces of violent division to "get loose." "One real slip and we're done for," he would say again and again, as if both his power and the future of America were fragilely suspended by a gossamer thread. Fearing that the issues of the civil rights question would be "taken over" by the "extremists"— defined as a choice between the irreconcilable views of Southern segregationists and Northern liberals—Johnson felt "driven" to seek a middle course, a legislative formula, that would represent some real progress—enough to moderate liberal passions, but not so unacceptable that it would provoke an open break with the party and its leadership. "I knew," he later said, "that if I failed to produce on this one, my leadership would be broken into a hundred pieces; everything I had built up over the years would be completely undone."[27]

Less significant than the revelation of personal fear is the fact that Johnson exhibited the prescience to recognize that this issue had dimensions far greater than the difficulties of formulating practicable legislation. He seemed to understand that the issue of civil rights had created a crisis of legitimacy for both the Senate and the Democratic Party. Perhaps it was this understanding that helped Johnson not only to surmount his fears during this struggle but to transform them into instruments of leadership—influencing the action of others by persuading them to share in his apprehension of dangerous possibilities.

Johnson determined that his first task must be to persuade the "reasonable" Southerners to abandon their support for a filibuster, by demonstrating that even if it was successful the only result would be a Pyrrhic victory for the South. Northern passions were rising, becoming "hysterical," and would no longer accept defeat by filibuster; instead, the attack would focus on the filibuster rule itself. He began with Russell: "These Negroes, they're getting pretty uppity these days and that's a problem for us since they've got something now they never had before, the political pull to back up their uppityness. Now we've got to do something about this, we've got to give them a little something, just enough to quiet them down, not enough to make a difference. For if we don't move at all, then their allies will line up against us and there'll be no way of stopping them, we'll lose the filibuster and there'll be no way of putting a brake on all sorts of wild legislation. It'll be Reconstruction all over again."[28]

Worse, Johnson said, an attempt to kill the bill would plunge the Senate and the South into the paralysis that results when issues of status or morality remain unresolved and are the object of constant challenge, making it impossible for Senators or the South itself to act on its most fundamental problem—economic growth. Johnson argued, and he probably believed, that the South was on the verge of new possibilities for rapid expansion. However, the realization of these possibilities was far from certain. Decisions made by the leadership and people of the South could determine whether it would become one of the most prosperous areas of the country or whether it would remain an economic backwater, subsisting on hominy grits. Among the most significant determinants of Southern prospects would be the willingness of Southern leadership to accept the inevitability of some progress on civil rights and get on with the business of the future, or its continued insistence on conjuring the ghost of Thaddeus Stevens.

Johnson assured Russell that if the Southerners discontinued the filibuster, he would personally take responsibility for revising the bill to eliminate its most objectionable feature—Title III, which authorized the federal government to dispatch agents into the South to protect a wide variety of civil rights—and he would add an amendment requiring a jury trial for all civil cases arising under the new statute. The jury-trial amendment provided Southerners with a face-saving explanation of their willingness to permit the first civil rights bill to pass without a filibuster. How, they could ask, could a Southerner fear a Southern jury?

Having secured Russell's agreement to let debate proceed, Johnson turned his attention to the North, where, as he put it, "the liberals could be divided into three classes," only one of which could be mobilized for his purpose. "First, there were the emotional liberals outside the Congress—the groups like the ADA that were held together only by a desire to create trouble. They believed in controversy and could never reconcile themselves with anyone who believed in achievement. To such men, the words 'compromise' and 'betrayal' are exactly the same. They cared less about delivering results than they did about the purity of their route to a nonexistent accomplishment.

"Second, there were the emotional liberals inside the Congress who were similar in psychology to the woolly ADAs, but at least they were checked to some extent by the responsibilities of office and the desire to be re-elected. This meant they would charge a brick wall but stop the charge just short of physical contact with the wall. The only workable approach to this group was the clipped-wing technique—accomplished by pushing forward the 'good moderate liberals,' who were outside the emotional camp, and identifying them with the leadership.

"Third, there were the good liberals or what I would call the true liberals, the men with specific programs they desired to put across, the men who were satisfied with achieving objectives. These men represented the best leverage for taking care of the emotional liberals since, no matter how irresponsible they got, they couldn't afford to be completely isolated and identified in the public mind as a crackpot outfit."[29]

Johnson saw an opening in the possibility of persuading moderate liberals from the mountain states that if they did not help him to eliminate Title III, then the Southerners would be forced to filibuster and the issue would become insoluble—with terrible consequences for the Democratic Party, the U.S. Senate, and the U.S.A. But Johnson did not rely solely on appeals to reason and the national welfare. "I began with the assumption that most of the Senators from the mountain states had never seen a Negro and simply couldn't care all that much about the whole civil rights issue. But if they didn't care about the Negro, I knew what they *did* care about and that was the Hell's Canyon issue. So I went to a few key Southerners and persuaded them to back the Western liberals on Hell's Canyon. And then, in return, I got the

Western liberals to back the Southerners in cutting out Title III, and then, with Title III gone, I was able to show the reasonable Southerners that some progress was necessary and that as long as they trusted me the progress would be slow and easy."[30]

Withholding any expressing of his own judgments until all points of view had been heard and their relative strength had been measured, Johnson moved from one side of the cloakroom to the other, assuring one side, then the other. He'd tell Senator Douglas to ready his troops and arguments so "we can make sure this long-overdue bill for the benefit of the Negro-Americans will pass." Later, in another corner, he would whisper a warning to Senator Sam Ervin that the worst part of "the nigger bill" was coming up.[81] Throughout the long debate he remained on the floor, correcting extreme statements from both sides, continually striving to prevent the conflict from being defined in irreconcilable terms, trying to prevent a variety of publics from forming impressions of the issue that would make them unwilling to accept any achievable results.

On August 7, 1957, when the bill was finally approved by the Senate—the first civil rights bill enacted by that body in eighty-seven years—it was not Eisenhower's bill or the Democrats' or the liberals'; it was Lyndon Johnson's. Assessed by Dean Acheson as "among the great achievements since the war," and by the *New York Times* as "incomparably the most significant domestic action of any Congress in this century,"[82] passage of the bill was a wondrous victory for Johnson. It gave him what he most valued, a significant achievement that could be described to each of his constituent groups in terms they would accept and even applaud.

To his conservative voters in Texas, he could boast of his leadership role in "cutting out Title III, the notorious troops in the South provision," which would have permitted the federal courts to move into any field categorized as "civil rights." Thus, by securing Senate approval of the substitute bill, he had prevented "a punitive sectional monstrosity." "We were faced with a combination of forces capable of ramming down the throat of the South vicious, punitive legislation," he told Texas voters. "The bill could not be blocked. The only alternative was to convince reasonable minded men to pass instead a reasonable measure . . . and we succeeded in doing so. No better results could have been obtained for Texas."

Indeed, it would be, as Johnson told his constituents, "a serious mistake to regard this legislation as a civil rights bill—all the objectionable features were eliminated. It is more proper to call what was passed a voting rights bill."[33]

To other Democrats, Johnson could boast that the party, which seemed on the verge of an irreparable rupture, had, instead, achieved its greatest unity in two decades. "The real story of the Civil Rights Act is that five states left the Confederacy voluntarily—the healthiest thing that could have happened to this country in years. The ultra-liberal position would have left eleven states solid—cut off from the rest of the country, dividing the Nation in an hour of peril. But now—by opening a division between those Southerners who have always been uncomfortable at the denial of so basic a right as the right to vote, and those who are determined from unshakable habit and prejudice to stand against everything for a Negro, we have passed a bill and have bought for ourselves needed time—time to reconcile the North and the South so we can present a united front in 1960."[34]

To his colleagues in the Senate, he could argue that the moderate and dignified manner in which the issue had been resolved had reflected the best and most honored qualities of representative institutions and had recovered the national respect for the Senate that had been impaired during the McCarthy days. "We've shown the Nation and the world that this legislative body really works even on the toughest issue of all time, and that's a critical thing to prove. It'll give us a reputation for many years to come."[35]

And finally, to the nation, he could explain that the bill was a historic turning point. For once the right to vote, the most fundamental of all rights, had been secured, everything else was possible. "A man without a vote," he said, "is a man without protection . . . he is virtually helpless. A man with a vote has his destiny in his own hands. We've started something. Now, don't worry, it's only the first. We know we can do it now, we know the ropes."[36]

Was Johnson's leadership—his unique abilities and the power he had gradually accumulated—essential to passage of the Civil Rights Act? Admittedly, a wide variety of forces were already moving in the same direction. Nevertheless, there was no inevitability about the passage of this bill at this time. The forces were closely matched and fragmented among themselves. The manner in which the issue was conducted was vital in adding support and moderating opposition. And it was Johnson's leadership that determined the manner and terms of conduct, which alone made it possible for the Democratic Party to pass a bill and still remain intact.

There were a few who disagreed with the overwhelmingly favorable assessment of Johnson's leadership in producing the Civil Rights Act of 1957. Wayne Morse spelled out his own dissent on the floor of the Senate: "I disagree with my Majority leader on the nature of the bill. I consider it a corpse. I think this so-called Civil Rights Bill shows that civil rights for the time being for millions of colored people are dead, so far as effective protection of their right to vote is concerned."[37] But he stood virtually alone.

Naturally, no one expected Johnson to produce answers for all the important problems of the country. But he occupied the highest and most powerful office held by any Democrat. And there were some who argued that his position imposed an obligation to make a commitment for himself and his party—to an ideal and comprehensive program of goals, which he would then set forth in order to stimulate a national debate about values and priorities. Johnson totally disagreed. "What the man in the street wants," he responded, "is *not* a big debate on fundamental issues; he wants a little medical care, a rug on the floor, a picture on the wall, a little music in the house, and a place to take Molly and the grandchildren when he retires."[38]

Johnson's response contained a reiteration of his basic belief that ultimate values and goals could be taken for granted, that the essential wants of all Americans were the same. The logical consequence of this assumption was his conviction that disputes which divided the country resulted from misperceptions or lack of understanding rather than from genuine clashes of conflicting interests. Thus Johnson could always believe that "in time, the underlying consensus will *have* to emerge. . . . So long as men try conscientiously to resolve their differences by negotiation, so long as they follow the prophet Isaiah to 'come now let us reason together,' there is always a chance."[39] Johnson insisted that most of the country's troubles came from defective methods and organizations, from people's failure to understand how best to achieve their goals. It rarely occurred to him that conflicts might arise from differences in the ends themselves. Much of his effectiveness is due to the fact that the pragmatism and consensus that were the key to his successful style of leadership were also important elements of his belief. And in the 1950s his style, not that of Stevensonian confrontation, also matched the belief and temper of the times.

"Just look at the election results," Johnson said, "and you've got the perfect way to measure the success of my leadership against that of all those intellectual liberals who supported Paul Butler and Adlai Stevenson. After all, their method of campaigning—with their search for big issues and big fights with the Republicans—was tried twice and it failed twice, producing the greatest defeat ever suffered by the Democratic Party. Now you put that dismal record beside my method of campaigning for a Democratic Congress on the basis of the positive achievement of the Democratic Party, striving all the time to work out solutions rather than merely creating electoral issues, and what do you see but an unbroken string of successes for me and an unbroken string of failures for them? I was winning Democratic seats in the Congress while they were losing the Presidency."[40]

In his avoidance of ideological questions, Johnson was in harmony with the emerging pluralism of the decade. A variety of historical experiences—such as World War II, a frustrating cold war, fear of Communist intentions, dazzling advances in technology, and the advent of a seemingly irreversible prosperity—combined to produce a general distaste for ideology, an unwillingness even to consider that there were problems which might require changes in basic beliefs or social structures, and a widespread commitment to the almost ideal nature of American institutions. It seemed that if the magical, emotional, and traditional elements of life could be replaced by systematic, rational, and instrumental modes of action, then society could work effectively and rationally to benefit all its members. When Daniel Bell wrote of "the end of ideology" in 1959, he was providing a systematic and illuminating expression of dominant moods and convictions.[41]

This description of dominant American attitudes and convictions is also, of course, a description of Lyndon Johnson, elements of his thought and behavior for decades. The pluralist theory, which denied the authority of ideological systems, found concrete expression in Johnson's practice of seeking political ends by trying to establish agreement among a variety of concerned groups, usually organized on the basis of some common interest. Once the process of trying to reconcile these interests had begun, it committed the groups that were involved to at least some effort to achieve a result. This meant bargaining, perhaps through an intermediary like Johnson—and bargaining among organized groups, which are far less likely than individuals to act on the basis of transient impulses or irrational decisions. Thus the procedures and nature of "group politics" tend to decrease the intensity of political and personal emotions and to produce conflict which, even if not resolved, is conducted in an orderly manner. "The biggest danger to American stability," Johnson argued, "is the politics of principle, which brings out the masses in irrational fights for unlimited goals, for once the masses begin to move, then the whole thing begins to explode. Thus it is for the sake of nothing less than stability that I consider myself a consensus man."[42]

Johnson's detractors believed that unless it took a position on important issues, the Democratic Party would have no chance of capturing the White House in 1960. The most effective way of establishing a Democratic position, and drawing clear and credible lines, would be for the party to use its congressional majorities to pass the entire Democratic program, even though the President was certain to veto such legislation. Indeed, the veto itself would dramatize and clarify the differences between the Democratic and the Republican parties, thus helping to persuade the voters that the country would be better served by returning the Democrats to the White House.

Johnson had a different view of political conditions and possibilities. To him, the fundamental political fact was that "America loved Ike."[43] He understood the appeal of Eisenhower's values. Of course, there had been many reasons for Eisenhower's election—the Korean War, a desire for change after two decades of Democratic rule, etc. But Eisenhower had not really been elected on the strength of his platform or because of objection to specific acts or policies of the Democrats. He had been chosen most of all as a symbol of the nation's longing for tranquillity. Johnson saw the attraction of the Eisenhower optimism: the appeal of a President who limited his statements to the enunciation of lofty principles that seemed to purge his leadership of partisanship; the respect for a leader who followed—slowly and with calm deliberation—when the people moved. Johnson felt that to attack Eisenhower would be "like telling children that their father was a bad man"—an exercise in self-defeating politics. So Johnson refused to involve himself or the Senate in what he defined as "gallant operations"—doomed to defeat by presidential veto—designed to dramatize Republican deficiencies. "I have never believed," he said in 1956, in a tone reminiscent of his critique of the debunkers thirty years before, "that a political party should ask for votes because its opponent has shortcomings." (Especially, he might have added, when the target must be an extremely popular President who might be more than a match for Johnson and the Senate.)

"The American people," Johnson continued, "are tired of wrecking crews. They want builders—people who construct. They will entrust their affairs to the party that is constructive. They will turn their backs on the party that is destructive. . . . If we go forward as positive Americans and not negative oppositionists I am convinced that the time is not too far distant when the Democratic Party will again be in the majority. The party that can produce a record of service to the people . . . the party that is the least partisan and the most patriotic . . . that party will win. A party that is overly partisan, overly quarrelsome and obsessed solely with politics will lose."[44]

Johnson rejected with equal vigor the liberals' demand that the parties should offer the nation a clear-cut choice between fundamental principles. In his opinion, "the phantom of the big choice," if such a choice were actually made and acted on, would result in only one thing: a nation grinding to a halt, consumed by irreconcilable argument, powerless to produce anything for anyone. He was convinced that an insistence on "principled platforms" would wreck the two-party system by making impossible an alliance between men of disparate convictions, and encourage the emergence of many single-issue parties. Against those who called for cohesive parties and crusading leaders, Johnson advocated "loose parties and unifying leaders." It is easy, he argued, for a party representing only one group or one section to produce a consistent program, but it is far more difficult to keep such parties alive. And effective government is not possible without relatively stable political parties: "They come and go," and "once they go, we are left with the same need we've always had—the need for large, unifying parties that unite us rather than divide us."[45]

"With few rare exceptions," Johnson contended, "the great political leaders of our country have been men of reconciliation—men who could hold their parties together. Lincoln never permitted the radical Republicans to drive more moderate elements out of the party. Woodrow Wilson appealed to elements throughout the nation and only went down to failure when he became too doctrinaire and too arbitrary. FDR successfully maintained a coalition that ranged all the way from Jimmy Byrnes to Leon Henderson. Theodore Roosevelt was a great political figure up to the point that he split his own party. . . . A true leader is a man who can get people to work together on the points on which they agree and who can persuade others that when they disagree there are peaceful methods to settle their differences."[46]

To Johnson, the merits of the party system were tested not by its forthright advocacy of virtuous ideals but by its actual contribution to the creation of tangible and beneficial conditions—by results and consequences. And, he claimed, by this test the American party system had proven itself not only valuable but indispensable; with one exception (the Civil War), it had provided stability and unity without the sacrifice of diversity. Indeed, what the critics saw as "defects" in the party system—its fuzziness and its fragmentation—he saw as virtues. That fuzziness, he contended, was not simply a political expedient, but an authentic reflection of the American people's own ambiguities of conviction and purpose, their refusal to act consistently within categories that purport to characterize attitudes and conduct in relationship to public questions. "I am," he announced in 1958, "a free man, a U.S. Senator, and a Democrat, in that order. I am also a liberal, a conservative, a Texan, a taxpayer, a rancher, a businessman, a consumer, a parent, a voter, and not as young as I used to be nor as old as I expect to be—and I am all these things in no fixed order. . . . At the heart of my own beliefs is a rebellion against this very process of classifying, labeling and filing Americans under headings."[47]

To require precision is to create division: "The people of this country," Johnson asserted, "are tired of the kind of political thought that divides Americans into blocs . . . I doubt whether the carpenter who built this rostrum thinks of himself only as a laboring class. And I doubt equally whether the man who paid his wages thinks of himself only as part of the managerial class. They think of themselves first as American men and their wives think of themselves as American women. And they are perfectly right in doing so."[48]

These statements of belief are consonant with the assumption of pluralist thought that if people do not exclusively identify themselves with a single category—such as class, occupation, or system of belief—political cleavages will be limited in intensity. Thus it is likely that successive disputes will draw different lines of separation: in the absence of such unitary identifications, positions are likely to be determined more by the content of particular disputes than by the characterizing identity of other participants. Thus it is likely that successive disputes will draw different lines of separation. And when politicians or other representatives of groups or interests contend within a system in which today's opponents may be tomorrow's allies, where they confront an adversary who was yesterday's supporter, conflicts are almost certain to be less severe. Those on all sides will tend to seek solutions that do not create irrevocable ruptures and endanger the possibility of changed relationships under different circumstances of need and interest. Once this was understood, Johnson thought, it became clear that the very imprecision and ambiguity that many censured was, in fact, the "balance wheel" of American politics. Failure to perceive this came from viewing the process not in terms of its consequences but as an end in itself. From this perspective the Senate would seem to consist of the continual satisfaction of special interests and personal needs. "That is the way the Senate works"—and so, Johnson might have added, does the marketplace. Each Senator calculates the preferences and vulnerabilities of others who share in authority; politicians act in their self-interest. The task of leadership is to unite these fragmented intentions into some more general agreement. That is, the leader's own interest lay in effective leadership which can make the Senate function by assembling support for interests that are larger and more general than those which compose the alliance.

Thus the process of bargaining, the continual interplay of individual ambitions and concerns, results in actions that benefit the "public interest." Of course, the opposite can happen. The consequence can be opposed to the public interest. Nevertheless, the fundamental principle is the same: a process of fragmented bargaining in a body like the Senate where authority is widely dispersed must always have more general consequences. It is the essence of Johnson's argument that it is by these consequences that the institution is measured. Of course, the process is flawed, vulnerable to a variety of corruptions. But if one accepts Johnson's assumption, then those who advocate a changed process—one closer in operation to some principle of democracy or virtue—have the burden of proving that it would result in actions of greater benefit to the country.

Johnson's concept of politics and leadership can be supported by an ample body of argument and theory, but only if, in fact, no legitimate interests are excluded from the process. However, as some critics of pluralist politics have pointed out, access is limited to those interests categorized as "legitimate," and not all interests are considered legitimate.[49] Business, labor, agriculture—these groups are; but the poor, the minorities, and the migrant workers—in other words, the people with the least resources—are not. And a refusal to acknowledge legitimacy is equivalent to imposing exile. Consequently, these critics have argued, the territory of American politics is like a plateau with steep, insurmountable cliffs on all sides. On the plateau are the interest groups considered legitimate who can at least be heard; far below are the outsiders, marginal and impotent, ignored and sometimes scorned, their claims inaudible.

Johnson's description and justification of the varied elements of the political system that he inhabited and helped to lead—the Senate, the party, relationships between governing institutions—contained no acknowledgment of this reality. The greatest flaw in his argument is not a weakness of concept or theory, but a distortion of realities. Ironically, this most practical of men accepted an assumption contradicted by the facts. Of course, he knew the facts, he had experienced the reality. If he did not acknowledge them, it was probably because, in the 1950s, there was nothing he could do about it. The times were inauspicious; there could be no reasonable expectation of support for programs to elevate the status and improve the life of the excluded. Moreover, such an effort was beyond the Senate's capacity. It would require the determined use of presidential power. And that would not come—at least not then.

There can be no doubt that Lyndon Johnson was among the most effective and powerful leaders in the history of the United States Senate. He had his critics, but at any time during his leadership he would have received, had he asked for it, an overwhelming vote of confidence and approval from his colleagues, the press, and the public. As a result of this impressive support combined with his own formidable personality and record of accomplishments, few bothered to consider or evaluate the criticisms of his conduct, yet they raise troubling questions. Lyndon Johnson was an impressive leader responsible for some of the most significant achievements of his time. And the current incapacities and failures of Congress demonstrate that there are many virtues in strong leadership. Still, there is a significant difference between the political leader who mediates among existing structures and forces and the leader who sets out to reshape the circumstances amid which he operates, not only to enhance his power, but to make it possible to pursue new purposes.[50]

Lyndon Johnson was a brilliant mediator within the established order, but the possibilities of his leadership were confined by the same traits, experiences, and values that made his mediation so successful: his insistence on face-to-face relations, his secrecy, and his pragmatism. As a result of his preference for private negotiations and his penchant, even need, for concealment, he virtually abolished debate in an institution where debate, although frequently frivolous and often ignored, had also served to publicly expose problems and warn of error. His insistence on subordination to the executive on all issues of national security—denying even Congress' right to information—seriously reduced the Senate's ability to participate in decisions on foreign policy. By insisting that the Senate yield to the President, he reduced the right to share in foreign policy that had been established by custom. Now the body whose support had been cultivated and considered indispensable to significant presidential action only a few years before—in the days of Arthur Vandenberg—could be ignored or limited to the forms but not the substance of authority. By conceding the right of defining national goals to the White House, he eliminated a forum that might have revealed those important national problems which were to remain concealed and untended until they erupted in the 1960s. At least partly, his final failure was the bitter fruit of his earlier success, for in the Senate his was the success of power more than of purpose.

Chapter 6

The Vice-Presidency

If the Democratic members of the U.S. Senate had been given the power to select the Democratic candidate for President in 1960, Lyndon Johnson would have been their choice. But a fact of political life Johnson never fully grasped was that the Senate did not possess this power. A dozen years after his abortive campaign, Johnson believed, on the one hand, that no matter how shrewdly he had planned his strategy, his Southern heritage would have prevented his nomination and, on the other hand, that his ignorance of national politics was responsible for his humiliating defeat at the hands of John Kennedy.[1]

As it happened, Johnson never really got to the point of running a full-fledged campaign. Insecure about his legitimacy as a national politician, longing for the Presidency, yet terrified at losing his prestige in the Senate, he became muddled and ineffective in his actions. Without the single-mindedness that had propelled him to power in the Senate, removed from that assembly of men he knew so well and over which he had possessed boundless influence, Johnson's instincts failed. New experience ceased to educate. Johnson remained the perpetual tourist in the alien land of national politics. Confusing the national campaign with bargaining in the Senate, he wrongly assumed that each Democratic Senator controlled the delegates from his state. While John Kennedy and his men crisscrossed the country, winning primaries, attending state conventions, and rounding up delegates, Johnson remained in his office in Washington, expecting somehow to make the right deals with the right people. Johnson's experiences in the Senate might have been considerably more relevant in 1952 or even in 1956, when conventions were still the vast bargaining arenas they had been since Andrew Jackson's time. But 1960 brought a different breed of Democratic Convention. It was, in some ways, the first postbroker convention. By the time the party convened in Los Angeles on July 10, 1960, all the important deals had already been made. John Kennedy captured the nomination on the first ballot.

This left Johnson with only one chance to move up in the political world, and he took that chance. He accepted Kennedy's offer of the second spot. It was a decision few understood at the time. Friends and colleagues could not imagine why Lyndon Johnson would exchange the real powers of the Majority Leader for the ceremony of the Vice-Presidency. "Power is where power goes," he explained to a friend who was counseling him to reject Kennedy's offer.[2] Johnson believed he could carry his powers with him. Give him time, and he would make the Vice-Presidency powerful. That Johnson should believe it possible to do what no other political figure had been able to do was characteristic. Again and again—as assistant to President Evans at San Marcos, as speaker of the Little Congress, as party whip and leader— Johnson had taken positions with no apparent base of power and then, by recasting and expanding their functions, he had pyramided meager resources into substantial political holdings. Why should this experience be different? At the very least, the Vice-Presidency was a way of shedding his regional image once and for all and placing him in line to succeed John Kennedy at the end of his two terms in office.

There remained an additional reason for accepting the offer. Lyndon Johnson recognized that his power in the Senate had depended in part upon having a passive Republican President in the White House. Under the shadow of an active Democratic President, the Majority Leader would be reduced in size. No matter what Johnson decided about the Vice-Presidency, the election of 1960 would affect the Senate leadership in uncomfortable ways; the world he had mastered so well would no longer be his. Even if Kennedy lost, Richard Nixon would be no Eisenhower; he would not accord the Majority Leader the respect or the power Johnson had enjoyed in the 1950s. Better, then, to help young John Kennedy win. For whether he won or lost, the contrast with the 1950s Senate would be real; indeed, Johnson's anticipation of the difference made him ready, perhaps eager, to leave, thereby sparing himself the agony of watching his prestige diminish day by day.

In the past, Johnson's willingness to accept a subordinate position had come from the conviction that initial deference was but a means to eventual replacement of the figure in authority. Repeatedly, Johnson had played the role of apprentice with consummate skill. Cecil Evans, Harry Greene, Franklin Roosevelt, Sam Rayburn, Richard Russell: all these men had served as his master, teaching him the skills and the secrets of their trade. In return, Johnson had given the full measure of his attention, talent, and respect. Now Lyndon Johnson was Vice President; and to the outsider looking in, the role of apprentice appeared ideal for both the man and the office. The Founding Fathers had created the office of the Vice-Presidency precisely for the purpose of providing an understudy to the President in the event the Chief Executive's office fell vacant. Beyond this major role, they had given the Vice President only two functions: to preside over the Senate—a duty that could easily be delegated—and to cast the deciding vote if the Senate was equally divided—a rare occurrence. In a political system where seven Vice Presidents—one of every five—had succeeded to the Presidency, clearly the Vice President's most important role was as an apprentice, participating in the daily decisions, soberly learning the main tasks of the Presidency.[8]

Kennedy tried, at the start, to provide Johnson with meaningful work and to keep him informed on all major issues. He appointed Johnson chairman of the President's Committee on Equal Employment Opportunity and Chairman of the National Aeronautics and Space Council. He invited the Vice President to attend his staff meetings, his Cabinet meetings, and his briefings before news conferences. He asked Johnson to represent him in numerous functions abroad and at home. He sought Johnson's opinion on speeches and strategy. They were, to be sure, very different men: the one a disciplined, precise, and detached New Englander; the other an emotional, expansive, and intimate Texan; yet they respected one another. Indeed, they even developed a measure of affection few would have guessed possible. On his part, Johnson exhibited complete loyalty and self-discipline. When he disagreed with the President—as he did, among other issues, on his handling of the steel crisis, on his approach to the Soviet Union, on his policy toward Diem, and on foreign aid—he kept his disagreement to himself. Reporters, trained in the ways of provoking reluctant politicians to speak, found it impossible to get Johnson to criticize Kennedy in public. Even among friends at the dinner table, Johnson talked about Kennedy as if he were speaking before a formal audience; he measured his phrases. For the man who had for many years taken great pleasure and received much satisfaction from mocking his colleagues, friend as well as foe, behind their backs, Lyndon Johnson's Vice-Presidency was a triumph of self-restraint.[4]

But, in the end, tradition joined with personality to prevent Kennedy and Johnson from sustaining a commitment to their respective roles as master and apprentice. No matter how often Kennedy spoke about including Johnson in the daily work of the White House, the fact is that no President in history has ever shared the major tasks of office with his Vice President. Wary of a potential rival and aware of past habits, Presidents have been inclined to leave their Vice Presidents with little more than special assignments; traveling abroad or chairing a council on space or heading a committee on employment are fair first steps toward vice-presidential participation, but they are only first steps, and somehow the process never seems to move forward. The second and third steps are untaken, and Vice Presidents are consigned to essentially peripheral tasks. As one observer put it: "The very fact that a problem is turned over to the Vice-President argues that it is not very important or that the Vice-President actually is going to play a far less critical role in solving it than announced or that the President recognized the impossibility of solving the problem and therefore wants to stay as far away from the whole thing as possible."[5] No good politician willingly cedes power to another politician he cannot control. And unlike the members of the White House staff—to whom recent Presidents have given considerable power—the Vice President cannot be fired.

In Johnson's case, personality compounded the problem. It was not easy for him to apprentice himself to a backbencher nine years his junior. Nor was it easy for Kennedy to play the role of master. After all, Kennedy once explained, "I spent years of my life when I could not get consideration for a bill until I went around and begged Lyndon Johnson to let it go ahead."[6]

Within a matter of months, the inevitable followed. Had arrogance and ambition not blinded his vision, Johnson's instinct and intelligence would have led him to foresee this.

Like every Vice President before him, he found himself stifled in the Vice-Presidency, reduced to the role of an on-looker, in office but out of power. The only exception was in the field of civil rights, where Johnson's work on equal employment clearly occupied his energies and evidenced his talent.

Johnson reckoned the days spent in the office described by its first occupant, John Adams, as "the most insignificant office that ever the invention of man contrived or his imagination conceived." Perhaps the only useful purpose the Vice President served, he later suggested, was to remind the President of his mortality—a ghastly function at best. "Every time I came into John Kennedy's presence, I felt like a goddamn raven hovering over his shoulder. Away from the Oval Office, it was even worse. The Vice-Presidency is filled with trips around the world, chauffeurs, men saluting, people clapping, chairmanships of councils, but in the end, it is nothing. I detested every minute of it."[7]

Nowhere did Johnson feel his loss of power and his uselessness more painfully than in his relations with Capitol Hill. When the Senate Democrats convened in caucus on January 3, 1961, Mike Mansfield of Montana, the new Majority Leader, proposed to change the rules and elect the new Vice President the chairman of the Democratic Conference, which would make him the presiding officer at formal meetings of the Senate's Democratic members. Mansfield's proposal, which he had discussed with no one but Johnson, met with strong opposition. Liberals and conservatives joined in arguing that such a move would surely violate the spirit of the separation of powers. When the motion came up for decision, seventeen Senators voted nay, a number large enough to persuade Mansfield and Johnson to let the motion die.[8]

Johnson interpreted the vote as a profoundly personal rejection. All the hopes he had entertained of leading the Congress from the Vice President's chair were discarded. Suddenly he felt separated forever from the institution to which he believed he had given the best part of his life. Time and the success of the Eighty-ninth Congress under his presidential leadership would alter this perspective, but in 1961 Johnson was so hurt and angry after the seventeen negative votes that he simply retired from the Hill. From that day on he was of minimal help to Kennedy on legislation, the area in which the President most desired his help. At the weekly White House breakfasts for legislative leaders, Johnson rarely said a word. As observers have described him, his face appeared vacant and gray; he looked discontented and tired. He offered an opinion only when asked directly by Kennedy to give one; and even then, he tended to mumble, his words barely audible to the person sitting beside him. On rare occasions, when he was particularly excited or perturbed, he would suddenly raise his voice for a few moments to its customary shout, only to let it quickly sink again into an unintelligible murmur.[9]

No matter how much he longed to participate in these meetings on legislative strategy—especially because he believed the Kennedy men were blundering badly—Johnson could not bear being treated as one of many advisers. Shortly after the inauguration, he sent an unusual Executive Order to the Oval Office for President Kennedy's signature. Outlining a wide range of issues over which the new Vice President would have "general supervision," it put all the departments and agencies on notice that Lyndon Johnson was to receive all reports, information, and policy plans that were generally sent to the President himself. It led to remarks in the White House that compared Johnson to William Seward, Abraham Lincoln's Secretary of State, who had sent his President an equally preposterous memo on how the government should be conducted and how he, Seward, should be the lead conductor. Kennedy's response was similar to Lincoln's; in both cases, the memos were diplomatically shelved.[10]

The loss of a leadership position amounted to political death. There were times, Johnson later admitted, when he felt that he would simply shrivel up. What inflamed him the most was that no one seemed to appreciate his loyalty and self-discipline. On the contrary, the same critics who had originally predicted that Lyndon Johnson would be a runaway Vice President, arrogating too much power to himself, were now putting him down for his quiet demeanor. "Whatever happened to Lyndon Johnson?" they asked, implying that in the glitter of the Kennedy administration Johnson had simply faded away.

Johnson was angered by political criticism, but he was used to it; far more difficult for him to accept was the cultural critique, the implicit comparison between the Western cowboy and the urbane aristocrat. It is easy to imagine the uneasiness

Johnson felt as John Kennedy came to be admired more and more for the very qualities Rebekah Johnson had always hoped to find in her first-born son. The more praise Kennedy received for his oratorical ability, for his skill in debating, and for his brilliant parries at press conferences, the more uneasy the Vice President felt in front of even the most friendly audience. Worse still was "all the fuss and excitement,"[11] to use Johnson's words, about Kennedy's transforming Washington into a cultural center. After a state dinner in October, 1961, scenes from several Shakespearean plays were performed; it was, the *New York Times* reported, the first time in anyone's memory that this had happened in the White House, and for it, Kennedy was "ranked with such Presidents as Lincoln, Jefferson, and Adams in their demonstrated love of Shakespeare." The following month Pablo Casals performed for guests at a formal party; it was his first appearance at the White House since 1904, when he had played for Theodore Roosevelt. The evening of chamber music reaped praise from artists in every field. There was more. In the spring, the White House sponsored a performance by Jerome Robbins' "Ballets: U.S.A."; it was the first ballet ever danced at the White House.

Apprehensive of being culturally inferior, Johnson groaned at every announcement of another luncheon for writers and scholars and loathed each new invitation to a formal dinner. He read the lists of the invited guests: Thornton Wilder, Tennessee Williams, Arthur Miller, Paddy Chayefsky, Edmund Wilson, Elia Kazan, Leonard Bernstein, Fredric March, Sir Ralph Richardson. He knew at most the names of two or three. He could never think of more than ten words to say to any of them. In the hush of these formal settings, when, as Johnson later put it, the White House smelled like a musty museum or a university lecture room, he felt called upon to talk about music or literature or art. Perhaps he mistook his own projected ideal for the expectations of others, but he was convinced that "high" conversation was required. At such functions, he felt himself launched upon waters where he was never meant to sail. Sorely conscious of being seen as an outsider, assuming that politics had no currency with these people, he stood in the corner, his hands in his pockets, his mind detached.

Yet in some things Johnson tried to imitate the Kennedys. When, on a trip abroad, he read that John Kennedy loved soups, he insisted that his plane be stocked with dozens of soups. He watched McNamara once in a restaurant ordering shrimp salad with three shrimps. For weeks after that Johnson ordered exactly the same thing.[12]

Vice President Thomas Marshall in 1920 compared the Vice President to a cataleptic: "He cannot speak; he cannot move; he suffers no pain; yet he is perfectly conscious of everything that is going on about him." Marshall anticipated the nature of Johnson's difficulties. During this period, Johnson said, he dreamed again of physical incapacity, recreating at night the condition of utter powerlessness he experienced during the day. The dream that stood out in his memory found him seated at his desk in the Executive Office Building, a few yards in space, but an infinite distance in significance, from the West Wing of the White House. "In the dream, I had finished signing one stack of letters and had turned my chair toward the window. The activity on the street below suggested to me that it was just past five o'clock. All of Washington, it seemed, was on the street, leaving work for the day, heading for home. Suddenly, I decided I'd pack up and go home, too. For once, I decided, it would be nice to join all those people on the street and have an early dinner with my family. I started to get up from my chair, but I couldn't move. I looked down at my legs and saw they were manacled to the chair with a heavy chain. I tried to break the chain, but I couldn't. I tried again and failed again. Once more and I gave up; I reached for the second stack of mail. I placed it directly in front of me, and got back to work."[13]

When Johnson, at the age of fifteen, had a dream that resembled this one—the dream in which he saw himself enclosed in a small cage—he had escaped by running away from home to California. Now, forty years later, Johnson found a similar escape from a different cage; during his Vice-Presidency he made eleven separate foreign trips, visiting thirty-three countries, including Italy, Great Britain, Senegal, Jamaica, Scandinavia, Cyprus, Greece, South Vietnam, and Israel. Away from the United States, Johnson shed his mantle of restraint. When he landed on foreign shores, his energy gathered force again. In striking contrast to the sluggish image he projected in Washington, this Lyndon Johnson was characterized by high spirits, joyful emotion, and readiness for all kinds of action.[14]

He was once again the spoiled, demanding, and exuberant

child. Before each trip he compiled a long list of the things he needed to have with him: an oversized bed to fit his six-foot, four-inch frame, a shower attachment that emitted a hard needlepoint spray, two dozen cases of Cutty Sark, five hundred boxes of ball-point pens, six dozen cases of cigarette lighters. The pens and the lighters were brought along by the thousands as gifts. In the poorest slums of India, on the crowded streets of Dakar, in the markets of Thailand, Johnson passed among the people distributing LBJ-inscribed pens, shaking hands, patting heads, inviting a camel driver to America. The Vice President's personal diplomacy and impulsive behavior appalled many officials in the Foreign Service. He provokingly refused to take their rules of etiquette seriously; he was, they believed, confusing diplomacy with campaigning. Yet with all the confusion of pens and crowds and abrupt changes in plans, Lyndon Johnson was clearly successful as an ambassador of goodwill, though none of this restored even a measure of authority. His energy and his friendly manner were contagious; but then he came home, ending his brief return to center stage and retiring to his cage once again.

Curiously, Johnson, with little else to do, seemed to learn little or nothing about international relations from these trips. Conceivably, foreign travel could equip the American statesman with a feel for another culture, or at least with the ability to comprehend differences in political and economic structure from one country to another. Johnson's utter lack of prior experience with people from outside the United States ill-prepared him to ask questions that might have elicited a deeper understanding.[15] Without informal contacts among foreigners, he seldom strayed beyond carefully planned stops. When he was removed from his native ground, Johnson's sensitivity to nuance, tone, and inflection diminished. He saw each country and all the people he met through an American prism. In 1961 Johnson made a trip to Vietnam at Kennedy's request. In the report he wrote as a follow-up, he spelled out in the strongest terms his belief that our failure to stand in Vietnam would lead to a crisis of confidence throughout Southeast Asia and would consign all the mainland countries to eventual Communist rule. "I felt a special rapport with all those Asians," Johnson later said. "I knew how desperately they needed our help and I wanted to give it. I wanted them to have all the dams and all the projects they could handle."[16]

Thus the circumstances of the Vice-Presidency seemed to conspire against Johnson, imparting wrong lessons, impeding the development of his talents, stifling his spirit. For all this, Johnson did not resign himself to life as he found it. In the summer of 1963, he no longer even guessed what the years ahead had in store, but he still looked with a flicker of hope toward the future. A change of circumstances, the challenge of new work—there was still a chance that, in some later engagement, he might turn the tables on the world, that his energies and talents, gathering force, might join together once again.

Chapter 7.

The Transition Year

"I took the oath," Johnson later said, "I became President. But for millions of Americans I was still illegitimate, a naked man with no presidential covering, a pretender to the throne, an illegal usurper. And then there was Texas, my home, the home of both the murder and the murder of the murderer. And then there were the bigots and the dividers and the Eastern intellectuals, who were waiting to knock me down before I could even begin to stand up. The whole thing was almost unbearable."[1]

Yet scarcely four months later the new President, firmly established in office, had effected a transfer of governmental authority so smooth and dignified that his own nomination for the Presidency seemed absolutely assured. How did Lyndon Johnson bring it off? Part of the answer lies in the institutional advantage available to any new President in Johnson's position. The American system provides a set of well-defined procedures for a Vice President's succession to office, which ensure unquestioned and immediate acknowledgment of his newly acquired powers. The executive bureaucracies and the institutions of government have a momentum of their own; their activities continue, uninterrupted even by the death of a President.[2] But an ease of transition was not inevitable. An alternate scenario could be sketched in which the new President, facing a convention in eight months, displayed qualities that created doubts about his abilities, or aroused strong and divisive hostilities in his own party. In the absence of skillful presidential leadership, a legislative stalemate could have developed. Such failures of leadership might well have encouraged the ambitions of others, and the new President could then have confronted a serious struggle for the nomination at the Democratic Convention.

Clearly, there were both opportunities and dangers in Johnson's situation; the point is that Lyndon Johnson capital-

ized on the advantages. Here was a case where the exercise
of talent joined with personality and opportunity to produce
a brilliant display of leadership and political skill. Despite, or
perhaps because of, his own fears of illegitimacy (fears, as
we have seen, rooted in the conflicts of his childhood, which
plagued virtually every step of his political rise), Johnson
demonstrated a valuable insight into the national mood, an
acute understanding that Kennedy's assassination had produced a crisis of legitimacy for his country as well as for
himself. Kennedy's death had unexpectedly brought fulfillment of his greatest ambition in circumstances that must
have inspired awesome guilt and doubts. For Johnson, the ex-
hilaration of power was nearly always accompanied by deep
insecurity, the consequence of a sense, deeply concealed from
conscious awareness, that his authority had been wrongfully
acquired and would be taken away when its illegitimacy was
discovered. The troubling impact of these inaccessible fears
could only have been intensified by the events that had now
endowed him with the highest authority.

The dominant tone of public sentiment—reflected in television reports, newspaper columns, and public opinion polls—
echoed Johnson's anguish, shame, and vulnerability.[3] The people of America responded to the news of Kennedy's assassination and the continuing televised reports of every subsequent
happening with a state of shock that went beyond mourning to
something approaching melancholia,[4] a serious collapse of
self-esteem. With the assassination, something more than a
man had been lost, something more abstract and more compelling—a part of America's faith in itself as a good society.
Literary critic Irving Howe described the national mood:

> Two assassinations, each ghastly in its own right, and
> each uncovering still another side of our social pathol-
> ogy; callousness, maybe planned negligence on the part
> of the Dallas police; fourth-grade children in the South
> cheering the news that a "nigger loving" President had
> been murdered; subversion of the processes of law en-
> forcement to the demands of television . . . it is all too
> much.[5]

It was especially too much for a country that prided itself
on the possession of common values and the rule of law.
"Everything was in chaos," Johnson later recalled. "We were

all spinning around and around, trying to come to grips with what had happened, but the more we tried to understand it, the more confused we got. We were like a bunch of cattle caught in the swamp, unable to move in either direction, simply circling 'round and 'round. I understood that; I knew what had to be done. There is but one way to get the cattle out of the swamp. And that is for the man on the horse to take the lead, to assume command, to provide direction. In the period of confusion after the assassination, I was that man."[6]

Johnson expanded on this theme in his memoirs:

> I knew I could not allow the tide of grief to overwhelm me. The consequences of all my actions were too great for me to become immobilized now with emotion. I was a man in trouble, in a world that is never more than minutes away from catastrophe. . . . There were tasks to perform that only I had the authority to perform. A nation stunned, shaken to its very heart, had to be reassured that the government was not in a state of paralysis . . . that the business of the United States would proceed. I knew that not only the nation but the whole world would be anxiously following every move I made—watching, judging, weighing, balancing.[7] . . . It was imperative that I grasp the reins of power and do so without delay. Any hesitation or wavering, any false step, any sign of self-doubt, could have been disastrous.[8]

Johnson understood that a great many Americans were simply incapable of instantly placing their trust in his leadership. An immediate acceptance would have reinforced the vague apprehension that somehow we, because it had occurred in our country, might all be implicated in the crime. Johnson's own fearful doubts, inevitably reinforced by the fact he had first been Kennedy's antagonist, then his understudy, and was now his inheritor, demanded relief. He found that relief by achieving a unique synthesis between the two patterns of behavior that had long characterized his approach to authority.

Throughout his life Johnson had most successfully attained power in one of two situations: under conditions that allowed him to play apprentice to a master, whose power, by careful deference and emulation, he would use to increase his own authority until he had surpassed the other man's accomplishments or position; or under conditions that allowed him to assume the role of the caretaker, the strong protecting the weak. In both cases Johnson saw himself serving others, a perception that allowed him to rationalize his use of the relationship to gain power for himself and to do so without guilt. In the terrible wake of John Kennedy's assassination, Johnson was able to act as both apprentice and caretaker—faithful agent of Kennedy's intentions and the healing leader of a stunned and baffled nation.

The living President armored himself with the passionate admiration, intensified by his death, that many felt for John Kennedy and with the still unfulfilled goals of the Kennedy administration.[9] By carrying out what his predecessor had started, Johnson argued that his call to continue was in effect John Kennedy's call. Johnson was but "the dutiful executor" of his predecessor's will. Throughout the transition period the slain President was invoked in a powerful and decisive fashion. In the early weeks and months after the assassination, Johnson's public addresses were filled with allusions to John Kennedy. In fact, references to his predecessor were more than double the references to anyone or anything else in that period.

Johnson's storied arrogance, his compulsion to assume center stage, was checked. Without undue self-deprecation or timidity, he conveyed a deep humility, yet one consistent with confident determination that Kennedy's goals would be pursued and reached.

Now able to transcend the impotent anger at the rejection by Senate colleagues that had kept him away from Capitol Hill throughout his Vice-Presidency, Johnson selected the Congress as the forum of his first major address. For thirty years the Congress had been his home. Now, "in this strange and difficult time," as Johnson later called it, he felt the need to return to what he considered the source of his own and his country's strength—its political tradition. On that November 27, 1963, speaking from the rostrum of the House before an assembled body of Senators, Congressmen, and Supreme Court Justices, Johnson sought to reassure the nation: "Let us continue," he began, striking upon the befuddled nation's deepest need. "And now," Johnson went on, "the ideas and the ideals which [Kennedy] so nobly represented must and will be translated into effective action. ... In this critical moment, it is our duty, yours and mine, to do away with uncertainty and delay and doubt and to show that we are capable of decisive action; that from the brutal loss of our leader we will derive not weakness but strength, that we can and will act and act now. . . . John Kennedy's death commands what his life conveyed—that America must move forward."

If at the beginning of his address one missed the clipped delivery of John Kennedy, by the end one was grateful for the measured steadiness of Lyndon Johnson. Substantively, that address delineated the new leader's resolve to urgently implement the priorities of his predecessor in the days ahead. The most important of these was civil rights. On this issue, one that aroused the most complex and intense public feelings, Johnson expressed his views with a direct simplicity, more a profession of faith than a political position. "First," he said, "no memorial or oration or eulogy could more eloquently honor President Kennedy's memory than the earliest possible passage of the civil rights bill for which he fought so long. We have talked long enough about equal rights in this country. We have talked for one hundred years or more. It is time now to write the next chapter and write it in the books of law."

Survey after survey reflected a widespread conviction that extremism was the cause of Kennedy's death. It was to this sentiment that Johnson spoke in his peroration: "Let us put an end to the teaching and the preaching of hate and evil and violence. Let us turn away from the fanatics of the far left and the far right, from the apostles of bitterness and bigotry, from those defiant of law and those who pour venom into our nation's bloodstream."[10]

By the time he finished, the audience was on its feet, fervidly applauding the new President for the tradition he had summoned and so well embodied, and for the dead President whose programs he had taken as his own. And also because the formidable and elusive Majority Leader of the United States Senate sounded like a President.

Johnson's skillful handling of the transition is nowhere better illustrated than in his treatment of the members of the Cabinet and the White House staff. It was a far more delicate and difficult job to strike the right tone with these men than with the public at large. "I constantly had before me the picture that Kennedy had selected me as executor of his will, it was my duty to carry on and this meant his people as well as his programs. They were part of his legacy. I simply couldn't let the country think that I was all alone."[11] So Johnson met personally with each of the Kennedy men and, through a powerful mixture of rational argument and emotional appeals, convinced all of them to stay on. Although Johnson approached these men differently, according to their various relationships with John Kennedy, and to what he knew of their own feelings and ambitions, all his appeals ended in the same way: "I know how much *he* needed you. But it *must* make sense to you that if he needed you I need you that much more. And so does our country."[12]

In order to conciliate and reassure this inherited Cabinet and the White House staff—Robert Kennedy, Robert McNamara, Theodore Sorensen, McGeorge Bundy, Kenneth O'Donnell, Dean Rusk, Richard Goodwin, Lee White, Lawrence O'Brien, Henry Hall Wilson, and all the others—Johnson showed continuous restraint. Never once did he permit himself even to imply that, however things were done before, this was now *his* White House. Where one might have expected bitterness—for all the slights received from some of these same men when he was Vice President—Johnson showed only benevolence.[13] "I knew how they felt," he later said. "The impact of Kennedy's death was evident everywhere—in the looks on their faces and the sound of their voices. He was gone and with his going they must have felt that everything had changed. Suddenly *they* were outsiders just as I had been for almost three years, outsiders on the inside. The White House is small, but if you're not at the center it seems enormous. You get the feeling that there are all sorts of meetings going on without you, all sorts of people clustered in small groups, whispering, always whispering. I felt that way as Vice President, and after Kennedy's death I knew that his men would feel the same thing. So I determined to keep them informed. I determined to keep them busy. I constantly requested their advice and asked for their help."[14]

In these early days Johnson spoke to the Kennedy men with a subdued tone. He requested rather than ordered; he spoke of his shortcomings and shared his doubts. This solicitous manner coming from a President disquieted, shamed, and thereby induced in these men the very cooperation and submission that Johnson was after. Although some key men of the former administration were soon to leave (Sorensen resigned and Robert Kennedy rarely showed up for work), the large majority stayed on. Gradually, Johnson added his own men to the White House staff—Walter Jenkins, George Reedy, Jack Valenti, Bill Moyers, and Horace Busby—but they, too, were expected to show nothing but deference to the Kennedy men.

Eventually, Walter Jenkins became, if not chief of staff— an authority Johnson never allowed to anyone—the first among equals. His was a gentle, quiet presence around which the entire staff, Kennedy and Johnson men alike, could unite. "I've often wondered," Johnson's private secretary later mused, "what would have happened to them if Walter Jenkins had remained throughout Johnson's Presidency. He was the only one who knew Johnson well enough to judge when to carry out an order verbatim and when to exercise discretion. He was the only one who had both the entire staff's and Johnson's complete trust. He was a natural link between the Johnson and the Kennedy men."[15]

Use of the imperative for a man of Johnson's turbulent and infantile nature was never difficult. With his own men, Johnson commanded, forbade, insisted, swaggered, and swore. Verbal tirades and fits of temper became an integral part of his image. On occasion, it seemed as if Johnson *needed* to make his staff look ridiculous; that he was strengthened by his exposure of inadequacies in others. In addition, Johnson's outbursts with his own men helped him to deal with the Kennedy men from a position of strength. His modesty and deference could command their loyalty, but he wanted their respect as well, the respect due a strong man— although he chose to display this strength by implying a capacity to inflict a fearful revenge for even slight errors.

He defied Machiavelli's warning that "a new prince should organize the government entirely anew . . . he should appoint new governors with new titles, new powers and new men . . . he should leave nothing unchanged in that province so that there will be neither rank, nor grade, nor honor, nor wealth, that should not be recognized as coming from him."[16] Yet in 1964 Johnson had little opportunity to create this condition. If he had chosen to follow Machiavelli's advice and Harry Truman's example—in less than five months after Roosevelt's death, Truman replaced holdovers with his own appointees—

it is likely that he would have had far greater difficulty in re-
cruiting than did Truman. After all, Truman had three years
and six months before he had to face the electorate; Johnson,
eleven months. Moreover, so flagrant a disavowal of his predecessor's choices would have been thought to belie his public
expressions, and would have endangered his support among
those who had allied themselves with Kennedy's political
career, many of them active participants and leaders in the
Democratic Party. And, in any event, he had a lot to do in a
short time and he needed them.

The puzzling question is not why Johnson kept the Kennedy men during that first year, but rather, why, even after
the election, he did not swiftly recruit more of his own men.
Part of the answer is supplied by understanding that Johnson
had always considered himself a good judge of talent and
that he saw a great deal of talent in the Kennedy entourage.
He considered Robert McNamara, for example, one of the
most talented men he had ever met in public life. "I had a
good impression of McNamara from the first day I saw him,"
Johnson said in an interview in 1965. "And he has exceeded
my expectations. He is always prompt and always prepared.
He does his homework. He is an expert on economic matters,
prices, strikes, taxes and other things as well as defense. He is
the strongest poverty and Head Start man except Shriver. He
is the first one at work and the last one to leave. When I wake
up, the first one I call is McNamara. He is there at seven every morning, including Saturday. The only difference is that
Saturday he wears a sport coat. He is the best utility man. I
would make him Secretary of State or Secretary of Transportation tomorrow—he is that qualified. He is smart, patriotic,
works hard. I never heard him say, 'I told you so.' We usually agree, but he presents his arguments dogmatically. And
he always advises me where I am wrong, although most Cabinet officers do not. If I had my way, I wish he would play
more, have more personal friends, be a little more sentimental. He's like a jackhammer. He drills through granite rock
till he's there. Limitations? One would be health. No human
can take what he takes, he drives too hard. He is too perfect.
Russell says he is too good, that he wishes he would stumble
once. He never had a military man bad-mouth McNamara,
never had seen one criticize him. He does not impose himself
in Rusk's business; he and Rusk work very well together. . . .
McNamara has a deep understanding of the diplomatic side

and Rusk was only twenty minutes from being a professional military man so they understand each other's job. They know everything there is to know about their departments because they've been there a long time. I needed them."[17]

A more revealing answer to the question of why Johnson kept the Kennedy men is supplied by another Johnson statement: "I needed that White House staff. Without them I would have lost my link to John Kennedy, and without that I would have had absolutely no chance of gaining the support of the media or the Easterners or the intellectuals. And without that support I would have had absolutely no chance of governing the country."[18]

And if he needed them, they needed him. "Everything I had ever learned in the history books taught me that martyrs have to die for causes. John Kennedy had died. But his 'cause' was not really clear. That was my job. I had to take the dead man's program and turn it into a martyr's cause. That way Kennedy would live on forever and so would I."[19] Nevertheless, gradually, over the next few years most of the Kennedy men departed the White House; none, however, because Johnson had asked them to leave.

As self-styled executor of the legacy, Johnson assumed responsibility for transforming Kennedy's proposals into legislative victories. With great caution, never permitting himself to depart from the display of deferential humility, he began to create the impression that he, the doer, might succeed where the thinker had failed. He thus gradually de-emphasized *his* need for Kennedy by hinting that perhaps Kennedy needed him. Thus step by step he made his familiar and predictable shift from a passive to a dominant position, abandoning at a barely perceptible rate his somewhat feigned apprenticeship to a dead man's image. It was, given the complexity of timing and tone, a difficult shift to make, but Johnson carried it off, becoming more and more his own man in the eyes of the Washington community.

Instinctively, he sought to identify himself with the sources and objects of presidential power.

His energy—so striking in the Senate, so dormant in the Vice-Presidency—seemed redoubled. He talked with chiefs of state; sent messages to the Congress; issued orders to the executive branch; met with businessmen, labor leaders, and civil servants. The hours between 2 and 6 A.M. were all that Johnson grudgingly gave to sleep. Endowed with an encyclopedic memory, he had a command of the details of matters significant to his power and its exercise that was prodigious. In one sitting, he would deal in turn with issues of education, finance, poverty, and housing. His mind remained resilient even when his body was fatigued. He tended to rest from one kind of activity by engaging in another.

The most important decision a President makes concerns what he wants to do with the office, what range of issues he wants to recognize. The challenge is to create boundaries for the office, to select among possible goals. John Kennedy had set that agenda for his successor: tax reduction, the civil rights bill, federal aid to education, executive action to improve life in the cities, medical care for the aged, and plans for a poverty program. In the two years and ten months before November, 1963, Kennedy had defined for himself and for his Presidency a series of purposes, or what Richard Neustadt calls "irreversible commitments to defined courses of action."[20] The commitments implied the selection of a particular clientele and the shaping of an institutional core—a White House staff and a Cabinet—that understood the kind of Presidency John Kennedy wanted.

Commitments, clientele, and core had given the Kennedy Presidency a character that could not be altered in weeks or even in a year. Kennedy's day-to-day decisions about what to do with his time, how to allocate his resources and where to put his energy, had generated precedents, alliances, symbols, loyalties, and pressures that, taken together, had given life to the structure of the presidential office. And this was the construct that now contained Johnson's presidential authority.

It would be difficult to imagine circumstances better suited to his peculiar talents. The goals had been set. The immense task now required was the mobilization of political support. Although Kennedy had set forth these goals with a style that attracted the admiration of many Americans, his endeavor to pass legislation that would materialize these goals had been largely obstructed by the congressional opponents of his programs. His death proved a sufficiently powerful explosive to break past that obstruction. Johnson tried, not to conceal or deny the force of that explosion, but to organize and direct its power. He immediately began to focus public attention on the skillfully ordered legislation that was to mark his transition.

The essence of presidential leadership is the ability to appeal publicly to large and widely different constituencies at the same time.[21] The necessity for this sort of appeal, where one addresses all factions at once, would seem likely to hamper rather than reinforce a President like Johnson whose forte lay in one-to-one relations behind closed doors. How could he now lead his nation, please his party, adopt a regal stance, and knock heads together from such a visible platform? The Senate with its cloakroom mode of operation had allowed him to speak public nothings while the real business was accomplished discreetly.

However, he succeeded, and for many reasons: one, the circumstances of his assumption of office, creating a mood of strong national unity; two, the fortuitous state of Kennedy's administration at the time he was killed—the legislative programs had been articulated but not passed; and three (the most important reasons, but dependent on the first and second), his transformation of the conduct of the Presidency in such a way that he could utilize those techniques that had served him so well in the Senate: one-to-one relations, bargaining, consensus, and insulation from choice. This transformation could not take place overnight. But the unusual unity of national mood, the common desire for some renewal of purpose, permitted Johnson, in the first months of his Presidency, to address the general public as one in mind and spirit, as he would a single group—in terms of their ambiguous but shared interests. At the same time he could deal with a dozen little publics, soothing the leaders of each of the major interest groups with the same flair and skill he had practiced with each of sixty Democratic Senators.

An unprecedented number of public leaders were summoned to the White House the first ninety days—congressional leaders, union leaders, governors, mayors, businessmen, and civil rights spokesmen.[22] Everyone with a substantial constituency was invited in, one by one, group by group. These meetings served a variety of purposes. Through them, Johnson acquired information about each of the men with whom he would have to deal—George Meany, Roy Wilkins, Frederick Kappel, Martin Luther King, Henry Ford, and so on. He was interested in their conceptions of themselves and their hopes for their organizations, their range of skills, and, most importantly, their feelings and attitudes toward him. In the immediate presence of another man, Johnson felt utterly confident of his ability to judge what that man really wanted.

Johnson understood that the first impression of his Presidency would be crucial. Even though, as Senator or Vice President, he had previously met most of these men, as President he would now have to start over again, and it would have to be right. He knew they were looking at him afresh; he knew they would be thinking what he would have been thinking on seeing an old friend or an associate suddenly become President.[23] The initial definition of the situation would provide the basis for all future meetings. Before every meeting, Johnson was briefed by one of his aides; together they would mull over the facts and the figures of the political landscape. About each visitor, a dozen questions were discussed: How strong was his base of power? Who was his opposition? Who were his friends? Where had he staked his future? What issues were critical to him, and in what sense?

All these conversations in these early days were appropriately staged: for some the Oval Office was best; for others, the small room to the right of the office, an intimate walk around the White House grounds, or a group meeting in the somewhat austere Cabinet Room proved more relaxing or suitable. The key to Johnson's success in these meetings was his ability to communicate something unique to each and every person. Even if Johnson had spoken the same words of praise ten minutes before to someone else, the words still held a fresh and spontaneous quality. In a meeting of four or five important persons at once, Johnson managed at some point to take each one aside and say something special. The repetitive and stylized nature of the performance, therefore, was never perceived unless one stayed by his side as one audience left and a new one entered.

After the meetings Johnson would send each visitor a photograph to commemorate the event and to remind him that this was just the beginning of a long line of services. Over time, depending on the rhythm of the relationship, the mode of address on the pictures would shift. If the alliance prospered, the original form of signing—"To Roy Wilkins, from Lyndon Johnson"—would give way to "Dear Roy, My best, Lyndon"; within a couple of years "Roy" was addressed as "My Esteemed Friend" and two years later "Lyndon" became "Your friend and admirer, Lyndon." If things soured, as they did with Wilbur Mills over the course of the surtax struggle, the salutation—"To my friend and colleague Wilbur, from your good friend and greatest admirer, Lyndon"—was devaluated—"To Wilbur Mills from Lyndon Johnson"—to finally "To Mr. Chairman from Mr. President."

Eventually, Johnson created for himself a mental dossier of data portraits to remind him, for example, that union leader George Meany "liked the visible signs of consultation, the formal appointments to commissions and boards and delegations, the invitations to White House functions, the pictures of the two of us together," whereas business leader Henry Ford "preferred for the most part that our meeting remain strictly informal and off the record."[24] So during the course of his administration, Meany served on over a dozen commissions. His constant appearances at the White House always found their way into the mass media, and his invitations to White House social events doubled each year; whereas Henry Ford's visits, while nearly as numerous, received little mention in the papers and his name appeared on only two commissions.

Johnson understood that Roy Wilkins would fidget uncomfortably in a conversation if the main point of the meeting was to ask for a favor, whereas Everett Dirksen would blatantly and without hesitation send long memos to the White House detailing his requests for that week: a judgeship in the 5th District, a post office in Peoria, a presidential speech in Springfield, a tax exemption for peanuts. The following interchange well shows the serious nature of the banter between Johnson and Dirksen. It took place on June 23, 1964:

DIRKSEN: General Graham is going to appear before the Public Works Appropriations Subcommittee tomorrow. There is planning money in the bill for the Kaskaskia River navigation project. Now all I want him to do is say that the engineers do have construction capability for fiscal year 1965 and it is only $25,000 to $50,000. Now it is in that area of Illinois that is distressed. The total cost of the project is $30 million. And it is going to be the making of the southern thirty counties of the state.

PRESIDENT: Let me get on that and I will call you back. Now you are not going to beat me on excises and ruin my budget this year. Please do not beat me on that. You can do it if you want to and you can ruin my budget but you are hollering economy and trying to balance it.

DIRKSEN: Well, look at the pressure I'm under.

PRESIDENT: I know it, but you are also for good fiscal prudence and you know that the way to do this is through Ways and Means. You know they are not going to let you write a bill over in the Senate on taxes. Please do not press me on that. Give me a few of your Republicans because I just do not have the votes to do it without you.

DIRKSEN: You never talked that way when you were sitting in that front seat.

PRESIDENT: Yes, I did, when my country was involved. I voted for Ike many times when Knowland voted against him.

DIRKSEN: You are a hard bargainer.

PRESDENT: No, I'm not. I will look at this and see what I can do and call you right back.

DIRKSEN: That'll be fine.

Early that same evening the President phoned Dirksen:

PRESIDENT: I got in touch with Major General Graham and he says that if I want him to he will testify . . . that the engineers have a construction capability for 1965 contingent on favorable restudy of the economics of the project and that he believes it'll be a favorable restudy because he's got $100,000 wrapped up in it. I told him to go as strong as he could and he said he'd go $60,000. So please don't tell anybody now that you have a back door to the White House. But you go up there and please do not kill my tax bill tomorrow.

DIRKSEN: You left me upset 100 days on that civil rights bill.

PRESIDENT: You got yourself in debt. You are the hero of the hour now. They have forgotten that anybody else is around. Every time I pick up a paper, it's "Dirksen" in the magazines. The NAACP is flying Dirksen banners and picketing the White House tomorrow.

DIRKSEN: I could not even get you to change your tune about that damned House bill.

PRESIDENT: The hell you couldn't. I told them whatever Dirksen and the AG agree on, I am for. This is what I sent him up there to agree for. You know you never got a call

from me during the whole outfit. But do not mess up that
tax bill tomorrow, Everett, please don't.

DIRKSEN: Well, I have to offer this, but we shall see.

PRESIDENT: Offer it, but John Williams is not for raiding the
Treasury—so get him to save you. Okay. Goodbye.[25]

For Dirksen, Johnson was Tammany Hall—their brazen
exchange of memos stretches six inches in the LBJ Library
files. The character of these transactions was not so much an
expression of Johnson's nature as an accommodation to Dirksen's. If he could easily, in private, share the candor of such
manipulations, he could cut a very different figure in the
presence of a different personality.

In a conversation with Roy Wilkins, Johnson spoke of his
"desperate" need for Wilkins' advice on a matter he had obviously decided—recalling black Ambassador to Finland Carl
Rowan, in order to appoint him head of the United States Information Agency.

PRESIDENT: I want to do something a little unusual and I'm
going to get me in some trouble, but I want to get you behind me before I do it. Be sure I'm doing the right thing
and nobody will know I ever talked to you except you. I
want to bring Rowan back from Finland to run this shop.
He has good judgment, he's worked with me around the
world and he started out peeved at me and prejudiced
toward me and he wound up being a real devotee of mine
and a real friend. Now what is your reaction and your
judgment of Carl and tell me frankly.

WILKINS: He has excellent training as a newspaperman and
is familiar with the media. The only chink in the armor I
can think of right now is that he lacks the radio and communications media. I know he's a good administrator and
furthermore he's a Southerner. I think he's a good man
and able to survive personal antagonism. . . . Yes, yes, a
good man.[26]

By the end of the conversation, Wilkins was somehow
asking Johnson to appoint the very man Johnson had been
planning to appoint all along and Johnson was letting the
civil rights leader know that at some point in the future the
President might ask a return favor from him. Two dilemmas
remained: the current head of the USIA, Ed Murrow, though

dying, was still alive, and the appointment was bound to meet opposition in the Appropriations Committee, whose chairman was John McClelland, a conservative Democrat from Arkansas. Later that day Johnson called McClelland:

PRESIDENT: John, I've got a little problem. I don't want to embarrass you in any way and the best way to avoid it is to talk to you about [it] beforehand so you know what the problem is. Ed Murrow is dying with cancer of the lung. I've got to get another man. I've got a good solid man that's gone around the world with me and spent a good deal of time working with me and writing stuff for me and helping me and he's a good administrator and he'll listen to me, but he's a Negro. His name is Carl Rowan. He's the Ambassador to Finland. USIA is in your department under Appropriations and I don't want you to cut his guts out because he's a Negro. I've seen you operate with a knife.

McCLELLAND: I wouldn't say that. I wouldn't put it on that account. . . . On things like this, when you tell me, I always show every leverage, I appreciate your calling me and I know you have problems and you're going to do a lot of things I wouldn't do—unless I was President.[27]

And so, with Rowan sounded out, Murrow still living, Wilkins searching black attitudes toward Rowan as head of the USIA, and McClelland willing to "show every leverage," the way was clear, its potential for serious controversy defused by this seeming collaboration, and upon Murrow's death, Carl Rowan was appointed and confirmed as Director of the USIA.

Black appointments remained a chronic source of irritation among Johnson's former colleagues from the South. His achievements in the field of civil rights were made possible by his intimate knowledge of these men, on which he could base his capacities to influence or manipulate. In private with Richard Russell, Allen Ellender, John McClelland, Harry Byrd, and others, his Southern accent deepened, his manner suggested that although he understood or even shared their attitudes toward blacks, he was the President, and, as they well knew, in the difficult position of having to answer for the entire nation. Such dissembling could be accompanied, even made more credible, by a teasing humor that also implied intimacy. He told me of one such conversation with Senator Russell Long of Louisiana.

"Russell Long had recommended some man from Louisiana for a position on the Federal Reserve Board. I had him checked out. McChesney Martin [head of the Board] didn't want him. Besides, there was no vacancy in Louisiana and you had to appoint members from particular districts. One night Long came to see me about it. I knew he'd be mad as hell, always was mad when he'd had a couple of drinks, and that night he had already had a couple before he came and he wanted some more as soon as he sat down, and he started talking right away about *his* man. I explained about the district problem. He said, 'Hell, why, I'm chairman of the Senate Finance Committee. I'll get that amended.' 'It won't do no good,' I responded. 'I can't name your man. I've already made up my mind. It's going to be Andrew Brimmer.' 'Brimmer? Who the hell is he?' 'Why, Russell, he comes from your state, from —————— you see, I am naming a Louisianian after all, but you see he doesn't live there any more, he moved away.' 'Why, that's KKK territory,' Russell said; 'by God, I never heard of him.' 'Hell, Russell, you've already approved of him as Assistant Secretary of Commerce. The Senate confirmed that appointment. I know. I've got a picture of him in my drawer. I know you'll recognize him when I show it to you.' I opened the drawer, took out the picture, and showed it to Russell. 'That's who you're going to name?' he asked. 'Really?' 'Oh, yes, I just wanted you to know ahead of time.' 'You better give me another drink,' he said and then he smiled and said somewhat less gruffly, 'My God, do you realize what this means? . . . When they all jump on me because I couldn't get one Louisianian on the FRB, I can say I did get one—a nigger.' "[28]

Often he could make his own choices appear as favors to others. Those "favors" became credit to be drawn upon in some future bind. Opposition to his decisions might be placated by the promise of future favors or the collection of past debts. In this manner he was able to create a coherent mosaic consisting of a prodigious number of incongruous bits and pieces.

Johnson's willingness to compromise in order to achieve results, his political malleability, was confined within limits imposed by the requirements of the Presidency and his knowledge of just how far a particular man or group could be pushed. "The challenge," as Johnson later described it, "was to learn what it was that mattered to each of these men, understand which issues were critical to whom and why. Without that understanding nothing is possible. Knowing the leaders and understanding their organizational needs let me shape my legislative program to fit both their needs and mine."[29]

Over time, each of the leaders most important to his leadership had made tentative claim to influence matters that were vital to him but not immediately critical to others. In exchange for this, he would remain silent or uncommitted on matters important to others but not immediately important to him. And Johnson also attempted to tie the leaders together in a host of ways. As he described it, "I wanted each of these men to participate in my administration in a dozen different ways. The key was to get men from different groups so involved with each other on so many committees and delegations covering so many issues that no one could afford to be uncompromising on any one issue alone."[30]

In cementing ties among the group leaders, Johnson was at the same time laying the foundation for the politics of consensus, which, before the end of 1964, would yield a major tax cut, a billion-dollar antipoverty program, and a sweeping civil rights bill.

Kennedy had left behind a tax reduction bill that had already passed the House and was awaiting action in the Senate. But it was not known whether the new administration could mobilize the support of the business community behind the tax cut; if not, it would be difficult to get the bill through the Senate Finance Committee. From the beginning of his Presidency, when he insisted, with great public drama, on keeping the budget below $100 billion, Johnson had his eye on the business community. He recognized how important fiscal responsibility was to the leaders of industry and commerce. Johnson's legerdemain with the budget thus set the stage for a series of meetings to discuss the tax cut with the Business Council—a group of one hundred corporate and financial executives, chaired by AT&T chairman Frederick Kappel.

In these meetings, Johnson marshaled argument and forestalled objections so well that he astounded the businessmen, who had expected a fairly crude piece of jawboning. He began by demonstrating that, with the stimulus provided by the tax cut, there would be a general increase in resources, which, in turn, would significantly reduce the possibility of class conflict. So long as the economic pie continues to grow, Johnson argued, there will be few disputes about its distribution among labor, business, and other groups. But as soon as it begins to slow down, the conflict over who gets what begins: "I want you to make just as much profit as you reasonably can. If you make 100 million instead of 100 thousand, then Johnson gets 50 million instead of 50 thousand. There is no need to worry because I'm not going to be going around telling you how to run your business. I think that you know better than I do how to do that and I believe that I know how to run the government, so let's leave it at that. You're not afraid of me and I'm not afraid of you."[81]

Thus Johnson established an immediate rapport with the leaders of business. The tax cut was signed into law on February 8, 1964, and two months later *Fortune* magazine addressed this encomium to the President:

> Lyndon Johnson ... has achieved a breadth of public acceptance and approval that few observers would have believed possible when he took office. ... Without alienating organized labor or the anti-business intellectuals in his own party, he has won more applause from the business community than any President in this century. ... A large part of Johnson's success can be summed up by saying that he is the Democratic President who drew his party closest to the traditional Republican position of an active, effective federal government encouraging the development of a free enterprise economy.[32]

In the year before Kennedy's death, the issue of poverty had attracted the attention of the President himself and of high-level bureaucrats in the Council of Economic Advisers and the Department of Labor. Plans for a poverty program were in the preliminary stage of development when Johnson took office. Learning of these, Johnson responded instinctively: "Go ahead. Give it the highest priority. Push ahead full tilt."[33]

When Johnson spoke of poverty, he spoke, he claimed, "from experience, the experience of a boy who knew what it was like to go hungry, the experience of a boy who saw sickness and disease day after day." Through this revised, and exaggerated, picture of his past, he better accommodated the American dream of rags to riches. It is said that in the 1950s, when Rebekah Johnson first heard about Johnson's description of his childhood, she felt hurt and angry. She had worked to give her son everything: why was he now telling the world that he had had nothing?

Yet the tales should not be dismissed entirely. In spite of the distortions and exaggerations, there were, nonetheless, times of hardship during his childhood when his father went bust, and he had witnessed real poverty during his brief teaching career at Cotulla. To Johnson, the poor would never be "the disadvantaged," an abstract class whose problems must be solved. They were familiar men and women suffering a circumstance he well understood.

Johnson worked incessantly to make poverty an issue of public concern. He met with groups ranging from the Daughters of the American Revolution to the Socialist Party, from the Business Council to the AFL-CIO. He made dozens of speeches. He made personal visits to poverty-stricken regions. What had been largely the concern of a small number of liberal intellectuals and government bureaucrats became within six months the national disgrace that shattered the complacency of a people who always considered their country a land of equal opportunity for all. From this base, Johnson went to the Congress to declare an "unconditional war on poverty." "This program," he said, "is much more than a beginning. It is total commitment by this President and this Congress and this nation to pursue victory over the most ancient of mankind's enemies. . . . On similar occasions in the past we have often been called upon to wage war against foreign enemies which threaten our freedom today. Now we are asked to declare war on a domestic enemy which threatens the strength of our nation and the welfare of our people. If we now move forward against this enemy—if we can bring to the challenges of peace the same determination and strength which has brought us victory in war—then this day and this Congress will have won a more secure and honorable place in the history of the nation and the enduring gratitude of generations of Americans to come."[34]

This genuinely dynamic conception of political responsibility foreshadowed the Great Society, his ultimate expression of "good works." And here, as with the tax cut, Johnson handled the issue with remarkable deftness. By shaping the political consensus beforehand through an elaborate courtship of leaders of the relevant groups, he paved the way for legislative success. On August 20, 1964, the Economic Opportunity Act became the law of the land.

Yet if consensus produced legislation, it also exacted its price by limiting the range of the possible. Alternatives were necessarily excluded from the outset. The first of these discarded alternatives called for stimulating the economy, not by accepting the existing tax structure and simply cutting taxes across the board, but by reforming its structure: closing loopholes, reducing inequitable benefits for the few, lowering the burden of rates on the many. Another rejected alternative—and one also rejected by Kennedy—was massive public spending that could stimulate the economy while simultaneously improving the conditions of life, especially among the poor. Tax-cutting, it was argued, would accomplish only half as much; it was reactionary Keynesianism, providing what the country needed least—more conspicuous consumption—at the expense of the things it needed most—schools, housing, hospitals, and environmental protection.

Either of these alternatives—tax reform or massive spending—required difficult choice and promised substantial conflict. But Johnson stubbornly maintained a conception of America in which no one seriously disagreed with what was to be sought, retaining to the end a belief that so long as the Gross National Product continued to rise, all conflict could be contained; although perhaps more important was the political judgment that it would be impossible to enact either alternative. "Helping some will increase the prosperity of all"—this was the administration's refrain as it embarked on a contradictory course: reducing taxes and cutting the budget with one hand, while fighting poverty and raising spending with the other. As seen through Johnson's eyes, however, the two courses were perfectly compatible, and in this vision he was not alone. The best known of America's columnists, among many others, fully agreed. "This is," Walter Lippmann remarked,

> the post-Marxian age. A generation ago it would have been taken for granted that a war on poverty meant taxing money away from the haves and turning it over to the have nots. For until recently, it was assumed that

there was only so much pie and the social question was how to divide it. But in this generation, a revolutionary idea has taken hold. The size of the pie can be increased by intention, by organized fiscal policy and then a whole society, not just one part of it, will grow richer.[35]

And so Johnson could wage war against poverty and at the same time win substantial backing among the well-to-do. "He is the only President," remarked Leonard Hall, chairman of the Republican National Committee, "to have prosperity and poverty going for him at the same time."[36]

"Both the period of mourning for Kennedy and of experimentation for Johnson are over," James Reston wrote in the spring of 1964.

> Washington is now a little girl settling down with the old boyfriend. The mad and wonderful infatuation with the handsome young stranger from Boston is over—somehow she always knew it wouldn't last—so she is adjusting to reality. Everything is less romantic and more practical, part regret and part relief; beer instead of champagne; not fancy but plain; and in many ways more natural and hopefully more durable. This may not be the most attractive quality of the new Administration but it works. . . . The lovers of style are not too happy with the new Administration but the lovers of substance are not complaining.[37]

Johnson's greatest exertions in his first months as President were made in the field of civil rights. There, consensus politics would not be enough. He recognized that retreat on this issue would jeopardize not only the transition but the approaching nomination. Before Kennedy's death, it was generally thought that the civil rights bill as finally enacted would fall considerably short of the original Kennedy draft. Johnson shared this view: "Even the strongest supporters of President Kennedy's civil rights bill in 1963 expected parts of it to be watered down in order to avert a Senate filibuster. The most vulnerable sections were those guaranteeing equal access to public accommodations and equal employment opportunity. I had seen this 'moderating' process at work for many years. I had seen it happen in 1957. I had seen it happen in 1960. I did not want to see it happen again."[38]

There is in this statement more than a little dissembling; in saying that he "had seen" the moderating process at work, Johnson leaves the impression that he was outside looking in, when in fact he was the very instrument of the process. Sitting in the White House in 1963, he demanded a different, and far more difficult, approach. Populist instincts about the equality of men, inherited fears of national fragmentation, fond dreams about ending the Civil War once and for all— all these combined with the responsibilities of the Presidency to invest his conduct with an unusual steadiness of conviction about a public issue. This time Johnson's personal means were committed to an unconditional victory. While still making use of his capacity to convey privately subtle differences in tone with the liberal Democrats, the blacks, the Southerners, and the Republicans, Johnson openly proclaimed a unifying and consistent purpose—to secure a strong, sweeping civil rights bill.

In pledging that there would be "no deal" on civil rights, even if it required suspending all other activity in the Senate for months, Johnson replaced his practiced methods of maneuver with an untypical, inflexible determination. "I knew," Johnson later said, "that if I didn't get out in front on this issue, they [the liberals] would get me. They'd throw up my background against me, they'd use it to prove that I was incapable of bringing unity to the land I loved so much. . . . I couldn't let that happen. I had to produce a civil rights bill that was even stronger than the one they'd have gotten if Kennedy had lived. Without this, I'd be dead before I could even begin."[39]

So Johnson did on civil rights the thing he always feared the most. He refused to bargain his position with his onetime mentor, Richard Russell. Johnson's steadfast refusal gave positive shape to the six-month struggle. Accepting Johnson's firmness, Russell, too, "went for broke." He mobilized his troops for a filibuster, hoping the liberals could not organize a two-thirds vote for cloture, but knowing that if they did, the bill would pass intact. Although Russell and Johnson split on this decisive issue, the tone of the separation was more of sorrow than of anger. Johnson approached Russell with sympathetic understanding, not vindictiveness, manifesting his hope for a future when Southerners would no longer stand against the rest of the nation.

While reaching out to the South in hope of eventual reconciliation, Johnson also reached out to the Republicans. "I knew right away that without Republican support we'd have absolutely no chance of securing the two-thirds vote to defeat the filibuster. And I knew there was but one man who could secure us that support, the Senator from Illinois, Everett Dirksen."[40] In working on Dirksen, Johnson used both subtle and blatant devices of politics. He turned first not just to Dirksen himself but to Roy Wilkins and Whitney Young. "When are you going to get down here and start civil-righting?" he asked them. "I think you are all going to have to sit down and persuade Dirksen this is in the interest of the Republican Party and I think that he must know that if he helps you then you're going to go along and help him. And let [the Republicans] know that you're going to the presidential candidate that offers you the best hope and the best chance of dignity and decency in this country and you're going with a senatorial man who does the same thing."[41]

While fostering this indirect tactic, Johnson also approached Dirksen on a direct level, offering, as we have seen, favors which ranged from personal notes to federal projects, from photographs to judgeships. On June 10, 1964, Dirksen joined the forces for cloture, thereby defeating the Southern filibuster and opening the way for Congress to pass the most sweeping civil rights bill in history. On July 2, 1964, in the presence of the leaders of all the major civil rights groups, Johnson signed the Civil Rights Act of 1964.

Only two weeks later, the strength of Johnson's alliance with the civil rights groups was severely tested when large-scale rioting broke out in Harlem. Johnson immediately called a meeting at the White House. There, he persuaded Roy Wilkins, Whitney Young, and Martin Luther King of the necessity to join together against the forces of chaos. At the end of the meeting a surprising statement emerged in which the leaders of the various civil rights groups called on "their people" to stay off the street.

> Our own estimate of the present situation is that it presents such a serious threat to the implementation of the civil rights act ... that we recommend a voluntary temporary alteration in strategy and procedures. ... The greatest need now is for political action. ... We call on our members voluntarily to observe a broad curtailment if not total moratorium of all mass marches, picketing

and demonstrations until after Election Day, November 3.[42]

That statement assumed a sharing of interests between officials in government and rioting youth in the streets, an assumption that, within two years, would become untenable. But at the time both Lyndon Johnson and the civil rights leaders were confident—and they seemed to have good reason for their confidence—that leaders and followers alike were united by common goals and common agreement on the rules of the game.

Johnson took office at a time when cold war tensions and fear of military conflict between the United States and the Soviet Union had diminished substantially. Many knowledgeable observers believed that the resolution of the Cuban missile crisis in 1962 and the Nuclear Test Ban Treaty that followed in 1963 were preludes to an eventual détente with the Soviet Union. There was no sign of approaching crisis in Berlin or Cuba, those earlier hot spots of the cold war. In South Vietnam, there were only eighteen thousand American advisers; and although there had been considerable political upheaval in the wake of Diem's assassination, very few Americans foresaw that Vietnam might become the arena for serious international crisis. "It was," as Johnson later described it, "almost as if the world had provided a breathing space within which I could concentrate on domestic affairs."[43]

Obviously, no twentieth-century President could ignore foreign policy completely. There were speeches to be made, meetings to be chaired, and leaders to be met. And even though there were no international difficulties of urgent public concern, there are always problems, and continual need for presidential decisions. And the American people still wanted to be both beloved and envied by those in other countries. And when Johnson told them it was so, no one could have realized that this was the last Presidency for some time and almost the last year in the decade when Americans would hear or believe such words. "My plane has landed in many continents," Johnson said in a speech in February, 1964, "touched down in more than thirty countries in the last three years. The wheels have never stopped and the door has never opened and I have never looked upon any faces that I didn't think would like to trade citizenship with me. . . . Since

World War II we have spent a hundred billion dollars trying to help other people ... so, regardless of what you hear and regardless of what some of the bellyachers say, we are a much beloved people throughout the world."[44]

This statement is not simply an expression of nationalism; it hints at a belief in the universal applicability of American values, the existence of a global consensus. In Johnson's first meeting with a group of foreign diplomats, he described his visit with an African family during his Vice-Presidency, letting them know that he was gratified, but not surprised, to discover in the heart of the continent a replication of Americana. "I stood," Johnson said, "in a mud hut in African Senegal, and I saw an African mother with a baby on her breast, one in her stomach, one on her back, and eight on the floor, that she was trying to feed off of $8 per month. As I looked into her determined eyes, I saw the same expression that I saw in my mother's eyes when she, the wife of a tenant farmer, looked down on me and my little brother and sisters, determined that I should have my chance and my opportunity, believing that where there was a will, there was a way."[45]

To Johnson there were foreign customs, foreign religions, foreign governments, but there were no foreign cultures, only different ways of pursuing universal desires—in this case, the transition from rags to riches. He knew about poor mothers with children—what else but determination could he see in her eyes? This defect, almost an inability to conceive of societies with basically different values, was the source of his greatest weakness as President.

Naturally, economic development was Johnson's panacea for the ills of the planet. America was the missionary nation, destined to defeat the ancient enemies of mankind—poverty, ignorance, and disease—and in so doing to serve as a model and a source of determination to the world. "When I first became President," Johnson told me, "I realized that if only I could take the next step and become dictator of the whole world, then I could really make things happen. Every hungry person would be fed, every ignorant child educated, every jobless man employed. And then I knew I could accomplish my greatest wish, the wish for eternal peace."[46]

It was this belief in universal values, combined with his confidence in his powers of persuasion, that led Johnson to conclude that he need only arrange a meeting, face to face, in order to straighten out American disagreements with other countries. "I always believed," Johnson later said, "that as long as I could take someone into a room with me, I could make him my friend, and that included anybody, even Nikita Khrushchev. From the start of my Presidency I believed that if I handled him right, he would go along with me. Deep down, hidden way below, he, too, wanted what was good, but every now and then, this terrible urge for world domination would get into him and take control and then he'd go off on some crazy jag like putting those missiles in Cuba. I saw all that in him and I knew I could cope with it so long as he and I were in the same room."[47]

In January, 1964, Panama broke diplomatic relations with the United States. American students illegally had raised the American flag over their high school, precipitating a riot that led to the death of several American soldiers. Johnson's initial reaction was prompt and man-to-man. "Hey, get me the President of Panama—what's his name, anyway?—I want to talk to him."[48]

As seen through Johnson's eyes, the behavior of world leaders was influenced by the same grammar of power; whatever their countries' size or shapes, they shared a common concern with questions of rulership: which groups to rely on, which advisers to rely on, and how to conduct themselves amid the complex intrigues of politics. "When Chancellor Erhard came to my ranch at Christmas time in 1963, we knew very little about one another, but before he left we'd come to understand each other so fully that I knew that no matter what issue came between us we'd be able to sit down and reason it out. This is what I wanted to happen with every leader I met and most of the time I was successful. President de Gaulle was the hardest to get to. I always had trouble with people like him, who let high rhetoric and big issues take the place of accomplishments. But even with De Gaulle I refused to get my back up and eventually we learned to live with each other."[49]

Without personal contact, Johnson tended to see foreign leaders as remote, uncanny figures and was uncomfortable with their strangeness. During three decades at the seat of the government, he had learned the accepted concepts of international conflict, containment, bipolarity, limited war. But he didn't think in that language. He thought in terms of personalities, power, and good works.

South Vietnam was ten thousand miles away. Johnson had visited it once, for three days. He had then met Ngo Dinh Diem, but now Diem was dead and he knew almost nothing about his successor. Skeptical of his own ability to sort out the complicated strands of religion, party, and culture, Johnson turned to others for guidance, in particular to John Kennedy's men: Robert McNamara, McGeorge Bundy, Dean Rusk, and Maxwell Taylor. All these men had previously committed themselves to the maintenance of an independent non-Communist South Vietnam. All of them shared the view that Vietnam was a critical testing ground of America's ability to counter Communist support for wars of national liberation. Moreover, they reflected the generally held position of the foreign policy establishment that had dominated America's conduct of foreign affairs since the cold war began.

That Johnson was strongly influenced by these advisers is clear; they were Kennedy's men and they had expertise in the one area he knew the least about. But he was not, as some have pictured, a passive figure, a dupe to their advice. He accepted their advice to continue the policy of supporting South Vietnam because it accorded with a set of assumptions he had long held about the nature of Communism and the importance of Southeast Asia.[50] These assumptions are delineated in this conversation with William Fulbright on March 2, 1964:

PRESIDENT: If we can just get our foreign policy straightened out.

FULBRIGHT: Get that damn Vietnam straightened out. Any hope?

PRESIDENT: Well, we've got about four possibilities. The only thing I know to do is more of the same and do it more efficiently and effectively and we got a problem out there that I inherited with Lodge. I wire him every day and say what else do you recommend? Here is the best summary we have. (1) In Southeast Asia the free world is facing an attempt by the Communists of North Vietnam to subvert and overthrow the non-Communist government of South Vietnam. North Vietnam has been providing direction, control, and training for 25,000 Vietcong guerrillas. (2) Our objective, our purpose in South Vietnam, is to help the Vietnamese maintain their independence. We are providing

the training and logistic support they cannot provide themselves. We will continue to provide that support as long as
it is required. As soon as the mission is complete our
troops can be withdrawn. There's no reason to keep our
military police there when the Vietnamese are trained for
that purpose. (3) In the past four months there've been
three governments in South Vietnam. The Vietcong have
taken advantage of this confusion. Their increased activity
has had success. At least four alternatives are open to us:
(1) Withdraw from South Vietnam. Without our support
the government will be unable to counter the aid from the
North to the Vietcong. Vietnam will collapse and the
ripple effect will be felt throughout Southeast Asia, endan-
gering independent governments in Thailand, Malaysia and
extending as far as India and Indonesia and the Philip-
pines. (2) We can seek a formula that will neutralize
South Vietnam à la Mansfield and De Gaulle but any such
formula will only lead in the end to the same results as
withdrawing support. We all know the Communist attitude
that what's mine is mine, what's yours is negotiable. True
neutralization would have to extend to North Vietnam and
this has been specifically rejected by North Vietnam and the
Communist China government, and we believe if we attempted to neutralize, the Commies would stay in North Vietnam. We would abandon South Vietnam. The Communists would take over South Vietnam. (3) We can send
Marines à la Goldwater and other U.S. forces against the
sources of these aggressions but our men may well be
bogged down in a long war against numerically superior
North Vietnamese and Chicom forces 100,000 miles from
home. (4) We continue our present policy of providing
training and logistical support of South Vietnamese forces.
This policy has not failed. We propose to continue it. Secretary McNamara's trip to South Vietnam will provide us
with an opportunity to again appraise the prospects of the
policy and the future alternatives open to us.

FULBRIGHT: I think that's right ... that's exactly what I'd arrive at under these circumstances at least for the foresee-
able future.

PRESIDENT: Now when he comes back though and if we're
losing with what we're doing, we've got to decide whether
to send them in or whether to come out and let the domi-

noes fall. That's where the tough one is going to be. And
you do some heavy thinking and let's decide what we do.
FULBRIGHT: Righto.[51]

Although Johnson shared the general outlook of his advisers, he was far from deciding what means should be employed—whether, indeed, the objectives were possible of fulfillment. He had, after all, not approved an earlier proposal
to use American military force to prevent Ho Chi Minh's victory over the French. He did know that these were difficult
decisions to be made. But he needed time, and in any event
an election year was no time to make them. The word went
out that tough decisions on Vietnam should be deferred as
long as possible. The glimpses of the President revealed in
The Pentagon Papers show a man determined to achieve the
goal of an independent non-Communist South Vietnam, yet
holding back on actions to achieve that goal until he believed
they were desperately, absolutely necessary.

In the spring of 1964, opinion surveys showed that more
than two-thirds of the American public said they paid little or
no attention to what was going on in Vietnam. Johnson
wanted to keep it that way. Rejecting proposals to expand the
war into North Vietnam, or to introduce combat troops in
the South, Johnson believed that he was, for now, left with
only one choice: incremental and covert escalation of military pressure, designed to convince Hanoi that the United
States was serious and to reassure Saigon. Nonetheless, in the
next few months, the situation in South Vietnam continued to
deteriorate and the Saigon regime was shaken by one crisis
after another. Yet the established official consensus on Vietnam and its significance held firm.

The only time his will seemed fully engaged in Vietnam
policy came in August when an American destroyer was sup-
posedly attacked by the North Vietnamese. He saw it as an
opportunity to show the seriousness of our commitment to
South Vietnam. Within twelve hours after news of the incident reached Washington, American bombers were
dispatched on a reprisal raid over North Vietnam. Two days
later, the administration asked the Congress "to approve and
support the determination of the President as Commander in
Chief to take all the necessary measures to repel any armed
attack against the forces of the United States to prevent further aggression. . . . The United States regards Vietnam as vi-

tal to its national interest and to world peace and security in Southeast Asia."[52]

William Fulbright guided the Tonkin Gulf Resolution through the Senate, with only Wayne Morse and Ernest Gruening in dissent. In the House, the vote was unanimous, 416 to 0. Congress had, without knowing, established the formal foundation that would later be used to support a full-scale war.

In one stroke, Johnson had been able both to flex his muscles and to show restraint, to act abroad as he had done at home with the tax cut and the poverty program: pursue contradictory policies and apparently make them work. Running as the "man of peace," the man who would "never send American boys to do the fighting that Asian boys should do themselves," Johnson nonetheless had no intention of permitting Goldwater to usurp the role of defending America's pride and patriotism. The single bombing raid against Communist attackers of United States ships provided an ideal opportunity. He was able to demonstrate that the "man of peace" was not a man of weakness or timidity. And on the verge of the campaign, the Tonkin affair allowed this consensus President to speak by his actions to each of his constituencies, satisfying all of them in one stroke.

But the rhetoric of restrained commitment to South Vietnam, so effective during the campaign, later provoked serious difficulties when Johnson finally had to choose between massive escalation or the defeat of Saigon. As the country learned the less innocent reality of the United States role at the Gulf of Tonkin and saw hundreds of thousands of their fellow Americans being sent to war, millions of Americans came to feel that the President had betrayed them, lied, and deliberately tricked them to get their votes.

"The virtues of the politician," Hans Morgenthau writes, "can easily become vices when they are brought to bear upon the statesman's task."[53] The politician, Johnson's experience had taught him, could make promises without keeping them; words spoken in public had little relation to the practical conduct of daily life. But whatever justification a politician may claim for deceptions, the statesman must align his words with his action.

At the time, however, Johnson's action at the Gulf of Tonkin, along with his campaign statements, constituted a political master stroke. Though some uneasiness about Vietnam was reflected in letters to the editor in a few papers, in the two lonely Senate votes against the Tonkin Resolution, and in a handful of demonstrations and peace rallies, the American people and their politicians praised Johnson for the feat of riding two horses in different directions at the same time. Some wanted peace, even at the price of withdrawal. Some wanted victory, even at the price of a wider war. Others wanted, if not victory, at least to avoid defeat while keeping the peace. And most did not want to pay attention to the issue.

With unexpected elegance, Lyndon Johnson had done what few observers had imagined possible at his accidental accession: he had taken complete control of the levers of power; he had made himself the unquestioned choice of the Democratic Party for the presidential nomination. Yet even during this public acclaim Johnson was preoccupied with what became known in the White House as "the Bobby problem," the issue of the vice-presidential nomination.

"Every day," Johnson recalled, "as soon as I opened the papers or turned on the television, there was something about Bobby Kennedy; there was some person or group talking about what a great Vice President he'd make. Somehow it just didn't seem fair. I'd given three years of loyal service to Jack Kennedy. During all that time I'd willingly stayed in the background; I knew that it was *his* Presidency, not mine. If I disagreed with him, I did it in private, not in public. And then Kennedy was killed and I became the custodian of his will. I became the President. But none of this seemed to register with Bobby Kennedy, who acted like *he* was the custodian of the Kennedy dream, some kind of rightful heir to the throne. It just didn't seem fair. I'd waited for my turn. Bobby should've waited for his. But he and the Kennedy people wanted it now. A tidal wave of letters and memos about how great a Vice President Bobby would be swept over me. But no matter what, I simply couldn't let it happen. With Bobby on the ticket, I'd never know if I could be elected on my own."[54]

Johnson spent days and nights discussing "the Bobby problem." As Eric Goldman described it, Robert Kennedy commanded more attention and consumed more energy and raw emotion than any other single concern of state that the new President confronted after Dallas.[55] There was between them a dislike so strong that it seemed almost as if each had been created for the purpose of exasperating the other.

Moreover, Johnson identified Bobby as the agent of an effort to destroy his political career. At the 1960 convention, Bobby was sent to see Johnson when John Kennedy became increasingly concerned about the mounting liberal opposition to Johnson as his vice-presidential choice. But before Bobby arrived at Johnson's suite, Kennedy had decided to insist upon his choice of Johnson as his running mate. Unaware of his brother's resolve, Bobby subtly suggested to Johnson the possibility of taking himself out of the vice-presidential picture. Johnson took the discussion to mean one thing: Bobby and his friends had persuaded Jack to change his mind. And now Bobby was here to tell him that he was being dumped. Before Bobby finished, Johnson picked up the phone and called Kennedy, demanding a definitive answer. Kennedy, of course, gave him the assurance he sought. But the memory of that humiliating moment would never be erased. Unable, then or later, during the miseries of his time as Vice President, to express anger toward John Kennedy in public, or even in many private settings, Johnson projected his bad feelings onto the nearest target, and that was Bobby.

The response Robert Kennedy evoked in Lyndon Johnson was hugely disproportionate to the political realities. Robert Kennedy could not threaten Lyndon Johnson's power; not until 1968, after Johnson himself had virtually destroyed his own public support. Something beyond politics was at stake. Throughout his life, Johnson had desperately tried to keep alive the distinction between the doer and the thinker; a man was either one or the other. For years this dichotomy was Johnson's way of justifying his failure in becoming what Rebekah had wanted. Yet here was a man who seemed to combine both intellect and will. John Kennedy had never seemed to constitute the same kind of threat. From their first meeting, Johnson had typed the Massachusetts Senator as "weak and pallid," "a scrawny man with a bad back, a weak and indecisive politician, a nice man, a gentle man, but not a man's man."[56] With Bobby, it was different. If he was smaller, he was tougher, and a brutal bargainer. Johnson was nettled by pictures showing Bobby shooting rapids, climbing mountains, surrounded by the horde of children he had fathered. At the same time, the reports that Bobby liked to read, quote poems, and take long walks by himself connoted to Johnson a man of the mind.

Johnson made it absolutely clear to his friends that Robert Kennedy would, under no circumstances, be the vice-presidential choice. "If they try to push Bobby Kennedy down my throat for Vice President, I'll tell them to nominate him for the Presidency and leave me out of it."[57] But the speculation continued until Johnson could take it no longer. On July 29 he invited Kennedy to a private meeting in the Oval Office. The conversation is on record:

> I have asked you to come over to discuss with me a subject that is an important one to you and me.
>
> As you might suppose, I have been giving a great deal of thought and consideration to the selection of the Democratic candidate for Vice President. . . .
>
> I have reached a decision in this regard and I wanted you to learn of my decision directly from me. . . . I have concluded, for a number of reasons, that it would be inadvisable for you to be the Democratic candidate for Vice President in this year's election. . . .
>
> I believe strongly that the Democratic ticket must be constituted so as to have as much appeal as possible in the Middle West and the Border States; also it should be so constituted as to create as little an adverse reaction as possible upon the Southern States. . . .
>
> I am sure that you will understand the basis of my decision and the factors that have entered into it, because President Kennedy had to make a similar decision in 1960.[58]

The meeting lasted forty minutes; afterward, Johnson was euphoric. "It was," as Theodore White described it, "as if a coup had been accomplished, as if a tenuous control had been reinforced and confirmed by a stroke of action."[59] The larger problem of informing the public and the press remained, until Johnson hit upon what seemed to him the perfect evasion—a general principle to cover the specific case. On July 30, in a special television broadcast, he announced that he had reached the conclusion that "it would be inadvisable for me to recommend to the convention [as my running mate] any member of my Cabinet or any of those who meet regularly with the Cabinet."[60] In the writing of his memoirs,

Johnson insisted upon turning this sequence upside down, as if general principle came first and then, and only as a necessary consequence, the elimination of Robert Kennedy.

With all Cabinet officers eliminated from consideration, the list of vice-presidential possibilities narrowed to Hubert Humphrey, Eugene McCarthy, and Thomas Dodd, the latter two serving as stage props in the President's drama, designed to conceal to the end Johnson's inevitable choice of Hubert Humphrey. Johnson himself admitted that all along he had been 90 percent sure that Humphrey was the man he wanted. Humphrey, with his open, ebullient nature and his unswerving loyalty, had great appeal for Johnson. Yet with his own nomination already secured, Johnson wanted to provide some element of suspense that would strengthen interest in the convention, so Johnson would give Humphrey warm and visible signs of encouragement one day and back off on the next, engaging in speculation about McCarthy or Dodd.

This emotional seesaw took its toll on Humphrey. In the final weeks before the convention, Humphrey, seemingly drained of pride and dignity, repeated the poignant story of the girl whose hero was the handsome captain of the football team. He would keep phoning her—always to ask her opinion of some other girl and never for a date. His present political dependency only reinforced the psychological dependency long rooted in Humphrey's relationship with Johnson.

When the convention opened on August 24, 1964, Johnson still had not revealed his choice. Furthermore, Johnson's mood had led him to raise seemingly incredible doubts concerning his own availability for the presidential nomination. Always subject to extreme oscillations of mood, throughout the summer of 1964 Johnson had continued to alternate between periods of elation, excitement, and self-confidence and periods of severe depression, inhibition, and doubt. In depression, he invariably would turn his attention to running away. This was neither the first nor the last time that Johnson would contemplate leaving public life. He was nearing fifty-six. It was nine years since his heart attack. The thought of total responsibility for another four years was unsettling.

"I had," Johnson later recounted,

decidedly mixed feelings about whether I wanted to seek a four-year term . . . in my own right. . . . I knew clearly enough, in those early months in the White House, that the Presidency of the U.S. was a prize with a heavy price. Scathing attacks had begun almost immediately, not only on me but on members of my family. I knew that unfounded rumors, crass speculations, remorseless criticism, and even insult would intensify in a political campaign.

There was, in addition, the constant uncertainty as to whether my health would stand up through a full four-year term. . . . I felt a strong inclination to go back to Texas while there still was time—time to enjoy life with my wife and daughters, to work in earnest at being a rancher on the land I loved, to slow down, to reflect, to live.[61]

At first, it is hard to take this statement seriously. Politics and work went together for Johnson. What would he do back in Texas? How would he live without politics? "I believed," Johnson wrote,

that the nation could successfully weather the ordeals it faced only if the people were united. I deeply feared that I would not be able to keep the country consolidated and bound together. . . .

The burden of national unity rests heaviest on one man, the President. And I did not believe, any more than I ever had, that the nation would unite indefinitely behind any Southerner . . . the metropolitan press of the Eastern seaboard would never permit it. My experience in office had confirmed this reaction. I was not thinking just of the derisive articles about my style, my clothes, my manner, my accent, and my family. . . . I was also thinking of a more deep-seated and far-reaching attitude—a disdain for the South that seems to be woven into the fabric of Northern experience . . . an automatic reflex, unconscious or deliberate, on the part of opinion molders of the North and East in the press and television.[62]

Johnson may have been correct in asserting that America somehow resented a Southerner; yet he was unquestionably popular, and in a position to quash such resentment. In fact, personal insecurity more than political analysis informed

Johnson's assessment. As we have seen, he felt a recurring anxiety about losing hold, a sense of being scorned in some unexpected and dreadful way by those people whose love and respect he so consistently required. So once again the familiar pattern emerged: he controlled his anxiety by creating the possibility of his withdrawal: I don't want you. Do you need me? All right: but if you don't, I have already told you I don't want you.

On August 25, 1964, the day after the Democratic Convention opened, Johnson scrawled the following statement on a yellow pad:

> ... For nine months I've carried on as effectively as I could.
>
> Our country faces grave dangers. These dangers must be faced and met by a united people under a leader they do not doubt. ... The times require leadership about which there is no doubt and a voice that men of all parties, sections and color can follow. I have learned after trying very hard that I am not that voice or that leader.
>
> Therefore, I shall carry forward with your help until the new President is sworn in next January and then go back home as I've wanted to since the day I took this job.[63]

These must have been painful words for Johnson to write or even to think. But in the act of writing them and even more in the act of taking them back, Johnson found a way to control his anxiety. I'm strong enough to give it up, but I won't give you the satisfaction. When he finished the draft, he showed it to Lady Bird, whose response demonstrated as profound an understanding of her husband as Rebekah had demonstrated of her son:

> Beloved—
> You are as brave a man as Harry Truman—or FDR—or Lincoln. You can go on to find some peace, some achievement amidst all the pain. You have been strong, patient, determined beyond any words of mine to express. I honor you for it. So does most of the country. To step out now would be *wrong* for your country, and I can see nothing but a lonely wasteland for your future.

Your friends would be frozen in embarrassed silence and your enemies jeering.

I am not afraid of *Time* or lies or losing money or defeat.

In the final analysis I can't carry any of the burdens you talked of—so I know it's only *your* choice. But I know you are as brave as any of the thirty-five.

I love you always.

Bird[64]

"In a few words," Johnson later maintained, crediting Lady Bird with his reversal, "she hit me on two most sensitive and compelling points, telling me what I planned to do would be wrong for my country and that it would show a lack of courage on my part."[65] But something more than a note from his wife was involved in this decision; the situation bears the marks of what Freud has called "the repetition compulsion," which leads an individual to unconsciously arrange for variations of an original theme that he has not learned either to overcome or to live with. Like the child who repeatedly flings his toys into the corner when his mother leaves in the morning only to retrieve them in the afternoon as a way of "making her" come back, so Johnson, when he felt that he was losing hold, typically issued and then retrieved statements of withdrawal, as he did, for example, shortly before his election to the Senate—thereby mastering what seemed at first an unbearable situation. By escaping and returning, if only in fantasy, Johnson could reassert his personal and political autonomy; and thereby seem to himself the determining force of his own destiny.

Having reconfirmed his desire to run, on the next day Johnson summoned Humphrey to his office. He wanted both Humphrey and Dodd to fly with him to Atlantic City. His plan was to keep up the suspense for one more day, so that he could make the announcement in person in front of five thousand delegates and a national television audience. But the intoxication of the internal drama of the previous day diminished his self-control. Standing on the runway, minutes before the takeoff, surrounded by reporters, Johnson suddenly took Humphrey by the arm and announced: "I want you to meet the next Vice President of the United States."

Atlantic City in August, 1964, was, as Johnson said in his

memoirs, a "place of happy, surging crowds and thundering cheers. To a man as troubled as I was by party and national divisions, this display of unity was welcome indeed.... As I stood there warmed by the waves of applause that rolled in on us, touched to the heart by the display of affection, I could only hope that this harmonious spirit would endure times of trouble and discouragement as well."[66]

In the months before the conventions, it seemed almost inconceivable that Lyndon Johnson's shining political prospects could be improved—until the Republicans nominated Barry Goldwater. For any Democratic candidate, at any time, the candidacy of a Republican from the right wing of the party would have presented an unusual opportunity. For John Kennedy's successor in 1964, in an atmosphere permeated with a desire for continuity, Goldwater's nomination made a Johnson landslide inevitable. Johnson was urged by most of his advisers to conduct a low-key campaign. But the man who had been haunted for years by his first senatorial margin of eighty-seven votes wanted, not just any landslide, but the largest landslide in history. He wanted to prove that he was loved. Moreover, to sit in the Oval Office during the campaign for his own election as President, knowing victory was certain, would have required him to subdue every impulse of his restless nature. So Johnson began what one observer has called "the most peripatetic campaign in the history of the Republic. Eighteen hours a day ... twenty speeches a week ... motorcades ... dinners ... handshakes. Andy Jackson in a jetliner."[67]

The contours of the campaign exactly fit Lyndon Johnson's personality. When in the White House, he could project his presidential image, serenely coping with the business of the nation and the world, acting the nonpolitical administrator. On the stump, raw and natural, casting away prepared texts, forgetting the lessons of elocution, Johnson gesticulated wildly, shouting out the plain, blunt idiom of everyday America. Reaching out to touch and feel, Johnson recreated with the many an air of intimacy resembling the one he had once shared with the few in the corridors of the U.S. Senate. By focusing his gaze on one friendly face and knowing that this face represented most of the crowd, Johnson conquered his fear of large numbers. Gone was the stilted Southern preacher; here was a Southern rouser. The crowds, infused by the vigor and the sheer power of his performance, reacted with spontaneous enthusiasm.

Johnson was jubilant. The fall of 1964 seemed to him a perfect Indian summer, a moment of golden health and personal satisfaction when everything went exactly as planned. All Johnson's youth and political life had been spent in reconciling conflict; the desire for personal synthesis had lent momentum to the development of his consensual skills. Now with the candidacy of Barry Goldwater, these skills and this talent would become the central element in the 1964 campaign.

The campaign allowed Johnson to pursue his candidacy in the terms of his favorite political choice: the philosophy of consensus or the philosophy of extremism. The one, he believed, was rooted in the American way; it rested on the belief that all interests could be conciliated by persuasion and satisfied by compromise. The other was rooted in a belief hostile to American values and experience—that some conflicts were irreconcilable and could be resolved only by the total defeat of one or more contending powers. The philosophy that Johnson represented—the philosophy of progress and construction—had yielded, he told his audience, "a generation of democracy, social security, minimum wage and strong unions." "Where'd we be," he asked, "if the other—the philosophy of opposition and destruction—had prevailed? The wrecker can wreck in a day what it takes years for the builder to build. . . . And if the only choice before us is between surrender and nuclear war, then we'll all be dead."[68]

Through September and into October, Johnson remained in an expansive mood. Because the polls showed that his majority was overwhelming, it was unnecessary for Johnson to do what he never did well—to engage his opponent. Never in his life had Johnson fought a partisan campaign; politics in Texas had made this possible. Now Barry Goldwater was making possible a presidential campaign in which Johnson could run for peace, harmony, and prosperity, and the voters would gratefully accept his generalities—although television spots (in which Johnson did not appear) levied harsh assaults against Goldwater, even implying that his election would mean nuclear war.

Then came the only cloud of the entire campaign. On October 14 the news media picked up the fact, until then unknown to Johnson, that the week before Walter Jenkins had been arrested in the men's room at the YMCA for "disorderly conduct." The Special Assistant to the President of the United States had been found engaging in homosexual activity with a sixty-year-old veteran who lived in an old-soldiers' home. Moreover, the media had discovered that Jenkins had been arrested on the same charge in the same washroom five years before.

Johnson heard the news that night in New York City just as he was about to make a speech on foreign policy. His first reaction was shock. He denied the story, substituting for it a conspiratorial theory of his own. "I couldn't have been more shocked about Walter Jenkins if I'd heard that Lady Bird had killed the Pope. It just wasn't possible. And then I started piecing things together. The Republicans believed that the question of morality was their trump card. This was their only chance at winning; anyone who got in the way wound up as corpses. Well, the night of October 7, the night of the arrest, I had been invited to a party given by *Newsweek* which had been owned by Phil Graham, my good friend, who had told Kennedy to make me Vice President. I couldn't go, so I asked Walter to go in my place. Now the waiters at the party were from the Republican National Committee and I know Walter had one drink and started on another and doesn't remember anything after that. So that must be the explanation."[69]

Whether Johnson actually believed his own statement here is questionable, but his overreaction to the question of homosexuality and his fantasy of conspiracy testify to the disturbance he must have felt. He was also disturbed—and pained—at the recognition that this had been Jenkins' way of committing political suicide. Overworked, tense, and exhausted, Jenkins was, as one of Johnson's aides put it, "a desperate man seeking a way out of the kind of life he had been living."[70]

Johnson's second reaction was caution. Before making a statement he wanted to gauge the impact of the incident on public opinion and to determine whether the national security was in any way involved. Lady Bird, however, did not wait for politics. She issued a statement at once filled with compassion and love: "My heart is aching today for someone who has reached the end point of exhaustion in dedicated service to his country."[71]

In the span of seventy hours after the Jenkins story hit the papers, the Labour Party won the national election in Britain for the first time in thirteen years and China exploded its first nuclear bomb—events which dominated the front pages. The Jenkins incident faded swiftly, and the campaign continued on course.

Yet Mrs. Johnson's sadness over the fate of Walter Jenkins remained. "Today is our 30th wedding anniversary," she wrote weeks later in her diary. "But in spite of that a curious pall of sadness and inertia, a feeling of having come to a standstill and being bound up in gloom, which has enshrouded me for several days, does not abate. . . . In the afternoon I went out to see Marjorie and Walter Jenkins, who are going home to Texas. It was a strange hour—very much the same, and very different. To me, Walter is as much a casualty of the incredible hours and burdens he has carried in government service as a soldier in action."[72]

Lady Bird's reaction to Jenkins was characteristic. "If President Johnson was the long arm," Liz Carpenter wrote, "Lady Bird Johnson's was the gentle hand,"[73] often softening the hurts her husband inflicted on the members of his staff, mediating quarrels between aides, and winning over her husband's opponents. "People often compared her to Mrs. Roosevelt," Liz Carpenter continued. "While she admired Mrs. Roosevelt greatly, she was very different. Mrs. Roosevelt was an instigator, an innovator, willing to air a cause without her husband's endorsement. Mrs. Johnson was an implementer and translator of her husband and his purposes . . . a WIFE in capital letters."[74]

Yet if her main role was one of complementing her husband, Lady Bird Johnson also developed a few important projects of her own. She became an active champion of highway beautification; she used the White House as a forum for bringing the issue of the environment to national attention; she created the First Lady's Committee for a More Beautiful Capital: the many new gardens and flowers along the streets of Washington today remain a daily testament to Lady Bird Johnson's life and work. And whatever her feelings about the painful aspects of public life, and the burdens of campaigning, she always remained by her husband's side—indeed, her whistle-stop tour through the South in the 1964 campaign proved an enormous success.

On election day Johnson flew to Austin; he wanted to be home to hear the results. "It seems to me tonight," he said to one friend, "that I have spent my whole life getting ready for this moment."[75] By the time the last poll had closed, Johnson had gathered what was, until then, the greatest popular majority in history. And his margin in the electoral college, 486–52, had been exceeded only once in the twentieth century—by Franklin Roosevelt. He carried every state in the North, the Midwest, the Far West, and, excepting Goldwater's native Arizona, the entire Southwest. And in the South, the only area of the country where Goldwater had substantial support, Johnson still carried six of the eleven states.

"It was," Johnson later recalled, "a night I shall never forget. Millions upon millions of people, each one marking my name on their ballot, each one wanting me as their President. . . . For the first time in all my life I truly felt loved by the American people."[76] Once again the same expression: the connection of votes and love.

Chapter 8

The Great Society

In the spring of 1964, only four months after he had become President, Lyndon Johnson had spoken at the campus of the University of Michigan, and there he sketched the outlines for a program intended to go beyond the "Kennedy legacy"—one that would be his creation, his gift, and the monument to his leadership. In that address he spoke of a "Great Society"—a phrase used a few times before, but at Ann Arbor for the first time given substantial content and thus, by inference, intended as history's label for his administration.

Even now when commentators discuss the Great Society, they concentrate on programs for the relief of poverty, help to education, etc.—measures, in the New Deal tradition, for the just distribution of rising abundance. And, in fact, most of the specific proposals that Johnson was to advance were directed toward just such ends. The concept itself, however, as described at Ann Arbor, and as elaborated in a remarkable series of speeches and messages to Congress over the next eighteen months, rejected national wealth and personal income as ends in themselves. "The challenge of the next half century," Johnson said, "is whether we have the wisdom to use that wealth to enrich and elevate our national life," to prevent "old values" from being "buried under unbridled growth." A rising Gross National Product and full employment would not by themselves create a civilization "where leisure is a welcome chance to build and reflect, not a feared cause of boredom and restlessness ... where the city of man serves not only the needs of the body and the demands of commerce but the desire for beauty and the hunger for community ... where men are more concerned with the quality of their goals than the quantity of their goods ... where the demands of morality, and the needs of the spirit, can be realized in the life of the nation."[1]

These gigantic aspirations—although clearly unattainable within one Presidency, or one generation—were not, however, intended merely as rhetorical exhortation. They expressed Johnson's intention to embark on a mammoth program of social reform. The climate that made it possible for a President to adopt such large ambitions and to succeed in enacting so many of his proposals was the product of converging historical circumstances. The shock of Kennedy's death, the civil rights movement, an emerging awareness of the extent and existence of poverty, a reduction of threatening tensions between the United States and the Soviet Union, all helped Americans to focus public energies and perceptions on the problems of their own country. More important was the deepening confidence that sustained economic growth, steadily increasing affluence seemed now an enduring and irreversible reality of American life. Therefore the problem was no longer simply the creation of wealth—that would continue—but how best to apply our riches to the improvement of American life.

Moreover, the Great Society was a response to—indeed, part of—gradually emerging currents in American awareness—the sense that we were losing control of our own society, that the means we had devised to create wealth had consequences that were beginning to threaten and degrade humanity. Along with the civil rights and peace movements came consumerism, environmentalism, and women's liberation, all protests against the system, not just for its economic deficiencies, but at its constriction of the possibilities for human fulfillment.

Thus a multitude of changing conditions and attitudes conspired to convince a President who was bent on achievements that would leave his mark on the country's history that the Great Society was not a utopian vision, but the inevitable direction for progressive action. Indeed, without this conviction neither the concept nor the many successful efforts of implementation would ever have come from the White House. For political leaders in a democracy are not revolutionaries or leaders of creative thought. The best of them are those who respond wisely to changes and movements already under way. The worst, the least successful, are those who respond badly or not at all, and those who misunderstand the direction of already visible change.

As the full scope of Johnson's ambitions gradually became

apparent, public reaction seemed to demonstrate that he had accurately perceived the national will. Political leaders and men of independent influence—from Martin Luther King to Henry Luce—praised his program for the country. His landslide election in 1964 appeared to constitute popular approval and a mandate to proceed. And opinion polls confirmed what most men already knew: the people were pleased with their President and shared his confidence in the almost limitless capacity of the American nation. During 1964 and 1965, however, Johnson's virtuoso performance obscured the fact that all his achievements depended upon this essential harmony between his acts and popular desires; that without that all his skills and energies would have been futile, would have been, in Blake's words, throwing "sand against the wind."

There were then few critics to claim that the Great Society was a mistake or a fraud, that the nation was being misled by unfulfillable promises, that unreal expectations might stir up irrational discontent. And those who voiced such apprehensions went unheard. In his Inaugural Address, Johnson declaimed: "Is our world gone? We say farewell. Is a new world coming? We welcome it, and we will bend it to the hopes of man."[2] Few censured this arrogance, which was, after all, consistent with the strain of limitless faith in American possibilities that had been a national characteristic from the beginning.

Thus, in the first years of Johnson's Presidency, as twice before in the twentieth century—during the New Freedom and the New Deal—special circumstances produced a blend of interests, needs, convictions, and alliances powerful enough to go beyond the normal pattern of slow, incremental change. But if the resources of change were provided by the circumstances, Lyndon Johnson played the dominant role—as Wilson and Roosevelt had before him—in transforming opportunity into achievement. His formidable presence seemed to infuse all the decisions of government, and he exacted a compliance from Congress unprecedented since the beginning of the New Deal. Yet the perception of Johnson—one that was accurate and that he encouraged—as the gargantuan manipulator, the tireless practitioner of political skills, submerged awareness of another quality that contributed to his effectiveness: his own belief, and his need to believe, in limitless possibilities for the achievement of common purposes that would serve the welfare of every citizen. Even after failure and rejection, until the end he retained this belief. At the ranch in 1970, referring to criticism of what was termed "guns and butter," he affirmed: "We have enough to do it all. . . . We're the wealthiest nation in the world. And I cannot see why, if we have the will to do it, we can't provide for our own happiness, education, health, and environment. There are no controls now and everyone's a little selfish; there's no jawboning any more and big business wants to get everything out of our hide, and the worker, too, like dogs chasing their tails. We need to appeal to everyone to restrain their appetite. We're greedy but not short on the wherewithal to meet our problems."[3]

The election of 1964 had given an independent legitimacy to his Presidency, his own ambitions and intentions detached from any responsibility for another's legacy. This enabled him to accelerate and more openly express his uniquely personal influence over the conduct of national affairs.

For the five years between 1963 and 1968 Lyndon Johnson dominated public life as almost no one before him. Even under Roosevelt there had been room for a varied, often colorful, cast of officials—men of independent stature who often asserted their clashing views to press and public rather than concealing them in "eyes only" memoranda, individuals who acquired a significant public identity and, sometimes, a public following: Hugh Johnson and Jesse Jones, Henry Stimson and Henry Wallace, the "Whiz Kids" and the "braintrusters." Under Johnson there was no one, except, of course, Robert Kennedy, an exception Johnson's mind experienced as a serious threat.

In the first two years of his Presidency Johnson seemed to be everywhere—calling for new programs and for action on the old, personally organizing his shifting congressional majorities, signing bills, greeting tourists, settling labor disputes, championing the blacks, constantly on the telephone to publishers, businessmen, astronauts, farm leaders, in a working day that began at 7 A.M. when he watched, simultaneously, the morning shows of all three networks and that ended sometime in the early hours of the next morning. The pulling of his beagle's ears and the exposure of his abdominal scars became subjects of national discussion, evoking emotions and argument ordinarily reserved for more portentous matters.

In Washington itself Johnson's personality and conduct were the unavoidable topic of continual discussion. "Under

Kennedy it used to be ideas," remarked a columnist's wife, explaining why her dinner party guests had spent the entire evening gossiping about Johnson. "Now it is Lyndon Johnson's personality." Washington became, as one reporter described it, "obsessed by its President." Everything seemed to orbit about this compelling man who seemed to have an endless capacity to dominate every setting. Diplomats, reporters, and administrators alike, whether admiring or repelled, were all fascinated by the baffling ambivalence of Johnson's behavior: the mixture of primitive conduct with the exercise of imperial power, the commingling of cruelty and compassion, the suggestion of a wildness not fully tamed.

Lyndon Johnson was not a man who looked upon the acquisition of power and position as an end in itself. The reality and scale of power were defined by the extent to which it influenced or dominated behavior and conditions external to the man of authority. Since in the Presidency, as in every position of authority that he had held, Lyndon Johnson's ambitions were not confined by lack of confidence in his capacities, it was inevitable that he would want his administration to outdo all others in achievement. His concept of achievement was derived from the New Deal and Roosevelt—which dominated the formative years of his public life—and from those influences and conflicts of his childhood that had brought him to equate achievement with fulfilling the needs and expectations of others, a purpose whose nobility was not impaired by his belief that such accomplishments also strengthened the authority of the man who had achieved them.

Among Johnson's greatest satisfactions as a Congressman had been bringing electricity to the Pedernales Valley. Now as he looked at maps of the country, flew over great cities, campaigned in New Hampshire, led a motorcade through Los Angeles, he could envisage new houses, new shops and roads; community organizations being formed in churches and schools; men and women walking unafraid through the night streets; cities reborn. To Johnson, this meant that he must broaden his goals in proportion to the immense variety of needs and expectations contained within this constituency. He could no longer find satisfaction in his capacity to manipulate or influence other individuals or groups to direct their authority to his immediate ends. Responding to the dimensions of

his new office, Johnson became deeply conscious of the effect
he might have on the daily lives of ordinary men and women
for generations to come.

This consciousness of his ability to influence the future
combined with awareness of the past traditions and accomplishments of his office to exercise a large, partially transforming influence on Johnson's long-established conception of
the meaning and nature of his public life. "A President's
hardest task," Johnson said in the State of the Union message
delivered on January 4, 1965, "is not to do what is right but
to know what is right.

> Yet the Presidency brings no special gift of prophecy or
> foresight. You take an oath, you step into an office and
> you must then guide a great democracy. The answer was
> waiting for me in the land where I was born. It was
> once barren land. The angular hills were covered with
> scrub cedar and a few large, live oaks. Little would grow
> in that harsh caliche soil of my country. And each
> spring the Pedernales River would flood our valley. But
> men came and they worked and they endured and they
> built. And tonight that country is abundant, abundant in
> fruit and cattle and goats and sheep and there are
> pleasant homes and lakes and the floods are gone. Why
> did men come to that once-forbidding land? Well, they
> were restless, of course, and they had to be moving on.
> But there was more than that.
> There was a dream—a dream of a place where a free
> man could build for himself and raise his children to a
> better life—a dream of a continent to be conquered, a
> world to be won, a nation to be made. Remembering
> this, I knew the answer. A President does not shape a
> new and personal vision of America. He collects it from
> the scattered hopes of the American past. It existed
> when the first settlers saw the coast of a new world and
> when the first pioneers moved westward. It has guided
> us every step of the way. It sustains every President.[4]

Johnson's ideal—and hence the guide to his ambitions—
was an America in which every person shared in the progress
and the responsibilities of the country. The ideal as abstractly
stated is not novel. But Johnson seemed to mean something
more than equality of opportunity, that no one should be de-

prived of the essentials of a decent life. Everyone should be not only guaranteed an equal chance but insured against the possibility of total defeat. Johnson wanted to give his people everything this principle suggested, and he wanted them to have it at once. There was no justification for delay in providing what had been already denied. And Johnson, never patient in his ambitions, was anxious to hasten the recognition of his administration, along with the acknowledgment of historic leadership that would reward his achievements. Undoubtedly, he also sensed that the mood and circumstances, coupled with the mandate he had just received, created an unusual opportunity for successful action. So the agenda was established; the Great Society would offer something to almost everyone: Medicare for the old, educational assistance for the young, tax rebates for business, a higher minimum wage for labor, subsidies for farmers, vocational training for the unskilled, food for the hungry, housing for the homeless, poverty grants for the poor, clean highways for commuters, legal protection for the blacks, improved schooling for the Indians, rehabilitation for the lame, higher benefits for the unemployed, reduced quotas for the immigrants, auto safety for drivers, pensions for the retired, fair labeling for consumers, conservation for the hikers and the campers, and more and more and more. None of his fellow citizens' desires were, Johnson thought, wholly beyond his ability to satisfy.

Johnson's optimism and energy were accompanied by an intense anxiety that his popular mandate might be swiftly eroded. In January, 1965, the congressional liaison men from all the executive departments were assembled in the Fish Room to hear Johnson explain his rationale for pushing forward on every front at once. "I was just elected President by the biggest popular margin in the history of the country—16 million votes. Just by the way people naturally think and because Barry Goldwater had simply scared hell out of them, I've already lost about three of those sixteen. After a fight with Congress or something else, I'll lose another couple of million. I could be down to 8 million in a couple of months."[5]

Johnson felt that it was necessary to act swiftly, since he could not know how long his consensus would last. The speed with which he sought to define and prescribe for all the deficiencies of a society that was changing in unknown ways shaped both the substance and the style of the Great Society.

In addition, it produced a politics of haste. "Democratic men," Tocqueville observed long ago, "are more apt to complete a number of undertakings in rapidity than to raise lasting monuments of their achievements; they care much more for success than for fame."[6] So it seemed with Lyndon Johnson. While he dreamed of fame, he acted only for success. He shaped the effort to enact his legislative program, not with an eye to the needs of the next generation, but in response to the sensed urgencies of the moment. Every technique reflected the importance being given to movement and speed. While a typical schedule of presidential messages to the Congress consists of one or two a month, in 1965 Johnson transmitted sixty-three separate documents requesting action on a bewildering variety of legislation.

Most of these proposals had been produced by seventeen task forces designated to consider an extensive list of topics, which ranged from transportation and education to Indians and rural development. Consisting mainly of university professors, the task forces were asked to identify the major issues in each area, analyze the most significant problems, and recommend specific programs. Johnson charged the task force members with the responsibility of "developing the most creative and imaginative ideas," believing that he had found a structural format that would produce a flow of brilliantly conceived descriptions and solutions. But the politics of haste also injured the work of the task forces. Much of American liberal thought was in disarray, still seeking to understand and accommodate itself to swiftly changing conditions and attitudes. The formulas of political liberalism, largely derived from the New Deal, were directed at many important and unresolved problems, but there were now other afflictions not yet included in the categories of liberal thought. So long as millions remained in poverty, and large numbers of citizens could not find decent jobs and were denied adequate housing for their families and education for their children, the New Deal's effort to provide basic economic security remained a significant objective of liberal politics. However, it was also true that the economic and political structure that resulted from the New Deal's attempt to restore economic growth and increase prosperity had itself generated a different set of problems: monopoly, bureaucracy, technology, wasteful growth, fragmented social groupings, alienation. There was no established canon of thought for these problems; indeed, there was often little comprehension of—and less agreement on—what the problem was, even whether it was a problem at all. No task force, for example, could have drafted a description of the action necessary to rebuild the central cities, restore the bonds of community, or restructure the nature of work. In many cases, the basic knowledge necessary for the development of a convincingly reasoned analysis did not even exist.

And even in more familiar areas of public policy, the need for haste often resulted in a failure to define the precise nature and requirements of social objectives. Legislative solutions were often devised and rushed into law before the problems were understood. Since time was limited and agreement on ends could be assumed, since surely all reasonable men—especially those likely to be consulted by a liberal Democratic President—favored the elimination of poverty, the expansion of educational opportunity, and improvement in the delivery of medical care, most of the attention was focused on means. Yet it is far from self-evident, for example, what is meant by "educational opportunity," what forms of training are most useful or most desired, whether access to a classroom means access to knowledge. Yet if one fails to examine such questions, then the "expansion of educational opportunity" is necessarily assumed to mean more buildings and teachers, as if putting more money into a poorly conceived system will inevitably make it better.

Pass the bill now, worry about its effects and implementation later—this was the White House strategy. For now, the legislative architects must be guided by the need to design each program in the manner best calculated to attract support so as to make it politically easier for reluctant Congressmen to join with Johnson. The objective was to make laws, not raise problems. How could government best organize itself to implement the Great Society? Were there inadequacies or dangers inherent in trying to solve problems from the center of government? What was the appropriate relationship between different government departments which had responsibilities for programs directed at the same problem? On these, and on other equally significant questions, little time was spent. Discussions in the Cabinet and the White House amounted to little more than rehearsals for the arguments that one could expect from the advocates of "states' rights." There seemed to be few among the principal officers of government who were trying to determine how the programs could be made actually to work. The standard of success was the passage of the law—and not only within the administration, but in the press and among the public. By this standard, the Great Society was on its way to becoming the most successful domestic program in history.

In his determination to get Congress and America moving again, Johnson demanded support for the Great Society and confidence in the capacity of government to improve all the conditions of society as matters of faith. In seeking support for his often embryonic programs, he drew upon the skill of the entrepreneurs who went East in order to persuade people to leave their homes for settlements on the Western frontier. They described Western life in almost imaginary terms: towns were referred to as cities, small colleges described as universities; taverns became hotels; a tent containing rows of benches was transformed into an opera house.[7] Lyndon Johnson was a twentieth-century booster. His object was to persuade others to move, not to the West, but toward an America that was the creation of his own desires and convictions—Johnson's "promised land." The intensity of his own belief strengthened his formidable persuasive powers. It did not seem to matter that in his enthusiasm he sometimes confused the dream with present realities, that he sometimes presented as facts events that had not yet occurred, changes of condition that were still only intentions. In so expansive an era, filled with such benevolent intentions, the boundaries between fact and fiction, between the present and the future, no longer held.

Johnson seemed to regard the programs of the Great Society in the way overly fond parents look at their children. By building on the strengths of prosperity rather than on the necessities of depression, the program of the Great Society would fulfill all the hopes that had been beyond the reach of the New Deal. It would accomplish more for the nation than had the programs of any other administration, compelling history to acknowledge the greatness of its progenitor— greater, perhaps, than the already legendary FDR. In the urgency of his desire to persuade others and, perhaps, to reinforce his own belief, he often spoke of hopes and possibilities as if they were established certainties. "No longer will older Americans be denied the healing miracles of modern medicine," asserted the message on Medicare. Other messages proclaimed "a national war on poverty," whose outcome must inevitably be "total victory." And so it went in message after message. The subjects might change, but the essentials remained the same: in the opening, an expression of dire need; in the middle, a vague proposal; in the end, a buoyant description of the anticipated results—all contained in an analysis presented in a manner that often failed to distinguish between expectations and established realities.

More serious than the exaggerations, and deceptions, and illusory assertions, which were consequence and result of his impatient ambitions, was the failure to acknowledge—in description or in the actual design of programs—many of the most fundamental elements of social problems. Johnson ignored the obstacles to his intentions that were inherent in the distribution and forms of economic power, the force of habit and tradition, the stubborn preference of people for doing things in their own way.

This was less a deception than a consequence of limits to his own perception of the country and of himself. There could be, he believed, no fundamental or impenetrable barriers to changes that would be beneficial to all, and that everyone desired—or would desire—once they understood the purpose and the inevitable consequences of those changes. Nor were there basic elements of design and social process hostile to his objectives. There was almost nothing beyond the practical capacities of a united and determined America. This view of social problems was not uniquely personal, but characteristically American—part of the common wisdom that Americans derived from what appeared to be the self-evident lessons of our historical experience and a native confidence in the irresistible force of practical understanding and action. What was unique to Johnson was the confidence that he possessed powers of will and persuasion which could convince an entire nation that his policies represented the necessary and wisest course toward the kind of America that all should desire. There was much to justify this confidence, but it also made him unable to foresee the possibility of resentment based, not on objections to his social goals or to the practicality of specific measures, but on hostility to the implicit assertion of increased central authority to define the general welfare and confer benevolences which, however desirable in themselves, should not be imposed by presidential will.

However, these flaws were not to appear until later. During 1965 Johnson's faith in the country's ability to heal its afflictions and enrich human life—to build a Great Society—infused his insistent messages and public exhortations. In later years these speeches might seem bombastic or arrogant, but when they were spoken, they had the desired result. The American people were anxious for a renewal of belief, and Johnson was not only a great believer but a great persuader. Indeed, for a brief moment it seemed that this mammoth Texan might be able to impose his personal configuration of the world on an entire society.

Johnson was also the beneficiary of change produced by the presidential institution itself. His authority to formulate the Great Society derived from two decades of institutional development during which the preparation by the executive of a comprehensive legislative program, complete with detailed requests and drafts of bills, had become a routine practice. Patterns established in the New Deal and continued through the postwar decades had modified the previous structure of institutional relationship so that the President was now expected to present a programmatic agenda to the Congress. Indeed, it had become his responsibility to do this. This responsibility and the increased authority it implied had their inception during the Roosevelt Presidency, and were expanded with the development of elaborate and institutionalized methods for formulating and presenting programs—such as the Budget Bureau's requirement that the departments present legislative programs for review, the annual messages, the special messages, the White House briefings, etc.

"The President proposes, the Congress disposes." According to conventional theory, the President takes the lead in setting priorities and offering programs, thus initiating a process which Congress then completes by adjusting, accepting, or rejecting the President's bills. But that was not Lyndon Johnson's theory in the early days of the Great Society. And by ignoring customary functions and roles, he contributed to the scale and the success of his legislative program. He blended and obscured the usual relationship between the President and the Congress, mingling previously distinct functions together until he involved each branch in both proposing and disposing of legislation. He was seeking to fashion an American version of the British parliamentary system, arrogating to himself the role of the British Cabinet—"a hyphen which joins, a buckle which fastens the legislative part of the state to the executive part."[8]

Johnson believed that all legislators were influenced by two emotions, each of which stimulated a different direction for behavior: the desire for recognition and the fear of losing hold. Desire opened the door to the exercise of presidential power; fear closed it. The desire for recognition could persuade a legislator to risk allying himself with the effort to bring about change so that he might receive acknowledgment of his good works. Fear of losing the struggle immobilized him, influencing him to stand pat, to leave things as they were. Johnson's success in winning congressional support for change depended upon his ability to reduce the fear and increase the desire, which, in turn, required him to establish closer ties between the often warring branches. By having Congress participate in the initiation of the programmatic process, Johnson could increase the rewards of recognition. By inserting himself into the traditionally congressional dispositive stages of the process, he could reduce the risk of moving ahead.

"The trick was," Johnson later mused, "to crack the wall of separation enough to give the Congress a feeling of participation in creating my bills without exposing my plans at the same time to advance congressional opposition before they even saw the light of day. It meant taking risks, but the risks were worth it. Legislative drafting is a political art. The President is continually faced with a number of tough choices: how to strike a balance between the bill he really wants and the bill he's got a good chance of getting; how to choose between a single-purpose or omnibus bill; how to package the bill for the Hill, when to send it up. In all these choices the President needs congressional judgment, and if he's wise, he seeks it.

"My experience in the NYA," he recalled, "taught me that when people have a hand in shaping projects, these projects are more likely to be successful than the ones simply handed down from the top. As Majority Leader I learned that the best guarantee to legislative success was a process by which the wishes and views of the members were obtained ahead of time and, wherever possible, incorporated into the early drafts of the bill. As President I went one step further. I insisted on congressional consultation at every single stage, beginning with the process of deciding what problems and issues to consider for my task forces right up to the drafting of the bills."[9]

Each fall, in anticipation of the President's annual program, the White House established task forces to study and define major issues. Perhaps because their subject matter and memberships were kept secret from the public, Johnson managed to persuade selected Senators and Congressmen to serve on these task forces. In so doing, he implicated them in what is generally considered an exclusively executive function. Using the task-force reports as the basis for their work, staff members from the White House, the Bureau of the Budget, and the agencies developed the substantive message in each field. At this stage, Johnson again insisted on congressional participation, and sent his aides to the Hill for secret sessions with key Senators and Congressmen. To consider the provisions of the draft message or bill, they consulted Wilbur Mills on taxes, Warren Magnuson on consumer protection, Robert Kennedy on housing, Edmund Muskie on pollution, and so on. Johnson himself would not approve the draft until the relevant Cabinet member had presented him with a statement that he had carried out the necessary consultations with Congress giving proof that he had done his homework: "I have touched base on this message with the leadership from the Committee on Labor and Public Welfare in the House, where this bill is likely to start; the chairman has polled selected members for their first reactions. The following six are likely to be favorable for these reasons, four are likely to be in opposition. Our answers to the questions of the opposition are ready, our testimony is complete and we are anxious to move." Of course such discussions with members of Congress greatly increased the risk that something would leak to the press. But most of the time, so long as the discussion was prefaced by explaining, "The President hasn't decided to do this, but if he did, how would you respond?" the member of Congress would respect the privacy of the meeting.[10]

Johnson explained: "My father always impressed me with the importance of trying to know whenever you walked into a room where your friends and enemies were standing. These initial checks gave us that knowledge; they gave us an early and quick sense of where our friends and enemies were likely to be found."[11]

More than that, these early checks gave the White House an opportunity to redraft its bills so they would be assigned to different and more favorable committees. This was not always possible, but the staff was instructed to concede the impossibility of avoiding the assignment of a proposal to a committee likely to act unfavorably only after secret consultations with the official parliamentarian and discussions with the President himself.

After all these preparations had been completed, the message was ready for official transmittal. Even at this final moment, however, Johnson insisted on one more step—a White House briefing with congressional leaders, conducted the night before the message was to be sent to the Hill. The briefings generally took the form of dinner meetings in the White House mess, to which Johnson invited the chairmen of the appropriate committee and subcommittee, the party leadership, and other legislators who were likely to be influential on this particular issue. At such meetings, Cabinet members, together with the White House staff, would review the contents of the message, provide background information, clarify language, and answer questions.

"Everyone thinks it was simply crises or assassinations that produced legislation. No one knows about the hundreds or more briefing sessions we conducted for Congressmen and Senators. That's what did it. It's all in my diary. I'd do it like the British system. It was my version of the question period—an opportunity for the members of Congress to get an advance look at my documents and then to confront my Cabinet members with all sorts of questions. Allowing some to receive an advance look the night before may seem like nothing, but, in fact, it was everything. It gave the chosen ones—between the charts and the tables and the answers to their questions—a knowledgeable understanding of what often turned out to be complex legislation. This understanding put them in good shape the next day when reporters and cameramen began pounding the Hill for reactions. The ones who had been at the briefing had their thoughts in order; they made the best statements on the 6 P.M. news. They looked smart before their constituents and that made an enormous difference in their attitude toward the bill."[12]

By insisting on White House briefings, Johnson was applying a lesson he had learned as a freshman Congressman. He described the experience in his memoirs:

> I was standing in the back of the House behind the rail as Speaker Sam Rayburn listened to the House clerk read an important new administration message President

Roosevelt had just sent to the Hill. Several dozen Democrats were gathered around him. As he finished, a unanimous chorus of complaints rushed forth: "Why, that message is terrible, Mr. Sam—we can't pass that." . . . "That last suggestion is awful." . . . "Why in the world did you let the President send one up like that?" . . . "Why didn't you warn us?"

Speaker Rayburn listened to all the criticisms and then responded softly: "We'll just have to look at it more carefully. That's all I can say now, fellows. We'll have to look at it more carefully." The crowd scattered. Mr. Sam and I were left alone in the back. I could see that something was wrong. "If only," he said, "the President would let me know ahead of time when these controversial messages are coming up. I could pave the way for him. I could create a base of support. I could be better prepared for criticism. I could get much better acceptance in the long run. But I never know when the damned messages are coming. This last one surprised me as much as it did all of them." He shook his head sadly and walked slowly away.

I could see that his pride was hurt. So was the President's prestige and the administration's program. I never forgot that lesson.[13]

When particularly sensitive matters were involved, Johnson often conducted his own one-to-one briefings, in person and on the phone wielding the same skills that had served him at all stages of his career: knowledge of the levers of power—personal and institutional—over each particular matter, the capacity to understand the motives and vulnerabilities of others and how best to approach them. The technique imposed towering demands upon his energy; he had to know how much to involve which members of Congress in what bill, selecting for each member the kind of participation that promised him the greatest reward, deciding where to draw the line in order to avoid the kind of overinvolvement that might expose his program to crippling opposition in advance. And he had to know these things himself, directly, from face-to-face talks, because only Johnson was in contact with all the varied groups and subgroups in both Congress and the administration. He alone could know the full implications and possible consequences of decisions in the conduct of relations with Congress. Johnson's methods for implicating the Congress in the traditionally executive function of initiating legislation would have been hard and completely consuming work for any man. Yet they comprised only one-half of his approach to Capitol Hill. The other half—inserting himself deeply and systematically into the traditionally legislative function of enacting legislation—proved even more demanding of his time, energy, and skill.

Other Presidents had paid close attention to the Congress, but the scope and intensity of Lyndon Johnson's participation in the legislative process were unprecedented. He began with an inherited liaison staff, headed by Larry O'Brien. John Kennedy's liaison operation had been organized to provide consistent, orderly attention to the legislators on the Hill. It could provide legislators with invitations to White House dinners and ceremonies, advance notification of federal contracts, detailed data about a bill's effects, campaign help from the Democratic National Committee, and birthday notes from the President. Many carrots and a few sticks, these were the tools of O'Brien's men. And they had learned to manipulate them with increasing skill. As one who worked for both Kennedy and Johnson as a congressional aide described it: "The first couple of years were the years of learning. It takes time to learn the men and to understand the process. It takes time to build the links. In 1965, we were beginning to come into our own. In fact, if we had known in 1961 what we knew in 1965, we might have had far greater success in securing the passage of the bills John Kennedy wanted so much. But all that is impossible speculation. What is more important is the fact that when Lyndon Johnson came to us for help we were ready to provide it."[14]

Using many of the same men Kennedy had used, Johnson created the most successful liaison staff in the history of the Presidency. He expanded the range of its duties and the depth of its involvement, and participated constantly and personally in its work.

"There is," Johnson later explained, "but one way for a President to deal with the Congress, and that is continuously, incessantly, and without interruption. If it's really going to work, the relationship between the President and the Congress has got to be almost incestuous. He's got to know them even better than they know themselves. And then, on the basis of this knowledge, he's got to build a system that stretches from the cradle to the grave, from the moment a bill is introduced to the moment it is officially enrolled as the law of the land."[15]

Congress has the formal power to decide which bills to consider in what sequence. As a practical matter, however, the President can shape the legislative calendar by the order and the pace of the messages he sends to the Hill. Johnson offered the following account: "A measure must be sent to the Hill at exactly the right moment and that moment depends on three things: first, on momentum; second, on the availability of sponsors in the right place at the right time; and third, on the opportunities for neutralizing the opposition. Timing is essential. Momentum is *not* a mysterious mistress. It is a controllable fact of political life that depends on nothing more exotic than preparation."[16]

Even before his staff had completed the final draft of a message, Johnson personally decided who should introduce it in the House and the Senate. This was a delicate, dangerous business. Custom did not easily sanction White House interference in the internal operations of congressional committees. But since the fate of many a proposal depended on the intellectual capacity and personal force of its sponsor, Johnson was willing to run the risk. On several important bills, he directly sought out the sponsors he wanted—among them, Phil Landrum, the conservative Georgian, for the poverty program; and the Senator from rural Maine, Edmund Muskie, for Model Cities. While these preparations were going on, the White House staff worked with committee staffs to schedule hearings and to draw up lists of potential witnesses so that, if possible, Johnson could simultaneously announce the introduction of a program and the start of hearings on the 6 P.M. network news.

Maximum attention in minimum time was also Johnson's way to avoid what he looked upon as Congress' congenital disease, its tendency to bog down. And in 1965 immobility and inertia were among the principal obstacles to success in his legislative struggles. The battles began with Medicare and education.

Johnson's decision to push for health and education legislation ahead of housing proposals and the granting of home rule to the District of Columbia resulted from his carefully considered judgment as to the amount of time each of the bills would consume and which measures were most likely to provoke the kind of debate and controversy that would drain valuable energy. Recognizing that John Kennedy had lost a full legislative year in pursuit of federal aid to education, Lyndon Johnson refused to let the education bill go to the Congress until administration officials had secured the agreement of two major lobbying groups—the National Education Association, which spoke for the public schools, and the National Catholic Welfare Conference, which represented parochial schools. The seemingly irreconcilable conflict between these lobbies had been largely responsible for the earlier failure to pass an education bill. Now an agreement was fashioned by means of an ingenious formula by which assistance would go, not to the schools, but to impoverished children, whether they attended P.S. 210 or St. Joseph's. Immediately thereafter the President dispatched the program to the Hill, and within four months the Elementary and Secondary Education Act was the law of the land.

"In some ways," Johnson confided, "Congress is like a dangerous animal that you're trying to make work for you. You push him a little bit and he may go just as you want but you push him too much and he may balk and turn on you. You've got to sense just how much he'll take and what kind of mood he's in every day. For if you don't have a feel for him, he's liable to turn around and go wild. And it all depends on your sense of timing."[17]

Johnson's sense of timing told him that after the struggle over the Civil Rights Act of 1964, 1965 was not a propitious year to press for more civil rights proposals. He felt that the American people wanted an intermission, a period without renewed conflict, in order to assimilate the political and social impact of the earlier bill. The agencies involved in matters of civil rights wanted time for orderly incorporation of the new people and bureaus and their new responsibilities. The Congress wanted time to heal the wounds of division. Though, in January, 1965, Johnson directed Attorney General Nicholas Katzenbach to begin the complicated task of preparing legislation to protect the voting rights of black Americans, no action was expected until the spring of 1966. Then came Selma, and everything changed. Responding to his own need for continuing action and momentum in order to sustain support for the civil rights movement and for his leadership, Martin Luther King initiated an all-out drive for Negro registration by leading a protest march from Selma,

Alabama, to Montgomery on March 7, 1965. When Governor Wallace sent state police against the marchers, the televised scenes of unarmed blacks being brutally whipped with billy clubs aroused many people in the country. Demonstrations multiplied, and there was massive pressure on Johnson to protect the marchers by mobilizing the National Guard.

But Johnson refused to be pushed. Pickets surrounded the White House, carrying placards calculated to shame him into action: "LBJ, open your eyes, see the sickness of the South, see the horrors of your homeland." Telegrams and letters demanding action streamed into the President's office. Still, Johnson held back, fearing, as he described it in his memoirs, "that a hasty display of federal force at this time could destroy whatever possibilities existed for the passage of voting rights legislation," knowing that "such action would play into the hands of those looking for a states' rights martyr in Governor Wallace."[18] It was, in retrospect, a brilliant move. In the middle of the turmoil, Wallace requested a meeting with the President, who granted the request at once. In the Oval Office, they discussed the question of troops. Johnson appealed to the large ambition and the populist strain that he perceived in Wallace: How could there be any fixed limits, he suggested, to the political career of the first Southern governor to combine economic and social reform with racial harmony? Why not Wallace? The talk lasted three hours; afterward, Wallace was reported to have said: "If I hadn't left when I did, he'd have had me coming out *for* civil rights."[19]

Two days later, when Johnson finally sent troops to Alabama, the act was generally regarded, not as an imperious imposition of federal power, but as a necessary measure to prevent further violence. By waiting out his critics and letting the TV clips make their own impression on the country, he had succeeded in persuading most of the country that he had acted reluctantly and out of necessity, not because he was anxious to use federal power against a guilty South. Then, once the Justice Department had finished drafting a Voting Rights Act, he presented the bill in a speech to a joint session of the Congress conducted during the prime evening viewing hours of the television networks, all of which covered the President's address. With this event, Johnson gave his fellow citizens a specific outlet for inchoate emotion and assured himself of irresistible support for his next, and now become urgent, civil rights program.

The speech was Lyndon Johnson at his best—homely, compassionate, audacious, and noble—a hard practical appeal and a strong moral statement. "I speak tonight," Johnson began, "for the dignity of man and the destiny of democracy. . . . At times history and fate meet at a single time in a single place to shape a turning point in man's unending search for freedom. . . . So it was a century ago at Appomattox. So it was last week in Selma, Alabama. . . . There is no constitutional issue here. The command of the Constitution is plain. There is no moral issue. It is wrong . . . to deny any of your fellow Americans the right to vote. . . . This time, on this issue, there must be no delay, no hesitation, and no compromise with our purpose. . . . What happened in Selma is part of a far larger movement which reaches into every section and state of America. It is the effort of American Negroes to secure for themselves the full blessings of American life. Their cause must be our cause too. Because it is not just Negroes, but really it is all of us who must overcome the crippling legacy of bigotry and injustice."[20]

Here Johnson stopped. He raised his arms and repeated three words from an old Baptist hymn, now the marching song of the civil rights movement: "And . . . we . . . shall . . . overcome." At this moment, as an observer described it, "the whole Chamber was on its feet. . . . In the galleries Negroes and whites, some in the rumpled sports shirts of bus rides from the demonstrations, others in trim professional suits, wept unabashedly."[21]

Then Lyndon Johnson spoke of his own past. He talked of his teaching experience in Cotulla: "Somehow you never forget what poverty and hatred can do when you see its scars on the hopeful face of a young child. I never thought then, in 1928, that I would be standing here in 1965. It never occurred to me in my fondest dreams that I might have the chance to help the sons and daughters of those students and to help people like them all over this country. But now I do have that chance—I'll let you in on a secret—I mean to use it. . . . I do not want to be the President who built empires, or sought grandeur, or extended dominion. I want to be the President who educated young children . . . who helped to feed the hungry . . . who helped the poor to find their own way and who protected the right of every citizen to vote in every election. . . . God will not favor everything we do. It is rather our duty to divine His will. But I cannot help believing that He truly understands and that He really favors the undertaking that we begin tonight."[22]

It had been a summons and a sermon. It had been that rare thing in politics, rarer still for Lyndon Johnson—a speech that shaped the course of events. For once, Americans would honor him for a greatness of spirit as well as a mastery of technique. For on this issue he was more than a giver of gifts; he had become a moral leader.

During the years of Johnson's Presidency a cruel joke was often heard at Washington dinner tables, the raconteur first carefully determining that no one present had loyal access to the White House. Johnson, the story went, dismissed his Secret Service guards, got into his car, drove to a distant and deserted corner of his ranch, got out, looked carefully around, and then, throwing up his head, at the top of his lungs shouted "Nigger!" The story always got a laugh, for many reasons, but chiefly because it was difficult for many to accept the sincerity of his dedication to civil rights, believing it, at best, a sudden conversion stimulated by the political necessities of winning and then holding presidential office. But as time passed, and I listened, talked, and learned, it became clear that in this, as in Vietnam, Johnson was a true believer, although with a far more lucid sense of the human and political realities. For these were people, the blacks and their white adversaries, whom he knew and had dealt with, whose variety of circumstance and opinion he had perceived through his own senses.

"I never had any bigotry in me," he explained much later. "My daddy wouldn't let me. He was a strong anti-Klansman. He wouldn't join the Methodists. The Klan controlled the state when I was a boy. They threatened to kill him several times."[23] Perhaps coincidentally, the assignment which began the "domestic operations division" of the FBI—ordered by Lyndon Johnson in September of 1964—was to infiltrate and disrupt the Ku Klux Klan. Moreover, the outward manifestations of racism—segregation, violence, condescension—had not been part of Lyndon Johnson's youthful experiences, as they were for so many other Southerners. For there were no blacks in Blanco County, and not many in his congressional district.

"In the middle thirties we didn't know Lyndon Johnson

from Adam," recounted a venerable and distinguished Negro leader, describing the period when Johnson had directed the NYA in Texas. "We began to get word up here that there was one NYA director who wasn't like the others. He was looking after Negroes and poor folks and most NYA people weren't doing that."[24] Johnson did put together special NYA programs for the black young, often financed by secret transfers of money from other projects that had been approved at upper levels of the bureaucracy.

"We had to use most of our money for wages," Johnson explained, describing one of the less clearly illegal among his techniques, "the rest for equipment, shovels, etc., and nothing for fancy things like dormitories. What I did was go around and get people to donate money for the equipment in the white areas and then apply that saving to Prairie View [a project location for Negro youth] and use it to build dorms which they so badly needed. I'd stop over there to see how they were doing, on my way to the Houston office. Stayed overnight, ate with them. Well, the day I announced for Congress, which was soon after the funeral of the man who'd had the seat, by the next night the announcement had been in the Sunday papers. Four cars drove up to the apartment where we lived on the second floor, and out tumbled ten to twelve Negroes. They said they'd come to let me know that they'd find every Negro in my district and make sure they voted for me."[25]

We have seen that in the late forties and early fifties Johnson felt it necessary to consolidate his strength among his new constituency: one far more conservative and racist than his congressional district had been. In those years he avoided being identified with the cause of civil rights. Yet one must also remember that, in the same period, the cause of black Americans had few champions among white politicians. Harry Truman integrated the armed forces, which, under Roosevelt, separate and unequal, had fought World War II. But with that single exception, no important steps were taken to improve the conditions of black Americans. Indeed, the issue was barely an issue, rarely rose to the surface of public debate, and when it did, was formed and fought around issues, such as the poll tax or antilynching, which were purely Southern problems. More fundamental denials of political, legal, and economic equality were neither challenged nor debated. In that period six civil rights bills managed to make it to the floor of Congress; six were defeated.

"In the 1940s and early 1950s," Johnson later explained, "I did vote against the poll tax bill and the antilynching bill. I just never thought it should be the federal government passing the law. Now I did support a constitutional amendment repealing the poll tax, and in fact in the fifties I went around Texas arguing that Texas should repeal its own poll tax. As for lynching, well now, that's murder. You're not going to stop that by passing another law. They simply wanted to put a stain on the South, by implying that Southern lynchings were frequent, which they weren't.

"I'm not prejudiced nor ever was, but I will say that civil rights was not one of my priorities in those days. I had other concerns. My job took me all day. Nor did I have the power to do anything about them but to stand up and sputter out. That'd be nonsense, like swimming one-half the way across a lake or going to Dallas with one-half a tank of gas left, so you'd be left floating in the water or stranded on the road. But all that changed when I became President. Then I had the power and the obligation to do something. Then it did become my personal priority. Then something could happen."[26]

When he finally did become President, when he "had the power and the obligation," then, as he claimed, it did become his personal priority. In speeches, legislation, and continuing proposals, Johnson took the most advanced position on racial issues of any President in American history; appearing at times, ahead of the civil rights movement itself, until, sadly, the war in Vietnam extended its paralyzing hand to this as to his other domestic ambitions.

"Without constant attention from the administration," Johnson argued, "most legislation passes through the congressional process with the speed of a glacier."[27] In each chamber over ten thousand bills are introduced each year. Moreover, legislative activity is just one part of a Congressman's hectic life. Most members of Congress must also oversee the activities of a staff assigned to advise them on issues, write their speeches, answer their mail, and do their case work. In a sense, each Congressman is the proprietor of a small business. In addition, there are lectures to give, partisan obligations to meet, and necessary trips to their home district or state. House members begin campaigning for a next term almost from the time they are elected to their present one. And at any given moment, at least several Senators are using some of their time to run for President, or to think about running. In this context, the White House can perform an invaluable function—one that serves its own interests as well as those of the Congress—simply by helping the legislators focus on the major bills of the President's program. But the White House can do this only to the extent the President is willing to concentrate on the Congress, something which varies with the temperament of the President and the nature of his administration.

In words and deeds, Johnson made known his intention to concentrate on legislation. In his message on the State of the Union, he devoted more than three thousand words to domestic affairs. And more importantly, he committed most of his waking hours to the Great Society. He began and ended each day by reading a substantial amount of material related to the Congress. The *Congressional Record*, clipped and summarized, appeared by his bed at 7:15 A.M. Placed at his bedside at 11 P.M. each night were memos from the staff, which described in detail each of the legislative contacts they had made that day, reported noteworthy conversations with particular members, and called attention to special problems.[28]

Johnson had an impressive capacity to absorb these reports rapidly and in detail so that he was thoroughly prepared for his Tuesday breakfast meetings with the congressional leadership, where the legislative schedule was discussed in great detail. At these meetings Johnson stood beside an immense chart that rested on an easel in the corner of the room. There he went over the diagrams of the chart, which showed the course of each of his bills: which were still in subcommittee, which were ready for the mark-up, and which were ready for consideration on the floor. The chart, which seemed to accompany Johnson everywhere, was also used to prod the members of his Cabinet, allowing him to request or demand explanations from the Secretaries whose departmental legislation was shown to be lagging. In 1965—before Vietnam became the central concern—the major item on the agenda of every Cabinet meeting was "pending legislation." At least half of every Cabinet meeting that year was devoted to individual reports by each of the Secretaries on the progress of his legislative program.

After reviewing the latest chart, Johnson focused the Cabinet meeting on the major bills. The White House staff reported the results of the latest head count. The report was divided into five categories: right, probably right, uncommitted, probably wrong, and wrong. It also included richly descriptive material about the status of each member's position. The Congressman from New York's 5th District "is all for it but can't stay with us unless the New York delegation votes for it as well"; the Congressman from Nevada "campaigned last time against this and probably will have to honor that commitment": the Congressman from the 3rd District in Massachusetts "is absolutely right and doesn't want to be bothered again"; the Junior Senator from California "will catch an early plane to avoid a negative vote if necessary"; the Senior Senator from Oregon "will vote for it if needed but hopes we can spare him on this one"; the Congressman from Ohio's 1st District "will go with us only if an amendment on local control is included": the Congressman from Pennsylvania "is owned body and soul by his local paper; our only way to get to him is to get to the publisher"; the Senior Senator from Louisiana "is immune to pressure from anyone except the President"; the Senator from Idaho "is uncommitted but leaning wrong"; the Senior Senator from New York "could vote for it but only after the New York primary"; the Congressman from South Dakota "is uncommitted but leaning wrong, he will listen only to the National Farmers Union on this one"; the Junior Senator from Illinois "will stay with us provided no softening amendments are added." And on it went.[29]

The central question that these tallies were designed to resolve was whether the administration could win on the floor with the legislation that had come out of committee. The validity of that judgment depended on the accuracy with which the views and positions of the members had been assessed. And the ability to make accurate assessments required both knowledge and trust. If a liaison man knew his contacts well, he could determine their initial reaction in a simple meeting or phone call: if he did not, he might be unable to interpret critical subtleties of expression, nuance, and timing. If the bill being discussed seemed in trouble, Johnson began to consider the possibility of amendments that might increase support. "What," he would ask, "are we willing to concede on this one in order to salvage the bill? What do you say? How do you feel? Well, if we take that amendment, how many votes will it produce? What evidence do you have for that figure? What would you say?" Round and round he went until necessary decisions were made.

In the House, the Democratic leadership was working with the strongest majority in several decades—a total of 295 members. Although this made a tremendous difference in the substance of the legislation passed and the number of amendments that were needed, the process of decision was the same as it would be in subsequent years when the Democrats would have smaller majorities. Henry Hall Wilson, chief administration lobbyist for seven years, makes this point explicitly: "When we have a fat Congress as we did in the Eighty-ninth, then we can hike up our demands to fit the situation. When the votes are not razor thin in either case, then we are not doing a good job."[30]

Wilson's exposition reflected Lyndon Johnson's own view that the task was to push each Congress to its limits, to obtain the maximum legislative output that any particular Congress could be made to produce. Thus slim margins were expected and, indeed, planned for. But this approach often required interpretation by the President to restrain the natural congressional tendency to make legislative compromises when the forces are closely divided. On such matters, as the moment of decision nears, concessions are often made even though they are not necessary to passage. "It was my job," Johnson later explained, "to hold the line on the final stretch."[31] How Johnson held the line in that final stretch was, and will undoubtedly continue to be, a subject of continual discussion and conjecture. The popular image at the time—reflected most sharply in the cartoons of Herblock and Al Capp—was of a giant, forbidding figure roaming back and forth between the White House and the Congress, slapping backs, twisting arms, trading dams. In fact, the process was more subtle and less colorful. Once again, it required an accurate sense of timing and substantial preparation. In the first place, Johnson became involved only after a long winnowing process had taken place. He was the ultimate weapon, kept in reserve, to be brought into action only after everything else had failed. Generally, Johnson limited his personal calls to a small number of members who had been identified by White House tallies as among those who were "probably right," "uncommitted," or "probably wrong." He ignored those members who had indicated either strong support or strong opposition to the pending legislation. Within the selected group, Johnson focused his attention on those Senators or Congressmen who could serve as swing votes, influencing others to follow their lead. Before placing his calls, Johnson would study detailed memos prepared by his staff, which indicated the reason for the opposition of a particular Senator or Congressman, what it would take to change him, and what his vulnerabilities might be. Armed with these memos and with his own anatomical knowledge of the states and districts, Johnson proved formidable in personal debate. A freshman Republican, after receiving one such call, said: "It was like talking to my campaign manager—only I wish *he* knew that much."[32] Obviously, the amount of preparation and knowledge required in order to be effective meant that Johnson's interventions had to be limited.

In the second place, the President's contacts rarely involved direct and open "deals." "The reason for this," explained Henry Hall Wilson, "are simply and obvious if you just think about it for a minute. If it ever got around the Hill that a President was trading patronage for votes, then everyone would want to trade and all other efforts at persuasion would automatically fail. Each member would tell his neighbor what he got for his votes and soon everyone would be holding out, refusing to decide until the President called. You can imagine how impossible that would be when I tell you the awful difficulty we had at a much lower level. Johnson had a tendency every now and then whenever he was in a happy mood to pick up the phone and call every Representative who had celebrated a birthday that week. Within five minutes, each of these conversations had spread throughout the Hill, and for weeks the recipients would begin every conversation with 'Now when the President spoke to me about that bill, he said . . .' "[33]

The principle involved here is the well-known danger of rising expectations: "As people become accustomed to a certain level of gratification which they may have initially considered extreme, they come to take it for granted and to expect at least that much gratification from their associations in the future."[34] This is not to say that rewards were never dispensed to faithful Congressmen, nor that sanctions were never imposed on those who opposed the administration's programs. The point is that the carrots and the sticks were dispensed by the White House and the executive branch on the basis of a pattern of support and voting over time, not by the President personally in exchange for a specific vote. In other words, the members who cooperated with the administration developed a general store of credit and knew they would be remembered.

The rewards themselves (and the withholding of rewards) took a variety of forms. It might be something as unobtrusive as receiving an invitation to join the President in a walk around the White House grounds, knowing that pictures of the event would be sent to hometown newspapers along with hints from "White House sources" that the President valued and frequently sought this man's advice. Other inducements might take the form of a designation as sponsor of important administration legislation, or appointment to a special presidential delegation or commission. More direct rewards might consist of benefits to the districts: public works projects, military bases, educational research grants, poverty projects, appointments of local men to national commissions, the granting of pardons, and more.[35]

In the White House, as in the Senate, one of the most underestimated of all political resources is personal attention. Johnson knew the Congress intimately; it had been his life and love for thirty-four years. Coming from him, little amenities meant a great deal, and he knew what they meant. After each vote he would generally call the man most responsible for the victory: "They tell me you [a liberal Democrat] did a helluva job up there. I'm mighty proud of you and so is the *New York Times*. It was a great day for the House. . . ." "I want you [a Southern conservative] to know how proud I am of you today, how proud your country is. You did the U.S. a great service. You're a gentleman and a scholar and a producer and I love you."[36]

Multiple actions at multiple levels were intended to serve as a continual compulsion to action; they were designed to infuse the entire governmental process with Johnson's goal of legislative success. Johnson saw the problem of dealing with the varied components of the presidential institution—Cabinet members, departments, White House staff and the Democratic Party—as a search for ways to reduce their autonomy in the same way he had once broken the independent power of the Senate's inner club. Now, as then, he wanted his priorities and his personality to prevail. Now, as then, he was determined to centralize the resources of power under his control—of information, publicity, money, status, legitimacy, and access—thus making their redistribution subject to his terms. He would have admitted that the present task was larger and more complicated. It is one thing to obligate fifty or sixty Democratic Senators by the delivery of services; it is quite another to obligate the entire government establishment. But in 1965, fresh from his wondrous victory at the polls, Johnson was more certain than ever of his schoolboy belief that "what you accomplish in life depends almost completely upon what you make yourself do . . . a strong purpose, perfect concentration and a great desire will bring a person success in any field of work he chooses."[37]

Johnson concentrated first on fortifying his position with his own staff. He wanted to assure his control over his own men, and then, with their support, to stretch his influence through the rest of the government. "When you see an ambitious assistant thinking more of his own future than the President's," he explained, "you know at once you're in trouble."[38] At the same time, he wanted his staff to be "as strong as possible," composed of "the most intelligent and energetic men he could find," and in looking for the best, he recognized the connection between ability and ambition. Fearing men of independent ambition around him, yet forced to accept them by his need for able assistants, Johnson sought to ensure loyalty by keeping fixed staff assignments to a minimum, giving everyone jurisdictions that overlapped. Second, he reduced the staff's access to the media, insisting that he alone was to deal with the press, he alone would determine the news, and if anyone talked to a reporter, it was to be at his instruction. And third, he would keep each of his assistants continually off guard, giving praise one day and taking it back the next, drawing close and then pulling away. One week, an aide would be invited to participate in every aspect of Johnson's life and work; the next week he would find himself frozen out.

Although Johnson did receive loyalty from the men around him, it was not because he succeeded in destroying their autonomy, absorbing their identities into his own. They were loyal, for the most part, for their own reasons: respect and admiration for the man, as an expedient of ambition, as an obligation of office, etc. Even had he been able to employ his strategies for control of attitudes and feelings, he probably would not have been successful. And the most important of these earlier strategies—the device of changing fixed responsibilities and authority, which undoubtedly was drawn from his earlier observation of Franklin Roosevelt's style of operation—had been made impracticable by changes in the conduct and relationships of government. In the larger and far more institutionalized Presidency of the 1960s, certain fixed assignments were inevitable, among them the roles and the functions of the press secretary, the appointments secretary, the congressional liaison staff, and the national security staff. For help in developing policies and programs, Johnson had to depend upon expertise and sophistication, both in his own personal staff and in the institutional staff at the Bureau of the Budget, the Council of Economic Advisers, and the Office of Science and Technology. These functions could be performed only by men and staffs with fixed and continuing responsibilities, whose significance made it impossible to conceal or obscure public knowledge of their roles. Moreover, Johnson's desire to establish domination by creating uncertainty and apprehension among those who worked for him— as he had done with his Senate staff—was made impossible by the size of the modern presidential institution and the vastness of the bureaucracy it commanded. An orderly staff system was required to screen information, evaluate alternatives, and implement decisions.

Since Johnson could not achieve his objectives, the same impulse toward control that motivated his desire to create ambiguity and insecurity now—paradoxically—propelled him in the opposite direction. If the President was to be served by able men of autonomous will and identity—and that now seemed unavoidable—there was always a danger of conflict between the contending ambitions of his subalterns in the executive branch. Of course Roosevelt had thrived on the competition of many men's ideas. But to Johnson, conducting his leadership amid such competitive struggles, those that he did not initiate and whose content and participants he could not wholly control, was unwelcome, and even threatening. So he sought prevention, and even protection, in hierarchy; and as the pressures of his Presidency increased, the greater became his inclination to find refuge in an increasingly rigid and self-contained hierarchical structure. In contrast to both Franklin Roosevelt and John Kennedy, he adopted many of the orthodox administrative practices and techniques associated with the Presidency of General Eisenhower. "I talk to Dean Rusk," Johnson said, "not to some fifth-desk man down the line."[39]

Yet if Johnson's system resembled Eisenhower's in some of its aspects, it was markedly different in others. His hierarchy was an orderly structure with many fixed relationships, but he alone was at the top with direct lines of communication and authority to the several men who occupied the level below. In Johnson's administration there was no Sherman Adams. The President was his own chief of staff: he made the staff assignments; he received the product of his staff's work and reconciled or decided between the competing reports; he set the pace of action and the tone of discussion. And, unlike Eisenhower, the kind of personal control that Johnson could not establish over the government he retained over that more manageable domain—the White House staff. And he extended that control down to the least significant levels of activity, handling such details as approving the guest list for social functions, checking the equipment for the White House cars, determining the correct temperature for the rooms in the Mansion. Late at night he would wander through the offices in the West Wing, reading the memos and letters left on the desks of his aides. Both the random nature of these inspections and the whimsical quality of Johnson's personal attention to detail helped to create an atmosphere of permanent intimidation which, even though it affected only some among that small group of White House aides who were rather young and whose public careers had been Johnson's creation, nevertheless seemed to serve as a safety valve for his fears of becoming dependent on those who worked for him.

In the end, no organizational chart could define Johnson's system of White House control. His techniques were essentially psychological. He elevated a smile, a glance, or a courtesy above all political honors. The system included as well an endless series of psychological collisions with the master himself. In this atmosphere, as one observer described it, "The group of assistants fragmented even more than the White House staffs usually do. Bundy's foreign affairs operation went largely its own way. Cater, Califano, Goodwin and McPherson moved principally in Moyers' orbit. Valenti and Watson worked in uneasy relationship to each other, and both to Moyers. Busby and Reedy were off by themselves, sometimes functioning together, mostly singly. To a considerable extent, the staff was turning into a shifting band of individuals and groups moving in mutual suspicion around the commanding demanding figure of Lyndon Johnson."[40] Johnson knew what he was doing in fragmenting the White House staff. By splitting it into more than a dozen pieces, he made it just one aspect of the kind of hierarchy he was constructing. By compartmentalizing the members of his staff, he clarified the fact that their authority and position came directly from Lyndon Johnson alone.

Lyndon Johnson demanded a great deal from his staff, and they received much in return: participation in great matters and an enormous arena for their talents, a relationship with a brilliant man who, though sometimes harsh, often honored them with benevolent intimacies. He exacted a precise account of how each staff member spent his time, whom he talked with, and where he went. Minutes became valuable, holidays a misfortune. Johnson considered it something dangerously close to treason for a staff member to spend Sunday afternoon with his family instead of at the office. Even if they complied, however, some of the people around Johnson occasionally suffered treatment that was harsh and even degrading. The price Johnson exacted for the gifts he bestowed upon his aides—personal intimacy, access to the presidential office, power for themselves—was often nothing less than their dignity. Some willingly paid the price. But Johnson also understood that some would not give up their dignity, that they could be pushed only so far, and with them he seemed to sense the point of no return and restrained himself from crossing it. And he never drove an assistant harder than he drove himself.

Sometimes, in the middle of a meeting, Johnson declared a swimming break for everyone. And everyone followed him into the White House pool. To save time, Johnson said, he often swam in the nude. Stripping down by the side of the pool, he invited others to do the same. Some found it difficult. Those who didn't want to undress in front of everyone else, however, were badgered and mocked until they complied. After the swim, the grudging swimmers were given towels. Standing in quarters so close that the drops from one body would splash onto another, they were expected to rub themselves dry, put on their clothes and return to the meeting.

Few Presidents have permitted the kind of intimacy between themselves and their staffs that Johnson encouraged. When he had to go to the bathroom in the middle of a conversation, it was not unusual for him to move the discussion there. Johnson seemed delighted as he told me of "one of the delicate Kennedyites who came into the bathroom with me and then found it utterly impossible to look at me while I sat there on the toilet. You'd think he had never seen those parts of the body before. For there he was, standing as far away from me as he possibly could, keeping his back toward me the whole time, trying to carry on a conversation. I could barely hear a word he said. I kept straining my ears and then finally I asked him to come a little closer to me. Then began the most ludicrous scene I had ever witnessed. Instead of simply turning around and walking over to me, he kept his face away from me and walked backward, one rickety step at a time. For a moment there I thought he was going to run right into me. It certainly made me wonder how that man had made it so far in the world."[41]

From the beginning Johnson realized that his methods of working with his staff could not be duplicated in his relationships with the members of his Cabinet. "When I looked out at the heads of my departments, I realized that while all of them had been appointed by me, not a single one was really mine. I could never fully depend on them to put my priorities first. All too often they responded to their constituencies instead of mine. Here I was working day and night to build the Great Society, conquering thousands of enemies and hurdling hundreds of obstacles, and I couldn't even count on my own administrative family for complete support. I felt like a football quarterback running against a tough team and having his own center and left guard throwing rocks at him. It was an impossible situation and I was determined to change it. I was determined to turn those lordly men into good soldiers. I was determined to make them more dependent on me than I was on them."[42]

Resonating through this statement can be heard Johnson's familiar conception of power as one-sided dependence, resting on the ability of the leader to give and withhold the services needed by others.

Johnson's drive to expand his power over the Cabinet was consistent with long-established historical trends. Over the first six decades of the twentieth century, the power relationship between the President and the Cabinet had turned sharply in favor of the President. By the time Johnson took office, the creation of presidential task forces to help design new legislation and the institutionalization of presidential authority in the Bureau of the Budget to approve legislative requests for appropriations, and to monitor some aspects of performance, had made the departments increasingly dependent upon the White House for programmatic ideas and for the translation of ideas into legislative proposals. With the creation of the legislative liaison staff in the White House and the consequent subordination of congressional liaison offices in the departments, this dependence was extended to the passage of legislation and congressional approval of appropriations. Even at the stage of implementation, frequently, overlapping jurisdictions had forced the departments to rely on the White House to help in sorting out bureaucratic tangles and arbitrating conflicting claims. Once this last function was established, a convenience rapidly became a virtual requirement, and public struggles between department heads—once frequent—virtually ended. Such matters were to be discussed in White House offices, and the decision accepted with silent loyalty.[48]

All this was in striking contrast to the situation in the nineteenth century, when the relationship of dependence tended to run the other way. In the early days, the President had no staff of his own. George Washington had one secretary; Abraham Lincoln had one clerk. The Presidents were forced to rely on their Cabinet members to answer mail, discuss newspaper stories, formulate legislative programs, develop legislative strategies, receive visitors, plan tours, and prepare speeches. Nor did they have the means to monitor or control the performance of their department heads, except on matters of the greatest significance—and not always then. Throughout the nineteenth century, Presidents tended to appoint men of public stature and independent political power to the Cabinet. Indeed, the earliest Cabinets were composed of the leading public figures of the day. Powerful as individuals, the early Cabinet officials also possessed collective power vis-à-vis the President through the institution of the Cabinet meeting, which at one time regularly, and with serious intent, discussed and debated alternatives of national policy, even to the point of taking a vote on the various options.

The twentieth century brought a sharp reduction in the power of the Cabinet. The Reorganization Act of 1939 provided the President with an institutional staff of more than a thousand people, while the President's personal staff grew from one to several dozen members. As a result, most of those functions traditionally performed by Cabinet officers that involved direct personal assistance to the President—e.g., mail, visitors, trips—were transferred to the President's staff; assumed by a swelling assemblage of ceremony coordinators, advance men, travel agents, assistants in charge of correspondence, etc. For advice on legislative strategy, the President now had his own liaison staff. For help in writing and delivering speeches, he had his own speechwriters and consultants on techniques of delivery. For help in formulating programs, he could call on skilled staff members on a "brain trust." Thus the extent to which the President had necessarily to rely on his Cabinet officers was substantially reduced. And a self-reinforcing process of decline had begun. For example, the diminished prestige and power of the Cabinet made it more difficult for the President to recruit men of the highest stature; the lack of such men reduced even further the prestige of the Cabinet. And the further expansion and institutionalization of the Presidency during the postwar decades led to those substantial accretions in the President's power to dominate his Cabinet which, as we have seen, Johnson inherited, and on which he was to build.[44]

Applauded by the liberal theory of his time, which saw the decline of the Cabinet and the rise of the White House staff as one aspect of a more general movement toward concentrating power in the hands of "the one institution that represented the public interest," Lyndon Johnson moved effectively to exploit his advantage. He used every tool at his disposal, most prominently his budget and his White House staff, to concentrate information, publicity, and decisions in the Oval Office. A variety of presidential orders were directed at the same purpose. He decreed that all major pronouncements on policy and program would be issued directly from the White House. And he warned his Cabinet officers that he would cancel their projects if he found them making unauthorized disclosures to the press, thus keeping them dependent on the President for publicity. He assumed personal control over decisions on the budget and on personnel, forcing his Cabinet to plead with him directly for money and staff. He refused to allow the findings of his commissions and task forces to be released to the public; the information and ideas they contained would be distributed when, and if, he wanted. He alternately encouraged and rejected requests for private meetings. In these and other ways, Johnson made the members of his Cabinet act as courtiers.

Implicit in Johnson's intention to expand presidential power was the need to strengthen his control over the Democratic Party, of which, as President, he was now the acknowledged leader. He had always regarded political parties, strongly rooted in states and localities, capable of holding him accountable, as intruders on the business of government. Moreover, he believed that excessive partisanship was bad for the country and dangerous to his leadership. The consensus that Johnson now needed could be formed only with the support of people from all constituencies and both parties. All the forces and groups of American life must be assembled under the same huge tent: labor, management, farmers, blacks, browns, yellows, Republicans, Democrats, dirt farmers, and Wall Street brokers. So once the election was over, Johnson ordered a drastic cutback in the activities of the Democratic National Committee; he slashed the committee's budget in half, reduced the staff by two-thirds, and removed the long-distance telephone lines. The White House regularly and as a matter of deliberate practice bypassed the committee in the distribution of patronage and funds. Johnson's principal fund-raising device, the President's Club, diverted money and contributions from party organizations at all levels, concentrating control over party funds in the President's hands, and thus further contributing to the disintegration of the local party.[45]

Here again the President's efforts were consistent with established trends of modern political history. Much earlier, in the nineteenth century, party leaders had essential resources at their disposal to secure their power: jobs, food baskets, medical care, legal aid. Involved with the daily lives of people and able to help them, the party bosses were able to create and sustain high levels of party identification, thus making it natural for many people to vote along strict party lines. Rooted in the local neighborhood, the party organization also provided a major source of entertainment and fraternity for large numbers of people.

With their power securely rooted at the local level, the party leaders brought obedient delegations to the national convention, giving them the power to select the nominee. And on election day the parties were responsible for printing and distributing the ballots. Nor did party discipline stop at the conventions or the polling places. In those days, the party's strength extended to the Congress. The Speaker of the House had enormous powers to implement his party's program. As chairman of the caucus at which important party positions were determined, and as the man who made all the committee assignments and decided who should speak on the House floor, he possessed an impressive authority to punish or reward with which to keep his party members in line.

The turn of the century marked the beginning of a decline in the strength of party organizations. Reacting to the strict and conservative control exercised by House Speaker Joseph Cannon, the Progressives (a combination of Midwestern Republicans and liberal Democrats) instituted a number of reforms designed to reduce the party's capacity to strangle liberal legislation: they curtailed the powers of the Speaker, introduced the direct primary, and fostered the establishment of nonpartisan elections and city managers. By redistributing the Speaker's powers to various committees and calendars, the reformers intended to open up the legislative process to the individual Congressman or Senator. By giving the voters the chance to nominate candidates before the convention, the reformers intended to reduce the power of the party barons at the nominating stage. But their actions had unforeseen and devastating consequences for the Congress and the party system. Deprived of centralized party leadership, fragmented by committees, the Congress lost its collective voice—a circumstance that contributed to growing presidential supremacy. To the extent it was deprived of the opportunity to nominate the candidates, the party organization lost its central function and most important source of cohesive authority. As this process continued, the focus of campaigning was gradually to shift from the party to the candidate.

Changes in the economic and social structure contributed to the decline of the political party The organization of unions, the development of the Civil Service, and the rise of the welfare state deprived the party of its capacity to provide jobs, food, and services to loyal constituents, thus severing its connection with the daily lives and needs of the people. Increasing mobility weakened the ties to neighborhood and community around which local parties were organized. Technology provided access to new forms of amusement and recreation, such as movies and then television, which were more diverting than party-sponsored dances and made it unlikely that people would attend political meetings and speeches for their entertainment value. During the 1960s more and more people declined to affiliate themselves with a party and identified themselves as independents. Straight party voting became an increasingly rare exception. And voter turnout precipitously declined. Thus the changed conditions of political life strengthened and helped to vindicate Johnson's drive to reduce the significance of party, and to substitute leadership by consensus, designed to transcend the merely political, and appeal to voters on the basis of shared interests and their common stake in the progress and well-being of the country. And the liberal theory of his time greeted his style with acclaim. "We are entering another era of good feelings," one commentator remarked, "and Lyndon Johnson is the gargantuan figure making it all possible."[46]

Johnson's expansion of the President's power over the Cabinet and the party was accompanied by an energetic campaign to build his influence with the press to consolidate his gains. For he believed that no President could lead effectively for very long if the media did not support him; unfriendly media would make him vulnerable to assaults on the power he was building. Johnson regarded members of the press as similar to the membership of any other interest group. And he acted on the assumption—congenial to his natural traits and conduct—that he could find a way to bargain with them for good coverage and favorable stories. "Reporters are puppets," Johnson said. "They simply respond to the pull of the most powerful strings. Every reporter has a constituency in mind when he writes his stories. Sometimes it is simply his editor or his publisher, but often it is some political group he wants to please or some intellectual society he wants to court. The point is, there is always someone. Every story is always slanted to win the favor of someone who sits somewhere higher up. There is no such thing as an objective news story. There is always a private story behind the public story. And if you don't control the strings to that private story, you'll never get good coverage no matter how many great things you do for the masses of the people. There's only one sure way of getting favorable stories from reporters and that is to keep their daily bread—the information, the stories, the plans, and the details they need for their work—in your own hands, so that you can give it out when and to whom you want. Even then nothing's guaranteed, but at least you've got the chance to bargain."[47]

Modern Presidents have the ability to command the nation's attention. They are the only public leaders with the ability to select issues for public discussion, and establish the terms of that discussion. Although every President must respond to events and circumstances of great public concern, the importance of their office means that whatever they say or do will be considered news. At any moment they can divert attention to themselves simply by arranging for what Daniel Boorstin has called a "pseudo event." Because the Presidency is the object of unrelenting attention and mandatory "coverage," Johnson was able to use routine procedures as political instruments. Private interviews were no longer given solely because they were thought the best and most effective way to communicate the President's news or qualities. They were disposed as reward or denied as punishment. Reporters in favor were given long and intimate interviews, filled with colorful detail and personal revelation. Reporters out of favor were simply denied access, a denial aggravated by the unsubstantial nature of Johnson's formal press conference—the institution originally designed to counter precisely this kind of favoritism. In theory, the press conference was to be a restraining influence against the Chief Executive, giving reporters an equal opportunity to question the President directly, and, in so doing, to expose the shortcomings of his administration. But in the hands of timid reporters and a dominant President the press conference became simply another tool for the strengthening of presidential power.

Johnson avoided, as much as was politically feasible, the type of press conference the newsmen wanted: formal sessions, scheduled regularly and announced in advance. Determined to escape the well-informed and difficult questions that might result if sufficient time was allowed for preparation, he deliberately announced his press conferences at the last minute and generally scheduled them on weekends, when the White House correspondents—who necessarily had little knowledge about the substance of particular issues and comprised the group of reporters most dependent on the President, whose activities were the sole target of their jobs—were the only Washington newsmen at work. Johnson opened his press conferences with a long statement that served to consume a third to one-half of the allotted time, and responded only indirectly to questions, often dodging an answer to the main point by discussing peripheral areas. The frequency of his press conferences varied with his changes of mood: when he felt good, he would hold four or five conferences within a few weeks; when he felt persecuted, he could go for months without any conferences at all. Still, even this whimsical behavior helped to strengthen the impression that news of presidential activity was dispensed as the President wished, not as the press demanded.

Unpredictability served Johnson in other, even more arresting ways. If a reporter learned in advance that the President was going to do something on Thursday, and reported that fact in Tuesday's paper, Johnson would often change his plans in order to embarrass the reporter, who had then to explain his error, and to serve notice on those who leaked the story that such indiscretion was a serious act of insubordination. The tales of such behavior are legion. When James Reston saw a copy of the speech Johnson was about to make to the UN in 1965, and wrote about the President's proposal for ending that organization's financial crisis, Johnson not only dropped the proposal, but he gave an entirely different speech. When the word leaked out that James Farmer had been appointed director of a new literacy drive in the Office of Economic Opportunity, Johnson canceled both the program and the Farmer appointment. When a story appeared in the Baltimore *Sun* describing Johnson's plans for a new Food for Peace program two days before they were to be announced by the White House, Johnson canceled the program and ordered his staff to burn the already prepared and mimeograped releases. Equating predictability with weakness, Johnson found occasions to deliberately throw reporters off guard; sometimes he speculated in great detail about plans he never intended to carry out; other times, he denied the existence of plans already under way.[48]

So during 1965 Johnson absorbed the Cabinet, the party, and, to a lesser extent, the press into the legislative process that was the focus of his Presidency. Cabinet Secretaries were there to do his bidding, rarely to question it. The party organization was hardly there at all, which meant one less source of potential criticism. And the press was everywhere Johnson was, judging him by his standards, celebrating his incessant transitions, from advancing a new idea to change the world to signing a new law that presumed to change, and might change, the lives of many Americans.

When Johnson signed a law, he brought to an end a legislative process that had begun with the preparation of a presidential message. Another program had come home from the Congress to the White House. This process was the center of Johnson's life, and the ceremony of successful completion was also a personal celebration. Every such occasion, whether it was a small gathering in the Oval Office or an elaborate affair in the East Room of the White House, was designed, conducted, and dominated by Johnson himself. The ceremonies were also a public forum in which Johnson bestowed upon the nation his most valued creations—the laws of the Great Society. And within that forum he assembled the people who had made the greatest contribution to the result. But Lyndon Johnson never ceased his labors. The ceremony was also a summons to the next series of legislative endeavors.

When major legislation was to be signed, Johnson often chose a setting outside the White House. On April 11, 1965, he traveled to a one-room schoolhouse, a mile from his birthplace, to sign the Elementary and Secondary Education Act in the presence of his first teacher, Miss Kate Dietrich. On August 6, 1965, he signed the Voting Rights Act in the President's Room adjoining the Senate chamber where Lincoln had signed the Emancipation Proclamation in 1863. On October 3, 1965, he signed the Immigration Act in the shadow of the Statue of Liberty.

The signing of Medicare had originally been scheduled for Washington. But, at the last minute, the President changed his mind. He wanted to go to Independence, Missouri, so Harry Truman could attend. Wilbur Cohen, Under Secretary of Health, Education, and Welfare, along with other concerned officials, resisted the proposal. There would be chaos if they tried to fly all the people who had planned to attend halfway across the country and back in a single morning. There was also some concern that the symbolic choice of Independence would remind the nation of Truman's more radical plan for national health insurance; that it might even risk an AMA boycott of the ceremony. But the President insisted. "Why, Wilbur," Johnson said, "don't you understand? I'm doing this for Harry Truman. He's old and he's tired and he's been left all alone down there. I want him to know that his country had not forgotten him. I wonder if anyone will do the same for me."[49]

Chapter 9

Vietnam

"LBJ was great in domestic affairs," elder statesman Averell Harriman once observed. "Harry Truman had programs, but none got through. Kennedy had no technique. FDR talked simply during the crisis, but didn't act enough later. Johnson went back past the New Frontier all the way to the New Deal. He loved FDR, and it was fantastic what he did. If it hadn't been for . . . Vietnam he'd have been the greatest President ever. Even so he'll still be remembered as great."[1]

"If it hadn't been for Vietnam"—how many times this phrase has been spoken in conversations assessing Johnson's place in history. For it is impossible to disconnect Johnson from that war, and undeniable that the fighting abroad halted progress toward the Great Society. Indeed, from the beginning, Johnson later claimed, he himself foresaw and weighed the devastating consequences of war on domestic reform, but in the end, felt he had no choice but to escalate the war.

"I knew from the start," Johnson told me in 1970, describing the early weeks of 1965, "that I was bound to be crucified either way I moved. If I left the woman I really loved—the Great Society—in order to get involved with that bitch of a war on the other side of the world, then I would lose everything at home. All my programs. All my hopes to feed the hungry and shelter the homeless. All my dreams to provide education and medical care to the browns and the blacks and the lame and the poor. But if I left that war and let the Communists take over South Vietnam, then I would be seen as a coward and my nation would be seen as an appeaser and we would both find it impossible to accomplish anything for anybody anywhere on the entire globe.

"Oh, I could see it coming all right. History provided too many cases where the sound of the bugle put an immediate end to the hopes and dreams of the best reformers: the Spanish-American War drowned the populist spirit; World War I ended Woodrow Wilson's New Freedom; World War II brought the New Deal to a close. Once the war began, then all those conservatives in the Congress would use it as a weapon against the Great Society. You see, they'd never wanted to help the poor or the Negroes in the first place. But they were having a hard time figuring out how to make their opposition sound noble in a time of great prosperity. But the war. Oh, they'd use it to say they were against my programs, not because they were against the poor—why, they were as generous and as charitable as the best of Americans—but because the war had to come first. First, we had to beat those Godless Communists and then we could worry about the homeless Americans. And the generals. Oh, they'd love the war, too. It's hard to be a military hero without a war. Heroes need battles and bombs and bullets in order to be heroic. That's why I am suspicious of the military. They're always so narrow in their appraisal of everything. They see everything in military terms. Oh, I could see it coming. And I didn't like the smell of it. I didn't like anything about it, but I think the situation in South Vietnam bothered me most. They never seemed able to get themselves together down there. Always fighting with one another. Bad. Bad.

"Yet everything I knew about history told me that if I got out of Vietnam and let Ho Chi Minh run through the streets of Saigon, then I'd be doing exactly what Chamberlain did in World War II. I'd be giving a big fat reward to aggression. And I knew that if we let Communist aggression succeed in taking over South Vietnam, there would follow in this country an endless national debate—a mean and destructive debate—that would shatter my Presidency, kill my administration, and damage our democracy. I knew that Harry Truman and Dean Acheson had lost their effectiveness from the day that the Communists took over in China. I believed that the loss of China had played a large role in the rise of Joe McCarthy. And I knew that all these problems, taken together, were chickenshit compared with what might happen if we lost Vietnam.

"For this time there would be Robert Kennedy out in front leading the fight against me, telling everyone that I had betrayed John Kennedy's commitment to South Vietnam. That I had let a democracy fall into the hands of the Communists. That I was a coward. An unmanly man. A man without a spine. Oh, I could see it coming all right. Every night when I fell asleep I would see myself tied to the ground in the middle of a long, open space. In the distance, I could hear the voices of thousands of people. They were all shouting at me and running toward me: 'Coward! Traitor! Weakling!' They kept coming closer. They began throwing stones. At exactly that moment I would generally wake up . . . terribly shaken. But there was more. You see, I was as sure as any man could be that once we showed how weak we were, Moscow and Peking would move in a flash to exploit our weakness. They might move independently or they might move together. But move they would—whether through nuclear blackmail, through subversion, with regular armed forces or in some other manner. As nearly as anyone can be certain of anything, I knew they couldn't resist the opportunity to expand their control over the vacuum of power we would leave behind us. And so would begin World War III. So you see, I was bound to be crucified either way I moved."[2]

Did Lyndon Johnson believe all this? Yes . . . some of the time. Was it true? Some of it; and the rest was not simply pure illusion. For even Johnson's most grotesque exaggerations were always constructed on some fragment of reality, so that they could never be totally disproven by factual evidence or unanswerable logic alone, only by rejecting his judgment for one more reasonable, more consonant with the known facts.

Johnson's description of the nature of the challenge in Vietnam was, of course, a product of his unique personal qualities. But it is important to remember that many others shared this view, although they would not have expressed it with such color or hyperbole. And they, like Johnson, derived their convictions from historical experience.

When Lyndon Johnson entered his fifth year in Congress, Roosevelt was increasing his active opposition to Japanese expansion into Southeast Asia because that area, with its rubber and tin, was thought vital to America's interests. In so doing Roosevelt risked, and helped precipitate, a Japanese attack. For the next quarter-century, as Johnson was learning the ways of power and growing in influence, events in Asia preoccupied American foreign policy, subordinate only to our confrontation with Soviet power in Europe. Indeed, both concerns often appeared like different fronts in the same struggle. As Johnson observed and gradually began to expand his participation in public life, China "fell" with devastating consequences for politics, innocent individuals, and American liberties. Truman was cheered for his response in Korea, censured as the war dragged on, seemingly vindicated by the historical judgment of the next decade; while Eisenhower, although applauded for restoring peace, did so on the basis of a settlement that secured the independence of South Korea—the original target of invasion from the North. As a Senate leader, Johnson opposed a proposal by Dulles and Radford for an air strike in support of encircled French forces in Indochina, not directly, not denying our interest, but because we had not yet secured a promise of assistance from our European allies, thus invoking a then well-established principle of American foreign policy.

But probably the most important factor in determining Johnson's position at that time was the fact that American intervention in Indochina was strongly opposed by Richard Russell, his friend, mentor, and patron, then the most powerful and respected man in the United States Senate and the man chosen by his colleagues to deliver the refusal of Democratic cooperation. Yet many years later, in 1964, Johnson, then President, telephoned Russell to discuss Castro's action in cutting off water supplies to our naval base at Guantánamo. "There's a slowly increasing feeling in this country," Russell remarked, "that we're not being as harsh and firm in our foreign relations as we should be—that is, we're worried more about our image than about our substance. A demagogue with any strength could blow it up. I don't know of anyone who has enough strength however. People don't trust Goldwater's judgment."[3] Although the subject did not arise, and it was probably unknown to Russell, proposals to escalate our effort in Vietnam were already on Johnson's desk.

Thus, when Johnson took the presidential oath, behind him was a century of American involvement and concern with Asia, three Pacific wars, two decades of cold war accompanied by the feared possibility of a nuclear apocalypse, and a widely held belief—almost a dogma—that the arena of confrontation was shifting to the "third world."

But perhaps most significant of all was the fact that an entire generation, many of its members now come to leadership, viewed these events and other conditions of the postwar period from the perspective of their experience of World War

II—that shattering transformation of historical conditions which created an America, not only powerful but supreme, faced with the alternative of accepting international responsibilities or abandoning the map of Europe to the intentions—whatever they were—of that only other significant power, the Soviet Union. Those felt responsibilities, emerging more from circumstances than from choice—and the ensuing confrontation, known as the cold war—were given their distinctive form by the lessons of the war that had just ended—or by what was then almost universally accepted as an accurate analysis of how the war had begun and why the forces of darkness had achieved so much, and had come so perilously close to a decisive conquest.[4]

Indeed, for a long time events seemed to conspire to demonstrate that those lessons did, indeed, have a global validity. We stood firm, established clear commitments, seemed prepared, if necessary, to meet force with force—in Iran, Western Europe, South Korea, Berlin. And those nations were not conquered by the Soviet Union. Of course, one cannot prove that our policies prevented conquest, for that would require certain knowledge of Soviet ambitions and intentions. But for most of this period those who shaped American policies believed that were it not for those policies the Soviet Union would have attempted to conquer other countries with military force that no one but the United States could resist. As a result, the lessons of World War II were not regarded as precepts based upon the historical circumstances of the 1930s, whose validity under very different conditions must be challenged and reproven; rather, they assumed an almost ideological cast—matters of belief continually renewed by new experience, fresh illuminations. And, indeed, a quarter-century after Munich, and shortly before Johnson took office, there occurred what seemed to be another manifestation that America had discovered invaluable and enduring principles in the conduct of world affairs: the Cuban missile crisis.

Thus Johnson had inherited not only an office but a world view: criteria of American responsibility, principles of action, necessities of leadership, established standards for determining threats to American freedom and to our greatness as a nation. Beside him were advisers who shared that view, and who represented that difficult-to-determine group of men—the so-called foreign policy establishment—who, from Acheson to Dulles to Rusk and Bundy, had developed, applied, and believed in the entire mode of reasoning that had dominated and given continuity to American foreign policy.

In many ways Johnson felt uneasy with men like this, sensitive to any sign of their contempt or condescension toward this crude Texan. Nevertheless, he relied on them. Confident of his mastery of domestic politics and matters of substance, he never hesitated to override or ignore counsel that contradicted his own judgment. In dealing with foreign policy, however, he was insecure, fearful, his touch unsure. In this unfamiliar world, he could not readily apply the powerful instruments through which he was accustomed to achieve mastery. As a result, his greatest anxiety—unlike his attitude toward domestic affairs—was to avoid making a serious error rather than to achieve great things. He felt that so long as his policies were approved by those men who represented the established wisdom, he was, at least, insured against appearing foolish or incompetent. This feeling was reinforced by his perception that these same men also constituted the dominant influence of the public judgment on matters of foreign policy: the *New York Times* and the Council on Foreign Relations and the other important institutions and media were governed by an interlocking directorate. And this perception was fairly accurate, except that the influence could be dissolved by widespread and intense popular feelings. Thus Johnson, for whom the label "expert" meant almost nothing in domestic affairs, who knew just how wrong established wisdom could be, and how often unjustified a high "reputation" was, felt dependent on the wise experts of established reputation in foreign policy.

Johnson's insecurity, his incapacity to find, with his usual sure touch, the levers of mastery in international affairs, had another, more devastating consequence. Johnson's great strength and principle of conduct was to recognize, manipulate, and draw upon practical realities; he had always believed that unless there were practical possibilities of achieving a goal, to advocate or pursue it was wasteful, or damaging, and ordinarily deserving of contempt. Yet in foreign policy he lacked an intimate and detailed command of such realities—what could be done, how, by whom, etc. Thus he could not judge how and whether a goal could be reached or a principle applied, and he was unaware of this incapacity. So he tended to rely, was compelled to rely, on the principles and goals themselves, to guide his conduct by ends for which means might not exist. In the Senate he would not fight for legislation that could not be passed and whose consideration might create serious disruptions and divisions. His ability to avoid creating such a situation depended on his detailed and sure knowledge of how the Senate would behave and react. In foreign policy he lacked such knowledge.

When Johnson chose to pursue a legislative goal, having determined it to be realistic, he did so with a conviction that was often genuine. "Whatever conviction I had with people," he had explained, "resulted from a deep, intense feeling I was right . . . intensity of conviction is the number one priority."[5] He brought this same kind of conviction to the goals and principles of foreign policy, its intensity increased by the fact that he was not sure how to achieve them. For it was inwardly necessary to be even more certain of the rightness of ends that were established despite uncertainty about the means. Indeed, if Johnson's goals were generally thought to be noble, and he had insisted upon them despite the fact that they seemed impossible of achievement, it would be easier to accept that in this area he was what he always held in contempt—an idealist. Failure, while almost unbearable, did not diminish his conviction. He could admit to a mistake—although not easily—after a legislative failure, and learn from it. But mistakes could not be admitted in a situation like Vietnam, where the effort was defined solely by a goal and where failure, therefore, was a challenge to the rightness of belief, to some integrity of self, which must be even more fiercely defended when under attack.

It was, therefore, natural for Johnson to describe the situation in Vietnam with terms such as "appeasement" and "aggression"; and so was his tendency to interpret violent and ideological struggles on other continents as an aspect of the universal conflict of values between freedom and unfreedom and between the interests of the great powers that represented these values.

Thus every conflict in which one of the warring parties fought under the ideological banner of Communism was part of the continuing battle for domination of the future. This outlook made it possible to view wars among the people within a single nation as, in reality, an aspect of international aggression. In every such war, Johnson believed, the enemy is the agent of an alien force that is invading the home of an ally. Again, the words Johnson used to describe the dangers of appeasement were more colorful than most; the reasoning was that of a generation: "If you let a bully come into your front yard one day," he explained, "the next day he'll be up on your porch and the day after that he'll rape your wife in your own bed."[6] The only way to prevent conflict is to stop the aggressor from the moment his intentions are perceived, or even suspected.

World views, once formed, are difficult to change, especially for politicians. Always reacting and responding, their life largely one of movement among and contact with others, politicians are nearly always bound to the concepts and images formed in their minds before taking office, or those evolved from well-established and therefore safely followed sources of knowledge and guidance. If their ideas about the world sometimes sound like assumptions from a forgotten age, it is, in part, the price they pay for a life of continual motion. Except for those matters of which he has substantial personal knowledge, a political leader is unlikely to become aware that an established point of view is no longer considered valid until he is made aware of a universal consensus to that effect.

Johnson's perception that the situation in Vietnam was a war of aggression rather than a primarily internal struggle was also shaped by the systems of reporting in the Pentagon and the State Department: by the Pentagon's propensity— given its expertise, the nature of its responsibilities, those upon whom it relies for information, and the way in which such information is processed—to look primarily at all violent struggle in military rather than political terms; and by the State Department's lack of capacity to offset this military bias with effective political analysis. Having been purged of its best and most dispassionate men during the days of McCarthy, the State Department had never re-established a position of clear dominance over the Pentagon. Moreover, the State Department was still scarred by the memory of what had happened to those who had analyzed the Chinese revolution as an internal struggle; fear of similar retribution should Vietnam fall inhibited candid or detached assessment.[7]

Johnson's belief that no Democratic President could survive the loss of South Vietnam to the Communists was based on the assessment, then generally accepted, that the Democrats were particularly vulnerable at home to the charge of being soft on Communism abroad. But what were the dangers the Democrats faced at home? Certainly the American people, regarding strength of will as a virtue and unaccustomed to defeat, were likely to be angry and troubled by a Communist takeover in Vietnam. However, at least before the escalations of 1965, it was not an American war, and a Communist victory would be viewed as a defeat for the "Free World," but probably not as the defeat—far more serious—of American military force. And, in the end, after paying a huge and bloody price, the American people seemed hardly to care when Communist forces moved into Saigon. The principal constraint, then, was not the extent of current public concern about Vietnam. It was fear that political opponents might be able to blame a Communist advance on weakness of American will, and successfully convince people of the administration's "softness" toward Communism.

All these general fears were symbolized in Johnson's image of Robert Kennedy. It is difficult to understand how anyone could have rationally believed that Kennedy might be a crusading hawk. Indeed, there is evidence that, as early as 1963, Kennedy was pressing a softer line on Vietnam. But to be fair to Johnson, it must be remembered that in 1964 Kennedy had voiced no public opposition to the war, and that before he had decided to run for the Senate he had wanted Johnson to appoint him as Ambassador to South Vietnam. Finally, however, the vivid terms in which Johnson describes the Kennedy assault—"betrayer" of John Kennedy, "unmanly"—are further evidence of what we have already observed: that whatever realistic basis there was for dislike or fear, it cannot explain the almost obsessive intensity of Johnson's feelings about Robert Kennedy. Kennedy had come to stand for everything Lyndon Johnson hated in others (e.g., "betrayal") and feared in himself (e.g., "unmanliness"). Kennedy's mere existence intensified Johnson's terror of withdrawing from Vietnam. And when Kennedy became an open opponent of the war, the same sense of Kennedy as "the enemy" only helped to stiffen his unwillingness to consider any change in his policies.

Still, Johnson did worry about the loss of his domestic programs. As a boy of five, he had heard his Populist grandfather describe the devastating impact of the Spanish-American

War on social reform. He had lived through the periods of reaction following World War I and World War II, seen a virtual paralysis of domestic action in the aftermath of Korea. And one cannot doubt the intensity of this concern; the Great Society, after all, was to be his monument, his passport to historical immortality.

Nevertheless, American policy moved toward escalation with gathering momentum. "Losing the Great Society was a terrible thought, but not so terrible as the thought of being responsible for America's losing a war to the Communists. Nothing could possibly be worse than that."[8] America cannot lose to the Communists; Vietnam is a test of our ability to combat a new and dangerous form of aggression, the war of national liberation—these are the refrains running through the public dialogue of early 1965. The necessity to deal with daily events, immediate circumstances, inhibited careful reflection or re-examination of assumptions. The winter policy review informed Johnson that the Communists appeared, by every type of measurement, to be winning the war—by the number of battles won, by the territory secured, and by the number of recruits. In fact, they might be able to achieve a total victory within a matter of months. Johnson's effort to prevent a South Vietnam defeat by convincing Hanoi that the United States meant business, while, at the same time, avoiding any expansion of the war, had obviously failed. It probably did not occur to him that he may not have failed completely. Hanoi might have been convinced that the United States meant business, but so did they. The time for decision was near. Either he committed himself now, Johnson was told, or he stood to lose South Vietnam.

On January 27, 1965, McGeorge Bundy sent a memo to the President arguing—on behalf of himself and Robert McNamara—that the current policy could lead only to disastrous defeat. Both men recommended using military power in the Far East to force a change in Communist policy.

Both of us understand the very grave questions presented by any decision of this sort. We both recognize that the ultimate responsibility is not ours. Both of us have fully supported your unwillingness, in earlier months, to move out of the middle course. We both agree that every effort should still be made to improve our operations on the ground and to prop up the authorities in South Vietnam as best we can. But we are both convinced that none of this is enough and the time has come for harder choices.[9]

Still, Johnson hesitated. He asked Rusk "to instruct his experts once again to consider all possible ways for finding a peaceful solution." He also asked Bundy "to go out to Saigon immediately with a team of military and civilian experts for a hard look at the situation on the ground."[10]

In the midst of this period of indecision, Johnson was informed that Vietcong guerrillas had raided a U.S. advisers' barracks in Pleiku on February 6, 1965, and nine American soldiers had been killed. Johnson responded immediately to what was termed a "provocation," authorizing air strikes against four targets in North Vietnam. Discussing his decision with the National Security Council, he said: "We have kept our guns over the mantel and our shells in the cupboard for a long time now. And what was the result? They are killing our men while they sleep in the night. I can't ask our American soldiers out there to continue to fight with one hand tied behind their backs."[11] He did, however, fail to stress that the American troops were in Vietnamese territory, having been sent to help the South Vietnamese fight the Communists for the right to rule that territory. The following day Bundy returned to Washington to present his team's evaluation of the situation in Vietnam. The report called for a policy of graduated and sustained reprisal against North Vietnam, concluding that "without new U.S. action defeat appears inevitable.

The stakes in Vietnam are extremely high. The American investment is very large and American responsibility is a fact of life which is palpable in the atmosphere of Asia and even elsewhere. The international prestige of the United States and a substantial part of our influence are directly at risk in Vietnam. There is no way of unloading the burden on the Vietnamese themselves and there is no way of negotiating ourselves out of Vietnam which offers any serious promise at present.

There is one grave weakness in our posture on Vietnam which is within our power to fix—and that is widespread belief that we do not have the will and force and patience and determination to take the necessary action and stay the course. This is the overriding reason for our present recommendation of a policy of sustained reprisal.[12]

The recommendation for the sustained bombing was agreed to unanimously by Dean Rusk, Robert McNamara, McGeorge Bundy, Maxwell Taylor, General William Westmoreland, and General Earle Wheeler. The policy of escalation was advocated by every individual at the highest level of responsibility for actions related to national security: the Secretaries of State and Defense, the Special Assistant for National Security Affairs, the Ambassador to Saigon, and the Joint Chiefs of Staff. The consensus at the top did not preclude the expression of dissent at other levels. However, the final decisions on important matters of foreign policy were made by a small group of top officials. Others could ordinarily participate only by having one of the officials represent their views. Clearly, this kind of hierarchical structure considerably increased the influence of those at the most commanding levels, while reducing the importance and the likelihood of dissent by those below them. In this case, the structure operated to reinforce the claims of those arguing for some form of escalation.

In early 1965 Under Secretary of State George Ball presented a critique of a policy of escalation. Rejecting the dominant and virtually unquestioned assumption that underlay the entire debate about policy, he argued that South Vietnam itself was not vital to America's national security. If we did nothing, its collapse would not be serious. However, if escalation was tried and failed—and he thought failure was likely—then the consequences would be profoundly serious; the French Republic had almost collapsed under the weight of its failure in Vietnam. Senate Majority Leader Mike Mansfield told the President that he feared that escalation might lead to a larger war, possibly with China. Richard Russell warned that the venture would be more difficult and complicated than the experts were saying. And Hubert Humphrey worried that it would take years to achieve a military solution.[13]

Those dissenters were significant figures in government, but none of them was among the inner circle of decision-makers. The institutional forms of the decision-making process made it difficult for those outside the process to prepare or present coherent arguments and rebuttals because those within the structure, the advocates of escalation, had daily contact with one another and access to secret information, which allowed them to prepare elaborately detailed predictions of the consequences, both immediate and far into the future, of a failure to escalate in Vietnam. The dissenters, on the other hand, were scattered, each proceeding from his own perspective, each criticizing a different aspect of the war. Without adequate staff work and collective organization the dissenters could do little more than express personal judgments opposed to an extensively documented and argued opinion shared by nearly all the top officials of government.

This is not to say that Lyndon Johnson was the prisoner of a bureaucratic structure that had coerced or deceived him into escalation.[14] If Johnson had wanted different advice, or a wider range of opinion at the top, he could have changed his group of advisers. He could have dismissed Dean Rusk and elevated George Ball to Secretary of State. He could have replaced McGeorge Bundy with Bill Moyers. He could have promoted Westmoreland out of Vietnam and appointed a new commander more congenial to withdrawal. Moreover, many of those advocating escalation had taken that position as it became clearer that escalation would be the President's own decision. If he had shifted, most of them would have shifted. None of this would have been easy. Leading the country out of war in 1965 would have required delicate planning on the order, in reverse, of FDR's masterful job in leading the country into war in 1939–1941. The point is that Lyndon Johnson never tried.

"Suddenly," Johnson later said, "I realized that doing nothing was more dangerous than doing something."[15] The bombing plans promised relief, however temporary, from indecision. Hesitations, paradoxes, debate—all could be abated by the elemental act of doing something. In the end, the coolness with which Johnson agreed to the bombing betrayed the pressures he had endured. Action, after so much discussion, was always a relief for Johnson.[16]

The decision to escalate, though ultimately disastrous, was probably inevitable, given Johnson's nature and convictions: his belief that a Communist victory would be a serious defeat for America, that no problem was insoluble, that Americans could do anything. There was also his fear of appearing weak, and his self-deceiving conjecture that the struggle might end quickly and leave the Great Society unimpaired. And the immediate public response was encouraging. He benefited from the tendency to support the President in foreign policy and especially in times of apparent crisis, no matter what he does. At such times people react to the symbolic aspects of the office "first in war," and are willing to believe that the President is in the best position to know what the country needs. The problem is that one cannot count on a continuation of the original opinion unless events vindicate the presidential action or things end quickly. Confidence in the President, strong as it is, cannot overcome anger at costly failure.[17]

Looking back, Johnson claimed he was never optimistic about the potential results of bombing. He had read the studies of previous bombing programs, and he said he fully recognized the built-in limitations. He hoped only to restore the crumbling morale in South Vietnam. But in this recollection Johnson refused to admit to the hope that he must surely have entertained in 1965—that his show of force could convince Hanoi to come to the bargaining table. No small power could possibly resist America's sophisticated technology and enormous military strength. At least, Johnson wishfully believed, Hanoi would think this and be persuaded to a less dangerous course.

After Johnson's commitment to some form of bombing, the White House meetings discussed how and when to bomb. The Joint Chiefs favored large-scale strategic bombing, aimed at destroying the industrial base of North Vietnam. If all the American air power in the Western Pacific were used, they predicted, it would take only twelve days to complete the task. But most of Johnson's political advisers favored a more limited form of bombing. Fearful that China or Russia might be brought into the conflict if large-scale attacks were launched immediately, McNamara and Bundy argued, instead, for starting up slowly and then gradually increasing the scope and the intensity of the raids. Step-by-step escalation, they contended, would allow continuous monitoring of the reactions of China and Russia; it would emphasize America's limited objective; it might press Hanoi to negotiate in order to prevent the terrible damage that large-scale bombing would inflict. Johnson chose gradual escalation. It was a predictable choice, based, as it was, on the type of approach he found most congenial: bombing represented the moderate path between the competing extremes of massive destruction and total withdrawal. Of course, sometimes, as every automobile driver knows, the middle of the road is the most dangerous place to be.

In Johnson's view, limited bombing was seduction, not rape, and seduction was controllable, even reversible. "I saw our bombs as my political resources for negotiating a peace. On the one hand, our planes and our bombs could be used as carrots for the South, strengthening the morale of the South Vietnamese and pushing them to clean up their corrupt house, by demonstrating the depth of our commitment to the war. On the other hand, our bombs could be used as sticks against the North, pressuring North Vietnam to stop its aggression against the South. By keeping a lid on all the designated targets, I knew I could keep the control of the war in my own hands. If China reacted to our slow escalation by threatening to retaliate, we'd have plenty of time to ease off the bombing. But this control—so essential for preventing World War III—would be lost the moment we unleashed a total assault on the North—for that would be rape rather than seduction—and then there would be no turning back. The Chinese reaction would be instant and total."[18]

Johnson's metaphor suggests an effort to force the contest in Vietnam into a pattern drawn from the politics he knew so well. As long as he could use force as a means of bargaining, he could moderate his anxiety about the difficulties and unknowable dangers of this strange war in an unfamiliar land. Although Johnson recognized the "foreignness" of the Vietnamese, he simply could not accept the possibility that they might not share important qualities with Americans. Otherwise, how could Johnson hope to deal with them? Johnson needed to create a Vietnam in his mind so he could find the levers of persuasion and success.

Louis Hartz has pointed out that "From the time of Wilson, indeed even before then, if we take into account a stream of thought which accompanied our early imperial episodes at the turn of the century, the country has actually sought to project its ethos abroad."[19] Separated for two centuries from the ideological struggles of Europe, the American cultural tradition displayed little awareness that it had taken a unique, peculiarly indigenous, direction and form, that the people of other nations might be different in fundamental ways. This American tendency to project its values upon other countries was dramatized in the view held on the highest levels of decision that the Vietnamese conflict was a battle between two fixed groups of people with different but negotiable interests. By denying significance to irreconcilable moral and ideological issues in favor of calculations of bargaining and power, thus limiting the stakes to matters negotiable, Americans overlooked the reality, ultimately decisive, that the war in Vietnam was an ideological struggle, a social revolution.[20]

Johnson assumed that in war, as in the Senate, everyone knew the rules of the game, what kind of agreement would be reasonable, and that eventually an agreement would be reached. The need for continuing relationships required at least this much. But this assumption closed his mind to the argument Frances FitzGerald and others have since made: that the Vietnamese people were interested in unanimity, not pluralism. Their culture embodied the moral principles of Confucius; they believed in the possibility—indeed, the necessity—of finding the one true way of life. Politics was not a matter of negotiable opinion, a realm unto itself; in Vietnam, morality, politics, and society were inextricably joined. The war was a revolutionary war, which promised to affect not only the political system but the entire structure of Vietnamese society—its ethos, its customs, its religious expression.[21]

These cultural differences, profound as they were, seemed to be unknown not only to Lyndon Johnson but to all his top advisers. Moreover, Johnson had grounded his actions all his life on the conviction that every man had his price. That must also be true of Ho Chi Minh, except one could not discover it by reading reports. Johnson persisted in the belief that if he ever met with Ho, he would reach the private man beneath the public image. If Ho Chi Minh was a reasonable man, then he, too, would recognize superior resources, just as Richard Russell had done when he had finally recognized the strength of the forces against him on civil rights. The war, Johnson said, would be "like a filibuster—enormous resistance at first, then a steady whittling away, then Ho hurrying to get it over with."[22]

The President had another reason for confidence in his ability to bargain with the enemy. Characteristically, Lyndon Johnson had a plan and a generous promise—a billion-dollar project for the social and economic betterment of both Vietnams, and the rest of Southeast Asia. Ever since his first trip to Saigon in 1961, Johnson had been intrigued by the idea of developing the Mekong River to provide food, water, and power on a scale so immense as to dwarf even the TVA. Now, perhaps, this noble concept could also serve the cause of peace.

> These countries of Southeast Asia are homes for millions of impoverished people. Each day these people rise at dawn and struggle through until the night to wrest existence from the soil. They are often wracked by disease, plagued by hunger and death comes at the early age of 40.
>
> The American people have helped generously in times past. . . . Now there must be a much more massive effort to improve the life of man in that conflict-torn corner of our world. . . . I will ask the Congress to join in a billion-dollar American investment.
>
> The task is nothing less than to enrich the hopes and the existence of more than a hundred million people. And there is much to be done. The wonders of modern medicine can be spread through villages where thousands die every year from lack of care. Schools can be established to train people in the skills that are needed to manage the process of development. And these objectives are more within the reach of a cooperative and determined effort.[23]

He could see it all in the years ahead just as he had seen it in his hill country forty years before, when the dams had first been built, bringing water, electricity, and hope to the poor farmers. He could see the fields of rice, rich in harvest, and surrounding the fields, lively, bustling villages. New houses. New schools. New hospitals. New roads. New forms of transportation making it possible for the people to travel beyond their place of birth. "I want to leave the footprints of America in Vietnam," Johnson said in 1966. "I want them to say when the Americans come, this is what they leave—schools, not long cigars. We're going to turn the Mekong into a Tennessee Valley."[24] As Johnson saw it, a bright future was within reach if only the North Vietnamese would stop their irrational war and turn to the task of improving society—with American help, of course.

The paradox cannot escape notice. Johnson was celebrating the possible reconstruction of a country even as his orders brought mounting destruction. Indeed, Johnson's grandiose visions for the future were being reduced to inadequacy by his bombs. The bombing devastated the forests, which had a critical part in the natural process of delta formation, depleted the organic layer of the soil and disturbed the natural checks and balances in the animal world. Defoliants did not distinguish between jungles and crops, and they spurred rapid runoff of rainwater, which crested into massive floods. Forced migration from the countryside to the city tore the peasants from the villages in which they and their families had lived for generations.[25]

Yet all this destruction, Johnson insisted, was necessary for the salvation of the Vietnamese. The Americans were in Vietnam not to wage war but to pursue peace. "We have helped," Johnson declared, "and we will help [the Vietnamese] to stabilize the economy, to increase the production of goods, to spread the light of education and stamp out disease."[26] It is difficult to imagine the leader of any other nation making such a pledge in the midst of conflict, and even more difficult to imagine the citizens of any nation other than America responding with anything but cynicism.[27] But Johnson was not simply playing politics. The rhetoric of reconstruction was traditional to American diplomacy. And the American people shared his faith. "We often say," Johnson said in 1965, "how impressive power is. But I do not find it impressive at all. The guns and bombs, the rockets and warships, are all symbols of human failure. They are witness to human folly. A dam built across a great river is impressive ... electrification of the countryside is impressive . . . a rich harvest in a hungry land is impressive. The sight of healthy children in a classroom is impressive. These—not mighty arms—are the achievements which the American nation believes to be impressive. And if we are steadfast, the time may come when all other nations will also find it so."[28]

Even if America's programs of foreign aid had failed in the past, Johnson believed, this one—coming at the height of the Great Society's social engineering at home—would be different. Here again Johnson fused Vietnamese culture and American values; as a result, what he viewed as the "demands of progress" would, had his program been implemented, have been instruments of cultural devastation. Johnson looked upon the Vietnamese wish to remain in the village of their birth as a confinement of the spirit; he saw their traditional customs as impositions; he viewed their sacralization of the past as an obstacle to the secular pragmatism needed for progress. Looking upon a system of individual competition as if it were a beneficent aspect of natural order, atomistic in his view of social relations, Johnson could not envisage a society in which the individual was an aspect of a more comprehensive organism. No word in the Vietnamese language corresponded exactly to the personal pronoun "I." Individualism was seen as selfish and immoral. The traditional Vietnamese had no existence outside his community.[29]

Although Vietnam was ten thousand miles away, the psychic distance was far greater. So powerful was the American conception of individualism that it resisted even the barest consciousness that another society might conceive of freedom in precisely the opposite terms, viewing exaltation of the independent person as the denial of freedom, not its fulfillment. Endowed with the assumption that the desire for private property was a universal impulse, Johnson found it difficult to believe that in Vietnam private property did not really exist: the father was less an owner than a trustee of the land to be passed on to his children; to the Vietnamese, the land itself, not the individual ownership of it, was the indispensable element.

Studies suggest that national leaders tend to fit incoming information about other nations into existing theories about their own nation. Experience with his own system typically determines what a leader perceives in another system. It is hard for any leader to see that issues important to him are not important to others, and even more difficult to realize that others may be governed by very different values and assumptions. Perception is always influenced by personal and historic memory. Historical analogies often precede rather than follow a careful analysis of the situation.[30] But these cognitive mechanisms, natural as they are, do not fully explain Johnson's insistence that the Vietnamese experience could be assimilated into his own framework.

He wanted to believe this about the Vietnamese because he needed to believe it about everyone. This master practitioner of bargaining and negotiation was also a man who perceived the fragility of that process. He preached rationality and compromise, but continually feared and imagined the emergence of unreasoning passions and unyielding ideologies. His conduct and words expressed a will to believe, a fear of his own doubts. Johnson was always afraid that he himself might give way to irrational emotions; control came to appear a requirement of survival of the self. By treating the struggle in Vietnam as an exercise in bargaining, he sought to deny that it might exist somewhere beyond the healthy bounds of reasonable negotiations. Thus the purpose of the bombs was not to hurt or destroy; that was a by-product. They were a means of bargaining without words. Since Johnson, if not an expert on warfare, was a master bargainer, he would retain final control over when and where to bomb, so that his knowledge of detail could be both used and increased. The same attention to the minutiae of power that had characterized his relations with the Congress would now characterize his conduct of the war.

Long hours of discussion preceded the choice of each bombing target. Tracing his fingers across the map of Vietnam, the President would point to various potential targets—railroad bridges, army barracks, oil-storage depots, airfields, armored-truck convoys, factories—demanding to know the costs and benefits of attacking each one. "How many tons of bombs will it take to destroy this?" he would ask, while waving a photograph of a railroad bridge twenty miles from Da Nang. "How important is that [a petroleum-storage depot] to the North Vietnamese? If we choose these army barracks fifteen miles from Haiphong, how can we be certain of the accuracy of our aim?" So it went, one by one. In developing his list of permissible targets, Johnson operated on the fundamental premise that he could bomb only up to a certain point. To move beyond that point—for example, to mine Haiphong Harbor or bomb the Red River dikes—might risk war with Russia or China. Suspicious that the North Vietnamese had entered into secret treaties with the Communist superpowers, Johnson lived in constant fear of triggering some imaginary provision of some imaginary treaty.

There, of course, was little basis for a belief in such agreements except Johnson's own need to believe. How else could he explain the caution, the personal, endlessly debated selection of particular targets for particular missions? In a dozen jungle-shrouded spots the Communist powers had placed secret limits, tripwires whose passage would automatically precipitate Russia or China into armed conflict with the

United States. And it was up to Johnson to outguess them. This belief was linked to, became part of, his continued magnification of the stakes—no longer just a "test case for wars of national liberation," a "lesson for aggressors," a necessity to "prevent the fall of Southeast Asia," or part of the "containment of China." America fought in Vietnam to prevent the otherwise inevitable onset of World War III. It was an aspect of Johnson's own dimension, the size of his personal needs and his huge ambitions to satisfy the needs of all others, that only the largest cause of all—to forestall world-wide destruction—could justify actions that were now so threatening to the public's admiration, his life as a public man, and his capacity to lead others, in their own interest, to accept his grandly benevolent intention. He had so much to give, but he must first preserve before he could build.

"I never knew," Johnson later said, "as I sat there in the afternoon, approving targets one, two, and three, whether one of those three might just be the one to set off the provisions of those secret treaties. In the dark at night, I would lay awake picturing my boys flying around North Vietnam, asking myself an endless series of questions. What if one of those targets you picked today triggers off Russia or China? What happens then? Or suppose one of my boys misses his mark when he's flying around Haiphong? Suppose one of his bombs falls on one of those Russian ships in the harbor? What happens then? Or suppose the fog is too thick or the clouds are too high or the target too small and the bomb drops by mistake within the thirty-mile radius of Hanoi?" The more questions he asked, the more agitated he became. "I would then begin to picture myself lying on the battlefield in Da Nang. I could see an American plane circling above me in the sky. I felt safe. Then I heard a long, loud shot. The plane began to fall faster, faster, faster. I saw it hit the ground, and as soon as it burst into flames, I couldn't stand it any more. I knew that one of my boys must have been killed that night. I jumped out of bed, put on my robe, took my flashlight, and went into the Situation Room."[31]

After hours of being alone, he felt so weary that he sought the world of action. At 3 A.M. the Situation Room was the perfect escape. There, at any time of day or night, he could find what he needed: people, light, and talk. Around the table in the middle of the room sat five or six men on loan from the Pentagon and the CIA, responsible for receiving messages from Saigon and Da Nang. As the pilots completed their bombing missions, they would report the results over their radios to American headquarters at Saigon: mission accomplished, bridge destroyed. The message would then be transmitted to the White House in the form of a summary telegram. With these Telex reports before them, the Situation Room staff would make the appropriate markings on a giant map, indicating which strikes had destroyed what targets.

As it turned out, the classified tickers and reports were endowing illusion with the appearance of precision. Johnson had reason to worry about whether the bombs were actually hitting their targets, but it was not the reason he thought. The real concern was not that a mistaken strike might provoke China or Russia, but the fact that the bombers, flying over hundreds of hamlets and hillocks and villages, could not even begin to separate enemies and innocents, soldiers and civilians. A seismic detector cannot tell the difference between a truck full of arms and a school bus; a urine sniffer cannot tell a military shelter from a woodcutter's shack. Forced to identify targets while passing over them at high speed, the pilot's glimpse might last only a second or two. If the target was small—a bridge or a truck or a railroad car—it was often necessary to make several bombing runs before the mission was accomplished. At times, a large area might be saturated with bombs to compensate for the difficulties of accurate aim. This was combat by proxy; it was war waged at a distance. It looked impressive from the air. But on the ground one could see that it was like "trying to weed a garden with a bulldozer."[32]

The difficulties of target identification were described by reporter Jonathan Schell, who for several weeks accompanied pilots on their missions:

> ... the ground commander guided Captain Reese to the target by describing it in relation to landmarks on the ground. "It's five hundred meters east of that pagoda on the road there. Have you got the pagoda?" the ground commander asked. Captain Reese ... answered, "I see a church but no pagoda." "It's right under you now." "I don't see it." "O.K. Well, there's one hootch [a house identified as the source of an enemy sniper position] down there about a klik south of us that we want you to get. We've got sniper fire out of that tree line." Captain

Reese flew over the area indicated, and found that it was occupied by a village of sixty or seventy houses. . . . "I see a village down there," he said. "No, this is just one hootch," said the ground commander, who was apparently unable to see the village from his spot on the ground because of a thick cover of trees. . . . [After more discussion and the firing of some marker rockets, without success:] "That's the general area," said the ground commander, apparently tired of trying to pinpoint the one house. "Do you want us to pretty well cover this general area?" Captain Reese asked. "Affirmative. Hit the whole area. We've seen activity all through this area." "O.K. I'll put in a can of napalm and see what it looks like." . . . "Any civilians in the area are Charlies, or Charlie sympathizers, so there's no sweat there."[33]

In the end, the entire village was destroyed. But the evaluation form simply said that "an enemy sniper position" and seven "military structures" had been hit. None of the forms had any space on them for reporting civilian damage. Success was measured simply by the number of sorties per aircraft deployed, by counting which planes and which pilots delivered the most ordnance. In competing with one another for initiating more strikes and dropping more tonnage, the Air Force and the Navy frequently inflated their "killed by air" claims. Volume became an end in itself. Concentration on the technical aspects of the bombing program substituted a set of short-term physical objectives for long-term political goals. By narrow military criteria, American bombs were not effective in destroying preselected targets, but such destruction was not easy to translate into political success. The enemy's capacity to recruit more men and rebuild structures never seemed to enter into the military calculations. We could, after all, just continue to bomb. But where would the cycle end?[34]

As the military increased its involvement and responsibility, errors in reporting became standard operating procedure. Exaggerated descriptions of American success were matched by diluted reports of North Vietnam's strength. The estimates of progress improved with each step of the journey from Army headquarters in Vietnam to the Situation Room in the White House. Soon it became almost impossible for anyone in Washington to really know what was going on in Vietnam.

But Lyndon Johnson was not about to question a process of reporting that provided him with what he wanted to hear. If the enemy body count seemed inordinately high, that was to be expected when poorly trained men without photo equipment or spotting devices were engaged in battle with the most technologically accomplished civilization in the history of the world. How could America possibly fail to force the North Vietnamese into bargaining? Lyndon Johnson wanted one thing from his nightly visit—the feeling that he was still in control—and that was the only thing that the maps and the men and the messages were able to provide.

"The realist," observed Randolph Bourne in describing the chain of events leading to American participation in World War I, "thinks he can at least control events by linking himself to the forces that are moving. Perhaps he can. But if it is a question of controlling war, it is difficult to see how the child on the back of a mad elephant is to be any more effective in stopping the beast than is the child who tries to stop him from the ground."[35] The drift of events in the spring of 1965—the inexorable movement from bombs to troops—can be described in similar terms. Seated on the back of a beast that was far wilder than he had imagined, Johnson found himself carried along by its momentum, moving inexorably toward the wider war he did not want.

When Johnson first decided to escalate the bombing, he hoped to keep the involvement of "his boys" to a minimum. "If there is one thing," he said in February, 1965, "that the American people will not take, it is another shooting war in Asia."[36] So Vietnam would be different. Mechanically concentrated firepower would substitute for conventional manpower. Warfare by remote control would keep America's sons at home and America's sight away from this remote conflict.

Yet the situation markedly worsened in the months after the bombing had begun. The Vietcong kept the initiative and were hurting Saigon's army badly. As guerrilla activity mounted, the South Vietnamese government was able to provide security for fewer people in less territory. The cities and towns were being isolated by successful Vietcong attacks on their power and communication lines. The desertion rate in the South Vietnamese Army was rising weekly. In contrast, the Vietcong were able to replace their losses more easily than before. There was no sign that the bombing had stopped the flow of supplies from the North; indeed, more weapons were now in Vietcong hands. America might control the sky, but the land was still being captured by the Communists.[37]

The more the situation deteriorated, as our military efforts met with failure, the more susceptible Johnson became to requests for increased use of American power.[38] If bombing was a failure at present levels, then an increase in the number of sorties and an expansion in the choice of targets would bring success. If South Vietnamese soldiers were fighting badly, or hardly at all, then an increase in America's tanks and guns and training would make them fight hard and well. If the presence of fifty thousand American troops could not stave off defeat, then more troops would assure victory. Moreover, Johnson felt that dwindling public support for the war made it necessary for him to rely less on manpower than on technology and firepower in the kind of situation where they would have the least effectiveness. As long as the Vietcong had firmly established roots in South Vietnam, they could and would replace lost supplies with the assistance of the local population. If the guerrilla's railways and highways were destroyed, he could and did resort to bicycle and foot. Designed to break the will of North Vietnam, the bombing had the opposite result: it built North Vietnam's morale.

Our involvement seemed only to strengthen our enemy and to weaken our ally. America's sophisticated equipment could destroy objects and kill people, but it could not bend the human spirit to America's aims. On the other hand, the more aid we gave South Vietnam, the more dependent South Vietnam became. Our increased effort was met with decreased effort on their part. Each new grant or combat division generated a demand for additional help, for reassurance that the United States would not go away.[39] President Johnson unwittingly impaired South Vietnam's strength with too many foreign goods and too many foreign services, just as surely as young Lyndon had destroyed Huisso's horse with too much food and too many races.

From one perspective, Johnson's power now seemed more imposing than that of any Chief Executive in history. Throughout the cold war, the American Presidency had steadily accumulated instruments of control over the conduct of foreign policy. Information, expertise, money, troops, publicity, etc., were concentrated in the White House. Ultimately, the American President exercised more power over his country's decisions of war and peace than did the Premier of the Soviet Union. Yet from another perspective, the President was like the Wizard of Oz, an ordinary man concealed behind a giant screen, pulling strings, pointing at targets, playing with the illusion of power. In the end, the most awesome arsenal of weaponry in the modern world could not ensure results, which turned out to depend upon less tangible qualities—in both Vietnam and the United States.

From the start, the Joint Chiefs of Staff had been more realistic than Johnson's civilian advisers in foreseeing that the bombing would not make it possible to avoid sending troops. But they refrained from voicing this judgment at the beginning of 1965—when pessimism about the bombing might have persuaded Johnson not to do anything at all. Better to settle for half-measures than to risk a complete reversal of policy. So the requests for troops were made gradually, one after the other, in a succession of easy, incremental steps. First, the military requested a few troops to protect the air base near Da Nang from which American air strikes were launched. On March 10 two Marine battalions—fifteen hundred men—landed in Vietnam. A few weeks later there was a second request for more troops, this time to protect our boys—the same boys, of course, who were originally there to protect the airfield. By the end of April there were more than fifty thousand American soldiers in South Vietnam. And the mission expanded as the numbers increased. The original mission of the troops was simply to protect the air bases. In early April American troops were permitted active participation in combat if a nearby Vietnamese unit was in serious trouble. By June permission had been granted to commit American troops to combat, either in conjunction with Vietnamese forces or on their own. And all the while, Johnson still insisted that we were not at war.[40]

The movement from bombs to troops without the approval, discussion, or even the awareness of Congress was a stunning revelation of changes in the balance of power between the institutions of American government, and how far we had come from the original understanding. The Founding Fathers were convinced that most of the wars that had taken place in Europe were the product of crazy and destructive ambitions, reflecting the desire of the rulers to enlarge themselves by enlarging their countries. And history had another lesson:

power that was acquired in response to the necessities of war was not readily relinquished when peace returned. In Europe military exigencies had prepared the way for the rule of absolute monarchs. The monarchs had then become desirous of acquiring power over expanding domains, equating their ambitions for the good of the nation with the health of the nation. The iron ring of tyranny was closed: wars demanded monarchs and monarchs demanded wars.[41]

The framers originally intended to sever the potential connection between war and the possibility of despotism by giving the warmaking power to the elected representatives of the people. In the early drafts of the Constitution, the legislature was granted the sole power of "making war." In later drafts, the wording was loosened to allow the executive to act in case a sudden attack was made upon the United States while the Congress was out of session—as it was expected to be for all but one month a year. In an age when it took several days for the fastest horse to ride to the proposed capital in New York from the northernmost state of New Hampshire, and considerably longer from the southernmost state of Georgia, one could easily envisage a military situation that required that something be done in less time than it would take Congress to assemble. The executive's power to respond to attack was not meant to include the power to initiate hostilities. But history has a way of fudging theoretical distinctions; time and practical experience blurred the line between initiation and response. The framers gave the President substantial powers in the conduct of foreign policy: to receive ambassadors and other public ministers and with the advice and consent of the Senate to make treaties and appointments. He was also Commander in Chief of the armed forces.[42] If, as was often the case, the exercise of these powers created situations that provoked armed attack, to which Presidents replied with force, it becomes difficult to draw the line between initiation and response.

The difficulty is not just theoretical. On May 18, 1846, President Polk sent an Army unit under General Taylor into a disputed territory on the border between Mexico and Texas. As expected, Mexico felt compelled to resist, and a Mexican unit ambushed Taylor's unit, killing eleven men. The ambush enabled Polk to claim that the United States must act at once to repel Mexico's armed attack. "I call on Congress," Polk wrote in a presidential message, "to *recognize* the existence of war and place at the disposal of the Executive the means of prosecuting the war with vigor, thus hastening the restoration of peace."[43] While Polk's actions triggered some criticism in Congress, it was difficult to deny that the United States was now actually at war with Mexico—however the war had started—and therefore money and supplies could not be denied to American soldiers already in combat. So Congress acquiesced and war was acknowledged and continued.

FDR's destroyer deal presents a more complicated example of the difficulty of distinguishing between initiation and response. In the summer of 1940, after France had fallen, Hitler was making plans for an invasion of England; the success of the invasion depended upon whether the Germans could control a sea lane across the English Channel. In ten days, the Nazis had sunk eleven British destroyers. Churchill wired Roosevelt for help. If the United States could provide Britain with fifty or sixty reconditioned destroyers, then perhaps the seaborne invasion could be repelled; if not, the future looked darker than ever before. Churchill's request created a dilemma for Roosevelt. He knew he had to act immediately, but he also knew he could not get congressional approval. Instead, he drew up an executive agreement between chiefs of state, exchanging the destroyers for military bases. But the ingenious approach could not hide the fact that by providing destroyers to England, Roosevelt was placing the United States in a state of quasi belligerence, since the sale of destroyers was seen as an act of war.[44]

Presidents also enlarged the concept of defensive action to include their power to protect American citizens abroad (in the early twentieth century, Presidents Theodore Roosevelt and William Taft sent troops into the Dominican Republic to protect American citizens living there); to protect American prestige (in 1914 Wilson sent troops to Veracruz to enforce respect for the American flag); and, finally, to protect the free world against Communism (in 1950 Truman sent troops into South Korea to repulse the aggression of North Korea). Significantly, the test was not whether the American people believed that the welfare of the nation was at stake, but whether the President so determined. Since it was possible to find many reasons to support a claim that the nation's security required swift actions, the original constraint on presidential action had in effect been removed.

The necessities of national survival were also used to justify the expansion of presidential powers at home. In the course of the Civil War, President Lincoln undertook sweeping actions without congressional authorization: he arrested and detained people without warrant, paid out millions of unappropriated funds from the Treasury to private persons, seized railroads and telegraph communications, seized property, instituted a militia draft, suppressed newspapers, and emancipated the slaves. The nation's survival, as Lincoln saw it, was at stake and with it the survival of free government upon earth. The situation, Lincoln said, "forces us to ask, 'Is there in all republics this inherent and fatal weakness? Must a government of necessity be too strong for the liberties of its own people or too weak to maintain its own existence? Is it possible to lose the nation and yet preserve the Constitution?' " Lincoln's answer to his own question was that the Constitution was nothing without the nation. The law of necessity demanded that the nation save itself, and by extension the Constitution, even if in the process extraconstitutional means were required. "Often a limb must be amputated," Lincoln concluded, "to save a life but a life is never wisely given to save a limb."[45]

The presidential apparatus grew with the growth of military needs; the great steps forward in the expansion of presidential power were linked—whether as effect or cause—with the great wars: the Civil War, World War I, World War II, the Korean War. Time and again, the law of national self-preservation was seen to justify placing extravagant powers in the hands of the President.

The story of expanding presidential power is not, however, a story of rapacious Presidents tyrannically enlarging their control against the resistance of the people. On the contrary, the American people and their representatives in the Congress continually deferred to presidential action. And, over time, Congress acquiesced in the President's increasing domination of national security policy, and restricted itself primarily to monitoring the executive branch, using its power in order to limit programs rather than attempting to intervene in shaping the substance of policies.

Explanations of this evolution usually give first priority to structural factors. It is said that the making of foreign policy demanded information, secrecy, dispatch, and concentration of authority, and that these qualities were difficult to find in an institution as large and unwieldy as the U.S. Congress.[46]

According to this view, the Congress was an assembly of individuals lacking a collective voice, hopelessly fragmented into dozens of committees and subcommittees. Nor could the parties put together what the congressional structure rent apart. Over time, the centralizing capacity of the parties had diminished—so much so that in some ways their activity added to the fragmentation of congressional structure.[47]

Congress' lack of information also crippled its ability to deal with questions of foreign policy; the Congress was almost solely dependent upon the executive for information and expertise in the field of foreign policy. And despite the President's responsibility for informing Congress on the state of the union, the executive branch had progressively tightened its control over transmission of information to Congress. The claim of executive privilege, the growth of intelligence operations, and the farflung nature of America's foreign affairs had given a near-monopoly of information to the Presidency. Nothing had done more to secure this monopoly than the development of an institutionalized system of security classification, which, by giving the power to conceal, helped persuade the executive branch that foreign policy was no one else's business.[48]

But too much emphasis should not be placed on institutional factors. On the one hand, the need for secrecy and dispatch was enormously exaggerated. On the other hand, the congressional structure was not as incapable of making decisions as the critics implied. The problem was more ideological than institutional. Congress' difficulties in sharing responsibility for deciding issues of war and peace arose primarily from the fact that most Congressmen would not give the energy and time such important questions demanded. The average member of Congress spent little time on questions of foreign policy. Political necessity encouraged him to give first priority to the concerns of his constituents, and few of their problems related to foreign policy. Studies of voting patterns on foreign policy indicated little correlation between foreign policy issues and constituent attitudes. So, rather than taking his cues from his district, the average Congressman turned to the President for guidance in foreign affairs. For the average member knew that if Congress voted against the President on any foreign policy issue, and the result was bad, then Congress would be blamed. On the other hand, if he voted with the President and things went wrong, then the President would get the blame and not the Congressman. The legislators could always say: "Well, you see, I had my doubts but I voted to back my President." And the public would respect this decision.[49]

The concept that only the Presidency could deal with the complexities of foreign policy was a consequence of the Representative's perception of that complexity. The sense of being overwhelmed by the demand for expertise happened to fit the individual Representative's own political needs and his own images of how foreign policy should be made. Over time, these fears and desires created a habit of deference, and the congressional muscles of decision-making in foreign policy atrophied for lack of normal use.

So it happened that in 1965 Johnson was able to take the American people into a war that turned out to be the longest in its history, without a declaration of war or even a specific resolution of support from the U.S. Congress. Advisers led to bombs and bombs led to troops and gradually America was at war with North Vietnam. And the Congress was called upon simply to recognize the situation and support the President's actions.

Still, the illusion of public choice remained. In July, 1965, five months after the initiation of the bombing, Robert McNamara presented the President with three options: to cut our losses and withdraw, to continue fighting at the current level, or to substantially expand our military pressure. The memo, signed by Bundy, Rusk, Taylor, Westmoreland, and Wheeler, clearly reveals their preference for the third option.

> The Viet Cong seem to believe that South Vietnam is on the run and near collapse. There are no signs of their settling for anything less than a complete takeover.
> We must choose among three courses of action ... :
> (a) *Cut our losses and withdraw* under the best of conditions that can be arranged—almost certainly conditions humiliating the United States and very damaging to our future effectiveness on the world scene.
> (b) *Continue at about the present level*, with the U.S. forces limited to say 75,000, holding on and playing for breaks—a course of action which, because our position would grow weaker, almost certainly would

confront us later with a choice between withdrawal
and an emergency expansion of forces, perhaps too
late to do any good.

(c) *Expand promptly and substantially the U.S. military
pressure against the Viet Cong* in the South and
maintain the military pressure against the North Vietnamese in the North while launching a vigorous
effort on the political side to lay the groundwork
for a favorable outcome by clarifying our objectives
and establishing channels of communication. This
alternative would stave off defeat in the short run
and offer a good chance of producing a favorable
settlement in the longer run; at the same time, it
would imply a commitment to see a fighting war
clear through at considerable cost in casualties and
matériel and would make any later decision to
withdraw even more difficult and even more costly
than would be the case today. [Emphasis added.][50]

Not surprisingly, President Johnson also chose option No.
3. The process of decision is worth noting at this point.
Though the decision called for a massive expansion of American troops, raising the troop level to 200,000, the structure of
decision-making had become so narrowed that Lyndon
Johnson received the advice of only five or six men, consult-
ing the National Security Council, the Congress, and the
Cabinet only after the decision had been made.

Having chosen his policy, Johnson turned to the question
of implementation. There were two schools of thought: The
majority of his advisers recommended that the President ask
Congress for higher taxes to pay for the war, issue a
presidential declaration of a "state of emergency," put the
economy on a wartime footing, and order the mobilization of
235,000 reservists. Johnson recoiled from this dramatic display of presidential action. Going to Congress meant, in
effect, going to the nation with an announcement of war, letting the country know that this was a major war, likely to be
a long war, which would demand sacrifice on their part.[51] The
alternative strategy—which was Johnson's strategy—was to
tell Congress and the public no more than absolutely necessary. The administration would request an additional appro-
priation of only $1.8 billion, thus deferring the full revelation
of the conflict's mounting costs until the following year. It

called for announcing only that fifty thousand troops were to
be sent immediately, and folding that announcement into a
crowded press conference held at midday to ensure the minimum TV audience. It called for extending enlistments and increasing draft calls rather than mobilizing the reserves. It
called, in essence, for initiating a covert full-scale war.

In deciding against his advisers not to summon the country
to a costly and difficult struggle, Johnson had asserted his intention to control the decision-making process. If in 1964 his
decisions were shared by the similar experiences and convictions of his experts who had recommended increased military
pressures against the North, now, in the middle of 1965, Lyndon Johnson was the one leading rather than the one being
led. McNamara's war had become Johnson's war.

It is impossible for an outsider to know the weight of all
the factors that influenced Johnson's course. He himself chose
to present only one reason in public. At the time and later, in
his memoirs, Johnson justified his decision to minimize the
extent of the war by arguing that if he had asked Congress
for vast sums of money, called up the reserves, and warned
the country and the world of the length and breadth of the
war, he might have triggered one of those secret provisions in
one of those secret treaties. Then we would have been fighting China and Russia as well as North Vietnam. Better, he
reasoned, to have done what was necessary without informing
the Congress and the public. In private conversation, Johnson
admitted two other considerations: his fear of "touching off a
right-wing stampede" and his concern for the Great Society.
Convinced that McCarthyism was dormant but not defeated,
Johnson feared that if the full extent of our difficulties in
Vietnam were known, the political right—a force of unde-
termined size whose power Johnson almost certainly overesti-
mated—would seize the initiative and demand an invasion of
North Vietnam and the bombing of Hanoi. Johnson was
much more concerned with the kind of furor that men like
John Stennis, Richard Nixon, Gerald Ford, and others might
have created than he was about any dove opposition. This reflected his knowledge of the sources of congressional power.[52]
Dissembling was the only way to keep the stampede from beginning. By pretending there was no major conflict, by minimizing the level of spending, and by refusing to call up the
reserves or ask Congress for an acknowledgment or accept-

ance of the war, Johnson believed he could keep the levers of control in his hands.

He had worked hard to reach the position where he could not only propose but pass his Great Society legislation. In the summer of 1965, after a lifetime spent in the pursuit of public power, he had come so close that he "could see and almost touch [his] youthful dream of improving life for more people and in more ways than any other political leader, including FDR. . . . I was determined to keep the war from shattering that dream," Johnson later said, "which meant I simply had no choice but to keep my foreign policy in the wings. I knew the Congress as well as I know Lady Bird, and I knew that the day it exploded into a major debate on the war, that day would be the beginning of the end of the Great Society. . . . I was determined to be a leader of war *and* a leader of peace. I refused to let my critics push me into choosing one or the other. I wanted both, I believed in both, and I believed America had the resources to provide for both. After all, our country was built by pioneers who had a rifle in one hand to kill their enemies and an ax in the other to build their homes and provide for their families."[53]

A full-scale public commitment to Vietnam would have required Johnson to accept the fact that he would not secure all the goals he desired. It would have required him to admit that even this leader must make choices and accept limits. It would have meant defining priorities and settling the conflicts among them. But here, as always, Johnson attempted to compromise conflict instead of choosing sides, manipulating and orchestrating the political process in order to shape a formula that would satisfy every competing claim.

How could Johnson have imagined that he could conduct a major war in virtual secrecy while simultaneously summoning the American people toward a Great Society? In early positions of leadership Johnson found that he could move in contradictory directions, so long as he compartmentalized his leadership, and kept his dealings with one group a secret from the next. Even in the search for votes, the process of campaigning permits, indeed requires, stressing some facts and minimizing others. The politician's talent, as Johnson interpreted it, was the ability to embrace and enter into the habits and ways of life of many different men. This required control over information. Johnson could not allow his immediate audience access to contradictory information about the particular "self" he was playing to them, permit a person who had seen him in the "right" role happen upon him in the "wrong" role. And when his leadership proved effective, Johnson had been praised by the very Senate on which he had practiced his deceptions. The country, then, would also reward the President for "pulling off," as he described it, "both the war in Vietnam and the Great Society at home," even if he hadn't told them everything at the time.

Johnson's concept of the President's role in foreign policy reinforced his confidence that it would not be necessary to make full disclosure. As the Democratic Majority Leader under a Republican President, Johnson had supported Eisenhower on most matters of foreign policy. He had preached and practiced bipartisanship. Now he was the President, and he expected the same deference from *his* Congress. After all, partisanship and public debate were enemies of a sound foreign policy. It was in the public's best interest—given its tendency every now and then to "go off on a jag in one crazy direction or another"—to leave complicated questions of international affairs in the hands of the President. The public, Johnson reasoned, would only hurt itself by knowing too much. Democracy demanded good results for the people, not big debates.

In bequeathing him the problem of Vietnam, history presented Lyndon Johnson with issues alien to his experience, resistant to his methods of leadership, yet decisive for his Presidency.

That was a historic misfortune, for Johnson and for America. But Johnson was not simply a victim of circumstance. Destiny and victimization are not the same. The latter assumes neither an act of will nor even a motivating passion; the circumstances appear as exclusively external, arbitrary, and exorbitant. But Lyndon Johnson's decision to escalate the war in Vietnam was his own, the product of his beliefs, inward needs, and the public experience of decades. Admittedly, unlike his predecessors, he did not choose to be confronted with the need to decide whether the assumption that Vietnam was vital to our security—an assumption that was part of the still more encompassing world view—must now be acted upon to the full extent of its furthest implications. But his choice to go into Vietnam covertly, with force and with overtures of benevolent intentions, was an act of will that almost seems to sum up the character of the man.

The initial choice to intervene in 1965, including the decision to start with the bombing, probably was not significantly shaped by Johnson's own personality. Given the pressures for action, it is easy to imagine a Kennedy, an Eisenhower, or a Truman making the same choice. On the other hand, it does seem clear that the decision to attempt the coexistence of the Great Society and the war, and the consequent tactics of half-truth and deception, bore Johnson's own personal stamp to a unique degree. It is difficult to imagine another President, even in the same situation, making the same choice. Almost any other President would have decided differently, not necessarily out of principle, but surely on the practical ground that not even a President can "pull off" the impossible. Perhaps only Johnson would have dared to conceal the cost of the war from senior members of Congress, so that he might receive the Great Society appropriations before the truth came out.

Probably the fact that he was, in fact, a master of the Congress had allowed him to engage in so complicated and immense an undertaking. The very qualities that had led to Johnson's political and legislative success were precisely those that now operated to destroy him: his inward insistence that the world adapt itself to his goals; his faith in the nation's limitless capacity; his tendency to evaluate all human activity in terms of its political significance; his insistence on translating every disruptive situation into one where bargaining was possible; his reliance on personal touch; his ability to speak to each of his constituent groups on its own terms. All these gifts, instead of sustaining him, now conspired to destroy him.

The most important thing about a democratic regime is what questions it refers to the public for decision or guidance, how it refers them to the public, how the alternatives are defined, and how it respects the limitations of the public. Above all, the people are powerless if the political enterprise is able to take them to war without their consent. The business of war involves the severest sacrifices falling on the ordinary men and women in the country. Here more than anywhere, the people must have an opportunity to make a choice. For in the end, no statesman can pursue a policy of war unless he knows for what goals, and for how long, his people are prepared to fight.

Lyndon Johnson had wanted to surpass Franklin Roosevelt; and Roosevelt, after all, had not only won the reforms Johnson envied, he had also waged a war. But there was a critical difference: Roosevelt did not attempt the New Deal and World War II at the same time. Only Johnson among the Presidents sought to be simultaneously first in peace and first in war; and even Johnson was bound to fail.

Chapter 10

Things Go Wrong

"I figured when my legislative program passed the Congress," Johnson said in 1971, "that the Great Society had a real chance to grow into a beautiful woman. And I figured her growth and development would be as natural and inevitable as any small child's. In the first year, as we got the laws on the books, she'd begin to crawl. Then in the second year, as we got more laws on the books, she'd begin to walk, and the year after that, she'd be off and running, all the time growing bigger and healthier and fatter. And when she grew up, I figured she'd be so big and beautiful that the American people couldn't help but fall in love with her, and once they did, they'd want to keep her around forever, making her a permanent part of American life, more permanent even than the New Deal.

"But now Nixon has come along and everything I've worked for is ruined. There's a story in the paper every day about him slashing another one of my Great Society programs. I can just see him waking up in the morning, making that victory sign of his and deciding which program to kill. It's a terrible thing for me to sit by and watch someone else starve my Great Society to death. She's getting thinner and thinner and uglier and uglier all the time; now her bones are beginning to stick out and her wrinkles are beginning to show. Soon she'll be so ugly that the American people will refuse to look at her; they'll stick her in a closet to hide her away and there she'll die. And when she dies, I, too, will die."[1]

The commentary is authentic Johnson, truth mingled with censure and regret; the metaphors, uniquely his—the girl-woman, simultaneously his creation, his gift, and his own life—emerging from the inward structure of the mind. It omits, however, the fact that his progeny's growth had been halted, not in 1969, but some years before, during his own

Presidency—and not by Richard Nixon, but by Lyndon Johnson himself, as the consequence of his escalatory policy in Vietnam and his economic policy at home.

Nor was the Great Society—as Johnson pictured it in his metaphor—a single entity to be judged a success or failure, dead or alive. It was, in fact, a medley of programs—between 1965 and 1968, five hundred social programs were created—administered with varying degrees of success. Some of these programs—e.g., Medicare and voting rights—succeeded admirably in achieving their objectives; others accomplished far less than was originally hoped—e.g., Model Cities and federal aid to education; still others proved self-defeating—e.g., community action.

Some of Johnson's administrative problems stemmed from the incoherent structure of the federal government. As Chief Executive, he was expected to obtain concerted action from a sprawling feudal government comprised of hundreds of autonomous fiefdoms, each with its own clientele, traditions, and loyalties. In domestic affairs, the conditions that made for presidential supremacy in foreign affairs were not present. In dealing with controversial issues of health, education, poverty, and manpower, the President could not invoke his office as a symbol of national unity in the same way as he could in matters of war and peace; nor could he point to the widespread consensus of attitudes that underlay his conduct in foreign policy. And his only constitutional grant of authority in domestic affairs was to "take care that the laws be faithfully executed," but even this does not grant independent authority; it only gives him authority to look over other people's shoulders.

In the absence of national emergency and constitutional authority, each department tended to go its own way, following its particular traditions and habits. The leadership task facing Johnson as Chief Executive of the domestic establishment bore closer resemblance to the challenges he faced as legislative leader in the Senate, where he also confronted the problem of securing responsiveness from a structure of feudal barons, entrenched within independent committee domains, fortified by the system of seniority, than it did to his other presidential roles as Commander in Chief or Chief of State.

But if the problems of the administrator were similar in character to those of the legislator, they were very different in scope. As legislative leader in the Senate, Johnson had dealt with fifty or at most one hundred individuals, divided up into twenty-one separate committees. In the legislative phase of the Great Society, the numbers had increased to 535 individuals and 45 committees. Now as administrator of the Great Society, Johnson had to deal with a bureaucracy of one million employees, charged with implementing more than four hundred grant-in-aid programs, each involving dozens of institutions. One example illustrates the problem of scope. Title VI of the Civil Rights Act of 1964 barred discrimination under any program or activity receiving federal assistance against any person because of race, color, or national origin. Full implementation of Title VI required that racial discrimination be eliminated from the practices of any institution receiving or applying for federal grants—10,000 hospitals, 23,000 public school districts, 2,000 colleges—all in all, 35,000 institutions in 50 states.

In the Senate, with the aid of a small staff, Johnson was able to program staggering amounts of information, correlating complicated fragments of knowledge about the desires, whims, fancies, and fears of his colleagues with the myriad resources of the Majority Leader—committee assignments, trips, campaign funds, invitations—to produce an individualized read-out for each Senator. By necessity, the staff system became more elaborate when Johnson reached the White House and began to enact the laws of the Great Society. Providing the President with head counts, tallies, charts, and nightly memos about both individuals and the legislative timetable, the White House liaison staff expanded Johnson's capacity beyond one hundred Senators to the entire Congress, allowing him once again to intervene effectively and efficiently at critical points in the legislative process.

Presidential intervention in the administrative process, however, involved thousands, not hundreds, of individuals. Five federal bureaucracies were charged with administering the programs of the Great Society: Health, Education, and Welfare; Housing and Urban Affairs; the Office of Economic Opportunity; Labor; and Agriculture. Each of these was subdivided into dozens of bureaus and departments. Physical size and spread alone precluded Johnson from roaming the hallways in search of information. And unlike the circular hallways in Congress, where tramping tourists and open doorways created a welcome atmosphere within which Johnson could absorb information about individuals and bills, the departments' corridors, one gray office after another, created an atmosphere impervious to all outsiders, including the President.

With each department governed by its own traditions and habits in devising the rules and regulations to carry out the bills assigned to it, the President experienced considerable difficulty keeping track of, much less controlling, the administrative timetable. In the bureaucracy, unlike in the Congress, the passage of a bill is the beginning of the job, not the end. As Chief Executive, the President needed information about the effectiveness of his earlier efforts in order to weigh new programs against them. But program evaluation was not easy to secure, given goals that were often vague and even contradictory and a bureaucracy with no tradition of judging the relative effectiveness of services rendered.

An additional factor that aggravated the problem of evaluating program activities was the inevitable reliance upon operating interests for the preparation of evaluation reports. In the operation of the manpower programs in the Department of Labor, I saw how difficult it was to separate out objective information from the habits and customs of the people involved.

The Economic Opportunity Act provided support for new programs to train and employ the hard-core poor. But the new programs depended upon old institutions—the State Employment Services—for their implementation. Set up during the New Deal as an exchange between the business community and the unemployed, the offices of the Employment Service were primarily located in the business districts of the central cities, not easily accessible to the residents of the slums. For thirty years, the employees at each local office had filled out the same report, documenting the number of people serviced that week. Now there suddenly appeared a new clientele, more difficult to place in jobs. The forms to be filled out at the end of the week, however, remained the same, pressuring the employees to "cream the crop," servicing the least needy and least difficult to place first.

In an effort to reverse the situation, the executives in the Labor Department prescribed a new weekly form; local Employment Service employees were now called upon to report only the hard core's placement, those who'd been out of work for eighteen months and made under $3,000 a year. The shift in the pattern of incentives finally focused attention on the hard core, but now a different problem emerged. Evaluated only on the basis of how many of the most difficult people were placed in their training programs, the local employees began waving advance payments to drag in off the streets drug addicts, prison convicts, and anyone they could find. Evaluators of the training program in the Cardozo section in Washington, D.C., discovered that heroin addicts made up more than half the trainees. The word had spread in the heroin community that one had only to enter the program, stay long enough to collect the advance, and then return to the streets, providing a successful placement for the Civil Service employees and $50 to the addict for another day's fix.

The director of the Cardozo program knew what was going on, but could not admit it publicly. His program, he said to me, had to compete for money and staff with the program in Anacostia, the other slum area in the District of Columbia, and such a revelation would hurt his chances for funding in the following year. Better to keep it quiet and work from within to change the situation. The executives in the Labor Department also knew what was going on, but they, too, felt the pressure of competition—at that time, the Labor Department was locked in a bureaucratic struggle with the Department of Health, Education, and Welfare to determine which agency could best serve the poor—and decided simply to let the reports stand and change things from within.

When I went to the White House, I reported the situation to the President, who smiled at me as he said: "Of course I understand the difficulties of bureaucracy. But what you don't understand is that the President's real problem is with the Congress, not the bureaucracy. It is the Congress that demands numbers from us, insisting that we handle the most people at the least cost. If we went around beating our breasts and admitting difficulties with our programs, then the Congress would immediately slash all our funds for next year and then where would we be? Better to send in the reports as they are, even knowing the situation is more complicated than it appears, and then work from within to make things better and correct the problems."[2]

So it happened that the bureaucracy from top to bottom became involved in a public-relations charade, each level legitimizing its activities and covering its failures with the statistics of success. "I wish it had been different," Johnson said later. "I wish the public had seen the task of ending poverty the same way as they saw the task of getting to the moon, where they accepted mistakes and failures as a part of the scientific process. I wish they had let us experiment with different programs, admitting that some were working better than others. It would have made everything easier. But I knew that the moment we said out loud that this or that program was a failure, then the wolves who never wanted us to be successful in the first place would be down upon us at once, tearing away at every joint, killing our effort before we even had a chance."[3]

Was Johnson correct in presuming the public's unwillingness to experiment? Or was his assumption an unexamined premise, a legislative piety projected upon an unwitting public? "I knew from the start," Johnson added, "that the '64 election had given me a loophole rather than a mandate and that I had to move quickly before my support disappeared."[4] In this recognition, Johnson was correct. A study of public opinion in 1964 suggested that the consensus behind the Great Society merely signified an acceptance of the individual programs Johnson had sponsored—Medicare, education, voting rights; it did not represent a shift in underlying philosophy. On the contrary, the majority of Americans still resisted the idea of federal intervention. But if Johnson recognized the conservative bias of the public's underlying attitudes, the pattern of his behavior did not reflect this knowledge. Just the opposite: at a time when careful deployment of administrative and public resources was essential, Johnson squandered both.

In the early months of his administration Johnson shaped a public image of himself he could not sustain over time. Presenting himself to the people as a master technician, a consensual leader who could produce something for everyone without cost to anyone, he created expectations that only a consummate administrator could have satisfied. To say this is not to suggest, as several observers have done, that Johnson was simply ill-suited, because of his legislative background, for the administrative aspects of the Presidency. The job of administering the Great Society was essentially political in nature, involving Johnson in many of the same challenges he had brilliantly mastered in the Senate, in the NYA, in the Little Congress, and even in college, by developing a flow of detailed information, concentrating in his hands a maximum supply of carrots and sticks with which to reward allies and punish enemies, deciding when and where to intervene.

Admittedly, the scope of the task was far larger, but the President did possess substantial tools for tracking his subordinates' behavior and could have organized his government to provide others, just as he could have expanded the mixture of resources—top-level appointments, White House endorsements, presidential publicity for selected programs, invitations to White House functions, backing on the Hill, budget allocations—which he already had at his disposal for rewarding energetic bureaucrats and sanctioning recalcitrant ones. The point is not that Johnson was incapable of becoming a consummate administrator—that remains an open question—but that he never really tried. His priorities were elsewhere. The skills and resources he might have invested in shaping the bureaucracy to meet the Great Society's goals were channeled, instead, into the war in Vietnam.

In the beginning, Johnson did devote some energies and talents to the task of organizational output: he sponsored the installation of a new system—PPBS (Program, Planning, Budgeting System)—designed to evaluate programs according to defined objectives and to expand the President's control over the budget-making process; he appointed the Heineman Commission to study the question of governmental reorganization;[5] he considered bringing Robert McNamara from Defense to head a superdepartment of domestic affairs, incorporating all the Great Society programs with major impact in the urban area; he experimented with various institutional arrangements for securing greater coordination between departments—interagency committees, Executive Orders, and lead agencies—and he even toyed with the more promising idea of creating an Office of Program Coordination in the Executive Office with a mandate to monitor Great Society programs and settle jurisdictional quarrels.

The Office of Program Coordination was reminiscent of several innovations begun in President Roosevelt's time to rationalize the myriad New Deal agencies and to coordinate agency responses during World War II—to Budget Director Harold Smith's ambitions for the Budget Bureau, and the Bureau's field offices, and to the Office of War Mobilization and Reconversion, especially under James Byrnes. But after the war came a long period of legislative and administrative drought. The wartime machinery was never converted to peacetime use. For nearly two decades, the domestic affairs of the government were either shrinking or stationary.[6] During this period the Budget Bureau fell on bad days; its administrative arm grew weaker and weaker. Accustomed to sending up messages with little expectation of their passage, the Bureau developed the habit of screening substantive programs primarily in terms of financial implications, which diminished still further its sensitivity to administrative problems.[7]

Even long-standing habits, however, can be changed with the proper incentives. Subordinates who are aware that their leader is measuring his own success on the basis of their ability to implement his programs will inevitably exhibit more concern with output than those who feel their superiors basically do not care. Morale, obedience, and initiative are all qualities that good leadership can help to bring into play.[8] The key to the successful passage of the Great Society legislation in 1964–1965 was the constant attention Lyndon Johnson focused on his legislative program. Through nightly memos, Tuesday breakfasts, and Cabinet meetings, he imposed his priorities on the system; and his energy was transmitted to hundreds of key individuals in both the executive and the legislative branches.

This same combination of commitment, energy, and attention could have been focused on questions of administration in 1966–1968. Johnson could have mobilized the members of his White House staff and his Cabinet to provide frequent reports on the implementation of Great Society programs. He could have devised a collective forum—reconstituting the Cabinet meeting or creating a new institution—for discussing administrative problems. He could have reached below his Secretaries to energize lower-level bureaucrats and to keep his Cabinet members on their toes. He could have structured a system of participation within individual agencies so that those responsible for administering the departmental rules and regulations were involved in the process of drawing them up. The principle of involving participants in a process—which he had practiced so successfully on Capitol Hill—had as much force in the bureaucracy as it did in the legislature.

None of these actions would have been easy to carry out in a bureaucratic system that for years had exercised considerable autonomy, free from presidential control. Still, a concerted presidential effort—with the commitment of substantial blocks of time—might have made a difference. But time was the one resource Johnson failed to give to his administrative role. Indeed, as the months went by, consumed more and more by the war in Vietnam, Johnson saw the heads of his domestic agencies less and less. Gradually, an atmosphere developed in which the domestic Cabinet members stopped asking for private meetings, assuming the President was too busy to concern himself with their business, as if their business were no longer his.

In contrast to the systematic way in which he had involved himself in the legislative process, faultlessly preparing his every word and deed, Johnson carelessly delegated the administrative tasks of the Great Society to the members of the White House staff. Worse than noninvolvement was Johnson's sporadic need to reassert control by arbitrarily inserting himself, directly and deeply, into the operation of a particular program. Often provoked by a congressional complaint or a newspaper story, these raids drained the entire system. Demanding instant reports, spot checks on field operations, and sudden meetings with program heads, Johnson created one crisis after another, each lasting no more than one or two days and often totally disappearing once the President's attention returned—as it always did—to Vietnam.

So it happened that the man who had prided himself all his life on attention to fine detail approved a one-billion-dollar poverty program without even coming to grips with the possible implications of the major provision calling for local community-action agencies sponsored by private as well as public groups. "I thought we were just going to have the NYA," Johnson later said to Bill Moyers. "I thought we were going to have CCC camps and I thought we were going to have community action where a city or a county or a school district or some governmental agency could sponsor projects—the State Highway Department, for example, where we'd pay the labor and a very limited amount of the materials and a good deal of the supervision. I thought we'd say to high school boys that are about to drop out, 'We'll let you work at the library or sweep the floors or work in the yard and we'll pay you enough so that you'll stay in school.' ... Now I never heard of any liberal outfits where you could subsidize anyone. I'm against that. Now if we had 100 billion dollars we might need to but with all the government agencies in this country, I'd prefer that Dick Daley do it rather than the Urban League. He's got heads of departments and he's got experienced people that are handling hundreds of millions of dollars and every one of these I'd make them come in and sponsor these projects. This other way just leaves us wide open."⁹

While Johnson's instincts proved politically correct, he never followed through to ensure that his wishes were carried out, and the privately sponsored poverty projects became a major source of political controversy. This failure to address himself to substantial detail became more and more noticeable as the war drained away increasing reserves of psychic energy, intuition, and talent. In the course of working on his memoirs, I asked Johnson how he felt about this diversion. He responded gruffly at first, flatly denying even the possibility of a conflict between the war and the Great Society, but the next day he produced a large red and black chart, which compared the hours he had spent on the war with the hours he had spent on the Great Society. "You see," he said, pointing to the long, black columns indicating his domestic activities, "no matter what you say about how I abandoned the Great Society, the truth is that I gave more hours every day to my domestic programs than I gave to anything else. Look, there's the entry for May 8: 6 hours on domestic policy, 1½ on Vietnam. June 4: 10 hours on domestic policy, 3 on Vietnam. July 15: 8 on domestic policy, 2 on Vietnam."¹⁰

Beneath the statistics, however, lay the fact that more than three-fourths of the hours he counted as domestic activities involved Rose Garden speeches, formal meetings with group leaders, bill-signing ceremonies, and presentations of awards to the Girl Scout of the Year, the Beauty Queen of the Month, or the Handicapped Veteran of the Year. Subtracting these ritualized activities from the total number of hours recorded, the years 1966–1968 show a decided shift of time and attention from domestic politics to the war in Vietnam.

The diversion of Johnson's attention from domestic concerns took place in a period when the problems of the Great Society were no longer simply problems of administration but the erosion of Johnson's consensus and the disappearance of those economic conditions of national life that had made the enactment of the Great Society possible. The beginnings of the Great Society coincided with the happy realization that federal budget revenues were rising faster than projected expenditures for ongoing programs and allowed

Johnson to avoid difficult choices between constituents and programs. The first phase of the Great Society promised something for everyone, and the promises continued even as Johnson escalated the war in July, 1965. His cardinal rule in his conduct of the war was to keep it as painless and concealed as possible. Deliberately avoiding new taxes, he drew upon existing revenues to finance his bombs and his troops. But the painless phases of the Great Society and Vietnam came to an abrupt end as the rising costs of the war combined with increased consumer demand and rising expenditures for the Great Society to produce inflation.

Consumer demand had risen sharply in 1965 in response to the Tax Reduction Act of 1964. Business had spent heavily on new plants and equipment to meet this rising demand. At the same time the government was increasing its expenditures for programs of social reform. Still, all these demands were being met until the economy ran into the sudden and sharp expansion of defense requirements. Together with the other expansions, the defense costs pushed total demand beyond the speed limits at which production could be expanded. Something had to give. Prices started to move up in 1965. As living costs rose, workers sought higher wages. These in turn raised the costs of production. Faced with higher production costs and strong markets, producers sought to raise their prices still further. This was the chain reaction that resulted in the wage-price spiral known as inflation.

Johnson was warned by Gardner Ackley, the Chairman of the Council of Economic Advisers, in December, 1965, that unless expenditures could be contained, a significant tax increase would be necessary to prevent an intolerable degree of inflationary pressure. But the President was in no mood to listen to such warnings at the moment when the American people were enjoying all the favorable consequences of the boom: profits were soaring, consumer living standards were improving dramatically, poverty was declining sharply, and the goal of 4 percent unemployment was finally being reached. While listening to Ackley's concerns, he flatly refused to consider a tax increase, sticking to his initial position that the American nation could afford guns and butter alike. This decision not to recommend a general tax increase in 1966 was the critical decision that sent the economic system into a prolonged period of chaos, from which it has still not recovered. By refusing to administer counterinflationary measures in the early stages, Johnson allowed the economy to heat up to the point where even drastic measures could have little impact.

Nor was Johnson willing to impose wage and price controls, preferring to solicit voluntary adherence to the established guidelines by jawboning with business and labor. But with the economy soaring out of control, Johnson's patriotic appeals for restraint had only limited success. Once food and service prices began to accelerate, it was unrealistic to ask organized labor to accept low wage increases and equally unrealistic, once the wages went up, to ask business to lower their prices. By 1967 the guidelines were badly frayed.

Still, Johnson refused to institute wage and price controls. "I don't think," he later said, "we ever ought to have anything compulsory we can do voluntarily. I think by reasoning together we may perhaps avoid some of the harassing details that come in an overregulated economy. I lived through the OPA, WLB, WPB in World War II and the Korean War. I remember going home one time and going to see a farmer neighbor. I told him I wanted to bring back a ham to Lady Bird for a Sunday night buffet. I asked how much. He said three dollars. I pulled out my wallet and gave him three dollars. Then I said, 'How many stamps?' He said, 'How many which?' I said, 'How many stamps are required for this?' 'Oh,' he said, 'you're talking about the OP and A. Well, we just never did put that in down here.' And that was only one measure of how deeply the American people resisted wage and price controls. I didn't ever want to go through that period again."[11]

In the absence of either wage and price controls or a tax increase, the Great Society became the sacrificial lamb of the rising inflation. In early 1965 Johnson had projected that the Great Society would get fatter and fatter with each passing year, and in some respects his projection came true: In 1965 the combined expenditures for education, community development and housing, manpower, health, and welfare totaled $7.6 billion or 6.4 percent of the federal budget. In 1970 the figure was $29.7 billion or 15.1 percent of the budget, representing a quadrupling of outlay. But this increase was less substantial than it appeared because of the rise in prices between 1965 and 1970. And the total increase must be placed alongside the increase in the Defense Department budget in that same period from $46 to $77 billion, an

amount greater than the total combined expenditures for all
the new human resource programs put together.[12]

Yet all along, the precise costs of the war were kept from
the Congress and the American people. Budget Director
Charles Schultze remembered that in the spring of 1966 both
the President and Secretary McNamara clearly knew that Vietnam spending for fiscal year '67 would be considerably
higher—by $6 billion—than the $10 billion allotted for it.[13]
Still, they refused to admit how much defense spending
would rise, limiting their public statements to vague pronouncements.

Six years later, when I asked Johnson to explain to me how
the defense expenditures were so consistently underrated, he
responded angrily: "No human being is ever able to estimate
accurately the costs of a war. No one man can say from one
month to the next how many dollars' worth of bombs thousands of other men, thousands of miles away, will fire. No
one could estimate the atomic bomb. When Marshall went to
Rayburn, he said it would cost hundreds of millions of dollars; he couldn't be any more definite than that. All he knew
was that if we got it before the Germans, we'd be able to
preserve our people, if not, we'd all be slaves. Besides, all this
talk about our not knowing anything about controlling costs
is a lot of shit. We had a hell of a lot more control than
those guys did over in Medicare. Why, no military man could
spend a dime without McNamara's approval. He fought and
bled for the principle that the Joint Chiefs of Staff could not
get a mandate without a specific request. Otherwise we'd be
giving them money based on pie-in-the-sky figures. When he
told the Congress that he was assuming for political purposes
that the war would be over by June 30, 1967, it was not a
lie; it was simply the most efficient way to plan the military
budget and enforce the requirement on the Joint Chiefs of
Staff that they were not to receive one nickel without a plan.
And moving step by step was not only the best way to plan
the budget; it was the best way to save the Great Society."[14]

If Johnson had hoped to save the Great Society by moving
step by step, his secrecy had just the opposite effect. When
the inflation set in, in the absence of a wartime mood of
sacrifice, the centers of power in the Congress responded with
a conventional call to cut the budget. Succumbing to their
pressure, Johnson sent word to his agencies: hold the line on
budget requests. So just at the time when, according to

Johnson's original scenario, the Great Society should have been entering its second phase—in which the good programs were to be expanded and the bad ones scuttled—the program administrators were told to tighten their belts and adopt a program of austerity. And Johnson the benefactor was forced to starve his own programs.

The second phase of the Great Society also made it clear that some people would have to pay the cost of helping others, shattering Johnson's earlier hopes of sustaining a Federal Community Chest joining the blacks and the whites, the browns and the yellows, the rich and the poor, the young and old. Once it became apparent that more jobs for blacks meant less jobs for whites, that cheaper housing for the poor meant coming up against the building trade apparatus, that welfare reform meant redistributing income, and that restructuring education meant restructuring neighborhoods, the choices became much harder. To revitalize the cities or to reform the educational system required a restructuring of vested interests that lay beneath the Congress and the bureaucracy.[15] To accomplish this, Johnson had to meet the power of group interests with an organized movement of his own. Building that coalition from the bottom up, however, demanded a willingness to delineate friends and enemies that went against everything Johnson believed. The task of creating a social movement dedicated to redistribution and reform was very different from the task of creating a consensus behind a vague set of individual programs. All his life Johnson had believed in blurring rather than defining issues. Skeptical of party organization, he had weakened rather than strengthened the very vehicle he now needed to mobilize grass-roots support behind the Great Society.

Yet to recognize the strength of the patterns of the past is not to say that Johnson was inevitably imprisoned by them. Observing Johnson's immense growth in civil rights, it is possible—in the absence of Vietnam—to imagine an equally impressive growth in any number of areas. But Vietnam *was* there; indeed, at the very moment when new and imaginative thinking was essential, Johnson's mind was elsewhere. Many times, Johnson later recalled, he consciously and deliberately decided not to think another thought about Vietnam. Nonetheless, discussions that started on poverty or education invariably ended up on Vietnam. If Johnson was unhappy thinking about Vietnam, he was even less happy not thinking about it. Away from Westmoreland, McNamara, and Rostow, separated from his maps and his targets, he felt anxious. He found himself unwilling, and soon unable, to break loose from what had become an obsession.

I remember once asking him if he had ever felt imprisoned by bureaucracy.

"Yes," he said, "but not for the reasons you think. My problem was not bureaucracy with a capital B, but a few self-satisfied bureaucrats in the Defense Department who thought they knew what was going on better than the President. I barely knew or saw them, yet there they were disagreeing with my policy and leaking materials to the press. It was a real problem all right. A President is entitled to people who'll execute his views."[16]

Johnson's obsession with the war inevitably damaged his relations with the Congress, contributing to the frantic pace the Great Society tried to sustain, even after the first year of amazing output. Determined to show that the war had not diminished the Great Society, Johnson relentlessly pushed the Congress to prove his case by producing one law after the next. Before one bill on a particular subject could be implemented, a new bill on the same subject had been proposed. Before the standards for the Water Quality Act of 1965 had been developed, the Clean Water Restoration Act of 1966 had been passed and Water for Peace Act had been proposed, diverting both congressional and bureaucratic attention at a time when focus on administrative questions was essential. Under siege about Vietnam, Johnson interpreted pleas made by the congressional leadership to concentrate on questions of implementation as a disguised attempt to sabotage the Great Society.[17]

The more defensive Johnson became about the war, the more he demanded sole credit for the laws the Congress had passed. He violated his own principle of sharing publicity and credit in order to create a base of goodwill for the future. "There were a lot of us," one Senator later said, "who broke our backs on some of these bills, but Lyndon claimed he did it all himself. And you don't make friends that way." By constantly referring to "my Medicare bill," "my housing bill," and "my education bill," Johnson created congressional ill-will that exacerbated the difficulties the Great Society already faced.[18]

But Johnson's faltering touch with the Congress was most

clearly revealed in his tortuous struggle over the question of taxes. After hesitating for nearly two years to recommend a tax increase, Johnson finally asked the Congress for a 6 percent surcharge in September, 1967, but the price of the legislation—as Johnson had feared all along—was a crippling reduction in domestic programs.

"You have to go on TV," Wilbur Mills notified the President in 1967, and explain that "because of Vietnam we must cut domestic spending and pass a tax increase, and if you take this position you can count on me to go with you all the way. . . . I also want some commitments made in executive sessions of the Ways and Means Committee on major slashes in domestic spending."[19] The skillful trader, his bargaining position enfeebled, now had to give up what he wanted to get what he needed; for almost the first time in his public life he was on the wrong side of a bargaining process that he did not invent, but had improved, strengthened, and transformed into a uniquely effective instrument for the exercise of power. "If I were a dictator," he informed a Cabinet meeting in the spring of 1968, "and didn't have to be concerned with the city council or the legislative body and could just write my own ticket, I would add to the budget instead of taking from it and I wouldn't have a ten percent surcharge either."[20]

But Johnson was not a dictator—his request for the tax increase produced only wrangling on the Hill. For eighteen long months, while the economy slid into more and more trouble, the bill remained trapped in the Ways and Means Committee and Johnson was unable to spring it free. It was not until after he had withdrawn from the presidential race in 1968 and after the gold market collapsed that Johnson finally secured the passage of the surcharge.

In the beginning Johnson had expected that economic arguments alone would be sufficient to persuade both the liberals and the conservatives to join with him on the tax increase. But this assumption failed to account for the depth and the bitterness of the issues that separated liberals from conservatives on the question of taxes. While the conservatives linked their support of the tax increase to a demand that Johnson wrap the tax in the American flag and use the resources gained from it to prosecute the war in Vietnam, the liberals conditioned their acceptance on the promise that funds be used solely for domestic purposes without a single penny going to the war.

Building a consensus under these conditions was clearly not easy, but Johnson had faced even deeper splits in the past—notably on civil rights in 1957—and had still managed to produce viable legislative strategies. Why did the keys to this particular issue elude him for so long? Part of the answer lay in the tensions involved in his relationship with Wilbur Mills, chairman of the House Ways and Means Committee. The two men had never been close, but until now each had so fully respected and appreciated the other's base of power that they had skillfully managed to bury their personal dislikes in public policy. On this issue, however, all manner of personal feelings and animosities came to the surface. Reading the public sentiment against a tax increase and recognizing that the Congress would reflect that sentiment, Mills refused to let the surcharge reach the floor, where he was sure it would be beaten. But Johnson interpreted his actions as a purely personal show of force. "I saw Wilbur holding back my bill up there," he later said to me, "and I knew why he was doing it. Not because he didn't believe in it but because that prissy, prim and proper man was worrying more about saving his face than he was about saving his country. He was afraid to put his reputation behind a risky bill. But when you run around saving your face all day, you end up losing your ass at night."[21]

Fumbling with the Congress, Johnson also fumbled with the American people. "The [prince]," Machiavelli warned, "must arrange to commit all his cruelties at once, so as not to have to recur to them every day. . . . For injuries should be done all together, so that being less tasted, they will give less offence."[22] By refusing to ask for a tax increase early on, Johnson failed to prepare the public for the sacrifices the war would entail. On the contrary, everything he said and did in the early days of his administration promised a painless war and a profitable peace. Nothing creates more bitterness than promises made and not kept. When life got tough on the American people, when the war and the inflation began to intrude upon their daily lives, they aimed their frustration at the President. Between 1964 and 1968 Johnson's support rating dropped 36 percentage points.

This sweeping decline in Johnson's popularity can be traced in part to the one-dimensional image he initially projected of himself as a master technician. Once formed, the impression of a President tends to last a long time, but the values people assign to what they see can quickly shift.[23]

The public's notions of what a President should be are affected by what is happening in their daily lives. Between 1966 and 1968 the private prospects of millions of Americans were upset by war and inflation. As this happened, their expectations of the President changed. A country at war wants a Commander in Chief, not an evasive manipulator. A country suffering from social and economic crisis wants a public leader, not a private schemer. Shifting expectations produced shifting perceptions; with startling speed, the respected wizard became the wheeler-dealer, a man of shabby quality.

Johnson accelerated his problems with the public by his clumsy handling of the press. At the most basic level, he failed to recognize that the White House press corps was not the same as the Senate press corps. The techniques he had used so successfully in the Senate were ill-suited to the White House. If the Senate correspondents needed Johnson more than he needed them, the situation was reversed in the White House. To understand the inside workings of the Senate, the Senate reporters *had* to cultivate the Majority Leader. There were few alternative sources. This was less true in the White House, where correspondents could obtain information from other sources: from members of the White House staff, from the agencies, and from the Congress. Prior experience with a number of submissive correspondents led Johnson to the erroneous conclusion that his press relations could be solved by the art of seduction. He told various reporters he "would make big men out of them if they played ball." But if they agreed, they were immediately identified by other reporters as sycophants; their words were read as the President's, and their standing within the Washington community sharply declined.

In the Senate, Johnson could trust the regular reporters not to reveal too much of his private person in their reports about his public acts. The interest of the press in the Senate was more in what was happening than in personality. This was not so in the White House, where anything the President said or did, if known, was news. Little was sacred to a highly competitive press corps composed of more than fifty reporters. Taken by themselves, the reports of Johnson's colorful language and behavior might not have been so damaging; it was the contrast between this earthy man and the image of the pious preacher he projected that did Johnson in. But he remained a wolf in sheep's clothing before the public at large. Terrified of making slips swearing or using ungrammatical constructions, Johnson insisted on reading from formal texts. Facial muscles frozen in place, except for the simpering smile, he projected an image of feigned propriety, dullness, and dishonesty.

Johnson responded to criticism of his speaking style by commissioning a monstrous podium, which reporters nicknamed "mother" because it encompassed the orating President with enormous sound-sensitive arms. Teleprompters rose from the top but the microphones themselves remained invisible. Johnson took "mother" with him wherever he went, carefully wrapped in furniture padding. Without his podium, Johnson felt lost. Once, when he was scheduled to speak in Philadelphia, it was discovered minutes before the event that "mother" had been left on the plane. Fortunately, before he spoke a local minister was to give an invocation. In a state of panic, Johnson's aides seized the minister's own podium, and sawed it down to three-quarter size to make its height the same as "mother's."

Fundamentally, however, Johnson's failure with the public was one of purpose, not technique. His difficulties as a public leader were rooted in the choice he made in 1965 to commit American troops to an undeclared war in Vietnam while continuing to build the Great Society and while keeping the full extent of America's commitment from the public, the Congress, and even members of the executive branch. And taken together, these decisions produced an atmosphere of frustrated hope that contributed to the outbreaks of ugly riots in city after city for three turbulent summers.

In the middle sixties the civil rights movement shifted from the rural South to the Northern slums, from lunch counters and laws to employment, broken homes, and disease. With this shift, the earlier consensus on ends and means split apart; in 1964 only 34 percent of the American people believed that Negroes were trying to move too fast; by 1966 the percentage had increased to 85. Nearly one-third of the whites interviewed said they thought differently about Negroes now than before—they felt less regard and respect; the Negroes were demanding too much, going too far. This was not, the media said, a temporary downturn. It was, instead, "the end of the civil rights era." Initiative had passed from the leaders who had brought about the Civil Rights Act of '64 and the Voting Rights Act of '65—LBJ, Martin Luther King, Roy Wilkins, Whitney Young, Clarence Mitchell—to a new group of militants, young and angry blacks whose primary experience had been in the ghettos of the North, where the gains of the sixties had barely penetrated.

Or so the media claimed as it crowned the militants kings of the civil rights movement, summarily rejecting the old leaders as men of a forgotten age. From a later perspective, the media's image turns out to have been more myth than reality—studies indicate that even at the height of the radical activity, the old leaders still retained the overwhelming support of the Negro community—but the images presented by the media had a profound effect upon racial relations, as did the changes in vocabulary, hair, and life style that were initiated by a small segment of the Negro community but which ended up affecting large numbers of blacks.

Johnson was slow to recognize and slower to admit the significance of the confusing events set in motion by the riots and the backlash. News of the rioting in Watts, Los Angeles, in August, 1965—the first riot to capture national attention—reached Johnson at the end of a week that had begun with the signing of the Voting Rights Act, a victory Johnson described as "a triumph for freedom as huge as any victory that has ever been won on any battlefield." "How is it possible," Johnson asked, "after all we've accomplished? How could it be? Is the world topsy-turvy?" So dreadful was the fact of Watts that Johnson simply refused at first to acknowledge it. "He just wouldn't accept it," White House aide Joseph Califano recalled. "He refused to look at the cable from Los Angeles describing the situation. He refused to take the calls from the generals who were requesting government planes to fly in the National Guard. I tried to reach him a dozen times. We needed decisions from him. But he simply wouldn't respond."[24]

Watts was the precursor of more than one hundred riots that stretched out for three long summers, leaving 225 people dead, 4,000 wounded, and $112 billion in property damage. Initially, Johnson perceived only the harm the rioters had done to him, seeing in the flames of the stores and the houses his own betrayal. "It simply wasn't fair for a few irresponsible agitators to spoil it for me and for all the rest of the Negroes, who are basically peace-loving and nice. A few hoodlums sparked by outside agitators who moved around from city to city making trouble. Spoiling all the progress I've made in these last few years."[25]

Sometimes, though, Johnson seemed to understand the honest frustration that was a source of the riots, although never admitting that he himself might have been responsible for some of that frustration. "God knows how little we've really moved on this issue, despite all the fanfare. As I see it, I've moved the Negro from D+ to C—. He's still nowhere. He knows it. And that's why he's out in the streets. Hell, I'd be there too. It was bad enough in the South—especially from the standpoint of education—but at least there the Negro knew he was really loved and cared for, which he never was in the North, where children live with rats and have no place to sleep and come from broken homes and get rejected from the Army. And then they look on TV and see all the promises of a rich country and they know that some movement is beginning to take place in their lives, so they begin to hope for a lot more. Hell, when a person's released from jail or his parents, it is only natural that he takes advantage and turns to excess. Remember the Negroes in Reconstruction who got elected to Congress and then ran into the chamber with bare feet and white women. They were simply not prepared for their responsibility. And we weren't just enough or kind enough to help them prepare. So we lost a hundred years going backward. We'll never know how high a price we paid for the unkindness and injustice we've inflicted on people—the Negroes, Mexicans, and Jews—and everyone who really believes he has been discriminated against in any way is part of that great human price. And that cost exists where many people may not even think it does. No matter how well you may think you know a Negro, if you really know one, there'll come the time when you look at him and see how deep his bitterness is.

"But there are thousands of people out there who'll never understand this, people who've worked hard every day to save up for a week's vacation or a new store and they look around and think they see their tax dollars going to finance a bunch of ungrateful rioters. Why, that's bound to make even a nonprejudiced person angry. Prejudice—you know, my feeling all along has been that prejudice about color is *not* the big factor. Maybe the Poles do hate the Negroes, but I think fear is the cause of their hatred, not prejudice—anyone who's afraid of losing his job to another man will soon turn to hate that other man. Now I thought when we got unemployment down, we'd eliminated that fear. When I got the tax bill passed in '64, it made such a dent in unemployment I figured we were on the way. And when I got the stock market up and everyone was making money, with wages going up even higher than prices, I figured if there was a time when jealousy wouldn't assert itself, it would be this one. Now I knew that as President I couldn't make people *want* to integrate their schools or open their doors to blacks, but I could make them feel guilty for not doing it and I believed it was my moral responsibility to do precisely that—to use the moral suasion of my office to make people feel that segregation was a curse they'd carry with them to their graves. This guilt was the only chance we had for holding the backlash in check.

"Then when we got that voting rights bill passed, I figured the most constructive thing that could have come to the Negroes would have been to register and vote for the people who'd do a good job for them. And when I met all the time with the heads of the black organizations, I knew I was helping those organizations grow in the eyes of their constituents. Why, if Whitney Young or Roy Wilkins could hang a picture of me on their office walls, shaking hands with them, they'd be in good with their people for some time. And when I appointed Thurgood Marshall to the Supreme Court, I figured he'd be a great example to younger kids. There was probably not a Negro in America who didn't know about Thurgood's appointment. All over America that day Negro parents looked at their children a little differently, thousands of mothers looked across the breakfast table and said: 'Now maybe this will happen to my child someday.' I bet from one coast to the other there was a rash of new mothers naming their newborn sons Thurgood."[26]

The stance Johnson adopted toward the racial issue was courageous and humane. In the political world of the 1950s and early 1960s it would have comfortably occupied a position midway between the radicals and the conservatives. But the dimensions of the racial problem in the mid- and late sixties were so large, having grown larger with every year of neglect, that it could not be easily handled by traditional politics. Sparked by frustrated hope, the violent events strained the common frame of reference that had offered the earlier period its measure of certainty. Centrist leadership is possible in the last analysis because the individuals within the society carry around in their heads a similar picture of the means and ends of their political order. Common purpose is essential for the development of mutual trust. But the sense of common purpose seemed to have vanished with the riots; the media suggested that a significant portion of the American population had lost its faith in the rules of the game and in the leadership organizations designed to articulate their demands.

After the riots, the media described America in very different terms. It was as if overnight an innocent child had become a middle-aged man, as if within months the soul of America had passed from childlike mirth and unreasoning optimism to deep dejection. The pointless deaths were taken by the commentators as evidence of the bankruptcy of the earlier faith in gradual progress, making it clear that equality for the Negro was a far greater problem than anyone had imagined and its solution probably more remote than ever. Suddenly the hopeful attitudes of the past were seen as somewhat embarrassing, the symbol of youthful improvidence.

While Johnson expected thousands of mothers to name their children after his new Supreme Court Justice, birth certificates on file in Boston and New York City revealed seven Martins, ten Luthers, eleven George Washingtons, and fifteen Franklin Delanos, but not a single Thurgood. To say this is not to take away from Johnson's action in appointing the first Negro to the Court; it was a measure of the times that achievements which would have seemed monumental in 1960 were taken as tokenism rather than progress. Militant leaders argued that whites had traditionally exercised the prerogative of choosing their own Negro leaders and choosing them on the basis of which ones were the most accommodating.

Clearly the racial situation in the late 1960s presented Johnson with political liabilities no matter which way he moved. Public opinion surveys taken in the aftermath of the riots suggested a sharp polarization in black-white attitudes. Of the whites surveyed, 45 percent blamed the riots on outside agitators with Communist backing. Only 7 percent of the blacks took this view; 93 percent blamed general frustration. Two-thirds of the blacks felt the police had contributed to the riots; only one-sixth of the whites even acknowledged the presence of police brutality.[27] And what the riots began, the inflationary economy—which locked the blue-collar worker into a struggle with the blacks for jobs—finished: the collapse of the old coalition of organized labor, intellectuals, workers, minorities, and the poor that had functioned for nearly a generation to unite the Democratic Party.

The anger and bitterness on all sides presented Johnson with a task of leadership more difficult than any he had ever faced before. It is tempting, but wrong, to suggest that it was simply a task beyond the ability of this traditional Southern politician. Considering how much Lyndon Johnson had grown on the issue of civil rights, remembering his "We Shall Overcome" speech to the Congress, watching his persistent commitment to open housing long after most of his advisers suggested that he give up, I think the question remains open. Perhaps the symbolic aspects of reunifying the blacks and the blue-collar workers would have been beyond his grasp; perhaps he never could have projected an image that pointed toward the future instead of the past. The point is, we shall never know. For once again, the war in Vietnam mortgaged his leadership at home—exacerbating tensions with Martin Luther King, forcing Johnson into defensive postures, draining his resources.

And in his abdication of leadership on this critical issue, Johnson paved the way for the emergence of two of his greatest rivals: Robert Kennedy, who came to be seen by many in 1968 as the only man capable of rebuilding the Democratic Party and bringing back together the blacks and the whites; and, after his assassination, Richard Nixon, who shared and elaborated upon Johnson's means without any ends at all.

Chapter 11

Under Siege
in the White House

Johnson continued to believe that by taking what he regarded as a "middle course" in Vietnam and in pursuit of the Great Society, he would ultimately secure those achievements that would ensure him a place in history among the greatest of American leaders—one who, like Roosevelt, both transformed American society and succeeded in war. Even Roosevelt, however, had not pursued both goals simultaneously. On the other hand, Vietnam was not a world war, but a battle contained in a small country against an emeny whose military power, by traditional measurements, could not be compared with that of America. It was this "fact," and the disastrous misjudgments to which it contributed, that made it possible for Johnson to think he could continue the Great Society while prosecuting the war.

The strategy he developed, however, required a relatively swift and convincing demonstration that his objectives in Vietnam were close to fulfillment, as well as the sustenance of the economic conditions that supported the Great Society. When he was unable to achieve the success his strategy demanded—when the war continued with no sign that the Communist forces were being compelled to abandon their objectives and when deteriorating economic realities could no longer be dissolved by exhortation—his consensus began to dissolve. His "moderate course" was attacked by both opponents of the war and those who agreed with the premise that our national security was at stake but believed that the necessary victory could be achieved only by the swift and massive use of military power against North Vietnam. As Johnson had feared, growing awareness of the war's dimension stiffened congressional resistance to his Great Society program. The effectiveness of this resistance was enhanced because it tended to come from those same conservatives who supported his policies in Vietnam, and could command domestic concessions as a reward for that support.

At the same time, the peace movement expanded the size and scope of its activity. Teach-ins and marches were followed by sit-ins and lie-ins, by draft card burnings and demonstrations, by desertions from the Army and other acts of civil disobedience. The nation was in turmoil, and the disruption worked against the President. Yet Johnson persisted in his course in Vietnam. Why? Why did this most pragmatic of men obstinately refuse to alter his policy and cut his losses? The answer requires an understanding of both the institutional and personal momentums at work.

In the beginning, Johnson had feared his country would become obsessed with failure if Vietnam was lost. As the war went on, the obsession he feared for his country became his own. Indeed, as the Great Society disintegrated, the lower the President's popularity fell, the more Johnson *had* to see his decision to escalate as the only decision he could have made. He had committed everything he had to Vietnam. Regardless of all evidence, he simply had to be right. To think otherwise, to entertain even the slightest doubt, was to open himself to the pain of reliving old decisions, options, and possibilities long since discarded. "No, no, no!" Johnson shouted at me one afternoon as I tried to discuss earlier opportunities for peace. "I will *not* let you take me backward in time on Vietnam. Fifty thousand American boys are dead. Nothing we say can change that fact. Your idea that I could have chosen otherwise rests upon complete ignorance. For if I had chosen otherwise, I would have been responsible for starting World War III. In fact, it was the thought of World War III that kept me going every day. I saw how long the war was taking. I knew what it was doing to my Great Society programs. But all that horror, as horrible as it was, and I hated it more than anyone—do you know what it's like to feel responsible for the deaths of men you love?—well, all that horror was acceptable if it prevented the far worse horror of World War III. For that would have meant the end of everything we know."[1]

As Lyndon Johnson saw the situation, large forces were at work in Vietnam that others did not see but that he, privy to vast and undisclosed knowledge of the matter, clearly understood. Furthermore, these forces had their origin in the experiences of war. It was a test case for World War III; danger to the survival of the free world was the sole criterion for a just apprehension of America's actions in Vietnam. Johnson's thought simply followed to its furthest reach a system of logic rooted in a particular reading of history. But as the need to ward off threatening aspects of reality intensified, his reasoning tended toward rationalization, wishful thinking, denial, repression, and projection.

Apparently hoping that his words would conceal or even change established facts, and in an effort to halt the erosion of his support, Johnson indulged more and more freely in distortion and patent falsehoods: constant reference to "the progress" made in Vietnam, describing things as he wanted them to be, as if he believed that by the force of his will he could transform what was or had already happened. And because of the office he held, and the armor of institutions, access to media, and control of information available to support him, he was capable of projecting a confusing distortion across the nation. His optimistic public reports drowned the black and ominous analyses of dissenters simply because they were official and public. Publicly established and accepted propositions had a great advantage over whatever individuals privately knew and believed to be the truth.[2] And because Johnson wanted so desperately to believe, he was unable to deceive others without often deceiving himself. In persuading the public of the success of the bombing program, he persuaded himself.

But as time went by, neither the powers of Johnson's office nor the intensity of his own conviction could overcome the accumulating facts and evidence of the war's cost and American errors. In 1960 the United States troop strength in South Vietnam stood at 800. By the end of 1964 the number had risen to 23,000, a year later it hit 184,000, and two years after that it reached nearly 500,000. As the troop level went up, the level of casualties (killed, wounded, hospitalized, missing) increased, growing from 2,500 in 1965 to 33,000 in 1966, to 80,000 in 1967, to 130,000 in 1968.[3] As the promise of easy victory receded, the war critics became increasingly strident. Deprived of an atmosphere of public support, besieged at home and abroad, Johnson retreated more and more into the world of his imagination, directing an increasing part of his energies to the task of protecting himself.

In the heady days of the Great Society and at the start of the escalation, Johnson was confident that he could deal rationally and successfully with the small, scattered strands of criticisms on the war. His conviction (that he was right and his critics were wrong) allowed him to spend hours at a time with his opponents. He summoned them to his office for confidential interviews; he invited them to specially prepared White House briefings. At that time, Johnson was able to maintain a bantering, almost friendly, tone—so long as those critics remained few in number and confined their critiques to private conversations. "Well, Bill [Fulbright]," one conversation began in 1965, "what have you been doing today to damage the Republic? You say you've got a bad stomach. Well, that's because you've been so anti-Johnson lately. I told you that it's bad for you to take out after me. Now you tell your wife I love her and I am sorry you're so damned cranky and grouchy all the time."[4] But as the opposition proliferated and surfaced in the public forums and as support for the administration's policies plummeted in the polls, Johnson no longer debated or discussed the substance of the critics' charges. Increasingly, he endeavored to dismiss the content by discrediting the source.

Strangely, however, Johnson was probably least harsh toward the protesting young, although he heard each taunt and chant, and they wounded him deeply. But they were not, he believed, motivated by self-interest or personal animosity; their dissent sprang from the ignorance of their youth. "Why should I listen to all those student peaceniks marching up and down the streets? They were barely in their cradles in the dark days of World War II; they never experienced the ravages of Adolf Hitler; they were only in nursery school during the fall of China; they were sitting in grammar school during the Korean War; they wouldn't know a Communist if they tripped over one. They simply don't understand the world the way I do." And how else could he deal with the young? Certainly not as enemies. They were, after all, the future for which he had hoped to build, and for which, he believed, he was now fighting. If they marched against him because of what they did not know, then there was a chance that someday they would understand.

Johnson, however, could be unsparing of the professors who had failed to guide their students. All his life he had maintained a distinction between the doers and the thinkers; as if membership in one category walled off the other. Now his mounting stress served to reinforce that wall. The thinkers were the critics, a negative chorus jealously intent upon the destruction of all he had built. "The professors believe you can get peace by being soft and acting nice. But everything I know about history proves this absolutely wrong. It was our lack of strength and failure to show stamina, our hesitancy, vacillation, and love of peace being paraded so much that caused all our problems before World War I, World War II, and Korea. And now we're really up for grabs. We're the richest nation in the world. And the minute we look soft, the would-be aggressors will go wild. We'll lose all of Asia and then Europe and we'll be an island all by ourselves. And when all that comes to pass, I'd sure hate to have to depend on the Galbraiths and that Harvard crowd to protect my property or lead me to the Burnet cave."[5]

Suspicion of motive became his chief instrument in discrediting critics on the Hill. "Fulbright's problem," Johnson told himself, "is that he's never found any President who would appoint him Secretary of State. He is frustrated up there on the Hill. And he takes out his frustration by making all those noises about Vietnam. He wants the nation to stand up and take notice of Bill Fulbright, and he knows the best way to get that attention is to put himself in the role of critic. He would have taken that role whichever way I moved on Vietnam. And then beside Fulbright there were all those liberals on the Hill squawking at me about Vietnam. Why? Because I never went to Harvard. That's why. Because I wasn't John F. Kennedy. Because I wasn't friends with all their friends. Because I was keeping the throne from Bobby Kennedy. Because the Great Society was accomplishing more than the New Frontier. You see, they had to find some issue on which to turn against me and they found it in Vietnam. Even though they were the very people who developed the concept of limited war in the first place.

"And then," Johnson continued, "there were the columnists. They turned against me on Vietnam because it was in their self-interest to do so, because they knew that no one receives a Pulitzer Prize these days by simply supporting the President and the administration. You win by digging up contrary information, by making a big splash. Truth no longer counts so long as a big sensation can be produced. Every story is always slanted to win the favor of someone who sits higher up. The Washington press are like a wolf pack when it comes to attacking public officials, but they're like a bunch of sheep in their own profession and they will always follow the bellwether sheep, the leaders of their profession, Lippmann and Reston. As long as those two stayed with me, I was okay. But once they left me in pursuit of their fancy prizes, everyone else left me as well. But the more they screamed and squawked, the more determined I was to stick it out. I read about all the troubles Lincoln had in conducting the Civil War. Yet he persevered and history rewarded him for the perseverance."[6]

By supplying himself with such explanations, Johnson tried to devalue the merit of the dissenting idea. In doing so, he expressed a host of fears, biases, and assumptions that had been held for a lifetime, and which not only had informed his public career but had made it so successful, and to which now he steadfastly would cling.

If Johnson rationalized and sought to deflect pressures on the left, he overexaggerated those on the right. The President was indeed criticized by the Joint Chiefs of Staff and the members of the Armed Services Committees in the Senate and the House for talking too much about peace and for not bearing down harder to win, but his picture of himself as under their constant barrage had little relation to reality. However, the picture served not only a public purpose but an inner need. Johnson wanted to believe he was restrained in his conduct of the war. He wanted to believe he was pursuing a middle course, warding off the crazies on both sides. It was necessary to magnify the hawks to balance the doves.

Still, Johnson had to find a reason for the fact that the level of public support for his moderate position was steadily waning. At this point, more elaborate devices were brought into play, in particular the mechanisms of projection and conspiracy. The more his popularity slipped, the greater became his need for evidence that he was not at fault. The scapegoat emerged in a group composed of the intellectuals, the press, the liberals, and the Kennedys. As unpleasant as it was to feel "done in" by his opponents, it was not accepting the blame. Indeed, his ensuing feeling of martyrdom brought a temporary rise in self-esteem. That his polls were down meant only that the conspirators had been successful in creating a false image. This was something new, and ominous, in Johnson's internal pattern of thought. It was one thing to look for unworthy motives, however unfairly or inaccurately described. But to believe oneself the target of a giant conspiracy was such a leap into unreason that it could only mean some disintegration of Johnson's thought, that the barriers separating irrational thought and delusion were crumbling.

"No matter what anyone said," Johnson once argued, "I knew that the people out there loved me a great deal. All that talk about my lack of charisma was a lot of crap. There is no such thing as charisma. It's just the creation of the press and the pollsters. Deep down I knew—I simply knew—that the American people loved me. After all that I'd done for them and given to them, how could they help but love me? And I knew that it was only a very small percentage that had given up, who had lost faith. We had more than three million young people serving in uniform. I heard from a hundred of them every day. They didn't get the attention the TV people gave the exhibitionists. They didn't have anyone to make signs for them and parade around for them. They were just there, from daylight to dark, fighting for freedom and willing to die for it.

"The problem is that I was sabotaged. Look what happened whenever I went to make a speech about the war. The week before my speech, the St. Louis *Post-Dispatch* or the Boston *Globe* or *CBS News* would get on me over and over, talking about what a terrible speaker I was and about how awful the bombing was, and pretty soon the people began to wonder, they began to think that I really must be uninspiring if the papers and the TV said so. They began to think that I might be wrong about the war. And gradually they stopped coming to my speeches. And then the press gleefully reported a small crowd and an uninspiring speech. Why, it's just as if you were making a tour of the nation and I was an advance man going into every town ahead of you, telling people you were a prostitute, a mean woman, out to cheat them of their hard-earned money. Well, at first the people might still come to see you, dismissing all that talk as nasty rumor. But after a while, some of it would have to sink in. And then more and more. And then there would be absolutely nothing you could do to stop the tide."[7]

It is characteristic of obsessional, delusional thinking to piece together bits of fact. Johnson's critics did, in fact, have a reinforcing effect upon each other. The Eastern media did exaggerate the sentiments of the people. There were those in the Kennedy crowd out to get Johnson. But in the past

Johnson had displayed a fine sense of discrimination about
his political opponents, recognizing that his enemies today
might be his allies tomorrow. Now he became unrestrained
and reckless, creating a fantasy world of heroes and villains.
Members of the White House staff who had listened to the
President's violent name-calling were frightened by what
seemed to them signs of paranoia. Suddenly in the middle of
a conversation, the President's voice would become intense
and low-keyed. He would laugh inappropriately and his
thoughts would assume a random, almost incoherent quality,
as he began to spin a vast web of accusations.

"Two or three intellectuals started it all, you know. They
produced all the doubt, they and the columnists in the Washington *Post*, the *New York Times*, *Newsweek*, and *Life*. And
it spread and it spread until it appeared as if the people were
against the war. Then Bobby began taking it up as his cause
and with Martin Luther King on his payroll he went around
stirring up the Negroes and telling them that if they came out
into the streets they'd get more. Then the Communists
stepped in. They control the three networks, you know, and
the forty major outlets of communication. It's all in the FBI
reports. They prove everything. Not just about the reporters
but about the professors, too.

"The Communists' desire to dominate the world is just like
the lawyer's desire to be the ultimate judge on the Supreme
Court or the politician's desire to be President. You see, the
Communists want to rule the world, and if we don't stand up
to them, they will do it. And we'll be slaves. Now I'm not
one of those folks seeing Communists under every bed. But I
do know about the principles of power, and when one side is
weak, the other steps in. And that's just what the Communists
did when they realized the soft spots in the American liberal
community.

"You see the way it worked: The opponents of the war
went on jags which pretty much originated in the Communist
world and eventually found their way to the American critics.
One jag was that we were killing civilians. The next was that
we needed a bombing pause. The first bombing pause came
after a Communist diplomat talked to some influential Americans. Bobby Kennedy sat with me and told me that he knew
that if we ordered a pause something would happen. So I ordered a pause. We delivered a letter to North Vietnam and
they threw it back the next day. Later, Senator Morse came

in and told me the Soviet Ambassador said that such and such would happen if we stopped the bombing. They were telling the same thing to Fulbright, Clark, Mansfield, Church, and others. Then McGeorge Bundy had lunch with Dobrynin and suddenly he became an ardent advocate for peace. Fortas was against the pause. So were Rusk and Clifford. I also thought it was wrong, that it would make us look like a weak sister. But I hated to see history record that I stood in the way of peace. So again I ordered a pause and again nothing happened. Isn't it funny that I always received a piece of advice from my top advisers right after each of them had been in contact with someone in the Communist world? And isn't it funny that you could always find Dobrynin's car in front of Reston's house the night before Reston delivered a blast on Vietnam?"[8]

Sometimes it seemed as if Johnson himself did not believe what he was saying, as if all the surmises were a bizarre recreation, a way to relax. But at other times Johnson's voice carried so much conviction that his words produced an almost hypnotic effect. What is clear, however, is that this continual concentration on conspiracy squandered a large amount of energy. The worse the situation in Vietnam became, the more Johnson intruded his suspicions and his fears into every aspect of his daily work. Conversations with Cabinet members would begin with the question "Why aren't you out there fighting against my enemies? Don't you realize that if they destroy me, they'll destroy you as well?" Discussions on legislation would be interrupted by diatribes against "the critics." Private luncheons and dinners would be dominated by complaints about "the traitors."

In typical circumstances, of course, people who slip into fantasy are quickly set straight by the adverse criticism of those around them, which forces them to face the truth. In Johnson's White House there were no such correctives. To the contrary, his every self-deception was repeatedly confirmed in the men around him. How did this happen? Where were all the checks and balances that had been built into the American political system to guard against precisely this occurrence? The answer requires an understanding of some developments of the modern Presidency and its relationship to the surrounding institutions of the Cabinet, the White House staff, the Congress, the Party, and the public.

No matter how well a polity's institutions are designed, its leaders are subject to lapses from rational, functional behavior. Every society learns to live with a certain amount of irrational behavior at the top, but lest the irrationality feed upon itself and lead to general decay, the polity must have the capacity to marshal forces that influence or compel the faltering actors to revert to the behavior that is required if the polity is to function properly.[9] Those who framed the American system sought to protect against a malfunctioning executive through a structure that provided for competition between "separated institutions sharing powers." Presidential performance would be checked from deterioration by the powers of the Congress, the threat of public disaffection, and the workings of the free press. Believing that the necessity for consent would discipline the participants, the framers created a system of checks and balances that called for agreement among a variety of institutions before decisions could be made. The system was reinforced in the early days of the Republic by the development of two extraconstitutional institutions—the Cabinet and the party—which served, along with the Congress, the public, and the press, to check the President. Thus the system as a whole—legal structure and formal institutions—seemed to require a politics of bargaining in which the President's advantages were continually checked by the advantages of others.[10]

Bargaining continued throughout Johnson's Presidency, as did the structure of separated institutions sharing powers. But historical experience in the area of foreign policy—along with the increase in the executive's domestic functions—had fundamentally changed the distribution of resources among the actors. The President still had rivals for power in foreign affairs, but not one of these rivals was coherent enough in its dissent nor strong enough in its base of power to stay the President's hand. As we have seen, for decades the power of foreign policymaking had been absorbed by the executive. This consolidation, justified by the speed with which the President was able to act and the stores of information available to him, along with the dominant tendency in liberal thought that only a strong executive could be counted on to enforce the country's noblest and rational goals, had resulted in a constitutional imbalance between the President and the rest of the government.

In the course of the war in Vietnam several members of

Johnson's Cabinet, including the Secretary of Health, Education, and Welfare, John Gardner, and the Secretary of Labor, Willard Wirtz, developed substantial doubts about American policy. They were distressed about the massive drain of resources away from essential domestic programs. Privately, these men urged a limit to America's involvement. But the structure of executive decision-making offered little opportunity for heads of domestic departments to express their views on matters of war and peace.[11] The only individuals whose opinions on foreign policy could carry weight were those whose positions tied them in on a daily basis to the decisions made about Vietnam.[12] The rules of the game restricted all other players from real participation in decisions on Vietnam, thus inhibiting an expression of views on the basis of domestic considerations. Cabinet meetings were largely ceremonial, serving more as channels of information between the heads of departments than as adversary proceedings. The agendas of the Cabinet meetings called upon each department head to report on activities in his own jurisdiction. In this atmosphere of "show and tell," little exchange took place; questions relating to Vietnam remained unasked and unanswered.

With the decline of the Cabinet meetings as a forum for discussion of foreign policy, domestic department heads were deprived of the one institution through which collective complaints could be effectively lodged. Lacking an effective voice within the administration, individual members were thrown back on the defense of dramatic resignation intended to communicate their dissent, and, perhaps, stimulate debate.[13] However, knowing that his accumulated power, prestige, and alliances within the government would evaporate with his resignation, given the absence in the American system of a parliamentary backbench, the typical Cabinet member chose to stay and fight from within, reasoning and rationalizing at the same time that if he left, things in his own organization would go from bad to worse.[14] In the end, this quiescence, masquerading under the name of loyalty, served only to insulate the President from views and concerns that were essential to his understanding.

Johnson was ravenous for information when things were going well. Under siege, however, his operational style closed in and insulated him within the White House, where discussion was confined to those who offered no disagreement. As time went by, he tended more and more to bypass the National Security Council, believing it too unwieldy for secret diplomacy. And as suspicions of disloyalty and conspiracy began to dominate his thought, Johnson narrowed his circle of advisers to the trusted Tuesday lunch group—the Secretaries of State and Defense, the Special Assistant for National Security Affairs, the Director of the Central Intelligence Agency, the Chairman of the Joint Chiefs of Staff, and selected others. As Johnson explained it: "The National Security Council meetings were like sieves. I couldn't control them. You knew after the National Security Council meeting that each of those guys would run home to tell his wife and neighbors what they said to the President. That's why I used the Tuesday lunch format instead. That group never leaked a single note. Those men were loyal to me. I could control them, but in those larger meetings, why, every Defense Department official and his brother would be leakers at one time or another. And when I'd see some DOD official's picture in the paper with a nice story about him, I'd know it was the paper's bribe for the leaked story."[15]

Soon, all who did not share Johnson's convictions ceased to attend the Tuesday lunches. Johnson protected himself from contrary arguments and discussions by dismissing the doubters from his staff. First McGeorge Bundy left. Then George Ball. Then Bill Moyers. The emphasis shifted to Walt Rostow, who believed that Johnson was doing the right thing in Vietnam; soon Rostow became the man who screened what the President heard and saw. Under Rostow's regime, the most optimistic news was packaged and sent to the President with covering notes which said such things as "This will give confirmation to the statement which the President so wisely made to the Congressional leadership yesterday."[16]

In 1967 McNamara began to move away from the President's policy of escalation. As McNamara now saw the situation in Vietnam, the war was going badly and should be capped. But as McNamara's pessimism grew, his access to the President diminished. Johnson did not want to hear other people's doubts. He needed loyalty and support. So in November, 1967, the President suddenly announced that McNamara was leaving the DOD to accept the directorship of the World Bank. Here again Johnson conjured an explanation that precluded the necessity for dealing directly with the content of McNamara's doubts.

"McNamara's problem," Johnson later said, "was that he

began to feel a division in his loyalties. He had always loved and admired the Kennedys; he was more their cup of tea, but he also admired and respected the Presidency. Then, when he came to work for me, I believed he developed a deep affection for me as well, not so deep as the one he held for the Kennedys but deep enough, combined with his feelings about the office itself, to keep him completely loyal for three long years. Then he got surrounded by Paul Warnke, Adam Yarmolinsky, and Alain Enthoven; they excited him with their brilliance, all the same cup of tea, all came to the same conclusion after old man Galbraith. Then the Kennedys began pushing him harder and harder. Every day Bobby would call up McNamara, telling him that the war was terrible and immoral and that he had to leave. Two months before he left he felt he was a murderer and didn't know how to extricate himself. I never felt like a murderer, that's the difference. Someone had to call Hitler and someone had to call Ho. We can't let the Kennedys be peacemakers and us warmakers simply because they came from the Charles River.

"After a while, the pressure got so great that Bob couldn't sleep at night. I was afraid he might have a nervous breakdown. I loved him and I didn't want to let him go, but he was just short of cracking and I felt it'd be a damn unfair thing to force him to stay. When he told me in November that the only job he really wanted then was the World Bank, I told him any job he wanted in the administration he could have. Now the man who deserved that bank job all along was Henry Fowler; he'd been waiting for it all the way through. When I told him McNamara was going to get it, tears came to his eyes. But at that point, I had no choice."[17]

As the central forum for decision-making on the war, the Tuesday lunch had serious weaknesses.[18] It was not a place through which military, economic, and political programs could be coordinated. Nor was it a place to discuss the larger questions of the war. Men deeply involved in the daily course of events tend to concentrate on operational rather than strategic questions and on logistics rather than on structural considerations. A typical discussion of the Tuesday lunch would begin with the alternative targets for bombing, continue with the increased lift capacity of the newest helicopters, move on to the quality of meat in the mess hall, and conclude with the production figures for waterproof boats, never once calling into serious question the shared assumptions about the nature of the war or its central importance to national security. Someone once said as he watched Dean Rusk hurrying to the White House for a meeting of the Tuesday lunch, "If you told him right now of a sure-fire way to defeat the Vietcong and to get out of Vietnam, he would groan that he was too busy to worry about that now; he had to discuss next week's bombing targets."[19]

The secrecy of the proceedings created additional problems. In his fear of leaks, Johnson refused to let his subordinates draw up either a systematic agenda or a written report of the discussion. As a result, decisions were often reached on matters that had not been discussed and therefore were not fully reviewed in advance. The confusion was compounded by the President's habitual desire to keep as many people in the dark about as many things as possible. Under Johnson's surveillance, the participants in the Tuesday lunch group were afraid to discuss the content of the meetings even with their senior subordinates. Eventually a serious communication gap developed between the men at the top and the assistants who were supposed to serve them but found it increasingly difficult to translate a policy they did not understand into daily action.[20]

Moreover, the content of the meetings varied substantially with Johnson's shifting moods. If he felt momentarily good about something—some article of praise or some news from the field—he could focus well and hard on the decisions that had to be made. But during periods of depression he would spend hours in rambling talk, turning listlessly from one extraneous subject to another. At such times he reduced the Tuesday lunch to a stage on which to vent his emotions, a forum for his monologues, holding forth at great length with a diatribe against the critics or calling out in a self-pitying way for understanding of his plight.

Once Johnson started on one of his monologues, it was difficult to halt him. If one of the listeners interrupted, trying to pull him back to the business at hand, he would become enraged. Yet if the listeners acquiesced by a smile or a sympathetic nodding of the head, Johnson would feel encouraged and continue on.[21] In such moods, Johnson's vanity proved unappeasable. The constant encouragement he demanded deadened the critical faculties of those still allowed access, creating a vacuum around himself and making him a prisoner of his own propaganda. Screening out options, facts, and ideas, Lyndon Johnson's personality operated to distort the truth in much the same way as ideology works in a totalitarian society.[22]

Secure in his enclave at 1600 Pennsylvania Avenue, Johnson could depend upon his aides for a reassuring interpretation of the public mood. "According to my son," White House aide Ernest Goldstein wrote in October, 1967, at the time of the March on the Pentagon, "your storm trooper reference slowed down the Vietniks at his college. A decent majority are now pulling away from the rowdies."[23] Writing in the same vein, another White House aide told Johnson that he had much stronger support in the liberal community than he realized. "Hardly a day goes by without my getting a call from outstanding liberals who just want you to know they are backing you."[24]

Over time, Johnson tacitly developed an anticipatory feedback system that discouraged views that the President would not receive favorably from being communicated to him. Chester Cooper described how this process worked in a National Security Council meeting. "The President, in due course, would announce his decision and then poll everyone in the room—council members, their assistants, and members of the White House and NSC staffs. 'Mr. Secretary, do you agree with the decision?' 'Yes, Mr. President.' 'Mr. X, do you agree?' 'I agree, Mr. President.' " During the process Cooper would frequently fall into a Walter Mitty-like fantasy: "When my turn came, I would rise to my feet slowly, look around the room and then directly at the President and say very quietly and emphatically, 'Mr. President, gentlemen, I most definitely do *not* agree.' But I was removed from my trance when I heard the President's voice saying, 'Mr. Cooper, do you agree?' And out would come a 'Yes, Mr. President, I agree.' "[25]

The organizational dynamics remind one of a phenomenon in psychology known as *folie à deux*, in which strong, overbearing personalities are able to make others living under the same premises accept their own delusional systems. The recipients are generally weak, submissive persons who find it easier to accept the ideas of the leader (even if those ideas are manifestly wrongheaded) than to fight his authority. The unshakable conviction of the leader as well as the anxiety that a rejection of his authority would provoke in the recipients bring the latter to accept his delusions.[26]

To understand how the men in Johnson's White House, few of whom would be considered weak or submissive, eventually played a role in what might be called a *folie à plus*, it is important to understand the state of dependency imposed upon a President's top advisers by the modern structure of the White House. "The life of the White House," as George Reedy describes it, "is the life of a court.

> It is a structure designed for one purpose and one purpose only—to serve the material needs and the desires of a single man.... To achieve this end, every conceivable facility is made available, from the very latest and most luxurious jet aircraft to a masseur constantly in attendance to soothe raw presidential nerves. Even more important, however, he is treated with all the reverence due a monarch. No one interrupts presidential contemplation for anything less than a major catastrophe somewhere on the globe. No one speaks to him unless spoken to first. No one ever invites him to "go soak your head" when his demands become petulant and unreasonable.[27]

In this strange atmosphere, the men surrounding the President tend to become sycophants. The tendency is most striking in relation to the members of the White House staff, who possess no independent constituency of their own and are completely dependent upon the President for their decisions, publicity, and status. The members of the staff are appointed by the President, promoted by him, and fired by him. Access to him soon becomes the coin of the realm. In this competitive contest, there is little room or incentive for independent criticism. On the contrary, compelled to explain their actions to no one but the man at the top, the members of the staff tend to become mirrors for the chief. In Reedy's words: "No White House assistant can stay in the President's graces for any considerable period without renouncing his own ego.... Those I have known who had kept some personality either left after a while or were careful to unleash their personality only in the President's absence."[28] Nor did this requisite of deference stop with the White House staff. As the Secretaries of State and Defense began spending more time at the White House than in their own departments, their dependence on the President grew. And with the growth in dependence came an increasing submission.

The structure proved disastrous for Lyndon Johnson and the nation. He had always functioned best in relationships where the other person had independent power. Then Johnson had to pay attention to the necessities of bargaining, moderating his drive to dominate by a realistic perception of the limitations of his own resources. But when the structure reduced the external limitations, Johnson fell back on his need to dominate and positively overpower everyone in sight. Thus the White House machinery became the President's psyche writ large, transmitting his wishes throughout the Executive Office with a terrifying force.

Nor did the President *have* to listen even to the Congress. At any time in the course of the war, the Congress could have stopped America's involvement in Vietnam if it had wanted to. The formal institutional authority was there: for example, the Congress could have rejected any one of the annual authorization bills for the DOD, or it could have passed a bill requiring the President to stop the bombing. The point is that when it came to the making of rough decisions on recorded roll call votes, a majority of the members of the Congress chose to support the war. In 1967 Representative George Brown of California introduced a motion to recommit the DOD authorization bill to add a sense-of-Congress resolution that none of the funds authorized by the Act should be used to carry out military operations in or over North Vietnam. The resolution was not legally binding, but even this move was considered a radical step. The vote on the motion found only 18 members, all Democrats, in favor and 372 opposed.[29]

In the House, the antiwar faction tended to be composed of junior members with limited access to the key committees that were in the best position to exercise leverage over the course of the war. The top positions in these committees— Appropriations and Armed Services—were filled by pro-administration members, men with years of accumulated seniority, extensive tie-ins to the military, and long experience in deferring to the President on matters of war and peace. The antiwar members could have compensated for their institutional disadvantage with a firm knowledge of the written rules, which allowed the House as a whole to take positions above and beyond the committee deliberations. But in understanding the parliamentary rules, the Young Turks were no match for the powerful few who controlled the committees.[80]

The antiwar faction in the Senate had an easier time. The Senate is less committee-dominated than the House. A Senator with a strong interest in a subject not covered by his committee assignments has more options. Protected by the tradition of unlimited debate, he can take to the Senate floor to express his opinions at great length. But the general level of senatorial debate in the 1960s was nowhere near what it once had been. For one thing, the Senators were involved in more committees and more activities than they used to be and could not afford to sit in the chamber half the day listening to speeches and waiting to vote. To accommodate these increased activities, the Senate leadership continued the practice that Lyndon Johnson had established as Majority Leader, of scheduling all the important business of the Senate on the basis of unanimous-consent agreements. This allowed the Senate as a whole to establish a precise time for voting or to place a specific limit on debate so that each Senator could know when a vote would be taken and arrange his schedule accordingly. Lyndon Johnson's innovation had proved extraordinarily effective in expediting Senate action on legislation. In reducing the individual Senator's incentive for being in the chamber, however, it had a stultifying effect upon debate. A quarter of a century earlier sixty or seventy Senators were generally present to hear Senator Vandenberg's discussions of foreign policy. In 1966, when Senator Fulbright delivered his celebrated address "Old Myths and New Realities," he spoke to an audience of four.[81]

Some have argued that Fulbright's televised hearings helped compensate for the deterioration in the Senate debate and performed an even wider educational function. But the hearings merely tugged and hauled at the President through a series of disconnected statements. They never really debated the premises behind the war. A graver problem was the absence of connection between the concerns of public hearings and the subject matter of senatorial votes. Not once during the years of the escalation did the issue of the war reach the floor of the Senate for a direct vote on the policy itself. Only three roll-call votes on Vietnam were recorded in the years between 1965 and 1968; all three revolved around the yearly supplemental appropriations in 1965, 1966, and 1967. But these votes did not accurately reflect dovish sentiment since they were phrased as measures to "support our troops." Faced with voting yea or nay on providing resources for American soldiers already in combat, all but two Senators consistently voted yea.[32]

In the absence of a collective legislative decision on the war, Johnson felt free to disregard the adverse voices as "nothing but a lot of sound and poppycock stimulated by the personal needs of William Fulbright."[33] Moreover, most of the communications from the Hill left the President in the dark as to what precisely was wanted of him. When Republican members criticized Johnson for lack of credibility, for mismanagement of the war, and for not exercising *more* power in the area, their charges were phrased in general terms and were not translated into specific policy alternatives. And when the Democratic doves expressed their opposition to the bombing, they failed to recommend withdrawal, and never followed their criticism to its logical extreme. Lacking clear-cut alternatives, facing simultaneous demands from different directions—urged by some to bomb more and by others to stop the bombing—Johnson continued unimpeded upon his escalatory course.

The bipartisan tradition reinforced Congress' impotence to constrain the President on Vietnam. The ideology of bipartisanship persuaded (or conveniently allowed) the political parties to abstain from partisan divisions on foreign policy. Throughout the course of the war, the Republicans' criticism remained merely tactical, never once questioning the premises of the administration's policy. And when it came to the option of openly breaking with the administration on roll-call votes, not a single Republican voted nay. The divisions within the Democratic Party were more open, but the party leadership was forced into an even more difficult position of defending the actions of *their* leader.

In the absence of response from either party, the peace movement developed essentially outside the established political system. This was both the source of its strength and its undoing. Existing in its own world, it evolved a powerful critique of the war, based on a very different set of assumptions and premises from those that guided the administration. The peace movement was drawn largely from a younger generation; World War II and the cold war were not its formative experiences; the heritage of Munich and Pearl Harbor was mere history. Communism was not a monolithic conspiracy to rule the world, but diverse nations, all of which deferred to Marx, yet had varied interests and often invoked the same sentences to curse each other. Who really could believe that China and Russia wanted to use Saigon as a jumping-off point for the invasion of San Francisco? Shaped more by the civil rights movement in their own country than by the struggle with Communism abroad, the young dissenters found social evolution and civil unrest recognizable, even familiar phenomena. From perspectives like this, the peace movement interpreted the Vietnamese situation as a civil war within a single tiny country. What happened in that country had little relation to what happened in the rest of Southeast Asia. Nor would the loss of Vietnam diminish America's national security.

When Johnson invoked national honor, the dissenters spoke of the dishonor of bombing and napalming the people of Vietnam. Even when the facts were not in dispute, their implications were. As the body count of enemies multiplied, Johnson took comfort from this sign of progress, while his opponents condemned the mounting toll in human life. Long before the end of his Presidency, Johnson lost all ability to communicate with the peace movement. Divided in values and assumptions, they went their different ways, the peace movement to the streets, Johnson to the refuge of his adamant convictions. Perhaps for the first time in his life, he could not even fathom the position on the other side. No longer the mediator, he had become a righteous if ineffective advocate of his own inflexibility.

The depth of Johnson's feelings, and the distance between the different views, was brought home to me in a long conversation with him during the summer of 1970. In the course of the conversation, I expressed a feeling that too often the debate about Vietnam was confined to tactical questions, focusing on the means of war—the effectiveness of bombing, the viability of strategic enclaves, the success or failure of pacification—at the expense of understanding the rightness or wrongness of the ends. After I finished, Johnson talked uninterruptedly for nearly three hours.

"How in the world can you and your friends say that South Vietnam is not a separate country with a traditionally recognized boundary? That boundary was created and internationally recognized by the Geneva Accords. Fifty nations recognized it; the Communist states recognized Hanoi's regime as a sovereign entity. The final decision specified two zones. That's that. . . . Oh, sure, there were some Koreans in both North and South Korea who believed their country was one country, yet was there any doubt that North Korean aggression took place? And does the belief of some within a country determine the legality of the boundaries? As for your claim it's not aggression, why, when a man walks into your house with a gun and its hammer pulled back, that's aggression. And that's exactly what North Vietnam did when it walked into the house of South Vietnam. It's just perverted history to claim that it's civil war, just pure bad history manufactured by the Harvards and the Galbraiths. No understanding of the thirty years before. There was no insurrection before the Communists decided to take part. Ho was a Communist all his adult life. He was trained in Moscow Communist headquarters. He was the founding father of the Communist Party in Indochina. After the Geneva Accords thousands of guerrillas moved from North to South awaiting word from Ho. All under Communist discipline, directly under Ho's command. The myth these professors have that it's a nice family fight, papa and mama and children, is pure crap. Why, the decision to renew the fight was made in Hanoi in 1959. The NLF was organized by the Central Committee of the Communist Party in Hanoi and announced from Hanoi. Sure, there's some free movement, but look at who controls it, who determines its direction. It is Hanoi, loud and clear.

"As for the argument that it was our aggression, not the North's aggression, against the people's will, well, that's just nonsense and naïveté. What better proof do you want of 'the people's' will than the elections in September, 1967? What better proof of the existence of a large fraction of dedicated anti-Communists in the South than their struggle in this war? And when you and your friends speak of the peasants physically suffering at the hands of the South Vietnamese government, just compare that with the suffering at the hands of the Vietcong—where every village chief, teacher, and doctor is killed to destroy the infrastructure.

"And when you all speak of a consensus among well-informed writers that the pro-Vietcong element is larger, just recognize the stake that La Couture, a Frenchman, has in seeing it that way, and the academics and journalists make money and sell papers, not by agreeing with government policy, but by disagreeing with it. And you people read their history. While we read the security and intelligence reports of the CIA, the State Department, the DOD—men whose interest it is to find out what's really happening over there. You see, we just read different histories, that's all.

"You see, I deeply believe we *are* quarantining aggressors over there just like the smallpox. Just like FDR and Hitler, just like Wilson and the Kaiser. You've simply got to see this thing in historical perspective. What I learned as a boy in my teens and in college about World War I was that it was our lack of strength and failure to show stamina that got us into that war. I was taught that the Kaiser never would have made his moves if he hadn't been able to count Uncle Sam out because he believed we'd never come in. Then I was taught in Congress and in committees on defense preparedness and by FDR that we in Congress were constantly telegraphing the wrong messages to Hitler and the Japanese— that the Wheelers, the Lindberghs, the La Follettes and the America Firsters were letting Hitler know he could move without worrying about Uncle Sam. I remember those days in Congress. The liberal debate almost got to me. I even signed a petition for something called the Ludlow Resolution, calling for a popular vote before a war. But then I came to my senses and recognized that Hitler could take over America while we were holding our election, and I felt so silly I ran down and took my name off. I firmly believe we wouldn't have been involved in World War II if it hadn't been for all the vacillation.

"So I knew that if the aggression succeeded in South Vietnam, then the aggressors would simply keep on going until all of Southeast Asia fell into their hands, slowly or quickly, but inevitably at least down to Singapore, and almost certainly to Djakarta. Now I know these academics thought that all they had to do was to write a lot of words proclaiming the death of the domino theory and their words alone could make the Communist threat vanish overnight. But while the impotent academics were talking, Moscow and Peking would be moving to expand their control and soon we'd be fighting in Berlin or elsewhere. And so would begin World War III.

"Oh, sure, I recognize your argument about the diversity of Communism and your claim that nationalism is strong as well as Communism, but the question is: which is stronger?

And I believe that the Communists—in terms of resources, skill, leadership, and training—have the upper hand in every battle against nationalist uprisings. I wish it were otherwise. It would certainly make the world a safer place. But look at Czechoslovakia. Now there you had a deep and strong solid nationalist faith, but in the crunch of Soviet tanks how did that faith hold up? 'Spirit' cannot stand up to superior force. You've got to understand the facts of power.

"And then you all speak of a united Vietnam as the best bulwark against Communist aggression and you talk approvingly of social revolution as a base for popular government. Well, you tell me when was the last major social revolution that came out successfully while a country was carved up in a war? Well, that's something for your sociologists. And don't give me the Bolshevik Revolution; that's a lot different. And to talk about Vietnam as a bulwark against Communist China—that's sheer Fulbright nonsense. Only slightly less nonsense than Dulles' claim that Laos was a bulwark of democracy. Vietnam ain't a bulwark of anything right now. It's in the midst of a struggle against Communism. And if you think it is, it's just because you don't understand the country. You don't understand the way in which the Communists control the resources over there. You simply see a different country than I do. First, we've got to get the Communists out and *then* begin the process of building South Vietnam as a stronghold.

"But the most unfair part of all is your constant screeching about the bombing, like I wanted to bomb civilians. There is nothing I wanted less, which is why I made sure that I had more control over the generals than any other civilian President in history. I insisted on that. I knew what the generals wanted. To saturate the whole area. To bomb the hell out of the North. Look at what's happening under Nixon. He's already dropped more bombs than I did in all my years. I spent ten hours a day worrying about all this, picking the targets one by one, making sure we didn't go over the limits.

"As for your criticism of our pacification, you are right that war is devastating. But we are doing everything we could to limit that. We rebuilt as we went along. That was our Mekong River Delta project. Hospitals, schools, technology. We wanted to modernize Vietnam society. You talk of land enclosure as a good thing. Well, I see it as an enclosure of spirit and mind. The promise of America has always been freedom from narrow boundaries. The frontier. The future. And technology is essential for that freedom and that future. Sure, the Vietnamese will never be the same again, but they've had a whole world opened to them. More choices. Freedom from superstition. The freedom of alternative lives. You can't talk about the quality of life until food and basic minimums are provided. We *will* get those things there. As soon as this conflict is peaceably settled. America will do it. You'll see. We've got in our history a tradition of benevolence. It will show up here, too. I am as certain of that as I am of anything in my life."

At that moment Lady Bird's voice came over the car radio to announce that lunch was ready. Johnson turned to me for just one final comment. "Look, I know you don't agree with me, but you must know that I believe everything I've just said with every bone inside me. You must at least give me that. Besides, someday it'll be you and your generation running this nation and then you'll know what it's like to agonize every night over the tough decisions you've got to make. I can only wish you better luck than me."[84]

During my college and university years in the East, where half my friends were involved in the peace movement, avoiding the draft, or participating in radical activity, and where dropping out of school was so commonplace, it seemed that all young Americans were engaged in revolution, and that a fundamental change in American values had been effected. Accepting economic security as a given, we asserted that wealth was not enough, that America was spiritually empty, a country with no national purpose aside from increasing the GNP, with no tangible foreign goals except to roll back the Communist menace. Our discontent was reinforced by the popular literature and songs and movies that spoke of restlessness, desolation, and awareness of absurdity. Suddenly it was fashionable to see only the bad, to discover everywhere signs of failure. The songs of Bob Dylan and the lyrics of Paul Simon became the texts for a generation—such as Simon's "And we sit and drink our coffee/crouched in our indifference, like shells upon the shore/you can hear the ocean roar/in the dangling conversation/and the superficial sighs /the borders of our lives." "Ah," the Beatles began in "Eleanor Rigby," "look at all the lonely people . . . where do they all come from?"

The assumption of our underground papers, Dylan's lyrics, and images of loneliness and alienation contrasted sharply with the optimistic idealism permeating Lyndon Johnson's America. Johnson's heroes were winners—"Lucky" Lindbergh, Andrew Jackson, Franklin Roosevelt—men who made it. The heroes of the sixties were losers who survived or martyrs. Malcolm X and Che Guevara became symbols for the age. Again and again, the words of these two figures could be found in pamphlets, in underground newspapers, in conversation. The young not only kept posters on their walls but copied the hair, the beard, the beret and the style. The cult of failure spread. As Benjamin Braddock in *The Graduate*, Dustin Hoffman came to epitomize the unknown everyman who was the hero of the late sixties: uncertain, alienated, and, by any traditional standards, a loser.

"How in the hell can that creepy guy be a hero to you?" Johnson asked me after we saw *The Graduate* in the movie theater on his ranch. "All I needed was to see ten minutes of that guy, floating like a big lump in a pool, moving like an elephant in that woman's bed, riding up and down the California coast polluting the atmosphere, to know that I wouldn't trust him for one minute with anything that really mattered to me. And if that's an example of what love seems like to your generation, then we're all in big trouble. All they did was to scream and yell at each other before getting to the altar. Then after it was over they sat on the bus like dumb mutes with absolutely nothing to say to one another."[35]

It looked at first as if a complete reversal of values had taken place, yet the new culture was also a product of the old. "The values of any new generation," Erikson wrote, "do not spring full blown from their heads; they are already there, inherent if not clearly articulated in the older generation. The generation gap is just another way of saying that the younger generation makes overt what is covert in the older generation; the child expresses openly what the parent represses."[36] There was in the culture of the sixties a romantic nostalgia for the era of the Old West, the simple life, the life of adventure. Once again, the West was seen as an escape from the sober responsibilities and acquiescence to impersonal authority that characterized the civilized East.[37] For some, the vehicle of escape was the open road. For others, it was drugs. Beneath it all was a profound boredom with respectable middle-class life. The quest for simplicity also ex-

tended to the realm of political action. The tactics of the left
in the 1960s can be partially understood as a disgust with the
slow, meandering procedures of American liberalism. In the
words of an SDS troupe: "They took us through committees
and procedures and places we'd never been before." The
simpler, almost vigilante political tradition of the frontier was
a much more direct and emotionally satisfying political alternative. As Jerry Rubin said: "I didn't get my ideas from Mao,
Lenin, or Ho. I got my ideas from the Lone Ranger."

Beneath their wild flurry of activity, however, the young
dissenters lacked the sustained involvement of a radical
cadre. Their dissent was coopted as the revolutionary leaders
willingly sat on evening talk shows, and as participants in
marches left early to look for themselves on the 6 P.M. news.
As the war continued, propelled by a political process seemingly oblivious to their marches and meetings, this sense of
hopelessness spread. Yet the new hopelessness was as simplis-
tic as the earlier naïve beliefs. The overthrow of the old gods
resulted in the installation of new gods. Devotion to a strong
and benign central government was replaced by decentraliza-
tion and community control, integration by black power,
economic growth by zero growth, technology by pastoralism,
optimism by pessimism. In these mirror images the sense of
complexity was lost. The American as Adam had been replaced by the American as Satan. With equal arrogance,
many Americans had gone from believing they were the best
people in the world to believing they were the worst people in
the world.

Among many of the young, for all the misdeeds of America they had found a single symbol, a primal villain. And
Johnson knew this, and it saddened him. "I just don't understand those young people," he said in his last years. "Don't
they realize I'm really one of them? I always hated cops
when I was a kid, and just like them I dropped out of school
and took off for California. I'm not some conformist middle-
class personality. I could never be bureaucratized."[88] Of
course, it was unfair of the young to cast Johnson in so dark
a role, but he also did not perceive the genuine impulses behind their own, somewhat different, American dream.

More interesting and less understandable than Johnson's inability to relate to the critical few was his inability to retain
the support of that large majority which by and large shared
his attitudes about work, progress, economic success, and the

importance of maintaining America's position in the world. They, like Lyndon Johnson, tended to be patriotic and proud of the fact that America had never lost a war. And also like Lyndon Johnson, the majority of Americans still believed in anti-Communism and in America's right and responsibility to intervene in support of small nations threatened by the enemy. After investing so much, the people wanted to believe their investment had been worthwhile. However discouraged they became about the long and appalling course of the war, they strongly opposed the tactics of the critics, especially when the critique became associated with rioting, disruption, bomb-throwing, and desecration of the flag.[39]

But Johnson never took the steps that would have been necessary to mobilize this majority. Afraid of arousing the emotions of the masses, he refused publicly to turn his critics into enemies of the people and he kept his own public statements on the war to a minimum. Obsessed with criticism from the left and the right, he simply assumed the support of the middle, an assumption that could not be tested so long as the Congress, the party system, and the peace movement remained incapable of defining viable alternatives to the administration's policy. In the absence of these alternatives, it appeared that only a small minority was visibly in opposition to the President's actions in Vietnam. And it was the virtually unanimous belief of other politicians that his renomination was inevitable, and that his chances for re-election were good. But—as the next chapter illustrates—one of the constitutional checks on executive power remained intact: the requirement of periodic elections. And once the presidential primaries opened up the mechanisms of choice, this public consensus was tested and it was clear that Lyndon Johnson's support had collapsed.

Chapter 12

The Withdrawal

After three years of persisting in the same policy, Lyndon Johnson finally decided on March 31, 1968, both to de-escalate the war and to withdraw from politics. Why? This chapter suggests that the Tet offensive and the presidential primaries changed the prism through which Johnson viewed the war and his Presidency. Reality returned as the checks and balances of the American political system came back into play.

The success of the enemy's sudden attack against what had until then appeared to be impregnable areas deep within South Vietnam suddenly exposed the falsity of the administration's optimistic progress reports. Until Tet, Vietcong forces had chosen to fight in jungles or villages, striking quickly and moving on, their true vitality hidden and, therefore, more easily concealed from the American people. Now the news of captured cities, and the films of skirmishes shown on the TV screen night after night, exhibited the other side's strength.[1] Surely an enemy with the resilience and the resources to mount an attack on the scale of the Tet offensive was not on the verge of collapse. Though Tet may not have surprised Johnson—he later claimed in his memoirs that his advisers had predicted the offensive weeks in advance—it certainly made the man who proclaimed his foresight only after the fact look surprised. What happened at Tet taught the American public an entirely different lesson from the one Johnson had intended to convey.

As the ever-impending peace—created throughout the late fall of 1967 by the optimistic tone of administration statements—gave way to the reality of continuing war, public support for Lyndon Johnson dropped to the lowest point ever. In the space of six weeks, between late January and early March of 1968, the percentage of Americans who approved of Johnson's handling of the Presidency dropped from 48 to 36 percent, while the percentage of those who supported his handling of the war dropped from 40 to 26 percent. This decline in public support was both father and child of an equally dramatic decline in media support. Between January and March, seven major newspapers, among them the *Wall Street Journal*, the New York *Post*, and the St. Louis *Post-Dispatch*, moved from general support of the administration's war policy to sharp criticism. *Life, Look, Time, Newsweek*, CBS, and NBC, each in its own way, came out against the war. And the erosion of support did not stop with the public and the press; it also affected the Congress, the Democratic Party, the Cabinet and the White House staff. Even the members of the Senior Advisory Group, who, until Tet, had been among Johnson's strongest supporters, now turned against his war policy. In a March meeting at the White House, McGeorge Bundy reported to Johnson the group's consensus that the present policy could not achieve its objective without virtually unlimited resources, that it was no longer being supported by a majority of the American people, and that significant changes were therefore required.[2]

But Tet alone could not have produced the dramatic decline in Johnson's fortunes without the presidential primaries, which finally provided effective expression of the mounting dissent. Even before Tet, the mood of the electorate had begun to swing against the Johnson administration as exasperation at the President's handling of the war combined with a loss of confidence in his handling of the racial situation. When Johnson began his Presidency in 1963, eight out of ten Americans—as measured by the Gallup poll's question "Do you approve or disapprove of the way the President is handling his job?"—approved of his actions. By the end of the following year his level of support had dropped to seven out of ten. The year after that, 1965, it was down to six out of ten; by 1966 to five out of ten, and by 1967 to four out of ten. In other words, with each year in office, Johnson lost one supporter in ten.[3]

Commentators and journalists writing at the time interpreted Johnson's diminishing support as a reflection of changing attitudes: from hawk to dove on Vietnam, from liberal to conservative on civil rights. But later studies provide a different interpretation of Johnson's loss: they suggest that what changed between 1964 and 1968 was not people's attitudes toward the policies Johnson espoused—in 1968 the majority of Americans still supported Johnson's position on Vietnam, on Medicare, open housing, desegregation, and equal employment—but their level of trust in Johnson's capacity to cope with domestic and international problems.[4]

A leader's authority comes from the public's belief in his right and ability to rule, in the willingness of individuals to suspend their own judgment and accept their leader's because they trust him and the system he represents. By 1968 Johnson had lost this trust. The issue was not simply Johnson's loss of popularity; it was his loss of credibility. A majority of people believed he regularly lied to them. And that belief soon spread from matters of personal biography to high matters of state. When asked in 1964 which party was most likely to avoid a larger war, the majority of Americans had chosen the Democrats. This confidence was destroyed in the ensuing four years of bombing and fighting in Vietnam. In 1968 the same question drew a majority for the Republicans.[5]

Unhappiness about the war and the protesters, the blacks and the bigots, the young and their critics, attached itself to the man in the White House. Too much outcry, too many riots, too many demonstrations: the nation seemed in a state of continual unrest and, as the people saw it, the President—the man at the nation's center—was to blame. Accordingly, the turbulent sixties became Lyndon Johnson's problem just as the depression had become Herbert Hoover's problem and the "mess in Washington" had become Harry Truman's problem.[6]

Few politicians at the time gauged the depth of the public discontent or its political power to unseat an incumbent President. Even after Tet, notwithstanding the deprecating chatter in Washington, it was simply assumed—by Democrats and Republicans alike—that Lyndon Johnson would be the party's nominee. When, in December, 1967, Senator Eugene McCarthy, supported by thousands of antiwar activists, had entered his name on the ballot for the New Hampshire primary, his challenge was regarded by official Washington as a somewhat baffling exercise begun by a hitherto stable member of the Senate liberal establishment. Two weeks before the primary, a *Time* magazine poll showed McCarthy with only 11 percent of the vote. Weeks of canvassing, going from door to door in every part of the state, however, had shown that the voters were anxious and upset—about the war, the economy, the general state of the country, and Lyndon Johnson. "You know when I first thought I might have a chance?" McCarthy said. "When I realized that you could go into any bar in the country and insult Lyndon Johnson and nobody would punch you in the nose."[7] In the final days before the vote, these submerged feelings had surfaced, albeit too late to influence the calculations of observers.

When the polls of the New Hampshire primary closed, Washington was boggled by the results—42 percent for McCarthy, scarcely known to New Hampshire citizens two months before. McCarthy's "victory" was hailed by the doves as a triumph over the hawks, an expression of the public's reversal on the war issue. But McCarthy's support in New Hampshire came from hawks as well as doves; in fact, among his supporters, those who believed Johnson should exercise *more* force in Vietnam outnumbered those who believed in less force by a margin of 3–2. Apparently, the sole common denominator was a deep dissatisfaction with the Johnson administration. Though McCarthy's views on many issues were contradictory to the views of many of his supporters, he was an alternative to Lyndon Johnson, the best and only vehicle for expressing anger and frustration at the incumbent administration.[8]

The surprising totals in New Hampshire convinced Robert Kennedy to enter the race. Kennedy had considered running even before New Hampshire, but had concluded that if he were the first to step forward, he would be accused of running to express a scarcely disguised vendetta against Johnson, of splitting the party, of spoiling the election. But after New Hampshire the party was split anyway. Its prospects in the election seemed uncertain, if not already ruined. So Robert F. Kennedy seized his chance for a candidacy that the voters would no longer see as a vendetta. On Saturday morning, March 16, 1968, in the same Senate Caucus Room where his brother had announced eight years before, he began the second Kennedy quest for the Presidency.

"If I ever had any doubts about Johnson's running," James Rowe said, "I would have lost them the day Kennedy announced because he is not about to turn the country over to Bobby."[9] Lyndon Johnson, so formidable in the acquisition and use of power, so unyielding in the pursuit of those policies that were destroying his popularity, his programs, and his political support, would surely not refuse a challenge led by his most despised adversary.

In the days following Kennedy's entrance into the race, the President's actions seemed to confirm Rowe's and many others' assessment that at last Lyndon Johnson was riled and ready to fight.

On March 17, Johnson flew to Minneapolis to address a meeting of the National Farmers Union. Fists pounding the lectern, he truculently declared: "Your President has come here to ask you people and all the other people of this nation to join us in a total national effort to win the war, to win the peace, and to complete the job that must be done here at home. Make no mistake about it—I don't want a man in here to go back thinking otherwise—we are going to win." Back in Washington several days later, Johnson told the National Foreign Policy Conference at the State Department that "danger and sacrifice built this land." He continued: "Today we are the Number One Nation. And we are going to stay the Number One Nation."[10] In the meantime, a major speech was planned for the end of March. The early drafts spelled out a tough and uncompromising stand: a refusal to consider a bombing halt without clear reciprocity, a call-up of fifty thousand reserves, and a demand that Congress pass the surtax as a measure of patriotic support.[11] These were bellicose speeches, suggesting from the outside that Johnson had abandoned his middle-of-the-road approach in favor of all-out war.

But the predictions that Johnson would stand and fight, based as they were on familiarity with a number of his superficial traits—his tendency to overwhelm people in one-to-one confrontations or group sessions, his apparent pleasure in ridiculing his enemies in private, and his ruthless drive for power—ignored deeper layers of his personality. They failed to weigh his most consistent pattern of behavior: his profound aversion to conflict; his reliance, in the face of potentially disruptive situations, upon bargaining if at all possible; his terror of campaign speeches, where the size of the audience was beyond the reach of his personal abilities and skills. As we have seen, he had written out and, at the last moment, discarded a statement of withdrawal before the 1964 convention; just as, in 1948, he had prepared, and instructed an aide to issue, a resignation statement—an order ignored at Lady Bird's advice—three weeks before his election to the U.S. Senate.

All his life Johnson had believed that power was something you obtained if you had the energy and drive to work harder than everyone else. Power, in turn, made good works possible, and good works brought love and gratitude, which then provided the inspiration and vitality for further work. This formula informed Johnson's personal experience: time and again he had been able to parlay his limited resources into substantial political holdings, rising from Congressman to Senator to Majority Leader to Vice President and finally to President. But now, three years after his landslide victory, the American people had, Johnson believed, broken the cycle of power, energy, and good works by denying him the appreciation he deserved for all that he had produced. Indeed, by Johnson's assessment, his administration had produced more than any administration in history, and he could document his claim: he had given more laws, more houses, more medical services, more jobs to more people, than any other President. Surely, he had earned the love and gratitude of the American people. Yet as he looked around him in 1967 Johnson found only paralyzing bitterness. He could not comprehend the nature of the unrest or the cause of his unpopularity.

"How is it possible," Johnson repeatedly asked, "that all these people could be so ungrateful to me after I had given them so much? Take the Negroes. I fought for them from the first day I came into office. I spilled my guts out in getting the Civil Rights Act of 1964 through Congress. I put everything I had into that speech before the joint session in 1965. I tried to make it possible for every child of every color to grow up in a nice house, to eat a solid breakfast, to attend a decent school, and to get a good and lasting job. I asked so little in return. Just a little thanks. Just a little appreciation. That's all. But look at what I got instead. Riots in 175 cities. Looting. Burning. Shooting. It ruined everything. Then take the students. I wanted to help them, too. I fought on their behalf for scholarships and loans and grants. I fought for better teachers and better schools. And look what I got back. Young people by the thousands leaving their universities, marching in the streets, chanting that horrible song about how many kids I had killed that day. And the poor, they, too, turned against me. When Congress cut the funds for the Great Society, they made me Mr. Villain. I remember once going to visit a poor family in Appalachia. They had seven children, all skinny and sick. I promised the mother and father I would make things better for them. I told them all my hopes for their future. They seemed real happy to talk with me, and I felt good about that. But then as I walked toward the door, I noticed two pictures on the shabby wall. One was Jesus Christ on the cross; the other was John Kennedy. I felt as if I'd been slapped in the face."[12]

So strong was Johnson's need for affection, and so vital his need for public gratitude, that he experienced this rejection of his "good works" as an absolute rejection of himself. Denied the appreciation which not only empowered but sustained his self, the love which validated his identity, the anatomy which gave Lyndon Johnson's ego its shape was dissolved. His energy and capacity to direct that energy outward abandoned him. Every presidential responsibility (speeches, conducting meetings, greeting visitors) took inordinate effort. The man who had battened on the goodwill of crowds, accelerating his pace in proportion to the crowd's number and affection, now could not leave the White House without being harassed by demonstrators and pickets. He had once liked to unwind with reporters, Congressmen, and staff, holding forth upon his strategy for the Great Society. But now Vietnam dominated his every word and a savage rain of vituperation fell upon his staff, the Congress, and reporters.

Now he began to marshal all his resources to fashion a defense, and the energies absorbed in this task of defending the self were no longer available for the everyday demands of leadership. Even at small group meetings Johnson now seemed unaware of what those present were thinking or even talking about. He gave the impression of not seeing his audience at all, having lost his sensitivity to the subtleties of tone and emphasis. This was not simply the passive inattention of a tired mind; it was the active inattention of a preoccupied mind, a mind whose focus was increasingly limited in mobility and scope.[13]

Johnson had traversed 1965, 1966, and most of 1967 retreating into a dreamlike world in which the tide on both the war and the Great Society was just about to turn. By early 1968 this dream had died. Daily contact with the real world—with the evidence of a deepening inflation, with the results of the Tet offensive, and with the challenge of the primaries—was forcing Johnson back to reality. If the days of accomplishment were truly finished, as Johnson suspected, what then was the point? No good works, no love, no self-esteem. Only the endless repetition of sordid, unhappy days. Johnson's enthusiasm and vitality steadily receded. He was really tired, and he knew it.

Hating the days, Johnson hated the nights even more. He began dreaming again the dream of paralysis that had haunted him since early childhood. Only this time he was lying in a bed in the Red Room of the White House, instead of sitting in a chair in the middle of the open plains. His head was still his, but from the neck down his body was the thin, paralyzed body that had been the affliction of both Woodrow Wilson and his own grandmother in their final years. All his presidential assistants were in the next room. He could hear them actively fighting with one another to divide up his power: Joe Califano wanted the legislative program; Walt Rostow wanted the decisions on foreign policy; Arthur Okun wanted to formulate the budget; and George Christian wanted to handle relations with the public. He could hear them, but he could not command them, for he could neither talk nor walk. He was sick and stilled, but not a single aide tried to protect him.

The dream terrified Johnson, waking from his sleep. Lying in the dark, he could find no peace until he got out of bed, and, by the light of a small flashlight, walked the halls of the White House to the place where Woodrow Wilson's portrait hung. He found something soothing in the act of touching Wilson's picture; he could sleep again. He was still Lyndon Johnson, and he was still alive and moving; it was Woodrow Wilson who was dead. This ritual, however, brought little lasting peace; when morning came, Johnson's mind was again filled with fears. Only gradually did he recognize the resemblance between this dream and the stampede dream of his boyhood. Making the connection, his fears intensified; he was certain now that paralysis was his inevitable fate. Remembering his family's history of early strokes, he convinced himself that he, too, would suffer a stroke in his next term. Immobilized, still in office nominally, yet not actually in control: this seemed to Johnson the worst situation imaginable. He could not rid himself of the suspicion that a mean God had set out to torture him in the cruelest manner possible. His suffering now no longer consisted of his usual melancholy; it was an acute throbbing pain, and he craved relief. More than anything he wanted peace and quiet. An end to the pain.[14]

Through the fall and winter of 1967, Johnson later reported, the decision to withdraw from politics took hold. He discussed it, he wrote in a section of his memoirs that reads as if it were a defense attorney's brief, with a number of people, among them John Connally, George Christian, General Westmoreland, William S. White, Horace Busby, and, of course, Lady Bird. He claimed he had considered announcing it at the end of the State of the Union message in early January, 1968; he had asked Horace Busby to write a draft statement. But when he got to the Capitol that night—and his explanation is not entirely convincing from this man of meticulous detail—he reached into his pocket and discovered that he had forgotten to bring it with him. The announcement was not made.[15] Then between the end of January and the middle of March came the Tet offensive, McCarthy's victory, the collapse of the gold market, the publication of the Riot Commission Report, and, most importantly, Robert Kennedy's entrance into the presidential race.

"I felt," Johnson said, "that I was being chased on all sides by a giant stampede coming at me from all directions. On one side, the American people were stampeding me to do something about Vietnam. On another side, the inflationary economy was booming out of control. Up ahead were dozens of danger signs pointing to another summer of riots in the cities. I was being forced over the edge by rioting blacks, demonstrating students, marching welfare mothers, squawking professors, and hysterical reporters. And then the final straw. The thing I feared from the first day of my Presidency was actually coming true. Robert Kennedy had openly announced his intention to reclaim the throne in the memory of his brother. And the American people, swayed by the magic of the name, were dancing in the streets. The whole situation was unbearable for me. After thirty-seven years of public service, I deserved something more than being left alone in the middle of the plain, chased by stampedes on every side."[16]

All his life Johnson had held before himself the image of the daring cowboy, the man with the capacity to outrun the wild herd, riding at a dead run in the dark of the night, knowing there were prairie dog holes all around. It was this definition of manly courage, opposed to what he saw as a feminine tendency to run away from responsibility, that had deterred Johnson in August, 1964, from abandoning the Presidency—and at that point the only stampede he faced was his own fear that the memorial film of John F. Kennedy would provoke a rush of delegates to Robert F. Kennedy. How much more difficult it would be for him now—when the stampede had already started—to justify his running away!

So Johnson found himself in an untenable position in early 1968. It was impossible to quit and impossible to stay. If he left office and went back to Texas, he would be acting like a coward; if he stayed for another four years, he would be paralyzed before his term was out. For months his position was all the more untenable because he did not know that it was untenable. He was in the grip of that supreme despair which, as Kierkegaard says, is not to know one is in despair. No matter how hard he tried to think it out, he got nowhere. One line of action was as bad as the other. No matter how hectic his activity, he could not drive the demons away. But then, Johnson explained, one day—exactly what day is not clear— he realized the total impossibility of his situation. The realization came to him in a dream. In the dream he saw himself swimming in a river. He was swimming from the center toward one shore. He swam and swam, but he never seemed to get any closer. He turned around to swim to the other shore, but again he got nowhere. He was simply going round and round in circles. The dream reminded Johnson of his grandfather's story about driving the cattle across the river, where they, too, got caught in a whirl, circling round and round in the same spot.[17]

Aware now of the bind he was in, Johnson finally found a way to extricate himself. He ingeniously reasoned that he could withdraw from politics without being seen as a coward. To follow his reasoning, we must understand the intensity of his concern for the verdict of history. The desire to leave something permanent behind as evidence of the work of a lifetime had been with him from the days of his youth, but never had it been so preoccupying a force as it was in the spring of 1968. At a time when the present was filled with unhappiness, Johnson turned to the future for uplift. Widen the constituency, flee once again from the pain of intimacy, multiply your resources. Looking ahead to posterity, Johnson began thinking that his current difficulties might prove to be a blessing in disguise. There was still the opportunity to restore his reputation if he acted nobly at this critical moment. "If the American people don't love me, their descendants will."

Eyes fixed on the future, Johnson believed he would be judged by history for his success or failure in fulfilling three presidential functions: providing domestic peace and tranquillity, providing for the national security, and providing for the general welfare. In each area, he saw a conflict between his role as President of all the people and his role as candidate of the Democratic Party. In each area, he reasoned, he would be more likely to reach his goals if he was not a candidate, but a chief of state above the partisan battle.[18]

First, on questions of national security: Critics argued that Johnson's decision to halt the bombing north of the 20th parallel reflected a substantial change in policy shaped by the combination of the Tet offensive, the New Hampshire primary, his meeting with the "Wise Old Men"—George Ball, General Omar Bradley, Mac Bundy, Arthur Dean, Douglas Dillon, Abe Fortas, Robert Murphy, General Matthew Ridgway, and Cy Vance—and the appointment of Clark Clifford as Secretary of Defense. The critics were right in suggesting that Johnson was affected by these events, but they had not quite put their finger on the reason why. Johnson himself admitted that Tet had been a psychological victory for the North Vietnamese. He also admitted that his talks with Clifford and his meeting with his outside advisers reinforced his belief that many of his own people, not to speak of the public at large, did not understand the "real" situation in Vietnam. Clifford's growing doubts undoubtedly posed a special problem for Johnson. When McNamara changed his mind on the war, his shift could be written off for many different reasons—his "idealism," his distaste for blood, his friendship with Robert Kennedy. But none of these motives could explain Clifford's shift. He was neither a dissenter nor a turncoat, but an emissary from the corporate world, a world of men apart from the personal and political motives which Johnson believed characterized most of the dissent, where the only standards of judgment were interest, utility, and power. "Now, I make it a practice to keep in touch with friends in business and the law across the land," Clifford explained at a meeting in late March, 1968. "I ask them their views about various matters. Until a few months ago, they were generally supportive of the war. . . . Now all that has changed. There has been a tremendous erosion of support among these men

... these men now feel that we are in a hopeless bog. The idea of going deeper into the bog strikes them as mad. They want to see us get out of it. These are leaders of opinion in their communities. What they believe is sooner or later believed by many other people. It would be very difficult—I believe it would be impossible—for the President to maintain public support for the war without the support of these men."[19]

Then Johnson knew. The herald had finally arrived to report that the walls were crumbling. Johnson was losing the support of the barons, and with it, his ability to lead. So he would change his tactics, but not his objectives and never his convictions. For this man, a master of compromising other men's views, could not compromise his own, his record before his only remaining constituency, the judgment of history. The bombing halt would defuse the internal debate in the administration and particularly within his circle of officials and advisers. The compromise at the 20th parallel would—and did—have the effect of buying further time in the pursuit of military victory. It would—and did—afford Johnson the opportunity to initiate a policy of Vietnamization.

One might ask, then, what about all the military arguments that had repeatedly been made against curtailing or halting the bombing? Several new factors served to relieve Johnson of much of the pressure previously exerted by the military, as well as to neutralize the doubts in his own mind. First, Johnson had by 1968 let the military bomb almost everything they had previously complained they were not allowed to; the list of restricted targets had become very small indeed. By 1968 the only remaining options—closing Haiphong, bombing the agricultural dikes—carried in Johnson's mind much too high a risk of Chinese intervention. Not only had most other targets been bombed—over and over—but doing so had not reduced the size of the war in the South nor improved our bargaining position with the North Vietnamese. Second, if the United States was in fact doing as well as Westmoreland claimed, then the curtailment of the bombing could proceed as it had always been meant someday to proceed—from a position of strength, not weakness. Finally, the alleged military risk of a bombing halt could be lessened further by the judicious employment of bombing missions below the 20th parallel.[20]

So it was that, in finally offering an end to the air war

against the North, Johnson was not forced to see himself as a coward, running away from Vietnam. To the contrary, he convinced himself that he was the same man of courage, determined to save South Vietnam, daring a new initiative in a continuing course. Moreover, by coupling this initiative with withdrawal from the presidential race, he made sure that it would not be read as a political trick. If, on the other hand, it failed to produce negotiations, then at least Johnson had laid the groundwork for further escalation. If the situation in South Vietnam was as good as the military claimed, then it was just possible that Hanoi would finally come to the peace table. And if that happened, then Johnson believed that he would be honored by history for having mapped out a policy in Southeast Asia that had ensured America's national security for years to come.

If concern for the future affected Johnson's decisions about "national security," it also affected his thinking about "the general welfare." By the spring of 1968 the tax surcharge had become the most pressing domestic issue. Without the surtax the American economy was in danger and Johnson knew it. And the situation at home was substantially exacerbated by deepening financial problems abroad. British devaluation of the pound in late 1967 had triggered a general deterioration in the gold market and a crisis of confidence in the dollar. By the middle of March the gold market was in a state of panic. Speculation was rampant that the United States, too, might be forced to devalue.

Johnson saw the deepest fears of his generation reflected in this situation. He believed that the stalemate on taxes was being interpreted abroad as a failure of the democratic process and a clear indication that America had neither the will nor the ability to control its economic affairs. The specter of 1929 haunted him daily; he worried that if the economy collapsed, history would subject Lyndon Johnson to endless abuse. Yet as long as he was a candidate, Johnson was convinced, the Republicans in Congress would stall the surtax, so they could campaign in the fall against "Johnson's inflation" as well as "Johnson's war." Therefore, in this case, too, withdrawing from the race was the only answer. Here, too, posterity would see his abdication as an act of courage, not cowardice.

Withdrawing would also strengthen the President in his search for domestic peace. Johnson looked back to the previous summer and recalled the accusation that he had chosen a partisan course during the Detroit riots. If he reacted strongly to civil disorders, he would be accused of currying favor on the right; if he reacted temperately, he would be vulnerable to the opposite charge. Either charge might reduce his reputation in the annals of history. Johnson wanted to be remembered as the preserver of domestic peace, a man who had enforced the law with equity and fairness to all. But here, too, as with Vietnam and the tax bill, the favorable judgment of history could be better secured only by withdrawing from politics.[21]

Abdication was thus the last remaining way to restore control, to turn rout into dignity, collapse into order. It served to advance Johnson's immediate purposes and his long-term goals. As the situation stood, Johnson was about to lose the Wisconsin primary and the forecasts looked equally dim for the primaries in Oregon, Indiana, and California. To win the nomination under these circumstances would have been— though possible—a Pyrrhic victory. It would have torn the nation apart. Johnson recognized this. His concerns for the present and the future, for national unity and posterity, for the war and the economy, joined together. He decided to retreat with honor.

Having made his decision in private, Johnson now made plans to share it with his countrymen on March 31, 1968. He addressed a nationwide TV audience that night from the White House. He began unceremoniously by reviewing his administration's efforts to find a basis for constructive peace talks. He then moved directly to his proposal for a bombing halt: "I am taking the first step to de-escalate the conflict. Tonight I have ordered our aircraft and our naval vessels to make no attacks on North Vietnam, except in the area of the Demilitarized Zone." This meant, he said, stopping the bombing in areas inhabited by "almost 90%" of North Vietnam's population. "I call upon President Ho Chi Minh to respond positively and favorably to this new step of peace."

He spoke gravely, gently; gone was the undertone of sarcasm, and the appearance of piety. He finished the section on Vietnam in thirty minutes. Then the moment came which would startle the nation. Even those who had read the phrases of abdication could not be certain he would read them, nor could Johnson himself—he had, after all, written out other withdrawals only to pull them back—until the irretrievable words rolled up on the Teleprompter: he glanced at Lady Bird and he hesitated for an inexpressible moment, which must have compressed the stormy inward clashes of a lifetime, then continued because the words were there, right in front of him, and the only way he could master his contradictions—the only way he ever knew—was to move ahead:

"This country's ultimate strength lies in the unity of our people. There is division in the American house now. There is divisiveness among us all tonight. And holding the trust that is mine, as President of all the people, I cannot disregard the peril to the progress of the American people and the hope and prospect of peace for all people. ... With America's sons in the fields far away, with America's future under challenge right here at home ... I do not believe that I should devote an hour or a day of my time to any personal partisan causes. ... Accordingly, I shall not seek, and will not accept, the nomination of my party for another term as your President."[22]

There was a mood of euphoria in the capital the next day. Even Johnson seemed pleased. What huge tensions must have been released. A few days later, Hanoi agreed to negotiate in Paris. To many, it seemed that the road to peace might now be open. The polls showed a sharp increase in Johnson's popularity. And the President, who, a short time before, could speak publicly only at military installations, was once again cheered in the streets of Chicago.

Johnson began to speak excitedly of his plans for the Lyndon B. Johnson Library and the Lyndon B. Johnson School of Public Affairs, and the writing of his memoirs. He set up a schedule of seminars and lectures for the following years and took pleasure in the large numbers of schools which were asking him to speak: Yale, and even Harvard.

In May, he returned, solaced and refreshed, from a visit with Harry Truman, one of the two living members of that exclusive group to which he would soon belong. "You know the great thing about Truman," he told me, "is that once he makes up his mind about something—anything, including the A bomb—he never looks back and asks, 'Should I have done it? Oh! Should I have done it?' No, he just knows he made up his mind as best he could and that's that. There's no going back. I wish I had some of that quality, for there's nothing worse than going back over a decision made, retracing the steps that led to it, and imagining what it'd be like if you took another turn. It can drive you crazy.

"Truman was one of the few comforts I had all during the war," Johnson continued. "Reminded me of all the hell he'd been through, but somehow he managed to ride it out. Ike was helpful, too. Once I complained to him about the trouble Fulbright and friends were making for me. He told me, 'Why, I'd just go ahead and smack them, just pay no attention to these overeducated Senators, that's all there is to it.' Another time, when Fulbright was busy talking things over with his Russian friends, I said to Truman, 'Imagine him not wanting the Russians to stop and wanting us to stop.' Truman interrupted me: 'But you are the President. You make the policy, not him.' "[23]

In June, Robert Kennedy was shot. Afterward, Johnson said little; but some time later, reflectively, and with some bitterness: "It would have been hard on me to watch Bobby march to 'Hail to the Chief,' but I almost wish he had become President so the country could finally see a flesh-and-blood Kennedy grappling with the daily work of the Presidency and all the inevitable disappointments, instead of their storybook image of great heroes who, because they were dead, could make anything anyone wanted happen."[24] Later in June, he signed the Omnibus Crime Act. "I don't want to do it, but I have no choice. Nixon has forced me into it by all the election bullshit blaming the Democrats for crime in the streets. That label will be disastrous in November."[25]

After Kennedy was killed, as the summer wore on his mood changed; he became withdrawn, canceled previous plans for new, bold domestic proposals—including a plan for income maintenance that he had already approved. "Better not propose anything radical now because the Republicans will defeat it with an election coming up, and it will have less chance of passing later." So he would simply put the idea into a speech. Then he decided to wait for his last State of the Union, only to strike even the mention of such a program because "it will hurt its chances of ever being passed if it's connected to me."[26] In Vietnam, there was no change: a continuing stalemate on the battlefield and at the peace table. His feared rival, Robert Kennedy, was dead, while his chosen successor, Hubert Humphrey, was doing badly in appearances around the country and in polls, which showed him running well behind McCarthy—whose nomination would be unacceptable to the convention—and even Nixon.

"Senator Eastland was in to see me the other day," he said one evening in late July, "and he wants me to run. In fact, a lot of them have been in. Eastland says Hubert hasn't caught on. I'm the only one who can hold the South. I don't agree, but he is organizing something for me. And he says he is happy with Medicare. Can you imagine that? He also told me that Fortas will come out of committee in mid-November though Dirksen will leave us. He says that one thousand delegates can be delivered to Humphrey, but he's losing them. And he's afraid the convention will be a holocaust, with McCarthy walking out."[27]

Perhaps Eastland had said all this, but James Eastland of Mississippi had never before shown much knowledge or interest in national politics; and even at the time I suspected that I was hearing, attributed to Eastland, Johnson's own, not completely inaccurate, but wholly wishful, analysis. Humphrey did appear to be a weak candidate, and McCarthy was an impossibility. Much of Humphrey's strength had been assembled and delivered by Johnson in the drive to halt Kennedy. Under such circumstances, it was natural to think that anything might happen, or might be made to happen. It was all illusion, of course. Johnson's candidacy would have caused an explosion, fragmenting, perhaps irrevocably, the Democratic Party. It might have been possible had he never withdrawn, but now Convention Hall would be crowded with delegates originally selected to support Kennedy and McCarthy, along with many Humphrey delegates who opposed Johnson and the war.

His increasing irritation was accompanied by a sharp renewal of interest in the military situation in Vietnam. He stepped up his consultations with the military. I thought from what he said—just hints, but ominous hints—that he might be planning a major escalation, hoping for a military victory that would transform the political scene. Secretary of Defense Clark Clifford, and others in the administration, shared this apprehension.

There is little doubt that, as the convention neared, Johnson began to feel that his withdrawal might not be irrevocable, that he might find vindication more real and immediate than the verdict of history—in the vote of the Democratic Party and American people. "Nixon can be beaten," he said over and over again. "He's like a Spanish horse who runs faster than anyone for the first nine lengths and then turns around and runs backward. You'll see," he predicted, "he'll do something wrong in the end. He always does."[28] Indeed, Nixon lost several million votes in the closing weeks of the 1968 campaign, transforming a landslide into a squeaker. But not until he had become President was he to confirm that even a diminished Johnson was unequaled in his capacity to sense the weaknesses and potentialities of other men.

Johnson's increasingly irascible and frenetic manner cannot be attributed solely to resurgent hope; it was also a return of anguishing internal pressures, momentarily released by his withdrawal, and masked by the consequent public acclamation. He was beginning to go through it all, all over again. And, finally, with the same paralyzing result. There was no mobilization of support for the nomination, no stirring new proposals to memorialize his dedication to the Great Society. And what was to have been his final memorable act, a summit meeting with Kosygin to lay the groundwork for a new détente, was canceled when Soviet forces invaded Czechoslovakia. Nor was he able to bring peace in Vietnam; despite the bombing halt announced on October 31, the stalemate on the war continued.

On January 20, 1969, Richard Nixon took the oath of office as the thirty-seventh President of the United States, and later that afternoon, the man who had come to Washington as a legislative assistant in the third year of the depression at the age of twenty-three, and served thirty-two years in public life as Congressman, Senator, Vice President, and President, returned to the hill country, where, as his father had told him, "The people know when you're sick and care when you die."

Epilogue

"The long, hard effort was over now, and I was glad to see it end."[1] These were the words Lyndon Johnson used to describe his feelings upon his retirement from public life. The relief was both immense and genuine. Yet after thirty-two years of public service, with the end of his presidential responsibility, a terrible, perhaps impossible, transition to the hill country awaited him.

In the final months of his Presidency, Johnson had laid the groundwork for his retirement. Preliminary plans for the LBJ School of Public Affairs and the LBJ Library had been made as well as a tentative schedule for a series of lectures at colleges and universities. Hundreds of thousands of file folders had been shipped to Austin to be sorted through for the library and for the work on the memoirs. A sketchy outline of the memoirs had been drawn up.

Almost immediately, however, it became apparent that none of these projects really engaged Johnson. The one he talked about the most was the memoirs, and at the start it seemed that after a few months rest he might turn his energies to the task. But he never did. Though he spent many hours thinking and talking about the book, he never concentrated his whole attention on it. His mind would wander, his conversations digress. In retrospect, given everything we know about his character, his mode of behavior, and, particularly, his feelings toward the written word, this evasion of the book was inevitable.

All his life Johnson had made a distinction between the doers and the thinkers, between the contemplative and activist life. The written word of the intellectual, of the contemplative mind, he connected with stillness, paralysis, and death. To devote himself to the task of writing the memoirs would have meant sitting alone and becoming what he had been running from all his life. And since the subject matter was a summary of his life, it seemed that he was being asked to do nothing less than construct his own coffin.

The more promising possibility was to talk out the memoirs, to have his assistants take down his spoken word and render it into written form. This is, in fact, what he decided to do. Plans were made for long conversations in which we'd take notes or record him on tape and then draft the chapters from these notes, at all times retaining the flavor and style of his own patterns of speech. But it didn't work as we had hoped. Whenever Johnson sat down to talk in front of the tape machine, he froze; his language became artificial and he insisted on having sheaves of memos on his lap before he'd say a word. The audience was too far away, too abstract, too unknown. I later realized that the problem of speaking before unknown audiences had plagued Johnson all his life. When he first went to school, as we have seen, he spoke incomprehensibly in "a language all his own" until the teacher took him on her lap. When urged by his mother, who taught elocution and debate, to participate in public speaking classes, he was dismissed for mumbling too much. Yet over time, he did develop an extraordinary facility in conversation; he became perhaps the greatest storyteller of his age. The power of his tales lay always in the telling—in the gestures, tone, and timing. Inherited from his father and his grandfather, this facility drew its power from a long and rich Western tradition. But, for reasons connected perhaps with the relationship between his parents, he never accepted the validity of this mode of talk. It could only be used, he thought, in private; it was inappropriate for public meetings. Only when the setting afforded privacy—as did the cloakroom of the Senate or, in a peculiar way, the campaign stump so long as no one was there to record his words—was Johnson able to make use of his verbal skills, his mastery of words, gestures, imitation, and mimicry. Before a more formal gathering, or in front of the television screen, he feared that his audience would scorn his wild gesticulations and crude language. And in the Presidency these feelings were reinforced by his view that the office was a stately institution demanding decorous appearance at all times.

That this posturing would be as disastrous for the memoirs as Johnson's public and TV appearances had been for his Presidency was clear from the time the first draft was completed. I had worked on two chapters. Neither one was very good. The chapters came to life only in the places where, against instruction, I quoted directly from the anecdotes and stories I had heard him tell informally about his dealings with men like Russell, Dirksen, Mills, King, Young, Mitchell, and others. I had hoped that when he read these colorful passages and saw the difference, he would finally change his mind and begin to open up. Instead, he had just the opposite reaction. "God damn it, I can't say this"—pointing to a barbed comment on Wilbur Mills—"get it out right now, why he may be the speaker of the House someday. And for Christ's sake, get that vulgar language of mine out of there. What do you think this is, the tale of an uneducated cowboy? It's a presidential memoir, damn it, and I've got to come out looking like a statesman, not some backwoods politician."[2]

Johnson's concern with the future power Mills might hold illustrates another aspect of his relationship with words. It is in the nature of political life to view words as sticks for action, as tools for persuasion. The words themselves mean nothing divorced from the object of persuasion. In the absence of a goal, Johnson's words became unmoored. It was only when the author was pushed by contemporary events or by early evaluations of his Presidency in the newspaper that the old persuasive power came through. Someone sent him clippings of a series of news stories which claimed that Johnson had been forced out of politics because after the Tet offensive his senior advisers—men like Clark Clifford, Dean Acheson, and Douglas Dillon—informed him they could no longer support his policy in Vietnam. Johnson was enraged: "We must refute every word of these stories. Get out my diaries. Go through the files. Bring me all the memos leading up to my decision in March. I've never been forced by anyone to do anything in my life, and I can't let this drivel stand on the record. It was *my* decision to withdraw, mine alone, and I've got to prove it."

Thereupon he sat us down and in superb fashion related his story. There was something a bit unreal in his account of how he had never wanted to be President and had always wanted to withdraw, but he embellished the tale with such astonishingly vivid detail that it resonated with authenticity. It was as if he had made everyone in the room a testament to his version of the truth simply because we were there as he spoke. And it all made a kind of sense—if, that is, you accepted Johnson's premises. If the critics said that Johnson's failure at Tet had led to the de-escalation, Johnson now claimed precisely the opposite: it was his victory at Tet that had made the bombing halt possible. And if the Eastern press insisted on making Clifford a hero, Johnson would show that Dean Rusk was the real force behind the de-escalation.

The standard at this point was not the truth, but what Johnson wanted to believe and what he thought he could persuade others to believe. It had little to do with history. Still, the Lyndon Johnson who shows up in these efforts—captious, imaginative, brilliant, and impossible—was far closer to the real man than the peculiarly colorless figure who plods through the rest of his book.

Johnson's insistence on distancing himself from the material made the book's failure inevitable. Yet, ironically, it was in part the fear of failure that led to his lassitude and detachment. We have seen throughout our present study his tendency to withdraw from situations where failure was possible. And he believed that, no matter how good his memoirs were, no matter how hard he worked on them, it wouldn't matter in the end. History was the real judge now, not the contemporaneous public, and he knew that there was no way for his memoirs to affect historical judgment. "History makes the judgment on decisions made and actions taken," he wrote in his book. But history was, he knew, in the hands of the historians, none of whom could be trusted to handle his Presidency fairly.

At moments his concern came out peevishly, his voice filled with self-pity: "All the historians are Harvard people. It just isn't fair. Poor old Hoover from West Branch, Iowa, had no chance with that crowd; nor did Andrew Johnson from Tennessee. Nor does Lyndon Johnson from Stonewall, Texas. It just isn't fair. Oh, well, why should I care about the future anyhow? I'll be dead then. What matters is now. And I've got exactly what I want right now. A wonderful wife and two wonderful daughters and two beautiful grandchildren. I am happy, very happy."

At times, Johnson did seem genuinely happy. His relationship with his wife was uncommonly close. Outward signs of deep affection and love were observable on a daily level—in the gentle touch of his hand on her knee as they rode in the car, in his kidding jests about her financial management as they entertained at dinner, in the warm, crinkly smile with which he greeted her after being separated for less than a day. Close, too, was his relationship with his married daughters, Lynda and Luci, who had both presented him with beautiful, healthy, and energetic grandchildren. In his play with his grandchildren, Johnson exhibited the wonderful childlike qualities he himself had never lost. He could entertain them for hours with the same repetitious game long after most other adults would have lost their patience. Yes, there were much love and warmth and pleasure in his final years, and, at times, there seemed some truth to Johnson's claim of being happier in retirement than he had ever been.

But at other times, particularly in the process of writing the memoirs, the impression produced by his claims of happiness was immediately contradicted by one look at his face, which made it clear that he felt anything but happy. "They'll get me anyhow, no matter how hard I try," he said one day soon after work on the book had begun. "No matter what I say in this book the critics will pull it apart. The reviews are in the hands of my enemies—the *New York Times* and the Eastern magazines—so I don't have a chance." I tried to suggest that the reviews didn't necessarily determine the fate of a book like this, that if he wrote his story in his own style, the people would read it no matter what the reviewers said, but he wouldn't listen. Pain and contempt sounded in his voice as he spoke: "You just don't understand the way things work in this country. You're too young and too innocent. I know the power of that group. Believe me, I know."

The savagery of his invective tapped the same circumstances we saw in the worst days of his Presidency. The tone was equally strident, and the web of conspiracy, if not so vast, could count among its number many of the same people and organizations. During his Presidency they had tried to destroy him by twisting the public's true feelings about him ("Before I made a speech they'd go into the town ahead of me and sabotage me"). Now they were trying to twist future perceptions as well.

So, finally, he gave it up. "There's nothing I can do about it any more. So I might as well give up and put my energies in the one thing they cannot take away from me—and that is my ranch."

Just as it is no coincidence that the long harangues about conspiracy that went on for hours in the privacy of his office in the last years of the Presidency were mirrored in his reaction to writing the memoirs, so the operation of the ranch developed into a kind of parody of the protective framework he had evolved through the insulation of the White House. Here, as there, he surrounded himself with people who would tell him what he wanted to hear, do his bidding, and filter information according to their perception of his desires. His behavior was in sharp contrast to that of Truman and Eisenhower, who continued to be public figures in the months after they left office: Truman talked repeatedly with reporters, and Ike held three news conferences in three months; Truman visited Washington and received an honorary degree, Ike met with Kennedy at Camp David and attended a White House luncheon, and both of them made a number of speeches. But Johnson became a hermit. He granted only one interview, attended few public meetings, and rarely left the ranch. He made, as I understood it, a conscious decision to occupy a smaller space so long as everything in that space was completely under his control. So averse was he to any appearance of helplessness and weakness that he totally avoided situations where he was unable to assert himself.

Johnson's decision to withdraw to a world he could control, no matter how diminished that world might be, was powerfully confirmed by what he endured during the first public ceremony he attended after his retirement—the launching of Apollo 11 on July 17, 1969. As Johnson described it to me, the day of the launch was scorching. Arriving early, he had been ushered into the bleachers, where he sat for over an hour, the sweat pouring through his shirt. The VIPs slowly arrived: Congressmen, Senators, foreign ministers. Lyndon Johnson was one of thousands, waiting "under the glaring sun," as he put it, for President Nixon's arrival.

A few people walked over to shake his hand. But the attention of the crowd was elsewhere that day, their binoculars directed toward the lunar module that would carry the first men to land on the moon. Minutes before the countdown, the President's helicopter arrived, and as the band played "Hail to the Chief," a cool and unwrinkled Richard Nixon approached the speaker's podium. The crowd stood up.

"I remember that moment," Johnson later told me. "My trousers stuck like cement to the back of my legs, the sweat from my hair kept dripping down my neck, and my stomach was upset. I knew right then I shouldn't have come. I didn't want to go in the first place, but I just didn't feel right saying no to the President's invitation. But it was worse than I thought it would be. I hated being there. I hated people taking pictures of me when I felt so miserable. And I hated shaking hands with all those people, pretending I remembered who they were when I'd never seen them before in my life. I hated their questions: What do you think of this? How do you feel about that? Each conversation was like a goddamn quiz. I hated every minute of it. All I kept thinking of was how much I wanted to be home, walking through my fields, and looking after my cattle." The most extraordinary thing about Johnson's rendering of this tale is that President Nixon was there only in the telling, not at the actual event. It was Vice President Agnew who came by helicopter and was treated royally; Nixon remained at the White House; and yet in Johnson's memory, "Hail to the Chief" was played and Nixon *was* there.

The difference between this insulation, which was pathetic and sad, and the earlier one at the end of his Presidency, which was tragic, was obviously that if the structures were analogous, the power was not. Whatever vestiges of power went with the retiring President—the grant of $375,000, the office space, the mailing frank, the military helicopter, the Secret Service—the real power was gone. So the Secret Service men sat all day in a little shack in back of the ranch house, waiting for Johnson to call. They brought him his clothes in the morning and gave him a rubdown at night. When he went for a drive, they followed faithfully behind, supplying drinks and snacks upon command. If something went wrong with his boat or radio, they fixed it. However insignificant, these services were essential to Johnson's psychic well-being; they served as props easing the transition, as vestiges of the presidential armor without which the feelings of dislocation might have been more stunning than they already were.

Deciding to spend his time on the ranch rather than on the memoirs or in public arenas, Johnson set about to master the ranch's activities with the same energy he had previously put into everything else. All the skills, all the tools, shaped over decades of public life were now directed at four or five field hands. Control that had once spanned the world was now reduced to a small, rugged domain, as Johnson became the commander in chief of a vastly reduced Western world. As always, information, detail, and direction of staff were keys to a successful operation.

For hours every day, Johnson would drive around the fields checking up on his men, finding tasks undone, spotting problems, talking with them about the cattle or the tractors. "Look at that cow," Johnson said one day, noticing a cow stalking the fence. "Look at the way she is moving against the fence and listen to her moo sound. Something's wrong. I'm sure of it. And look at her bag. See how tight it is. That can mean only one thing, that she has gotten separated from her calf. Let's go over to Pasture Three and I'll bet we'll see some calf over there standing against the fence looking for its mother. See, there it is—I knew it. God damn it. Some of Dale's boys must have gotten the calves and cows mixed up this morning while Dale was in Laredo judging a cattle show. I simply can't depend on these field hands when Dale isn't around. I think I'm going to have to start my meetings with them at six in the morning from now on."

At these morning meetings, Johnson delivered his instructions to his field hands with the same tone of voice and with the same urgency I had heard at early-morning staff meetings in the White House. "Now," he began, talking with his hands, "I want each of you to make a solemn pledge that you will not go to bed tonight until you are sure that every steer has everything he needs. We've got a chance of producing some of the finest beef in this country if we work at it, if we dedicate ourselves to the job. And if we treat those hens with loving care, we should be able to produce the finest eggs in the country. Really fresh. But it'll mean working every minute of every day. Now I want you to write down the following symbols. 'HP' means 'high priority.' 'P' means 'priority.' 'S' means 'Hold for a slow day.' Here goes. Fix the fence in Pasture Two—HP. Get itch medicine in town—P. Start the sprinklers in Pasture Three—HP. Fix the right wheel in the green tractor—HP. Check the price of feed at the county fair—S. Get some itch medicine for the sore eye on that big brown cow in Pasture One—HP." So it went for ten minutes or more. "Any questions?" he asked. There were none, and he strode off.

"Night reading" in the White House days referred to the thick packet of memos and reports that Johnson read in his bedroom before he went to sleep. After retirement, the custom remained, though the subject matter of the memos was somewhat changed. Status reports on the administration's legislative program on the Hill were replaced by reports on the number of eggs that had been laid that week by the 200 chickens Johnson owned. "From Jockey Wade to the President: Monday (162), Tuesday (144) . . . Thursday (158) . . . Saturday (104.)" As before, Johnson initialed the memo and responded. "Only 104 on Saturday? Out of 200 hens? What do you reckon is the matter with those hens?"

Using the same phrases in which he had once discussed national issues, he would talk to me about his problems with the ranch. On one dry, hot day in the summer of 1969, Johnson returned from an inspection of his fields. I could see from his rigid posture and the jerky movement of his eyes that he was exceedingly tense. He asked me to join him for iced tea in a voice that I recognized—a tone that signaled the beginning of a monologue. As I sat beside him, he looked at me fixedly, and then, bending forward, he said: "It's all been determined, you know. Once more I am going to fail. I know it. I simply know it. All my life I've wanted to enjoy this land. I bought it. I paid it off. I watched it improve. It's all I have left now. And then this rotten spring comes along as dry as any we've had in fifty years. Everything that could go wrong goes wrong. First, the rains don't come. Then the Ford motor pump breaks down. Then the parts we order to fix it are delayed. And still the rains don't come. And if we don't get our fields watered soon, everything will be spoiled. Everything. Why, those parts were ordered weeks ago. They should have been here long before now. I can't depend on anyone any more."

Next morning he sat at the table, tired and gray. After a long silence, he said: "I couldn't sleep all night. Not a minute. I kept thinking about those pump parts and about the rain and about my fields. And I couldn't stand it. I must have those parts before the end of the day. I simply must. If I don't, everything's going to fall apart. Everything. Now let's see, it's eight o'clock here, that means nine o'clock in Cincinnati. I must get started." He picked up the phone in the kitchen and asked the operator to get a Mr. McDonald in Cincinnati. McDonald was the president of the company that made the parts for the water pump. "Hello, this is Lyndon Johnson from Stonewall, Texas, and I'm sorry to bother you so early, but it's an emergency. About five weeks ago I ordered some parts for my pump and they're still not here. We need them bad. Can you check up on this for me and call me back right away?" Twenty minutes later the phone rang. Johnson grabbed it before the first ring was completed. McDonald reported that the package had been sent the day before via Air Express, American Airlines, on a 3:20 plane from Cincinnati to St. Louis, with a connecting flight in St. Louis at 5:30, to reach Dallas by 8:00 and Austin by 10:00 P.M. Which meant the package should be sitting in Austin that very moment.

Evidently feeling that he would soon have his pumps, Johnson relaxed his shoulders and let out his stomach. He reached for a piece of toast and munching it heartily he thanked McDonald "for your help and support at this critical time." But his feeling of well-being ended as quickly as it had come when, after breakfast, Johnson called the postmaster in Austin and discovered that, despite McDonald's assurance the package had not yet arrived. Johnson then called a Mr. Corcoran, the head of A.A. Air Freight. Here, too, without raising his voice he made it very clear that without these parts his water pump wouldn't work and without the pump his fields and his cattle would die. Though he didn't say it to Corcoran, his voice suggested that it would be the end for him, too. So it just better be there by nightfall. Fifteen minutes later Corcoran reported back that because of a traffic jam in Cincinnati the package had failed to reach the airport by 3:20. It had gone on the next plane to St. Louis but had missed the connecting flight to Dallas and was still in St. Louis. The best that could be done now was an 11:00 A.M. flight, to reach Dallas by 12:30, and then a Trans-Texas connection at 2:30, to reach Austin at 3:30. "No," Johnson said. "That won't do. That means it won't get here till 4:30. Too late for installation tonight. Well, you let me worry about that. You just make sure it's on that eleven-o'clock flight to Dallas and I'll take care of the rest. Thank you."

Johnson then called the head of American Airlines in Dallas, who offered to meet the 12:30 plane and fly the package straight to the ranch in his private plane. The package thus arrived at 2:00 P.M.; Johnson's entire crew was standing by. It took five hours to assemble the parts. Johnson supervised, running from one field to another, testing each pump. The sweat poured from his face and arms. It was 90 degrees in the shade. Finally, the job was done. A triumphant Johnson came back to the house for a drink. Standing on the porch overlooking his land, he turned to me and said: "What a great day. Now for the first time I've got reasonable confidence I'm not going to fail. We *will* have two hundred head of cattle, well fed and ready to sell by October. It's going to work. Thank God. I feel better tonight than I can remember feeling in a long time."

If the memoirs had been evaded by this frenzied absorption in the operation of the ranch, history became comically reduced to a constant and watchful eye on the birthhouse. In afternoon walks to the birthhouse, Johnson liked to check the different license plates to see how many states were represented; he seemed to get a great deal of pleasure from the knowledge that people were coming from all over to see this memorial to his childhood. Sometimes he'd count the number of cars and then figure out how typical that figure was for that time of year and what could be expected at that rate for the annual number. He wanted more people to see his birthhouse than any other presidential home. Every week he required written reports from the people operating the birthhouse, which assumed a standard form: "The attendance this week was (2,828), average of 404 per day. Admission receipts (728), 100 per day; book receipts (223); postcards (213); total (1164). Expenses: Wages to 8 employees (481)."

On one of our frequent visits to the birthhouse down the road he confronted the woman in charge with the latest memo. "How do you explain the difference in attendance figures and admission receipts?" "Well, sir," she said, "some people come in through the gate, walk up to the house, take a picture, and go away. And some send their children in while they wait outside." "No good," Johnson responded. "Why don't you collect at the gate or say all children must be accompanied by an adult? We've got to make ends meet, you know." Then, turning to me: "You see, I care about making money there because I want to take the money and raise the salary of the girls to two dollars an hour. I'd like to do it now, but I can't, because I've got to build up a reserve in the summer, when attendance is good, to hold us through the lean months of winter."

On the ranch, as in the White House, the people who worked for him learned to anticipate his desires. When the Lyndon Baines Johnson Library opened, Johnson repeatedly said that he wanted more people to come to it than had come to any other presidential library in the country. He pleaded with his staff to open the doors early in the morning and keep them open late at night. Asked to supply daily attendance figures, knowing that Johnson would be angry at them if the figures were low, the staff—in a painful similarity to another staff in another place—tended, gradually at first and then more and more regularly, to escalate the body count.

Through the license plates and the attendance reports, Johnson seemed to be searching for hints of his fate; the number of visitors serving as a finger in the wind, suggesting which way the historical breeze was going to blow.

I often accompanied him on the afternoon walks. Once we saw a young black boy at the gate, standing with his mother. Johnson went up to the boy and asked him how old he was and where he lived. He was seventeen and lived in Waco. The boy was thin, with short cropped hair and large ears. He had on a striped blue and white T shirt and dungarees. In his hand he was holding a little booklet describing the birthhouse. "Well," Johnson said, waving his arms, "maybe someday all of us will be visiting *your* house in Waco." The boy wasn't quite sure what Johnson meant by this. Neither was I. But Johnson went on. "You see, we'll all be visiting Waco someday because you'll be the President and your home will be a national museum just as mine is. It'll take a while, but it'll happen, you'll see. In fact, we might have seen it in my lifetime if it hadn't been for all that crazy rioting which almost ruined everything. You got off on the wrong track. That's the damn shame of it. The wrong track. But the progress we made will continue anyhow. You'll see. And someday Waco will be a President's home."

The boy looked stunned through the whole harangue. One moment Johnson had elevated him to the Presidency, the next moment he was yelling at him for getting off on the wrong track. By the end of Johnson's talk, the boy's face, which had momentarily lighted up at the thought of being President, had absolutely no expression at all. Then Johnson turned to the mother: "Now you better get that home of yours cleaned up spick-and-span. There'll be hundreds of thousands coming through it, you know, wanting to see the bedroom and the kitchen and the living room. Now I hope you get that dust rag of yours out the minute you get home." At that point, the boy smiled faintly; it was now the mother who looked stunned.

The longer we stood there, the more uncomfortable I felt. I felt as if I were participating in a show rather than witnessing a conversation, a show in which the boy and his mother were the props and I was the audience. The conversation was a routine, almost a vaudeville act. The tone was abstract and silly, even dehumanizing. Yet so strong was Lyndon Johnson's narcotic effect that I simply stood there and said absolutely nothing.

This scene was evocative of countless scenes of Johnson's life. In an African hut he had found in an African mother the same determination and will he had seen in his own mother. In Cotulla he had told children whose parents could not vote that they, too, might rise to the top of the American system. To these poor Mexicans he had given foreign aid out of his own pocket, set the goals and engineered the means. As always, the intensity of his conviction and the understanding of his own capacities were his source of persuasive power. "Where there's a will, there's a way," he repeated again and again.

"All my life I built around a series of truisms from the Bible, folklore, honor your father and mother. The good Lord endowed me with a wonderful constitution, twenty hours a day; I was plenty sturdy and tough, I had reasonable perception and astuteness, I was not a temple of wisdom or a fountain of justice, but I could comprehend things. No one ever said I was a goddamn boob, no one from Bobby up or down ever said that. I felt I could comprehend things; I had enough organizing talents, awareness of history, tradition. But the real payoff, three chances on the slot machine, which contributed more to the successes I had was the belief that where there was a will there was a way. If at first you don't succeed, try and try again. Pure will power and determination. Just like here at the ranch: be the first man all week on the pipe, carry the end pipe, the heavy one, in your slippers if necessary, with sheer guts, sheer will power, and finally you'll get your own boots."

Yet no amount of determined thought nor even the ranch—where his power was more absolute than ever before—could protect Johnson from the harsh judgments he received in his final years from the outside world. He agonized over reports in the papers about the course of the war in Vietnam and the fate of the Great Society. One of those days, as we have seen, he evoked the image of a starving woman to describe President Nixon's devastating impact on his Great Society. "And when she dies," he concluded, "I, too, will die."

On January 20, 1973, Nixon was inaugurated for a second term. The next day a cease-fire was announced in Vietnam—the long war was finally coming to an end. Later that day a new Nixon plan was announced for the dismantling of the Great Society.

The following day, on January 22, 1973, Lyndon Johnson had what was diagnosed as a fatal heart attack. He had been alone in his bedroom taking his afternoon nap. Lady Bird was in Austin and his daughters were away. At 3:50 P.M. he had called the ranch switchboard and asked his Secret Service men to come at once. Before they reached his room, he had died.

Acknowledgments

For research grants and other assistance I am grateful to the Lehrman Institute in New York City, the MacDowell Colony in Peterboro, New Hampshire, and Yaddo in Saratoga Springs, New York.

For encouragement, conversation, and criticism I am grateful to many friends and colleagues: Francis Bator, Erik Erikson, John Kenneth Galbraith, Arthur Hepner, Stanley Hoffman, Arthur Maass, Janna Malamud, Studs Terkel, Abraham Zaleznik and the Group for Applied Psychoanalysis. And for help in research, I thank Bert Solomon, Tom Johnson, and Robin Mount.

My special thanks go to Nathan Leites, David Riesman, Michael Rothschild, and Robert Shrum, who spent many hours criticizing, commenting on, and helping me with this book.

My thanks go as well to Dick Passmore, who copyedited the book with the rare skill of a true professional.

Finally, my deepest thanks to my husband, Richard Goodwin, who gave so generously of his experience and editorial skills.

Lincoln, Massachusetts
March, 1976

Author's Postscript

Now that the story of Lyndon Johnson's life has been told, I would like to draw together a number of observations on personality and politics which come to mind by treating the material as a case study in the interaction of leadership, institutional momentum, and the forces of history.

I PERSONALITY

The picture of Johnson's early life suggests a childhood torn between the irreconcilable demands of his mother—who hoped to find in his intellectual and cultural achievement a recompense for her dead father, unhappy marriage, and thwarted ambition—and those of his father, who considered intellect and culture unmanly pursuits. This may not, of course, be a wholly accurate or complete description, but the evidence we have—Johnson's recollections, his early letters to his parents, and his later behavior—supports this conclusion. His parents, most significantly his mother, seemed to bestow or withdraw approval on the basis of his behavior at home and, later, his accomplishments at school. All her expressions of satisfaction and love were related to something her son had done, just as his implied appeals for approval were accompanied by descriptions of all the good deeds he had accomplished.

Thus as Johnson grew up, he identified the success of his performance as the source of love. He could not allow himself to doubt that his mother loved him or that her praise was evidence and expression of her love. Unfortunately, however, words of admiration, praise, satisfaction, joy, even of love, which seemed a response to Johnson's activities in the many worlds through which he moved, could never truly fulfill his need for love. For the "love" whose experience, denial, or withdrawal is basic to the configuration of a given psychic structure must be, psychoanalysts tell us, perceived as a response to one's own being, unqualified by success or failure, by mental or physical defects, or by relationships to the external world. When this fundamental love is denied, or, as in Johnson's case, attached to external performance, then no recognition of personal qualities and gifts, such as integrity, warmth, energy, and talent, can suffice to satisfy inward needs. Performance alone can prevent the sense of failure and that performance must be continually displayed since past effectiveness is swiftly erased and soon counts for nothing at all. Thus continual motion and limitless ambitions become the necessities of daily life.

Lyndon Johnson found the source of his achievement in the acquisition of power and control. Yet control is not the only road to success, even in public life. For Johnson, however, control fulfilled another need as well: mastery of the outer world was necessary to mastery of the self; controlling his home environment was the only means for reconciling the profound inward tensions imposed by the contradiction between his mother's demands for intellectual achievement and his father's notions of manly pride. And control of the external world was also the only way of containing the powerful mixture of hate, rage, and love he experienced at various times toward his mother, his father, and himself. Mastery of the outer world was necessary to mastery of the self. And the drive for control was a surrogate for his urgent childhood desires to control the earliest of his environments and change his position within his parental family, thus enabling him to compel love and prevent conditions that created inner conflicts, dangers, and fears.

This understanding of the inward forces that contributed to Johnson's pursuit of power should not diminish respect for his extraordinary achievements; on the contrary, it should increase our regard for the masterful way in which—most of the time—he was able to harness and direct his personal needs toward constructive, social ends. Why some men cope and others do not remains a mystery. While we are able to suggest a number of possible bases for Johnson's strength—his grandfather's reliability, his mother's early devotion, his father's interest and attention—we have no theory to connect these observations in a coherent pattern. The psychoanalytic literature is able to analyze sources of weakness better than sources of strength.

It is also important to recognize that, while the demands of psychic structure led Johnson to pursue power, they did not determine that politics would be the avenue for that pursuit. The larger social setting provided content for Johnson's ambitions. Had his father and his father's friends been engaged in business or finance, one can imagine Johnson pursuing a very different career. But the options for a poor boy from a poor place in central Texas were limited—practically, if not theoretically. Politics was the one profession that seemed to offer both a reasonable chance of entry and a limitless future. In short, the same drives set in a different society or in another age might have led to very different pursuits.

And one thing is certain: his childhood relationships, the manner in which he sought, out of necessity, to resolve conflicts, protect his identity, and find personal fulfillment, may have shaped and energized his ambitions, but they did not, and could not, ensure their realization.

Johnson's success and achievements—his performance— were made possible, to a very large extent, by his unusual capacities, his intellect, energy, talent, and insight into men and the nature of institutions, through which he developed techniques of incredible and intricate subtlety. To his knowledge and skill he applied an innovative genius to construct a large variety of instruments which increased the coercive powers that enabled him to impose his will. And that very success only strengthened and increased his ambition.

On the foundation of the basic elements of his psychic structure, Johnson constructed characteristic forms of behavior and conduct. We have seen how they recurred constantly throughout the various stages of his career. Indeed, most of the more significant and typical methods of advancing his ambitions had already been manifested, at least in incipient forms, at San Marcos.

Every time he entered an institution whose structure made such a relationship possible and productive, Johnson apprenticed himself to a man with superior power—Evans, Vinson, Russell, Kennedy; he became the invaluable helper, the deferential subordinate willing and able to perform a dazzling range of services for his master, until, step by step, the apprentice accumulated the resources that enabled him to secure the master's role.

But Johnson was not alone in playing the role of apprentice, a role marvelously suited to a political system marked at important institutional levels by seniority and gradual ascent. What distinguished his behavior from others' was the skill with which he managed to avoid remaining a completely loyal subordinate (a position that halted the ambitions of others), yet, even while changing his role, to retain his master's support. The skills he evidenced here resonated of ones he had shown much earlier in his life as he walked the even more treacherous path between his parents' conflicting demands. The boy's earliest relationship with his mother was shaped by the idea that she needed him, and the confidence that he was capable of fulfilling that need. But with his mother, more than with anyone else, the role of apprentice required a distance; nothing less than survival of the self was at stake. So Johnson instinctively reached for the only other base of power he knew: identification with his father provided the independence he needed to separate from his mother.

In the exercise of his power, Johnson used a related technique drawn from an old tradition: he obligated his followers by providing them with services or benefits which they desired or needed. But the line between obligation and coercion was often thin. In return for his gifts, Johnson demanded a high measure of gratitude, which could only be acceptably demonstrated by the willingness to follow his lead. Though with some colleagues (those not central to his pursuit of power) he was able to grant the leeway and independence he himself had demanded, his more typical pattern required a continuing proof of loyalty so extreme that their autonomy was endangered. These demands for submission invariably worked against him, insulating him from the give and take of an adversary proceeding. He seemed to fear that any relaxation of control, even in front of his closest colleagues, would open the door to unknown enemies.

Of course, this kind of behavior cannot be attributed solely to Johnson's inner needs. It was also a response to the nature of the political world. When every situation is translated into one of power lost or gained, all relationships, including friendships, are reduced to a series of shifting, undependable alliances. In such a world it is easy to succumb to the belief that even one's closest "friend" must be watched for signs of treason.

But the vicissitudes of the political career account for neither the urgency beneath Johnson's demands for submission nor the passions he projected onto his critics. These emotions can be understood only by recognizing the fears of illegitimacy and loss that plagued Johnson from his earliest experience with power (his position in his mother's home), where he knew that all the power he commanded, while momentarily great, was subject to instant removal the moment his father returned. And these fears of illegitimacy and loss were undoubtedly reinforced by the circumstances of a political career that depended over and over on death (Buchanan, Sheppard, Kennedy) and political defeat (Lucas and McFarland). Nor was his sense of the precariousness of his power relieved by the narrow victory that launched his Senate career.

Throughout his career, Johnson exhibited an unmatched capacity to persuade individuals in one-on-one or small private settings, coupled with a crippling incapacity to present himself effectively before large public audiences. This juxtaposition of traits has long served as a puzzle for Johnson watchers. Countless descriptions have been offered of his uncommon skill in personal encounters, his brilliant blend of calculation and instinct, his unmatched richness of language and tone. One can safely assert that no American political leader has ever equaled Lyndon Johnson in the capacity to know the motives, desires, and weaknesses of those with whom he dealt. He seemed to possess a wholly intuitive ability to perceive a man's nature so accurately and profoundly as almost to be unnatural. Yet this same man, forced to speak before a large public audience, invariably stiffened up, his words delivered in monotone voice, his smile frozen, his hands tightly gripping the lectern.

This contrast is partially accounted for by the recognition that formal settings were less suitable to Johnson's particular talents—crude and colorful metaphors are less appropriate in formal speeches, and the power of physical touch is obviously reduced when the speaker stands before an audience of ten thousand or sits alone in a bare television studio. And part of the explanation for the problem in his later years can be found in the concept of the President as a statesman above the fray, a concept that Johnson shared with many others.

Yet many of the skills involved in the one were applicable to the other, as Johnson's own successes showed. His best speeches were those in which he departed from the text, and by far his most effective television appearance as judged by a poll of viewers was a long, informal conversation with three reporters during which he alternately sat in his chair, roamed around the room, or stood beside his desk, raising and lowering his voice at will. After this appearance, the opinions of his advisers were unanimous: he must adapt his informal style to his public appearances. Johnson refused with a stubborn persistence that can only be understood by searching back in his past, to the contrast already mentioned between the rich and natural mode of talk he adopted from his father and his mother's very different standards of acceptability, which produced in him a measure of shame and a determination, at least in public, to meet his mother's ideal. Yet the son of the woman who taught elocution and debate was dismissed from his lessons in public speaking for mumbling too much—suggesting perhaps an unconscious impulse to take revenge on his mother—and he never conquered his terror of speaking before an audience.

Johnson's career was marked by a continuing effort to avoid confrontation and choice, to prevent passionate and emotional divisions over issues. This inclination can be understood as a response to his particular family situation. From his earliest days, as we have seen, he had learned that if he chose his father, he might jeopardize the love and respect of his mother; if he chose his mother, his identity as a man would be in danger. The challenge then, as always, was to find a method of satisfying both—to shape an intermediate path, to find consensus. But Johnson's drive for consensus was not simply a product of inner need; its roots can be seen in the traditions and historical experience of his cultural environment, in the prevailing attitudes and ideals that comprised his view of the world.

The political heritage of Johnson's hill country was that of populism. There Johnson absorbed the established concept that government existed to help the ordinary citizen, and that the ordinary people's basic wants were essentially the same. He built his first campaign for the Congress on the promise that he alone could bring the benefits of the New Deal to the people of his district. And once elected he kept his promise: he brought water and electric power to the 10th District; he developed a slum-clearance project for the poor; he focused on the problems of the Mexican-Americans. But the populism that influenced Johnson did not include a theory of class conflict. Johnson's family was poor, but it did not identify with the poor, choosing instead to identify with the great majority of Americans, who believed in the possibility of progress and quelled their resentments of the rich by the conviction that someday they, too, would be rich.

Over time, as Johnson stretched his ambition from the 10th District to the state of Texas, he stretched his conception of "the people" to include the oil and gas men, the big ranchers, the big builders, and the cotton growers. Needing the support and the money of these powerful men, Johnson revised his definition of governmental responsibility to include help for the few as well as services for the many. He became a specialist in defense, a friendly agent ready to deliver any number of government contracts in return for campaign contributions and political support. He moved up in the world, but he never forgot the place where he had been born; he simply added new constituents to the ones he had originally served. Separate packages separately designed for separate groups—this was the winning strategy as Johnson defined it. Thus Johnson built his career on a series of disparate layers; he added one incompatible constituency on top of another; he juxtaposed contradictory ideas without choosing between them. This was a source of his personal strength in rising to power, but it also reflected the nature of a political system that rewards those capable of appealing to a variety of interests.

Johnson wanted many things, but among them, without doubt, that every American should have enough nourishing food, warm clothing, decent shelter, and a chance to educate his children; and later, as the Presidency extended his reach, he wanted to restore nature, rebuild cities, even build a Great Society. He wanted to out-Roosevelt Roosevelt and, at the same time, thought that what he wanted, everyone wanted, or would want if only he could explain it to them.

So as President he took the course that was most congenial to his character, and probably the only course possible in 1963. He would persuade everyone—businessmen, union chiefs, bankers, politicians—that his goals were in their interest, an interest that he thought, perhaps naïvely, was buried somewhere in every man—the desire to contribute, to leave behind a mark of which he could be proud. This drive to avoid conflict was a source of his greatest achievements in using his power: his success in bringing the Senate to its peak of effectiveness in the 1950s and in forging a consensus on the Great Society that went beyond the splitting of differences. Yet the drive was also a source of weakness. The American political system, superb in developing the technique of consensus, proved less capable of providing direction. Where positive goals were lacking, consensus could not supply them. Where hard choices had to be made (between constituents and ideas), Johnson could not choose. He could not choose between the Great Society and Vietnam; not only when—as in 1965—that choice seemed unnecessary because of an expanding economy and a faith in technology, but, more revealingly, when the failure to choose was obviously destroying the Great Society, the prospects of the war, and Lyndon Johnson himself. Still refusing to face even the necessity of choice, Johnson evolved an elaborate and illusory system (statistics on the continuing progress of the Great Society, statistics on Vietnam proving that the war was indeed being won), which distorted his vision and limited his real options. But practical necessity could not shift his course; the fear of choice had its roots too deep in his character and experience.

II   INSTITUTIONS AND EVENTS

Experience would strengthen Johnson's capacities, modify and supplement his modes of behavior. Man's identity, as Erikson has pointed out, is not fixed; it continually evolves through different phases of life. Some experiences induce growth in character, others provoke regression or even mental disintegration. Johnson's life history shows that he could adapt his conduct to the requirements of different political settings, that his priorities and commitments could change with the circumstances of the time. But that adaptation was possible only within limits. Some of his techniques and his ways of dealing with the world were so deeply rooted in his character and his nature that alteration proved impossible, even when those techniques proved no longer effective.

Having examined these characteristic techniques, let us consider each of the successive institutions Johnson encountered in order to assess the impact of personality in varying settings. In the present state of knowledge, it is not possible to describe the interaction of men and institutions in full and accurate detail. Institutions like individuals change over time; history moves on. The process itself cannot be frozen for inspection. The requisites for success in the same institution are different at different periods of time. This does not, however, make it impossible to analyze the interaction of men and events at a specific period of time and to draw conclusions, which I shall now attempt to do by examining each institution in turn, beginning with the House of Representatives.

The House of Representatives

From the moment of his arrival at the old Dodge Hotel to begin his work as a legislative assistant in the House, Johnson displayed and put to use those capacities and forms of behavior which—sharpened, strengthened, and modified—were to characterize and advance his entire political career. In retrospect, one can see that—behind the bursts of excitement, the frenetic motion and shifts of attention, and his almost comic behavior as within a single morning he entered and re-entered the common bathroom so he could brush his teeth alongside different groups of his colleagues—there was already the single-mindedness of purpose of a complete but yet unacknowledged politician, the inexhaustible energy that he exhibited but seemingly never consumed for most of the next four decades, directed characteristically toward learning about his new environment. From the knowledge he gained and the ability to work harder and more effectively than most other legislative secretaries, he earned a reputation as a performer on the Hill which gained him the respect of older colleagues and peers and success in the Little Congress.

The problem was that no amount of success in impressing members of the House or colleagues with his qualities, no display of skill and energy, no increase of influence among congressional staff members—then a relatively small and manageable group—could gain him real power in the House of Representatives. It might have been possible over time for Johnson to have become the trusted intimate and adviser of the House leadership—and some congressional staff members have had a great deal of influence over the course of legislation—but that of course was not a role Johnson could have wanted, accepted, or even thought about.

In order to acquire power within the House, it was necessary to be a member. And no one in the U.S. government—neither the Speaker of the House nor President Roosevelt—could appoint him to membership. Johnson realized that the

indispensable foundation of power in the legislative process
was elective office. So he bent his behavior to the requirements imposed by the political structure. Taking advantage of
the leeway in his job, which allowed him to help Representative Kleberg in a variety of ways, he concentrated on fulfilling requests from constituents, making influential friends
for himself in Texas, and earning a reputation within the
Roosevelt administration. For though Roosevelt did not have
the power of direct appointment, he did have the power to
appoint him to other positions—such as the NYA—from
which he could better build his elective base. Obviously, it
was not difficult for any aspiring politician to understand the
necessity of building a political base of his own. However, the
acuteness and comprehensiveness, part instinct and part calculation, with which Johnson understood the process and
recognized his own goals within that process enabled him to
evaluate and act upon opportunity with startling immediacy.
It must have been apparent to him, the moment he knew
Texas would need an NYA Director, that the job would permit him to increase his reputation and widen his relationships
in Texas, especially because the task was ideally suited to his
particular energies and talents. All of this enabled him to act
swiftly and purposefully, giving him an advantage over others—who were also politically ambitious, perhaps equally
qualified and with even better credentials, but who required
time to consider and calculate. Later this capacity and consequent mode of conduct were to foreclose opposition from the
wife of the Congressman whose death created the vacancy
that was the object of his first campaign, and to abate opposition for the party leadership in the Senate, where, before his
opponents had finished planning the strategy, he had already
won the fight. The experience of Johnson's career suggests
that the capacity to recognize and reach for opportunity is a
significant asset for high achievement within the structure of
American public life. Though there is usually no paucity of
candidates for a particular job, elective or appointive, time
often matters and many hold back, finding it hard to put
themselves forward, waiting to be selected on merit. And
while the others wait, those who step forward define the field.
   Thus if events and circumstance created the moment of
opportunity—the New Deal, enactment of the NYA, establishment of statewide directorships—personal qualities
made the opportunity, Johnson's opportunity. And once he

had become Director, the same qualities and skills enabled him to build the political base that would make his next success—election to the House—possible.

When he entered the House, Johnson had all the skills and qualities that had brought him success before and would again, but he did not become a leader, or even a powerful figure. Understanding that unusual failure helps to clarify the ways in which institutional structures and events can obstruct and limit the accumulation of power by even the most formidable and ambitious of men.

In the House of Representatives of the 1930s, leadership went to those who calculated and acted through a long period of patient waiting. Important Congressmen had invested years, even decades, to increase the chances of accession to leadership positions. Such positions would not be handed over to a relatively junior member who had proven his loyalty and was anxious to assume irksome burdens. Moreover, the seniority system, which led to key committee chairmanships, was firmly established, and Johnson had no access to any means of modifying this structure. And without a chairmanship it was hard to influence the content of legislation or the course of national affairs.

Now had Johnson entered the House in another era, he might have risen to power more rapidly; in the nineteenth century leadership positions were available to even the youngest members; Henry Clay was thirty-four when he was elected Speaker; and at the turn of the century, committee assignments were made by the Speaker in a bargaining exchange at which Johnson might well have excelled. By his time, however, power was institutionalized and professionalized to such a degree that Johnson's typical pattern of apprenticing himself to his elders could bring only limited rewards. (With FDR's help he received a seat on the Committee on Naval Affairs, and with the administration's support he was able to bring to his district federal programs, such as rural electrification, that solidified his political base and increased his general reputation for effective action.) But no one—not FDR nor Rayburn nor Vinson—could shorten the period of waiting within the House.

One opening provided by the institutional structure was the possibility of Johnson's mobilizing a majority to reform the seniority system and revolt against the established leadership. There were, however, barriers to this. The House had a large membership, and one that was continually changing as a result of biennial elections. In such a situation Johnson could not build the network of personal relationships—gradually constructing support through his usefulness to others—that would enable him to expand his power. Nor did Johnson have anything to offer—he lacked the resources—relevant to their legislative, political, and personal priorities. Yet even these institutional barriers might have been overcome under vastly different circumstances. There had been movements before to reform the House—some of them successful. However, this requires an atmosphere in which reform is an important issue. This condition, though there was resentment against recalcitrant conservative opposition to the continuation of the New Deal, was not sufficiently realized. Nor was Roosevelt temperamentally suited to lead such a reform. Nor for that matter was his protégé, who all his life had avoided conflict, undue risk, and public advocacy.

So the structure of the House blocked his way to power. As a result, he did what he did worst—he waited. He waited eleven years for an opportunity to leave the House to run for the Senate, not because he wanted to but because of the compulsions of institutional process. Had he possessed a different set of ambitions, these compulsions might have been less compelling. He could have used his seat in the House to speak out on various issues, to become a crusader. But Johnson always sought power in the form of control within and over public institutions. Moreover, his ambitions required continual upward movement. At each stage in the political system, the number of possible routes to the next stage is diminished. If, for example, the NYA directorship had not been available, there still would have been many ways, many kinds of jobs and activities, with which Johnson could have built his first political base. Once in Congress, however, there was only one possibility, election to the Senate (by then the governorship, even had he wanted it, was foreclosed by the circumstances of Texas politics), and that institutional reality compelled him to conduct himself in a manner that was neither characteristic nor satisfying.

He was not, of course, inactive: directing his energies in ways that would be helpful in Texas, preparing for the advent of opportunity. As soon as a Senate seat opened up, he ran and lost. It was his only electoral defeat, and it plunged him into despair. This defeat and his reaction afford us a good opportunity to analyze Johnson's attitude toward elections. Of course, all politicians are nervous about the outcome of elections, and unhappy at defeat. But to Johnson, they had a special meaning.

His skills were personal, enabling him to persuade, influence, bribe, or coerce other individuals—to understand them well enough to know how to impose his will. He generally established goals he knew he could achieve, unwilling as he was to commit himself until he was certain that the situation was under his control. This was not possible in elections. Try as he would to shake every hand and look every voter in the eye, he could not hope to evaluate the intentions or manipulate the decisions of such large numbers. Nor could he modify the results, reduce his objectives, in order to enhance the possibilities of success. In an election, there was no form of compromise between victory and defeat. In Johnson's mind, confusion, uncertainty, and doubt assumed enormous and menacing proportions. He was always driven to withdraw from situations that would not yield to his particular powers of domination and control. But to withdraw from elections would also mean closing the door to power and domination, denying his most powerful and compelling desires.

So he was at war with himself, a combat that went on in the deepest levels of his mind. The same, most fundamental attributes of his nature that compelled him to run for office also insisted that he leave the scene. And finally, most of the time, he did run because he was strong enough to resist irrational impulses in favor of practical necessities, and because of an unusual awareness that, however great the risk or intense his fears, withdrawals were irrevocable, and that destructive inner conflict would soon supplant temporary relief. However, before each of three elections (1948, 1964, and 1968) he drew up statements of withdrawal. And before almost every other election (the 1937, 1941, 1966 by-elections) he fell ill and had to be hospitalized, his body asserting the desires that the mind was restraining.

And elections had another characteristic. He wanted and needed to control other men, to dominate institutions. Still, this was unsatisfying. People did as he wanted because, in varying ways, he had imposed his will, not because of who he was. Elections were different. The votes were for him an expression of love. The word is extravagant, a metaphor, but the closest one can come to the reality. And they help explain why he also despised his own greatest and most successful abilities: by exerting power over others he was forever prohibited from discovering or experiencing their true feelings toward him. For, we must remember, they were the same capacities he had evolved in order to conceal his own emotions from himself.

This lengthy digression will, perhaps, enable us better to understand some of his actions as President, confronted with problems he could not control and a constituency he could not influence or persuade. And the fear of electoral loss is also a quality that made this man—who overrode so many institutional restraints—vulnerable to one of the most important checks in our constitutional system: the power of popular opinion, more formally incorporated in the power to elect.

The Senate

When Lyndon Johnson became a Senator, he entered an institution extremely well suited to his capacities, and at a time in the history of both Senate and country that made it possible for him to exert those capacities with great effect. No matter how great his abilities, Johnson's rise to power would not have been possible if the institutional conditions of the Senate had, like those of the House, not been favorable.

First, power in the Senate was less institutionalized than it was in the House. It was, for the most part, exercised by an informal group known as the "inner club"—the chairmen of important committees, mostly Southerners and predominantly conservative—whose acknowledged leader was Richard Russell. The hierarchy was not rigid, nor did it attempt to extend control over all the details of Senate activity. The formal leadership positions had little actual authority, and were not sought by ambitious men who had invested years of service in anticipation of being selected; their occupancy was seen more as a duty than as a base of power. Moreover, as Truman's administration neared its close the Democratic Party was in disarray, the President himself preoccupied with the Korean War, his influence dwindling. Thus there was no external party influence either on the current leadership or on the process of selection, as there might have been under a strong Democratic President and a united Democratic Party.

All these factors contributed to a situation where Johnson was able by skillfully cultivating one man—Russell—to provide an entry for himself into the power structure without infringing on the authority and prerogatives of others. There was no need to displace existing leadership—happenstance opened the posts—or to fight the organized candidacies of others. He had simply to make himself both desirable to Russell and the inner club and at least acceptable to the Northerners. And meeting the requirement, he played a skillful game: he apprenticed himself to Russell, performing all manner of tangible and psychic services, yet he avoided being placed in an ideological category that would have made him totally unacceptable to the other Senators. Thus he was prepared for the leadership opportunity when it came through—the successive vacancies of the offices of party whip and Minority Leader. Here again swift and skillful action to secure the posts was essential, but success was possible only because he was also claiming a reward—a kind of compensation—that seemed of little significance to those with the power of bestowal.

Once he became minority whip and leader, Johnson was able to accumulate power by exploiting institutional vulnerabilities—some the very ones that had made his selection possible—and the changing conditions of national and political life.

Slack in the system was perhaps the most important condition. The inner club exercised its power only over those matters it considered important or of special interest. In other areas there was no real authority, nor was there any leadership concerned with the interest of the Senate as a whole. Moreover, the inner club tended to exercise its power along ideological lines, enforcing interests and attitudes that were generally conservative and Southern. Its members were not concerned with the inevitable resentments of other Senators who did not share their convictions, because their power was based not on majority vote but on control over committees and tacit acknowledgment of their right to authority. Nor did the inner club try to placate the inevitable resentment of an increasingly number of new Senators who felt that the established customs, leadership, and procedures barred them from a significant role in the legislative process, diminishing their opportunity to perform as they wanted and as their constituents expected.

Yet, if resentments smoldered and needs went unmet, there was no organized or coherent effort on the part of any group to displace the present leadership with a majority leadership of their own. The formal discipline that would have been required for such a revolt was hard to find in a body characterized by independent bases of power for each of its members. Each Senator had interests distinct from those of every other—derived primarily from the necessities of his own political career. While a Senator's concern for the effective functioning of the Senate as a whole was not absent, it was not generally a priority concern compared to his relationship with his constituents. Thus the alternatives history provided—strong, elective party leaders with party caucuses to bind votes and men—seemed even less appealing than a disorderly, uninstitutionalized Senate.

The situation was ripe for a personal leadership style: one that could lessen the tensions resulting from the Southerners' tight control, concern itself with the smoother operation of the Senate, gather central resources to help individuals, but always remember that a Senator's relationship with his constituency was the primary concern.

So upon taking over, Johnson assumed some burdens of leadership that had not previously been exercised—allotment of office space, scheduling of legislation, appointments to committee delegations. Able to comprehend the current structure of the Senate as a whole, he formed a mental picture of a different structure and moved toward it with such skill that he managed to bring everyone along with his changes, even those who would potentially lose power under the new system. He began by persuading the inner club to relax seniority just a little, to provide more seats on important committees to new members as a token means of quelling incipient resentment and as a way of making the Senate function more effectively. By this move, however, he obligated the freshmen Senators to him; he established the appearance that his authority was the source of their ability to do their work effectively. At the same time, the small size of the Senate allowed him to gather information about every Senator: what he was going to do, was likely to do, or might be persuaded to do. Over time, Johnson became the only source of authoritative information on the Senate as a whole. Thus he became useful, and often indispensable, to other Senators who were forced to rely upon his judgment about, for example, the chances of passing legislation in which they were interested, or what form of compromise could bring agreement, or when they could take a trip without missing a crucial vote. In addition, he made it impossible for others to separate the appearance of power from its reality. If, for example, he told a Senator that he would make sure of a favorable vote on his bill and the bill passed, one could not know whether Johnson had exerted his authority or whether he had already known what the result would be. In this way he secured obligations not only by rendering real services and rewards but by seeming to produce results that were not, in fact, of his doing.

The insulation of the cloakroom, where much of the Senate's business occurred, allowed Johnson to impose his will separately on each Senator and in such a way as to reduce awareness of the coercive nature of his leadership. Had there been collective forums of decision in which he had forced individuals to go his way, the coercive nature of his tactics would have been all too clear. And, in fact, Johnson drained the collective organs, the caucus and the conference, transforming most of the Senate's business to his own office, where his relations were seen as bargaining. And, true, his capacity to bargain and persuade was undoubtedly an important element in his leadership. Yet the process was essentially coercive; over time, Johnson's power became increasingly necessary to the capacity of others to sustain and exercise their own authority. Every time he bargained there was always the implicit threat—never voiced, but inherent in the very disproportion of power and rewards—that failure to go along might have damaging consequences. And in most cases the Senators yielded, except, of course, on matters of fundamental concern to their constituencies—a limit Johnson understood and respected. When he anticipated failure, he didn't try to persuade—a fact that only enhanced his reputation as a leader who accomplished what he set out to do.

The disguise was essential. For no Senator could afford to let others know he was being compelled to act by another, that he was submitting to Lyndon Johnson's will. The nature of the Senate required unanimous acceptance of the mask— continual recognition of the Majority Leader's skills, his brilliance in argument, his effectiveness in conducting the business of the Senate, his genius at compromise—but not of his power to enforce his will. It is true that Johnson disliked, even feared, direct and open confrontation. But he was essentially a coercive personality, working in a situation in which bargaining and persuasion were the necessary forms for the acquisition of power and the exercise of control. Such forms were also more congenial to his personal qualities, reducing the possibility of failure, since one could not be defeated in a discussion or defied and overcome by another's inability to understand the wisdom of one's advice and arguments.

If institutional process and structure made the most important contribution to Johnson's power and the manner of its use, he was also helped by historical conditions and political circumstances, which—and partly because they were so congenial to his own character—in turn, influenced his conduct in the Senate. It is, for example, difficult to imagine Johnson's achieving a similar concentration of power in the Senate of Daniel Webster or John Calhoun. He came to Senate leadership during a time of relative quietism. The economy was doing well, and occasional recessions seemed nothing more than transient interruptions in the steady growth of personal affluence. There were no passionate issues of the kind that led to deep and irreconcilable divisions along lines of fundamental interest or ideology.

And the political circumstances were also congenial: a President uninterested in social reform, whose popularity restrained most Democrats from too open or strong opposition, permitted Johnson to avoid disruptive debates whose outcome he could not control. And that same President, because he was a Republican, made it unnecessary for Johnson to subordinate his conduct to the White House as he might have had to do with a strong Democratic leader.

Let us now turn to the influence of his power on the structure of the institution and on national events.

Clearly, he had achieved more power as leader than any other leader in decades. And he had built that power from the qualities and structure of the institution. But he had not created institutionalized power. His powers had not, with a few exceptions, been incorporated into the formal authority of the Majority Leader. He had transformed a position of limited significance into one of great power. But he had used the majority leadership and not transformed it. His system depended on his capacities, knowledge, and command over a variety of procedures which he enforced but did not establish. As a result, when he left, the Senate had no centralized structure of leadership—unless it could find another Lyndon Johnson, which seemed unlikely, since it had waited two centuries for the first one.

Despite the failure to institutionalize his power, we must

conclude that Johnson did bring the Senate during his reign to unprecedented heights of effective function. Legislation was moved from introduction to committee to floor and then enacted smoothly and with dispatch. Conflicts were reduced and respect for the Senate increased. Johnson's leadership is also responsible for speeding up the process through which the powers of the conservative Southern coalition were redistributed to the Senate as a whole, a process made inevitable by population shifts and the loss of a one-party South, and for reducing some of the inequalities resulting from the seniority system. The old system had rested on accepted traditions and procedure, informal alliances based both on common outlook and mutual interest and on established procedure—seniority—for the acquisition of authority. Once that system had changed, then the belief that the way things were was the only way they could be was shattered. Nor was it likely that any new group of Senators would now deliberately grant authority to a group of committee chairmen dominated by Southern authority.

Yet the powers once held by the inner club were not, after Johnson, lodged in a new leader; they were simply fragmented to the benefit of individual Senators. These Senators have since developed a stake in the existing system of leadership. Any change now would entail a transfer of power, a probability that familiar modes of conduct would be changed; the ultimate consequences are uncertain and thus appear as risk. This is precisely why structures of power in the Senate are not codified, but, instead, continually evolve over a long period of time with changes in the nature of the Senate membership. Johnson's rise was exceptional in this regard. The Senate would never have voted to give him the powers of leadership that they so often praised. Nor are they likely to bestow the same powers on any other Majority Leader or on the position itself. That would require a sense of devotion to the Senate as a whole, which would only be possible in an institution that was a collective body—that is, in a different institution.

Johnson's system of power and leadership influenced not only the Senate as an institution but national conditions and events. For one thing, he inhibited the development of effective and coherent opposition on domestic issues. There were serious national problems—persisting poverty, inadequate health care, recurrent recession and unemployment—along with questions of defense policy and foreign affairs. There was debate on these issues, both in the country and, later, during the 1960 presidential campaign. But the Senate was potentially the most important forum for the expression of opposition. It could influence the national dialogue; many of its members were themselves significant political figures, and with a Democratic majority could force a confrontation. Historically, it had often taken this role (congressional opposition during the later New Deal, the great and partly decisive debate over the Marshall Plan, etc.). This does not mean that the Senate could have substituted its policies for those of Eisenhower, but it abdicated the possibility even of stimulating national debate; of influencing, if not decisively changing, the course of events and those administration policies that needed senatorial acquiescence. Yet the days of the Senate's involvement with legislation had been steadily waning even before Johnson, and on the other side of the ledger is the fact that Johnson's leadership was vital to the passage of the first civil rights act since 1867, and in forcing the government to initiate a large-scale space program. And there were other accomplishments. Nevertheless, we must conclude that while Johnson's leadership style—his avoidance of issues and his fear of confrontation—may have increased his power over the Senate, it lessened the influence of the Senate on the country.

Under Johnson's reign, floor debate was substantially reduced in importance, and with it, the role of the Senate in foreign policy. Again we must acknowledge an institutional evolution toward increased executive authority in foreign policy. Yet in the decades before, Congress had felt free to debate—often along partisan lines—to oppose, and occasionally to act against the President's foreign policy. Since then, the felt requisites of unity in the difficult period of the cold war had worked to reduce open debate. But Johnson led in a time of peace, in a time when the Senate might have—as Senator Joseph Clark repeatedly suggested—moved to increase its supply of information without threatening executive authority. But Johnson refused, preferring always to resolve issues by private compromise followed by public agreement, and thus contributed to the general weakening of the Senate's role.

And once the traditional responsibilities were abandoned, there was little move to reclaim them. Because Senate constituencies had little interest in most matters of foreign policy, the most important incentive to action was missing. And the irony was that Johnson's own performance in the Presidency would itself be seriously influenced by this weakening of the Senate—by reducing an important check that might well have constrained his decisions on Vietnam in ways helpful to him as well as to his country.

The Nomination Process

That Johnson ran a poorly conceived and poorly executed campaign for the Presidency in 1960 is a commonplace observation. My interest is in why this happened to a man so skillful at acquiring power in so many other arenas. Part of the answer lay in the changing nature of the nomination process. Had Johnson been trying for the Presidency in the early nineteenth century, when the legislative caucus nominated the President, his chances would obviously have been much enhanced. Or had the system remained as it was through most of the nineteenth and early twentieth centuries, one in which a national convention controlled the choice, we can imagine Johnson exerting his enormous persuasive powers at that convention, face to face, wheeling and dealing behind closed doors. But the system he confronted in 1960 had moved away from a pure convention choice. Although deadlock was still conceivable, making it possible for the dealings at the convention to be of primary importance, the more likely occurrence was that one of the candidates, through a rounding up of delegates and primary votes, would be able to produce a near majority before the convention even began.

That Johnson failed to recognize these changes can be attributable in part to his preoccupation with the Senate. Unlike Kennedy, he had not spent time in the states learning who the important powers were, who controlled the delegations. And without personal knowledge and touch his usually acute powers of perception were substantially reduced, leading him to the mistaken notion that the leaders of the Senate were also the leaders of the delegations, that if he could round up the Senators from Arkansas and Idaho, for example, he would secure their delegations. Viewing the election through the prism of the Senate also led to an underestimation of Kennedy's qualities. True, Kennedy was not an impressive Senator, but the qualities needed or desired for success within the Senate were not necessarily those that would produce success in the electoral arena. There, more public qualities were important—for those states where the primaries determined the delegation vote—as well as large-scale-organization skills, which were necessary for holding together a national campaign structure.

Moreover, Johnson's identification as a nonliberal was a principal obstacle to his ambitions. In modern times, the Democratic Party had always nominated a liberal candidate. The membership of the convention was more liberal than the national constituency needed to elect a Democratic President; just as the Republican Convention tended to be more conservative than the constituency they needed to elect a President.

To secure the nomination, Johnson needed some identification with issues. Yet he had always sought to avoid a campaign based on divisions over issues, just as he sought to avoid division in the Senate. Such divisions were uncontrollable, at least were not susceptible to his capacities and ingenious modes of control. To take a position on an important issue, at least in the context of an election, meant creating opposition that could not be won over by bargaining or techniques of informal coercion. Always before he had depended on performance rather than on his stance on issues (with the exception of his first campaign, where he distinguished himself by support for Roosevelt's court-packing, but in fact that support was read more as support for FDR and the New Deal, and in his district Roosevelt and the New Deal were not issues, but secular manifestations of divine goodwill). From then on, the particular structure of Texas politics, although not permitting him to avoid issues entirely, made election largely dependent on support from identifiable sources of political power—a varied assortment of bosses, some political, some representatives of dominant economic interests. Johnson knew these men, what they wanted, and how to convince them—in action and through persuasion—that his election was in their interests, that, in fact, he was to be desired over other, equally reliable men, since he would approach the task with greater energy and skill than anyone else. Moreover, the interests of the variety of men and groups who were necessary to political success, although different, were rarely in direct conflict. The minorities in the state of Texas were unorganized, politically impotent, and were not, at that time, capable of organizing or expressing opposition. It was unnecessary to appeal to them on issues, although it did help a candidate if he could demagogue a little—to establish an identification through manner and rhetoric—even if his votes and actions showed his allegiance was somewhere else.

But if Texas politics allowed an avoidance of issues, national politics did not. The primary object in a national campaign was to take a position most likely to win the election; this required a judgment of the motives, intentions, and governing influences—not of knowledgeable individuals, but of a great number of people whose views, and, more important, the intensity of whose views, could not be ascertained by Johnson's powers of perception, observation, judgment, and intuition in the presence of those he was trying to assess or influence. One had to guess, or make a judgment based on indirect information, and to Johnson—because his political techniques, although of great practical value, were related to inner needs—those kinds of judgments, which most politicians make constantly, seemed to involve almost unbearable risk, a source of terror that was an inevitable response not to external circumstances but to inner conditions.

Thus it was not possible for Johnson to stand on an issue, or on his personal qualities, or on an image of strength or honesty that could be projected before the people. The only appeal he could make was the one he had always made—that he deserved election on the basis of his past performance—and in 1960, at a time when the people were looking for a change, that appeal had no appeal.

The Vice-Presidency

In accepting the Vice-Presidency, Johnson thought he could do again what he had done before: take a position with limited power and then, by recasting and expanding its function, pyramid its slight resources into substantial political holdings. But this time Johnson miscalculated, and his miscalculation tells us something not only about Johnson's limits but about the limits of the institution of the Vice President.

Theoretically, Johnson's notion of the Vice President as apprentice to the President made sense, but the evolution of the office itself had made that role very difficult to work out in practice. Out of political rivalry and habit, Presidents had rarely been inclined to include their Vice Presidents in the central decisions, preferring instead to give them special assignments, occupying their time in essentially peripheral areas. Nor did Johnson have many services, once the election was over, to offer Kennedy in return for the master's rewards. The one resource he could have mobilized—his talents with the Congress—was removed from him because he overreached in his attempt to restructure his formal relationship by his proposition to allow the new Vice President to remain the leader of the Conference Committee. He took the rebuff—essentially a reassertion of checks and balances—as a personal affront and was unable to help Kennedy on the Hill. In the absence of this resource, there was little he could do of vital importance. Nor was he able, temperamentally or institutionally, to use his base to build his own power for the future. Recent tradition had eschewed open rivalry and Johnson was not temperamentally suited for the role; it would force him into a position of direct conflict, when he knew only how to be the loyal subordinate. All these difficulties were compounded by the presence of Robert Kennedy, who became the power behind the throne that Johnson had wanted to be and who was more likely than he to receive John Kennedy's support in any subsequent election campaign.

It is conceivable that Johnson saw more than he gave indication of seeing, that he did recognize the limits of the Vice-Presidency, but that he had to believe in its possibilities, however slim, because there was nowhere else to go.

The Presidency

In 1963 Johnson entered an arena vastly different from the legislative institutions in which he had spent nearly all his adult life. Yet for the first twelve months the circumstances of the transition period and the election allowed him to conduct his Presidency in a manner consistent with his previous efforts to acquire and exercise power.

Upon his succession to the Presidency, Johnson confronted a dual problem: he had to guide the country through a traumatic and uncertain moment and work to ensure his nomination at the Democratic Convention, which was only eight months away.

The course he chose to meet the first objective—the theme of continuity—was natural to his character and to the needs of his time. Moreover, he was helped in this endeavor by the institutionalized process of succession—established by constitutional and historical precedent—which immediately placed in his hands all the powers, institutional authority, symbolic functions, and impressive trappings of the American Chief of State—a transfer that was more than a transfer, but rather a replacement thought so necessary and appropriate that not a single dissenting voice marred the population's unquestioning acknowledgment of its legitimacy.

The circumstances of the public mood even allowed Johnson while in the Presidency to assume his accustomed role of the faithful follower—this time of the memory of a dead President. Now, unlike the Vice-Presidency, where he had nothing to give, he could, as he had done with Russell, provide a significant service (the enactment of the dead man's program) and then reap the rewards that would enable him to consolidate his power.

This was possible because he had come into the legislative cycle at the ideal moment for his particular talents. Kennedy had already articulated the goals—most of the issues on Kennedy's agenda were suspended between formulation and approval—leaving the new President the familiar task of mobilizing congressional support.

Moreover, 1964 was a year of relative tranquillity in foreign policy, while the country itself experienced relative economic stability, and there were no serious or turbulent manifestations of domestic distress. Serious and visible crises would have required him to devote attention to unaccustomed responsibilities. In their absence, the enormous resources and elaborate machinery of the modern presidential institution—bureaucracies, established hierarchies of authority and decision, experts, a White House staff large and specialized enough to exercise some form of White House jurisdiction over every activity of importance and make decisions in his name—could ensure that the activities of government were continued, decisions made, foreign leaders placated, etc., without compelling him to divert his attention to unfamiliar matters or to consider and resolve problems unrelated to his immediate objectives: legislative achievement and election.

In the election, too, the circumstances created an ideal situation for Johnson. He had always sought to avoid campaigns based on divisions over issues, trying instead to focus attention on his performance. Now his performance would be the main issue—a transition performance whose circumstances allowed him to combine a deferential dignity with a dazzling display of effectiveness, which brought first relief, then approval and even admiration from the press and the general public. Indeed, his display of large abilities and presidential stature was so significant that he could, even though he'd been in office for only a few months, run on the record; and the shortness of his incumbency enabled him to define that record as a demonstration of stature and performance rather than of the substance and directions of his policies, which would obviously be more divisive.

To these conspicuous and influential circumstances was added the nomination of Goldwater, reflecting the culmination of an evolution—a shift part ideological, part geographical—of power within the Republican Party. Goldwater's candidacy—his insistence that he was truly ideological, the nature of some of his support for the nomination, and some of his speeches—gave the impression that he wanted to eliminate many of the programs and institutions established in the decades since Roosevelt took office, which had come to be viewed by moderates and many conservatives not as liberal experiments or intrusions but as part of the established order. The same interests who had opposed Social Security and government regulation of business activity had no desire to tear apart a structure they were now accustomed to, had conformed their activities to, and under which, moreover, they were doing better than before.

One can hypothesize a moderate to liberal Republican candidate who could have made a serious issue of Johnson's already expressed intentions and their implication of greatly increased federal activity and spending, who might have accused him of dangerous incapacities in foreign policy, or have debated the Democratic Party's intention—already manifested by the actions of Kennedy and Johnson—to reverse Eisenhower's refusal to intervene militarily in Indochina; a debate that would have permitted the Republicans to exploit the public's recollection of Truman and Korea and the vague identification of the Democratic Party as the party of war. Instead, however, the Republicans nominated a candidate whose campaign imposed upon his candidacy the most serious traditional vulnerabilities of both parties.

This made possible the kind of campaign most congenial to Johnson's own temperament. His election was in everybody's interest: to the conservative, complacent or fearful, he was the protector of the system; to a people whose enthusiastic response to the Test Ban Treaty had surprised even Kennedy, he was the man of peace who would meet crises with restraint; to the poor and the blacks, he offered not only understanding but a demonstrated capacity for effective action; to the middle class, he could appear as both a guarantor of increasing affluence and, without seeming inconsistent, as one who understood and would try to alleviate many of the sources of middle-class discontent—the state of the environment, pollution, the conditions of urban life. He was under no compulsion to set forth a coherent program, which might have revealed the difficulties of fulfilling such diverse and often conflicting expectations, whose content and potential consequences would have increased opposition. The unusual conditions of political life in 1964 allowed him to rely, instead, on general statements of purpose, principle, and intention. His opponent not only did not challenge him from the middle, but made *himself* and not Johnson's policies the issue (McGovern was to perform a similar service for Nixon in 1972). Johnson was, therefore, in the fortunate circumstance of being able to combine elements of the kind that contributed to the disparate appeals of both Eisenhower and Roosevelt.

So everywhere he went huge crowds assembled to greet his arrival, attend his movements through the streets. Millions of people he hadn't met, didn't know, whose motives and interests he had not calculated in order to decide how best to impose his will, cheered, almost screaming, often jumping excitedly, in their enthusiasm at his presence. No advance men or organization could have produced such multitudes or intensities. He had accomplished some significant things, but less than several other Presidents, far less than he intended, yet he was hailed as if he were a national conqueror. And even if he didn't understand and only half-trusted it, he couldn't get enough of it, traveling from place to place, descending into every crowd, touching the few he could reach as if to reassure himself it was really happening, and more obviously out of an uncontrollable and understandable exuberance. And who could blame him? It was the closest he could come to feeling loved, and who would not express—in his own manner and to the extent he could—exultance at the unexpected approach toward satisfaction of this universal longing?

The election of 1964, both the victory and its size, changed the nature of Johnson's political constituency. The Democratic Party itself was no longer a factor in the exercise of power or its renewal. His election left the party apparatus in his hands, and he would soon move to eliminate any remnants of independent authority or access to resources that the Kennedy White House had left intact. As an incumbent, his renomination, if he wanted it, was assured—or so he had every right to assume, and must have assumed. It was, therefore, no longer necessary to direct efforts or policies to cultivate the support of groups because of their potential influence on the party. Their importance to Johnson now depended on their potential influence on the outcome of a national election, and—of more immediate and pressing significance—on the extent to which they could help or obstruct the achievement of his objectives, mostly the passage of legislation.

After the 1964 election, Johnson found himself in command of an institution very different from the institutional and political settings in which he had spent virtually his entire life, and through which he had pursued his ambitions with enormous, if not uninterrupted, success. He had great powers, whose acquisition he could now regard as the consequence of his own abilities and that could, therefore, be exercised for his own purposes. However, it is unlikely that he fully understood the extent of the differences in function and structure between the Presidency and the earlier settings for his activity and ambition, nor the extent to which presidential powers were not only greater but of a different nature.

In the Presidency, unlike in the Senate, the standards of achievement had to be established in relation to accomplishments external to the presidential institution. Here Johnson's own skill and natural inclination, reinforced by the experience of the transition, led him to establish standards of achievement based on his success in designing and enacting a program of domestic reform. Moreover, institutional relationships between the President and Congress required that he must also determine the substance of that program—the general policies and the content of the legislation he would propose. Here Johnson could benefit from the ideas of a liberal tradition institutionalized in his agencies and the Bureau of the Budget, which for twenty years had been proposing legislation that had never passed; now their time had come and they had a ready agenda.

However, neither Johnson's own ambitions and convictions

nor the ready agenda would have prevailed under adverse conditions. But in 1965 conditions could not have been more auspicious for domestic reform. Sustained economic growth combined with a relative stability of prices had strengthened a conviction that affluence was inevitable. Moreover, there was still a general desire for the re-establishment of some form of shared national purpose: a sentiment that had formed the theme of Kennedy's successful 1960 campaign. The absence of paramount domestic divisions made it unnecessary for him to take positions that would have aroused the kind of opposition that would have extended beyond the issues themselves to him and his administration. Economic conditions and, even more, established economic expectations made it possible to convince people that the poor and disadvantaged could be helped and that national problems—conditions of urban life, disintegration of the natural environment, transportation facilities, etc.—could be resolved without requiring any group to sacrifice income or significant interests.

Finally, there was the influence of Johnson's own leadership—his natural capacities and unequaled knowledge of Congress, which enabled him to confound the traditional relationship between President and Congress, mixing the two so that both branches were involved in the acts of proposing and disposing. Moreover, the familiar resources of the presidential institution enabled him to provide a great variety of benefits and services that would create obligation and various degrees of dependency. Most importantly, as President, Johnson could now bargain directly with leaders of powerful interest groups—business executives, leaders of financial communities, union chiefs, the acknowledged spokesmen for minority groups, etc. As President, he could virtually command their presence, allowing him to exert his formidable personal powers. Even more significantly, every important group in the society was affected by the activities of the federal government, especially by the executive branch Johnson commanded. Thus every encounter also involved an awareness—rarely, if ever, expressed—of mutual interest more direct and specific than their shared patriotism and belief in the American dream. Thus Johnson was able to enlist support, or, at the least, mute potential opposition, from those interest groups whose views could influence the decisions of Congress. They were important, not just because of their wealth or numbers, but because there was no member of Congress whose political base was not subject to the influence of one or more of them. As President, Johnson could thus do what he could not do in the Senate—extend his reach to the foundation and source of office.

Of course, without general public support this would have been to no avail. But the aspect of consensus politics that made effective performance possible was a consensus among a limited number of special groups, whose leaders could be identified, making possible the personal contact that was the medium through which Johnson could make the most effective use of his personal powers and tangible resources—to persuade, convince, bargain, obligate, or coerce. As long as the objective was congressional action—the passage of legislation—the presidential institution enormously increased the effectiveness of behavior that had been successful in other contexts.

In particular, in the area of civil rights Johnson's legacy is clear: his position on racial issues was more advanced than that of any other American President; had he done nothing else in his entire life, his contributions to civil rights would have earned him a lasting place in the annals of history.

But if the modern Presidency permitted Johnson an unparalleled authority in domestic affairs for the successful exercise of his qualities and abilities, modes of conduct and methods of exercising power, it also permitted an equally unparalleled failure when those same qualities and patterns of behavior were applied where all Johnson's talents and skills were not merely inadequate but irrelevant and, even more, counterproductive.

Lyndon Johnson did not create the framework within which his country defined its commitment to South Vietnam. That framework, developed in the space of more than twenty years by three previous Presidents and their many advisers, rested on a series of assumptions derived from historical experience: the experience of World War II and the events that precipitated it; the initial confrontations between the Soviet Union and the United States; the fear of making concessions to adversary powers; the identification of the potentially dangerous power—the Soviet Union—with the ideology of Communism, an identification which required that any political leader or insurgent chief who called himself a Communist was simply an extension of Soviet power.

Of course, experience was not all so one-sided. We had

resigned ourselves to the "loss" of Eastern Europe and China, accepted stalemate in Korea, refused to intervene in Indochina; in other words, had shown that our policies, the underlying convictions, and their sometimes violent expression by leaders such as Dulles had not destroyed our ability to assess realities, and to accept limits imposed by the calculation of practical possibilities.

But the institutional structure Johnson inherited in 1963–1964 narrowed access to the information and perceptions that might have placed Vietnam in one of the above categories. All Johnson's principal advisers agreed on the critical nature of the goal of a non-Communist Vietnam, on the interpretation of the internal struggle as a struggle against Communism, and on the possibility of achieving that goal with gradual escalation short of large-scale war.

Clearly, Johnson's own qualities influenced his initial decision to escalate. In domestic affairs, particularly in the passage of legislation, he was used to grasping practical realities first and then adapting his goals to those realities. But his lack of intimate knowledge about foreign policy and Vietnam led him to rely, instead, on the goals and principles themselves, losing sight of the question of available means. The failure to ask "Will it work?" was reinforced by a pristine concept of foreign policy as an arena of choice that should be removed from ordinary political consideration. Therefore his means were subordinated to his ends; his ends *became* his means. Lack of experience and confidence also produced in Johnson an unquestioning acceptance of the "experts'" advice, something he would never have accorded to anyone in domestic affairs. Moreover, Johnson's adversary in Vietnam—unlike nearly all his opponents at home—was unwilling to bargain. Even if Johnson had been able to sit down with Ho Chi Minh, there was nothing to talk about so long as the goals of the two countries remained irreconcilable. So, faced with a situation he could not control and an adversary who was unwilling to bargain, Johnson would force him to bargain. And since he could not compel in his usual way—the denial of rewards or necessities—he was forced to act more directly, in this case with the only instrument of compulsion he had: military force. And, given his character, that force would be exercised in graduated degrees (thus avoiding the even more uncontrollable situation of all-out war).

To say Johnson's qualities were expressed in the decision to escalate is not, however, to say that his character caused that decision. On the contrary, in late 1964 and early 1965, as we have seen, all the relevant elements of the governing process moved in the same direction, making it impossible to filter out the particular weight of personality. Indeed, given the momentum, the necessity of choice—since at this point not choosing would have meant turning South Vietnam over to the Communists—and the consistency of advice from almost every corner, it is easy to imagine many other Presidents, acting under very different internal compulsions, making the same decision.

The influence of Johnson's personality on the decision-making in Vietnam is easier to observe in his conduct of the war—in the decision to conceal its nature and extent from the American people. Here the advice was not unanimous; indeed, most of Johnson's principal advisers recommended a different course from the one Johnson chose, urging him to go to the Congress, declare a state of emergency, and put the economy on a wartime footing. Johnson refused, opting instead to hide the costs of the war in the Defense Department budget, keeping the pretense of a peacetime economy, and letting the public know as little as possible about the nature and extent of the war—all of which he assumed would allow the Great Society to continue on course.

This decision was Lyndon Johnson's decision. It is easy to imagine another President, less concerned with domestic reform, more capable of choosing between goals, less confident of his ability to move in contradictory directions at the same time, less experienced in the arts of secrecy, deciding differently. Indeed, this decision seems almost to sum up the character of the man. The very qualities and experiences that had led to his political and legislative success were precisely those that now operated to destroy him. His tendency to resolve conflict instead of accepting it—responsible for his rise to power and his success in the Senate—now led him to manipulate and orchestrate the political process in order to shape a formula that could accommodate both the Great Society and Vietnam. Years of experience in gaining and exercising power had taught Johnson that the leader could move in contradictory directions at the same time so long as he compartmentalized everything he did and kept his dealings with one group secret from those with the next. Finally, the bipartisan tradition in foreign policy, responsible for producing consensus behind World War II and the Marshall Plan, now led to the conclusion that complicated decisions of foreign policy should be left in the hands of the leaders; the people would only be hurt by knowing too much.

As it turned out, however, the people were not hurt by knowing too much; Lyndon Johnson was hurt by knowing too little. The loss of public debate on the war lessened the possibilities of judgment, depriving Johnson of the chance to test various responses to different policies and of the opportunity to dispel misconceptions. Nor, in the absence of any clear understanding of the goals in Vietnam, could he expect to sustain the public's support.

He had hoped that a middle course at home and abroad would secure his place in history as a leader of war and a leader of peace. Instead, halfway measures on both fronts produced a condition of half-war and half-peace which satisfied no one and created resentments on all sides.

Moreover, the failure to increase taxes produced inflation, which produced, in turn, a squeeze on moneys for the Great Society instead of the steadily expanding supply of resources Johnson had originally promised. (At this stage of the Great Society, the difficulties Johnson experienced on questions of implementation were similar in nature to those that plagued him on Vietnam. Here, too, because he was so sure of the ends and because the persons involved in implementing the means were so far away, he underestimated the problems of making his programs work.) Furthermore, diversion from the Great Society was not only a question of economic resources; the war drained time, energy, and attention as well.

As the Great Society crumbled and the war continued with no end in sight, Johnson's popularity began to drop. The effective performer was no longer performing effectively, and once that measure of favorable judgment was gone, there was nothing else on which to base his relations with the people—except all those qualities he had never trusted: public advocacy, personal integrity, credibility.

Gradually, and for almost the first time, Johnson now found himself amid events and men he could not master: Vietnam and the Kennedys, and, later, the press, Congress, and even the public whose approval was all he could experience of love. One could have anticipated the result. As his defenses weakened, long-suppressed instincts broke through to

assault the carefully developed skills and judgment of a lifetime. The attack was not completely successful. The man was
too strong for that. Most of Johnson—the outer man, the
spheres of conscious thought and action—remained intact,
for most of the time. But in some ways, increasingly obvious
to his close associates, he began to crumble; the suspicions
congenital to his nature became delusions; calculated deceit
became self-deception, and then matters of unquestioned belief.

Moreover, Johnson was aided—or, more accurately,
hurt—in this process of deception by the nature of the institutional relationships around him. The White House itself—as
opposed to the Senate—was not manned by individuals with
independent political bases and formal authority. Here
Johnson was in command, and, expectedly, the coercive aspects of his nature manifested themselves. He could impose
his will much more directly upon colleagues—members of his
staff and of his Cabinet—whose positions and power within
the government rested primarily on him. Of course, he, in
turn, depended on the abilities of these men, but that meant
that the only hold they had was the right to resign. And it
was not much of a hold. For Johnson knew that few men
easily relinquished their high positions in government. Both
Johnson and his subordinates knew that resignation involved
forfeiting recognized status and power in return only for escape. Under these conditions, the independence of the Cabinet members and of those in charge of the most important
White House functions was gradually reduced. The President's will, once expressed, was not challenged. Advisers
began to anticipate his reactions before they said or did anything; self-deceptions multiplied in this hall of distorting mirrors. The more Johnson's energies turned to his critics, the
more obsessed he became with the need to discredit his opponents, the less anyone tried to stop him.

Nor did the President have to listen to the Congress so
long as it continued, out of tradition, habit, and deference,
to appropriate funds for the war, and so long as it refused
to take a single vote on the war itself. Nor—for three years—
did any other external force break through. Surrounded by
the White House staff, cocooned in an institutional framework protecting him from the outside world (his schedule,
secretaries, planes and cars), Johnson effectively insulated
himself from information he did not want to hear.

But there was a limit to Johnson's insulation and his self-defeating belief in the possibility of turning the corner in Vietnam. The Tet offensive and the presidential primaries changed the framework within which Johnson had to work. Finally, the checks and balances of the political system came back into play.

Forced to confront a precipitous drop in his public standing, a sharp shift in editorial reaction, and the loss of support from key-interest-group leaders, Johnson finally accepted the fact that he was in a situation he could no longer control and that further escalation would produce only more uncontrollability. Faced at the same time with loss of love and gratitude on what seemed an irretrievable scale, Johnson had no choice but to withdraw. Nor did he have any choice but to believe, since he had to believe it in order to survive, that eventually his withdrawal would make possible even more control over and more love from history—the only constituency that really mattered in the end.

III GENERAL CONCLUSIONS

Lyndon Johnson's public career, with the exception of a single election defeat, was one of uninterrupted and unparalleled success in the accumulation of power and—although with less consistency—in the use of power to achieve practical results. This implies that varied repositories of public authority share common elements of structure, which are, moreover, relatively resistant to rapid historical change. Our examination of Johnson's leadership proved to be a study not only of particular institutions but of attributes and vulnerabilities which are common to several institutions, and which, therefore, probably derive from the more comprehensive institutional processes of politics and government.

I offer these general observations more by way of suggestion than conclusion, but useful, perhaps, in framing questions that might enable us to understand better the relationship between leaders and the qualities of leadership, events and historical circumstances, and institutional structure. I offer these as only a few possibilities. The reader hopefully will see many more.

First: Different institutions reward different qualities—although what constitutes "reward" depends not only on the institution but upon the nature of the individual leader's ambitions. Neither John Kennedy nor Richard Nixon wanted to become a great Senate leader; to them the Senate was a useful platform, though not the only one possible, to advance their careers. Of equal importance, the abilities and characteristic modes of conduct of both men kept them from attempting to become powerful Senate leaders, and would have kept them from accomplishing such an objective.

Johnson, on the other hand, in psychic nature, modes of conduct, and natural abilities, possessed all the qualifications required by the structure in the Senate as it existed at a particular moment for becoming an enormously powerful leader. The institution rewarded his qualities, and that reward was the object of his ambitions. Of course, he, too, had higher aspirations. But his qualities, forms of conduct, the demands and fears that were an aspect of his nature seemed to foreclose other routes. He had to depend, as he always had, upon effective performance—which meant controlling his institutional environment. He was further restrained by the fact that this performance not only was his means of advancing his ambition but was also an end in itself, and he was not capable of risking it for actions that might seem to enhance his chances for more significant power in another institution.

In fact, the qualities the Senate rewarded were not adapted to the institutional process of presidential nomination nor, probably, to that of presidential election, for it was unlikely that Johnson could have moved from Majority Leader to election as President on his own.

Not only do institutions reward different qualities, but their demands are often contradictory. The same qualities and capacities that make success probable in one setting may be inconsistent with success in another setting. Johnson was fortunate that conditions in 1964 and 1965 permitted him to use many of the abilities and qualities with which he had mastered the legislative process to conduct his Presidency with some success. However, when circumstances changed, these capacities proved ill-suited to the Presidency, which was a vastly different institution. He could not lead or inspire the nation by secret deals; he did not understand foreign policy; he could not deal with conflicts taking place in a setting where he could not establish personal detailed knowledge of the problems and the participants; and the same search for control that gave such force and direction to his legislative career caused him now to move toward coercive action and to transform the executive branch into a personal instrument, and a weapon for concealing facts and policies from other branches of government and the people.

Of course, Johnson was unique, as was his career. However, that career suggests that many of the qualities that make for success in the legislative branch—compromise, avoidance of conflict, secrecy, the effort to submerge personal responsibility for success or failure in a collective body, the vision of law as the end of the process, etc.—may be contradictory to those required for effective national leadership: indeed, that a career in the legislative process may inculcate modes of behavior or strengthen existing qualities inconsistent with the nature of the presidential institution. This conjecture, which I believe to be true, is of special importance at a time when the Congress has become a significant platform for presidential candidates.

However, it demonstrates that fact that talent for public life is not a unity, but that there are distinct, often contradictory, talents, which are relevant to success in one area of public life and not in another. This is important in assessing not only whether a leader is likely to achieve his ambitions in a particular setting, but—more significantly—whether his leadership is likely to benefit or damage the country.

Second: Johnson demonstrated hitherto unsuspected powers in the executive branch. There was, as many have observed, a growing evolution toward concentration of power in that branch. However, Johnson did not merely continue this evolution. He gave it a new dimension. Previous evolution had rested on changing circumstances, e.g., federal intervention in economic policy and problems of public welfare, the growing significance of foreign policy, the size of the defense establishment, involvement in war, etc. For the most part, this expanding power was exercised with the knowledge and acquiescence of Congress and the informed public. Johnson discovered that the resources of the Presidency allowed him to conceal much of the exercise of power; that presidential authority could be exerted on the basis of undisclosed information and the private interpretation of information; indeed, that in many cases even presidential actions and decisions could be concealed. Of course, the effects of many such decisions would eventually become visible, thus revealing the decision itself. But not all. Moreover, concealment of the decision-making process shut out the opportunity for public discussion that is an essential part of the institutional process in our representative democracy. Johnson's actions became known because they were directed toward public goals, their objectives were of a public nature, and, hence, their effects would inevitably be revealed. Nixon illustrated how this power of concealment could be used for other kinds of objectives so that the probability of continuing concealment was increased. The development or discovery of a capacity to exercise substantial executive power in secret is not simply an increase in the power of the Presidency; it represents a change in the relationship of institutions within the constitutional framework, a change which, in some part, has the potential of moving the presidential institution outside the framework itself.

Third: This aspect of institutional change, developed under Johnson, and reinforced by the fate of the Nixon administration, suggests that the most effective checks on presidential power are not the institutions that form the constitutional system of "checks and balances." They are the media and public opinion, catalyzed, in Johnson's case, by the presidential primaries. In both administrations these nongovernmental institutions were more effective restraints on presidential actions and usurpations than established governmental institutions.

Fourth: Johnson's career also helps to reaffirm the significance, probably the necessity, of consensus politics to effective presidential leadership. Historically, the only exceptions have been under special conditions—depression under Roosevelt, shifts and growth of population under Jackson—which produced large popular majorities whose interests were opposed to those protected by the dominant structure of economic and political power. Jefferson, after all, moved to placate the Federalists, even at the cost of disappointing some of his Republican followers, while Theodore Roosevelt took steps to placate his business supporters even while establishing a reputation as a trust buster. Johnson, however, showed that consensus could be a foundation for an extensive program of domestic reform even at a time when there were no serious class hostilities nor any economic crisis. That accomplishment requires a modification of what is meant by "consensus," or, rather, a recognition that the term is susceptible to different definitions. Eisenhower's consensus consisted of the fact that a large popular majority was satisfied with his policies, and no substantial proportion of the population was urging him in another direction. Under Johnson as well, there was no significant movement for domestic reform (with the exception, for a time, of the civil rights movement). He himself was the initiating force. Admittedly, the absence of serious division, and favorable economic conditions, made it possible for him to initiate such a program. However, he also saw that consensus did not require him to marshal public enthusiasm and support. He would achieve consensus among groups of special interests and concerns, usually organized and with identifiable leaders, who could influence congressional action directly. And each program required a different kind of appeal to different kinds of groups. By persuading religious and educational associations, he could remove obstacles to a program for aiding education. Certain programs of public welfare required union support and the willingness of business groups to, at least, withdraw opposition. Thus, in a manner similar to the way in which he imposed his will in the Senate, he constructed a consensus from an assembly of particular groups and interests, most of them led by individuals with whom he could deal directly. He created an interlocking web of services and obligations. Finally, many were willing to support particular programs about which they had reservations because they believed that, on the whole, Johnson's program was good for them and for the country. It was a pluralistic consensus, an agreement among groups of limited, often contradictory interests. This consensus, Johnson knew, would shape the actions of Congress. Popular support, that other form of consensus, would be a consequence of achievement, not its source.

We cannot determine, however, the extent to which Johnson had developed a method for public action that can be applied in other situations, and how much its effectiveness depended upon his unique qualities and capacities. And of course, events during the last years of his administration showed that even a consensus built on majority support and the desire for action cannot survive serious public divisions.

Fifth: Johnson's career also provides further evidence that the basic qualities of a leader do not change when he assumes new and larger responsibilities. It is more a metaphor than an accurate description to say, for example, that a man "grows" in office. Of course, individuals do learn from experience— some better than others, and some become more skillful. But basic abilities, ambitions grounded on inner needs, modes of conduct, and inclinations of behavior are deeply and permanently embedded. It may be that these qualities cannot be displayed in a particular setting, or are not suited to achievement within a particular institutional framework and/or under certain historical conditions; yet in another place they can be the basis of accomplishments and actions that others would not have anticipated. One thinks of Truman. Or it may be that the widened constituency of the Presidency allows a broadening of goals. Yet, while Johnson's landslide victory did stretch his aspirations, it did not change the essential elements of his behavior. Even his possession of the most powerful office in the country did not diminish his need to extend control or increase his capacity to deal with certain kinds of conflict or resistance. All his newly acquired ability to command did not reduce his drive to coerce. And under the right conditions, these qualities, which many had seen in him previously, were bound to emerge. And just as great office could magnify, if not change, his strength, so it could disastrously extend the consequences of his flaws. So, too, we discovered that the new Nixon was the old Nixon with much more power.

Therefore the best evidence of what can be expected of a candidate for high office—especially the Presidency—can better be found in an examination of his pattern of activity at other stages of his public life than in his statements or goals, and particularly in situations of stress, when he was confronted with difficult decisions that were bound to affect his ambitions, his leadership, and his concept of himself.

Sixth: The dilemma of the modern Presidency is not as simple as the contemporary talk of the imperial President suggests. Admittedly, the presidential institution has widened in power, as has the capacity of the President to concentrate that power in his own hands—a consequence less of tyranny than of the steady weakening of the various institutions designed to check the President—the Cabinet, the Congress, and the party. But the same centralization of resources that allows an almost unconstrained initiation of policies in some areas (the making of war and peace) and the exercise of almost unilateral authority in others (the dropping of bombs) incapacitates implementation of both domestic and foreign programs and eventually weakens the President's ability to lead. With a weakened Cabinet, the President has less chance of controlling his vast bureaucracy; with a shattered party and diminished Congress, he is unable to command that restrained public support essential for the continued viability of both his policies and his leadership. Thus the concentration of resources is at once enabling and constricting; the analytical problem is to understand not only where the President is too strong but also where he is too weak; to delineate what is meant by strong and weak and to describe the curious relationship between the two.

Seventh: The President's ability to focus national attention upon his every word and deed—which is made possible, and almost inescapable, by the nature of the national media—is a source of both power and illusion. And the same can be said of the enlarged White House staff and the use of a technological apparatus unparalleled in history. For five years, between 1963 and 1968, Lyndon Johnson dominated public life in Washington to such an extent that the Cabinet was *his* Cabinet, the Great Society *his* program, the Congress *his* instrument. With every technological innovation at his disposal, he could tape his own television shows, tell his pilots ten thousand miles away where and when to bomb, talk with the Soviet Premier on a moment's notice, and fly around the world in less than two days. But the man in the center when things are good remains in the center when things go bad, and the resources technology provides are often illusory, substituting the sense of control for real control. Thus the war in Vietnam became Lyndon Johnson's war; he personally was dropping the bombs, disrupting the economy, making prices rise, setting back the progress of black and poor. Obviously, neither image—villain or hero—is valid; historical circumstances and institutional conditions were vital to both success in the Great Society and failure in Vietnam. And this understanding is of more than intellectual interest, for exaggeration of the President's personal powers (both self-induced and media propelled) is an inevitable source of frustration as the President's actions invariably fall short of expectations, producing a destructive cycle for the man, the office, and the nation.

Notes

Prologue

1. Doris Kearns and Sanford Levinson, "How to Remove LBJ in 1968," *New Republic*, May 13, 1967, p. 13.
2. LBJ/DHK. For this as for all succeeding quotes that come from the notes I took during my work with President Johnson in the White House, on the memoirs and on the ranch, I shall use the designation: LBJ/DHK. These notes were taken verbatim with a combination of shorthand and speedwriting and then transcribed, typed, and placed in chronological order in a large notebook.
3. *Ibid.*
4. *Ibid.*
5. Marcus Cunliffe, *The Literature of the United States*, London, Penguin Books, 1970.
6. LBJ/DHK.
7. *Ibid.*
8. *Ibid.*
9. Hugh Sidey, *A Very Personal Presidency: Lyndon Johnson in the White House*, New York, Atheneum, 1968, pp. 22–23.
10. LBJ/DHK.
11. *Ibid.*
12. *Ibid.*

Chapter 1/Growing Up

1. LBJ/DHK.
2. Rebekah Baines Johnson's description of her father is taken from the small ancestral history she compiled in 1954, *A Family Album*, introduction by Lyndon Johnson, edited by John Moursund, New York, McGraw-Hill, 1965. "At an incredibly early age," Rebekah writes, "my father taught me to read; reading has been one of the great pleasures and sustaining forces of my life. He taught me how to study, to think and to endure.... He taught me that 'a lie is an abomination to the Lord' and to all real people the world over; he taught me obedience and self-control, saying that without them no one is worthy of responsibility or trust." P. 28. This picture is sustained by Joseph's brother, George, in the obituary column he wrote for the *Baptist Tribune*, December 13, 1906. "He hated dirt, he loved neatness. For clean speech and morals, he could hardly have been surpassed. To hear a preacher indulge in unclean jokes or suggestions gave him a real disgust, and he

never wanted to hear him preach or pray." Reprinted in R. B. Johnson, *op. cit.*, p. 79.

3. LBJ/DHK.

4. LBJ/DHK. Johnson never said what it was that caused his grandfather's ruin, though he left the distinct impression that it happened suddenly and had something to do with idealism and naïveté. George Baines provides a different account in the obituary column referred to above: "On account of disastrous droughts, protracted four years, his extensive farming operations brought financial ruin." R. B. Johnson, *op. cit.*, p. 77.

5. LBJ/DHK.

6. R. B. Johnson, *op. cit.*, p. 17.

7. See, for example, Erik Erikson's description of the life of the frontier woman in *Childhood and Society*, New York, Norton, 1963, pp. 291–292. "In frontier communities she had to become the cultural censor, the religious conscience, the aesthetic arbiter and the teacher. . . . Puritanism, we should remember, was once a system of values to check men and women of eruptive vitality, of strong appetites, as well as of strong individuality."

8. R. B. Johnson, *op. cit.*, p. 30.

9. LBJ/DHK.

10. *Ibid.*

11. *Ibid.*

12. See Joseph R. Gusfield, *The Symbolic Crusade: Status Politics and the American Temperance Movement*, Urbana, University of Illinois Press, 1963.

13. LBJ/DHK.

14. Sigmud Freud develops this concept further in his essay "On Narcissism: An Introduction," *The Standard Edition of the Complete Psychological Works of Sigmund Freud*, Vol. 14, London, Hogarth Press, 1957, pp. 69–102. "If we look at the attitude of fond parents toward their children, we cannot but perceive it as a revival and reproduction of their own, long since abandoned narcissism. The child shall have things better than his parents; he is really to be the center and heart of creation. His Majesty the Baby as once we fancied ourselves to be. He is to fulfill those dreams and wishes of his parents which they never carried out."

15. LBJ/DHK.

16. The full statement is: "A man who has been the indisputable favorite of his mother keeps for life the feeling of a conqueror, that confidence of success that often induces real success." Quoted in Ernest Jones, *The Life and Work of Sigmund Freud*, edited and abridged by Lionel Trilling and Steven Marcus, London, Hogarth Press, 1961, p. 6.

17. LBJ/DHK.

18. *Ibid.*

19. LBJ/DHK. Erikson suggests that the child's sense of being needed by a parent, which Gandhi also felt, may provide a source of the adult's leadership style. Speaking in words similar to those used by Johnson, Gandhi said, "There was nothing dearer to my heart than her [Mother's] service. Play had absolutely no fascination for me in preference to my mother's service. Whenever she wanted me for anything, I ran to her." Quoted in Erik Erikson, *Gandhi's Truth: On the Origins of Militant Nonviolence*, New York, Norton, 1969, p. 110.

20. The events described so far took place, as Johnson remembered them, during the years from three to six, the period described by Freud as the Oedipal period. Freud discovered that during this period there were regularly present in the mental lives of many people fantasies of incest with the parent of the opposite sex combined with jealousy, rage, and fear toward the parent of the same sex. See Charles Brenner, *An Elementary Textbook of Psychoanalysis*, New York, Doubleday, 1955, pp. 117–132.

21. See Karen Horney, *The Neurotic Personality of Our Time*, New York, Norton, 1937.

22. This story has been repeated in several of the early Johnson biographies. See, for example, Alfred Steinberg, *Som Johnson's Boy: A Close-Up of the President from Texas*, New York, Macmillan, 1968.

23. LBJ/DHK.

24. *Ibid.*

25. *Ibid.*

26. *Ibid.*

27. Portraits of Sam Ealy Johnson can be found in John Marvin Hunter, *The Trail Drivers of Texas*, Nashville, Tenn., Cokesbury Press, 1925, p. 329, and J. Speer, *The History of Blanco County*, Austin, Pemberton Press, 1965, Chapter 15. For an excellent description of the life of the cowboy, see James Frank Dobie, *The Longhorns*, Boston, Little, Brown, 1941.

28. LBJ/DHK.

29. *Ibid.*

30. For a description of the stampede, see Dobie, *op. cit.*, pp. 87–138.

31. LBJ/DHK.

32. The full text of the National People's Party Platform can be found in George Tindall, ed., *A Populist Reader*, New York, Harper & Row, 1966, pp. 90–96.

33. For a discussion of the mythic idealization of the cowboy, see Leslie Fiedler, *The Return of the Vanishing American*, New York, Norton, 1937, and Erik Erikson, *Childhood and Society*, pp. 304–305.

34. LBJ/DHK.

35. *Ibid.*

36. Johnson described this dream to me in two parts. In his last year in the White House he told me only the last part, in which he saw himself as Woodrow Wilson, lying immobile in the Red Room. The summer after he left office he told me more, suggesting the connection between the Wilson image and the childhood dream.

37. Sigmund Freud, *The Interpretation of Dreams*, translated by James Strachey, New York, Basic Books, 1955. Punishment dreams are discussed in a section on wish fulfillment, Chapter 7, pp. 557–560.

38. LBJ/DHK.

39. Quoted in article in Austin *Statesman*, September 23, 1948.

40. The story of Rebekah's efforts to get Lyndon to study are told and retold in each biography. See Booth Mooney, *The Lyndon Johnson Story*, New York, Farrar, Straus & Cudahy, revised edition, 1964, pp. 12–13, and Alfred Steinberg, *op. cit.*, p. 15.

41. LBJ/DHK.

42. *Ibid.*

43. Lyndon's mumbling is remarked upon by Alfred Steinberg in *op. cit.*, p. 31.

44. LBJ/DHK.

45. For a discussion of Sam Johnson's legislative career, see William Pool, Emmie Craddock and David Conrad, *Lyndon Baines Johnson: The Formative Years*, San Marcos, Southwest Texas State College Press, 1965, pp. 33–45.

46. LBJ/DHK.

47. Sam Johnson, *My Brother Lyndon*, edited by Enrique Lopez, New York, Cowles, 1970, p. 10.

48. LBJ/DHK.

49. *Ibid.*

50. *Ibid.*

51. Arthur Schlesinger described a visit President Kennedy once made to the ranch during which he was given a rifle by Johnson and expected to shoot a deer. Kennedy shot the deer and Johnson sent the mounted head to the White House.

52. LBJ/DHK.

53. *Ibid.*

54. *Ibid.*

55. The mechanism at work here, which appears to be reaction formation, is discussed by Brenner in a chapter on "The Psychic Apparatus," in *op. cit.*, pp. 62–107.

56. LBJ/DHK. Johnson seems to be projecting here, a defense mechanism in which the individual attributes a wish or impulse of his own to some other person.

57. This tradition is discussed by Richard Hofstadter in *Anti-Intellectualism in American Life*, New York, Knopf, 1963. See especially Chapter II, "On the Unpopularity of Intellect," pp. 24–51.

58. LBJ/DHK.

59. *Ibid.*

60. The trip to California has been explained in various ways in different accounts. In his public version of the trip—given in speeches and to authorized biographers—Johnson said he left home because his father was in financial difficulty and it meant "one less mouth for my poor daddy to feed." See also Sam Johnson, *op. cit.*, pp. 20–22.

61. LBJ/DHK.

62. Reported in R. B. Johnson, *op. cit.*, p. 20.

63. LBJ/DHK.

64. For an interesting analysis of Johnson's character structure, see James David Barber, *The Presidential Character: Predicting Performance in the White House*, Englewood Cliffs, N.J., Prentice-Hall, 1972.

Chapter 2/Education and the Dream of Success

1. Lyndon Johnson, editorial, *College Star*, July 10, 1927, p. 20.

2. William Pool *et al., op. cit.*, p. 79.

3. *Ibid.*, p. 96.

4. LBJ/DHK.

5. William Pool *et al, op. cit.*, pp. 99–100.

6. LBJ/DHK.

7. Willard Deason, Oral History Project, LBJ Library. From now on material from this source will be designated OHP.

8. Lyndon Johnson, *College Star*, June 19, 1929, p. 2.

9. Willard Deason, OHP.

10. *Ibid*.

11. Lyndon Johnson, *College Star*, August 7, 1929, p. 2.

12. This letter is framed on the wall of the boyhood home in Johnson City; also quoted in Hugh Sidey, *op. cit.*, p. 12.

13. LBJ/DHK.

14. Lyndon Johnson, *College Star*, June 12, 1929, p. 2.

15. *Ibid.*, October 26, 1927, p. 2.

16. For further discussion of the tradition of benevolent service, see Ralph Gabriel, *The Course of American Democratic Thought*, New York, Ronald Press, 1940. In a chapter called "Wealth: The Gilded Age," Gabriel develops the linkages between Mather, Franklin, and Carnegie. See also Robert McCloskey, *American Conservatism in the Age of Enterprise: A Study of William Graham Sumner, Stephen J. Field and Andrew Carnegie*, Cambridge, Harvard University Press, 1951, pp. 135–153.

17. Lyndon B. Johnson, *College Star*, June 27, 1927, p. 2.

18. LBJ/DHK.

19. Lyndon B. Johnson, *Public Papers of the Presidents of the United States, 1966*, Washington, D.C., U.S. Government Printing Office. Hereinafter designated *Public Papers*.

20. This and most of the references to Carol Davis are drawn from LBJ/DHK. Sam Johnson describes the relationship but does not give the girl's name, referring to Carol Davis as his brother's high school girlfriend rather than his college fiancée.

21. Sam Johnson, *op. cit.*, p. 29.

22. For a discussion of the mood of the 1920s, see William Leuchtenburg, *The Perils of Prosperity, 1914–1932*, Chicago, University of Chicago Press, 1958.

23. Editorial, *Record Courier*, Blanco County, Texas, June 5, 1925.

24. This description of life in Johnson City in the 1920s is derived from a study of the local papers and records completed by a research assistant, Burton Solomon.

25. Lyndon Johnson, *College Star*, June 19, 1929, p. 2.

26. *Ibid.*, October 5, 1927, p. 2.

27. This theme is more fully developed in John William Ward, "The Meaning of Lindbergh's Flight," in *Red, White and Blue: Men, Books and Ideas in American Culture*, New York, Oxford University Press, 1969.

28. Lyndon Johnson, *College Star*, November 16, 1927, p. 2.

29. *Ibid.*, July 17, 1929, p. 2.

30. *Ibid.*, December 7, 1927, p. 2.

31. Lyndon Johnson, "Special Message to the Congress: The American Promise," delivered March 15, 1965. Reprinted in *Public Papers, 1965*, p. 281.

32. LBJ/DHK; see also Alfred Steinberg, *op. cit.*, p. 47.

33. LBJ/DHK.

34. *Ibid*.

35. *Ibid*.

36. *Ibid*.

37. Interview with Willard Deason, OHP.

38. LBJ/DHK.
39. *Ibid.*

Chapter 3/The Making of a Politician

1. LBJ/DHK.
2. Johnson's activities in this period are rescribed in Booth Mooney, *op. cit.*, p. 19.
3. Quoted in Clarke Newlon, *L.B.J.: The Man from Johnson City,* New York Dodd, Mead, 1964, p. 50.
4. Booth Mooney, *op. cit.*, p. 18.
5. This story is told by Gene Latimer in his oral interview, OHP.
6. The story of Johnson's takeover of the Little Congress is told in William White, *The Professional: Lyndon B. Johnson,* Boston, Houghton Mifflin, 1964, p. 110.
7. Clarke Newlon, *op. cit.*, p. 50.
8. The material on Lady Bird is derived from a variety of sources: LBJ/DHK; Eric Goldman, *The Tragedy of Lyndon Johnson,* New York, Knopf, 1969, Chapter 9; William White, *op. cit.*, pp. 115–120; interview with Dan Quill, OHP.
9. Eric Goldman, *op. cit.*, p. 343.
10. LBJ/DHK.
11. Eric Goldman, *op. cit.*, pp. 344–345.
12. *Ibid.*, pp. 339–342.
13. Alfred Steinberg, *op. cit.*, p. 87. See also Eric Goldman, *op. cit.*, pp. 343–344.
14. Eric Goldman, *op. cit.*, p. 346.
15. This letter is framed on the wall of the boyhood home in Johnson City.
16. I was witness to this several times at the LBJ Ranch.
17. Clarke Newlon, *op. cit.*, pp. 57–68.
18. LBJ/DHK.
19. *Ibid.*
20. Alfred Steinberg, *op. cit.*, p. 110.
21. LBJ/DHK.
22. This letter, quoted in Sidey, *op. cit.*, p. 13, is now on display at the LBJ Library.
23. LBJ/DHK.
24. *Ibid.*
25. This story is recounted in every Johnson biography. See, for example, Alfred Steinberg, *op. cit.*, p. 119.
26. In a radio address on January 23, 1938, Johnson spoke of the need for clearing up the slum areas: "Last Christmas when all over the world people were celebrating ... I took a walk here in Austin and there I found people living in such squalor that Christmas day was to them just one more day of filth and forty families on one lot, using one water faucet." Text included in the *Congressional Record*, February 3, 1938, p. 429. Hereafter I will use *CR* to indicate the *Congressional Record*.
27. LBJ/DHK.
28. *Ibid.*
29. *Ibid.*
30. *Ibid.*

31. Lyndon Johnson, *CR*, May 7, 1947.
32. Lyndon Johnson, *CR*, April 30, 1941, p. A1992.
33. LBJ/DHK.
34. Lyndon Johnson, *CR*, May 7, 1947.
35. LBJ/DHK.
36. Lyndon Johnson, *CR*, May 7, 1947.
37. Louis Hartz, *The Liberal Tradition in America: An Interpretation of American Political Thought Since the Revolution*, New York, Harcourt, Brace, 1955, p. 286. See also Stanley Hoffmann, *Gulliver's Troubles, Or The Setting of American Foreign Policy*, published for the Council on Foreign Relations, New York, McGraw-Hill, 1968.
38. Lyndon Johnson, *CR*, June 4, 1946, p. A3170.
39. *Ibid.*, April 20, 1947.
40. LBJ/DHK.
41. *Ibid.*
42. Lyndon Johnson, speech given before Texas State Network entitled "America in the World Today," and inserted in the *CR*, March 29, 1948, p. A1966.
43. Lyndon Johnson, *CR*, May 7, 1947.
44. *Ibid.*, July 29, 1948, p. 9533.
45. LBJ/DHK.
46. Louis Kohlmeier, Ray Shaw and Ed Cony, "The Johnson Wealth: How the President's Wife Built a $17,500 Outlay into a TV Fortune in Texas," *Wall Street Journal*, March 23, 1964, p. 7.
47. *Ibid.*
48. Louis Kohlmeier *et al.*, "Lyndon's Pals," *Wall Street Journal*, August 11, 1964, p. 1.
49. Quoted in *ibid.*
50. LBJ/DHK.

Chapter 4/Rise to Power in the Senate

1. The best writing on Johnson's Senate years is in Rowland Evans and Robert Novak, *LBJ: The Exercise of Power*, New York, New American Library, 1966.
2. The data on the relationship between Richard Russell and Lyndon Johnson are derived from my conversations with Johnson; from an interview with Bill Jorden, long-time Russell aide; from Meg Greenfield, "The Man Who Leads the Southern Senators," *The Reporter*, May 21, 1964; and from Douglas Kiker, "Russell of Georgia: The Old Guard at Its Shrewdest," *Harper's Magazine*, September, 1966, pp. 101–106.
3. LBJ/DHK.
4. Interview with Bill Jorden, January, 1972.
5. Evans and Novak, *op. cit.*, p. 33.
6. Quoted in *ibid.*
7. For a description of Johnson's shift in politics, see *ibid.*, pp. 26–49.
8. LBJ/DHK.
9. For analysis of conflicting organizational requisites, see Peter Blau, *Exchange and Power in Social Life*, New York, Wiley, 1964, Chapter 4, pp. 88–114.

10. Niccolò Machiavelli, *The Prince,* with an introduction by Max Lerner, New York, Modern Library, 1940, pp. 91, 20–21.

11. Johnson's selection as whip is discussed in an article by Leslie Carpenter, "Whip from Texas," *Collier's,* February 17, 1951.

12. This line of analysis is suggested by Lewis Dexter in Raymond Bauer, Lewis Dexter and Ithiel de Sola Pool, *American Business and Public Policy: The Politics of Foreign Trade,* Chicago, Aldine, Atherton, 1972, pp. 403–438.

13. DHK interview with James Rowe, January, 1972.

14. For a discussion of legislative effectiveness, see Donald Matthews, *U.S. Senators and Their World,* Chapel Hill, University of North Carolina Press, 1960, Chapter 5; William White, *The Citadel: The Story of the U.S. Senate,* New York, Harper & Row, 1957; and Ralph Huitt, "The Outsider in the Senate," in Ralph Huitt and Robert Peabody, *Congress: Two Decades of Analysis,* New York, Harper & Row, 1969.

15. LBJ/DHK.

16. *Ibid.*

17. *Ibid.*

18. Machiavelli, *op. cit.,* p. 21.

19. The analysis of Johnson's reform of the seniority system is built on discussions with Johnson, and Evans and Novak, *op. cit.,* pp. 63–64.

20. Alvin Toffler describes this process in "LBJ: The Senate's Mr. Energy," *Pageant,* July, 1958, pp. 102–109.

21. This letter, along with other correspondence and memos to be cited in this chapter, Johnson read aloud in the process of going over with me some of the materials in his files on the Senate years.

22. Further discussion of the Policy Committee can be found in Hugh Bone, *Party Committees and National Politics,* Seattle, University of Washington Press, 1958.

23. See note 21.

24. LBJ/DHK.

25. *Ibid.*

26. *Ibid.*

27. Evans and Novak, *op. cit.,* pp. 102–103.

28. *Ibid.,* p. 103.

29. LBJ/DHK.

30. Machiavelli, *op. cit.,* p. 8.

31. Evans and Novak, *op. cit.,* p. 97.

32. Quoted in Randall Ripley, *Power in the Senate,* New York, St. Martin's Press, 1969.

33. See note 21.

34. LBJ/DHK.

35. For an interesting case study, see Ralph Huitt, "The Morse Committee Assignment," *American Political Science Review,* Vol. 51, June, 1957, pp. 313–329.

36. LBJ/DHK.

37. *Ibid.*

38. The description of Johnson's private meetings is built on conversations with LBJ and interviews with members of the Senate and his staff.

39. The term is Ralph Huitt's in "Democratic Party Leadership in the Senate," *American Political Science Review,* Vol. 55, June, 1961.

40. LBJ/DHK.

41. *Ibid.*

42. This is described in *Outsider in the Senate: Senator Clinton Anderson's Memoirs,* by Clinton Anderson with Milton Viorst, New York, World, 1970.

43. LBJ/DHK.

44. Lyndon Johnson, *CR,* September 28, 1955.

45. Robert Merton, "Bureaucratic Structure and Personality," in Amitai Etzioni, *Complex Organizations: A Sociological Reader,* New York, Holt, Rinehart and Winston, 1961, pp. 48–61.

46. Erving Goffman, "Teams," in *The Presentation of Self in Everyday Life,* New York, Doubleday, Anchor Books, 1959, pp. 77–105.

47. LBJ/DHK.

48. Quoted in *Time,* March 17, 1958.

49. In his *Memoirs: Sixty Years on the Firing Line,* New York, Funk & Wagnalls, 1968, Arthur Krock describes the countless expressions of appreciation he received from Johnson: showers of memos in which Johnson set down his thinking on the immediate issues, signed photographs with the most complimentary inscriptions ("The Stud Duck of the Washington Press Corps"), letters on his birthdays and other red-letter days, Christmas gifts.

50. This is described by Joe Hall in an article for the Associated Press, July 27, 1956. See also in Toffler, *op. cit.,* pp. 104–105, and Ralph Huitt, "Democratic Party Leadership in the Senate," *op. cit.*

51. Stewart Alsop, "Lyndon Johnson: How Does He Do It?," *Saturday Evening Post,* January 24, 1959, p. 14. The members of the staff included Walter Jenkins, Gerry Siegel, George Reedy, Booth Mooney, Willie Day, Dorothy Nichols.

52. This point is made in Dorothy Nichols' oral interview, OHP.

53. DHK interview with Gerry Siegel, January, 1972.

54. The analysis of Johnson's relationship with Humphrey is built on conversations with LBJ, an interview with Humphrey in January, 1975, and interviews with aides to both.

55. DHK interview with Hubert Humphrey.

56. LBJ/DHK.

57. *Ibid.*

Chapter 5/The Senate Leader

1. For a discussion of the critics' complaints, see "The Struggle for a Liberal Senate: A Debate Between Senators Proxmire and Neuberger," *The Progressive,* June, 1959, p. A21. See also "ADA Statement" in October, 1959: "Early in this session Messrs. Rayburn and Johnson snuggled into the strait jacket offered them by the Administration. Instead of accepting the challenge to meet the country's needs, the leadership makes the divided government work by the simple expedient of surrendering to the President."

2. Senator William Proxmire, *CR,* February 23, 1958. Johnson responded, "If they cannot get their committees to go along with them how do they expect a fairy godmother or a wet nurse to get a majority to deliver it into their hands?" *CR,* February 28, 1958, p. 9260.

3. Reported by Howard Shuman, aide to Senator Douglas, interview January 26, 1972.

4. LBJ/DHK.

5. *Ibid.*

6. Quoted in Stewart Alsop, *op. cit.*, p. 14.

7. *The Washington Window*, Public Affairs Institute, March 13, 1958.

8. For further discussion, see Gerald Pomper, "After Twenty Years," American Political Science Association Convention, September 8, 1970.

9. LBJ/DHK. In Johnson's Senate files, there are two dozen or more memos which set down Johnson's thinking on issues such as these. George Reedy helped in their preparation. When I talked to Johnson about the Senate, he often took off from and elaborated on these memos.

10. LBJ/DHK.

11. Joseph Clark, *CR*, January 23, 1958.

12. Johnson response, *CR*, January 28, 1958. See also Ralph Huitt, "Democratic Party Leadership in the Senate," *op. cit.*, for a discussion of Johnson's conception of the Presidency.

13. Lyndon Johnson, *CR*, July 15, 1955.

14. LBJ/DHK.

15. See studies on McCarthy by Nelson Polsby, "Toward an Explanation of McCarthyism," *Political Studies*, October, 1960, pp. 250–271; and Michael Rogin, *The Intellectuals and McCarthy: The Radical Specter*, Cambridge, M.I.T. Press, 1967.

16. LBJ/DHK.

17. Lyndon Johnson, *CR*, February 15, 1953.

18. For a description of this skillful balancing act, see Evans and Novak, *op. cit.*, pp. 75–76.

19. LBJ/DHK.

20. The phrase is that of Professor Arthur Maass, Harvard University.

21. Lyndon Johnson, *The Vantage Point: Perspectives of the Presidency, 1963–1969*, New York, Holt, Rinehart and Winston, 1971, p. 272.

22. Lyndon Johnson, speech before Senate Democratic Caucus, January 7, 1958.

23. Television interview with Walter Cronkite on space in July, 1969.

24. The material on civil rights is derived from John Weir Anderson, *Eisenhower, Brownell and the Congress: The Tangled Origins of the Civil Rights Bill of 1956–1957*, University of Alabama Press, 1964; Douglass Cater, "How the Senate Passed the Civil Rights Bill," *The Reporter*, September 5, 1957; and Evans and Novak, *op. cit.*, "The Miracle of '57," pp. 119–140.

25. LBJ/DHK.

26. David Riesman and Nathaniel Glazer, "The Lonely Crowd: A Reconsideration in 1960," in Seymour Lipset and Leo Lowenthal, eds., *Culture and Social Character: The Work of David Riesman Reviewed*, New York, Free Press of Glencoe, 1961, p. 438.

27. LBJ/DHK.

28. *Ibid.*

29. *Ibid.* This conversation, again, was sparked by a Reedy memo on the same subject.

30. *Ibid.*

31. DHK interview with Harry McPherson, May 22, 1970.

32. Acheson statement reported in the *New York Times* and read by Johnson to Senate Policy Committee, August 13, 1957.

33. These "Letters to Constituents" were in the Senate material Johnson read to me. See note 21, Chapter 4.

34. Speech before Democratic Caucus, September 15, 1957.

35. Lyndon Johnson, *CR*, August 7, 1957, p. 13997.

36. *Ibid.*

37. Wayne Morse, *CR*, August 2, 1957, p. 13485.

38. LBJ/DHK.

39. *Ibid.*

40. *Ibid.*

41. See Daniel Bell, *The End of Ideology: On the Exhaustion of Political Ideas in the Fifties*, New York, Free Press of Glencoe, 1969.

42. LBJ/DHK.

43. The 1955 Gallup poll reported that 79 percent of the adults applauded the way Eisenhower was handling his job.

44. Lyndon Johnson, *CR*, January 16, 1956, p. 629.

45. LBJ/DHK.

46. Arthur Krock quotes this portion of a Johnson memo on this subject in the *New York Times*, July 13, 1956, p. 18.

47. Lyndon Johnson, "My Political Philosophy," *The Texas Quarterly*, Vol. I, No. 4, Winter, 1958, p. 17.

48. Lyndon Johnson, "Address Before Jefferson-Jackson Dinner, Raleigh, North Carolina," *CR*, March 18, 1957, p. 3885.

49. See Robert Paul Wolff, "On Tolerance," in Robert Paul Wolff, Barrington Moore, Jr., and Herbert Marcuse, *A Critique of Pure Tolerance*, Boston, Beacon Press, 1965, pp. 3–69. See also William Connally, *The Bias of Pluralism*, New York, Atherton Press, 1969.

50. For a discussion of this point, see James MacGregor Burns, *Roosevelt: The Lion and the Fox*, New York, Harcourt, Brace, 1956.

Chapter 6/The Vice-Presidency

1. LBJ/DHK.

2. Reported by Evans and Novak, *op. cit.*, p. 280.

3. See columns by David Broder, Washington *Post*, September 23, 1973, and October 1, 1970.

4. DHK interview with Lee White. See also Evans and Novak, *op. cit.*, p. 310.

5. Alan Otten, *Wall Street Journal*, August 13, 1972.

6. Quoted in Arthur M. Schlesinger, Jr., *A Thousand Days: John F. Kennedy in the White House*, Boston, Houghton Mifflin, 1965, p. 646.

7. LBJ/DHK.

8. This is described in Evans and Novak, *op. cit.*, pp. 305–308.

9. See descriptions of the Vice President as "morose" in Arthur M. Schlesinger, *op. cit.*, p. 648, and "not voluble at meetings" in Theodore C. Sorensen, *Kennedy*, New York, Harper & Row, 1965, p. 297.

10. Discussion with Professor Richard Neustadt, Harvard University.

11. LBJ/DHK.

12. DHK interview with George Reedy, 1974.

13. LBJ/DHK.

14. There is a description of Johnson's trips in Evans and Novak, *op. cit.*, pp. 305–335, and in Arthur M. Schlesinger, *op. cit.*, p. 705.

Schlesinger reports: "Once an American diplomat met him [Johnson] at the Rome airport and on the way into the city methodically instructed him, as if he were some sort of uncouth backwoodsman, on how to behave. Johnson listened to this singular performance with unaccustomed patience. When they arrived at the hotel, the diplomat said, Mr. Vice President, is there anything else I can do for you? The Vice-President, looking stonily up and down at his model of diplomatic propriety, replied, Yes, just one thing. Zip up your fly."

15. This is a point William Bundy has stressed to me by letter and in a seminar at the Lehrman Institute in New York City.
16. LBJ/DHK.

Chapter 7/The Transition Year

1. LBJ/DHK.
2. These institutional mechanisms are discussed by Richard Neustadt in "Presidency and Legislation: The Growth of Central Clearance," *American Political Science Review*, September, 1954, pp. 641–671, and "Presidency and Legislation: Planning the President's Program," in *ibid.*, December, 1955, pp. 980–997.
3. LBJ took office as an unknown quantity. Only 5 percent of the people felt they knew a great deal about Johnson, compared with 24 percent about Kennedy; 67 percent felt they knew very little, compared with 17 percent for Kennedy; 45 percent had seen or heard Rockefeller or Goldwater, only 22 percent Johnson. These figures are reported in a memo to Johnson from Horace Busby, January 14, 1964.
4. For a study of the assassination's effect on the American people, see Bradley Greenberg, *The Kennedy Assassination and the American Public: Social Communication in Crisis*, Stanford, Stanford University Press, 1965.
5. Irving Howe, "On the Death of JFK," in *Steady Work: Essays in the Politics of Democratic Radicalism, 1953–1966*, New York, Harcourt, Brace & World, 1966.
6. LBJ/DHK.
7. Lyndon Johnson, *The Vantage Point*, p. 12.
8. *Ibid.*, p. 18.
9. Talcott Parsons, *Politics and Social Structure*, New York, Free Press, 1969, pp. 125–156, 98–124.
10. Lyndon Johnson, "Address Before a Joint Session of the Congress," November 27, *Public Papers, 1963*, pp. 8–10.
11. LBJ/DHK.
12. *Ibid.* See also Eric Goldman, *The Tragedy of Lyndon Johnson*, p. 26.
13. DHK interviews with Lee White.
14. LBJ/DHK.
15. This point was made by Johnson's private secretary, Juanita Roberts.
16. Niccolò Machiavelli, *The Discourses*, with an introduction by Max Lerner, New York, Modern Library, 1940, p. 184.
17. Notes taken by staff aide in White House during interview with Neil Sheehan, March 24, 1965.
18. LBJ/DHK.
19. *Ibid.*

20. Richard Neustadt, "Afterword," in *Presidential Power: The Politics of Leadership*, New York, Wiley, 1960, p. 202.

21. Grant McConnell, *The Modern Presidency*, New York, St. Martin's Press, 1967.

22. David Broder, *The Party's Over: The Failure of Politics in America*, New York, Harper & Row, 1972, p. 71.

23. LBJ/DHK.

24. *Ibid.*

25. This was one of a dozen or so typed transcripts apparently made from phone conversations which Johnson showed to me with the suggestion that from these I "could learn more about the way the government really works than from a hundred political science textbooks."

26. *Ibid.*

27. *Ibid.*

23. LBJ/DHK.

29. *Ibid.*

30. *Ibid.*

31. Lyndon Johnson, "Remarks to the Members of the Business Council," *Public Papers, 1964.*

32. Editorial in *Fortune*, April 15, 1964.

33. Lyndon Johnson, *The Vantage Point*, p. 71.

34. Lyndon Johnson, "Total Victory over Poverty," March 16, 1964; reprinted from *The War on Poverty: The Economic Opportunity Act of 1964*, Senate Document No. 86, Washington, 1964.

35. Walter Lippmann column, "Today and Tomorrow," March 17, 1964.

36. Remarks of Leonard Hall, Republican National Chairman, May, 1964.

37. James Reston column, *New York Times*, March 22, 1964.

38. Lyndon Johnson, *The Vantage Point*, p. 157.

39. LBJ/DHK.

40. *Ibid.*

41. Transcript of conversations with Wilkins and Young. See note 25.

42. Statement issued as a press release, July 20, 1964.

43. Lyndon Johnson, "In Quest of Peace," *The Reader's Digest*, February, 1969.

44. Lyndon Johnson, "Remarks to Key Officials of the Internal Revenue Service," February 11, 1964, *Public Papers, 1964*, p. 289.

45. Lyndon Johnson, "Remarks to a Group of Editors and Broadcasters Attending a National Conference on Foreign Policy," April 21, 1964, *Public Papers, 1964.*

46. LBJ/DHK.

47. *Ibid.*

48. Quoted in Alfred Steinberg, *op. cit.*, p. 725. See discussion of Panama incident in Philip Geyelin, *LBJ and The World*, New York, Praeger, 1966, pp. 100–112.

49. LBJ/DHK.

50. See Leslie Gelb, "The Vietnam System Worked," *Foreign Policy*, November, 1971.

51. Transcript. See note 25.

52. Leslie Gelb, *op. cit.*

53. Hans Morgenthau, "The Difference Between the Politician and

the Statesman," in *Politics in the Twentieth Century*, Chicago, University of Chicago Press, 1971, p. 344.

54. LBJ/DHK.
55. Eric Goldman, *op. cit.*, pp. 196–200.
56. LBJ/DHK.
57. *Ibid.*
58. Lyndon Johnson, *The Vantage Point*, p. 576.
59. Theodore White, *The Making of the President 1964*, New York, Atheneum, 1965, p. 263.
60. Quoted in Eric Goldman, *op. cit.*, p. 199.
61. Lyndon Johnson, *The Vantage Point*, pp. 92–93.
62. *Ibid.*, p. 95.
63. *Ibid.*, pp. 96–97.
64. Lady Bird Johnson, *A White House Diary*, New York, Holt, Rinehart and Winston, 1970; Dell, 1971, p. 210.
65. Lyndon Johnson, *The Vantage Point*, p. 98.
66. *Ibid.*, p. 101.
67. James Reston column, *New York Times*, May 8, 1964.
68. Lyndon Johnson, speech remarks saved in the collection of campaign speeches in the LBJ Library.
69. LBJ/DHK.
70. Quoted in Eric Goldman, *op. cit.*, p. 251.
71. *Ibid.*, p. 250.
72. Lady Bird Johnson, *op. cit.*, p. 223.
73. Elizabeth Carpenter, *Ruffles and Flourishes*, New York, Doubleday, 1970, p. 56.
74. *Ibid.*, p. 57.
75. Eric Goldman, *op. cit.*, p. 253.
76. LBJ/DHK.

Chapter 8/The Great Society

1. The speech referred to as the "Great Society speech" was delivered at the University of Michigan at Ann Arbor on May 22, 1964.
2. Lyndon Johnson, "The President's Inaugural Address," January 20, 1965, *Public Papers, 1965*, I, p. 71.
3. LBJ/DHK.
4. Lyndon Johnson, "Annual Message to the Congress on the State of the Union," January 4, 1965, *Public Papers, 1965*, p. 9.
5. Quoted in Eric Goldman, *op. cit*, p. 260.
6. Alexis de Toqueville, *Democracy in America*, New York, New American Library, 1956.
7. See Daniel Boorstin, *The Americans: The National Experience*, New York, Random House, 1967.
8. Quoted from Bagehot by Sam Beer, in "The British Political System," in Samuel Beer and Adam Ulam, *Patterns of Government: The Major Political Systems of Europe*, New York, Random House, 1962. For a general description of the President's resources in the legislative area, see Louis Koenig, *The Chief Executive*, New York, Harcourt, Brace & World, revised edition, 1968, pp. 124–154.
9. LBJ/DHK.
10. DHK interview with Henry Hall Wilson, Chicago, January 20, 1972.

11. LBJ/DHK.
12. *Ibid.*
13. Lyndon Johnson, *The Vantage Point*, pp. 447–448.
14. Interview with Henry Hall Wilson.
15. LBJ/DHK.
16. *Ibid.*
17. Johnson's attitude toward Congress is discussed in Eric Goldman, *op. cit.*
18. Lyndon Johnson, *The Vantage Point*, p. 162.
19. *Ibid.*, p. 163.
20. Lyndon Johnson, "The American Promise," March 15, 1965, *Public Papers, 1965*, p. 281.
21. Eric Goldman, *op. cit.*, p. 322.
22. Lyndon Johnson, "The American Promise."
23. LBJ/DHK.
24. See William White, *The Professional*, for a discussion of NYA days.
25. LBJ/DHK.
26. *Ibid.*
27. Lyndon Johnson, *The Vantage Point*, p. 448.
28. The system of reports is described by Harold Sanders, White House aide, in his analysis of "The White House—Congressional Relations Operation." This analysis was in the material provided for work on the memoirs.
29. Sample work sheets are on file with the Sanders analysis mentioned above.
30. Interview with Henry Hall Wilson.
31. LBJ/DHK.
32. Quoted in Evans and Novak, *op. cit.*
33. Interview with Henry Hall Wilson.
34. This concept is discussed in Peter Blau, *op. cit.*, pp. 90–95.
35. These rewards are described in an address by Larry O'Brien at the Phillips Lecture Series, Technical High School, Springfield, Massachusetts, October 5, 1966.
36. Transcript. See note 25, Chapter 7.
37. See discussion of Johnson's college editorials in Chapter 2.
38. LBJ/DHK.
39. See James Thomson, "How Could Vietnam Happen? An Autopsy," *Atlantic Monthly*, April, 1968.
40. Eric Goldman, *op. cit.*, p. 275.
41. LBJ/DHK.
42. *Ibid.*
43. Richard E. Neustadt, "The Constraining of the President: The Presidency after Watergate," *New York Times Magazine*, October 14, 1973.
44. For a discussion of the evolution of the Cabinet, see Richard Fenno, *The President's Cabinet: An Analysis in the Period from Wilson to Eisenhower*, Cambridge, Harvard University Press, 1959.
45. See David Broder, *op. cit.*
46. See Walter Dean Burnham, *Critical Elections and the Mainsprings of American Politics*, New York, Norton, 1970.
47. LBJ/DHK.

48. See Louis Koenig, *op. cit.*, for a discussion of Johnson's relations with the press.

49. Told to me in an interview by Wilbur Cohen, Secretary of Health, Education, and Welfare.

Chapter 9/Vietnam

1. Discussion with Averell Harriman, Kennedy Institute, Harvard, 1972.

2. LBJ/DHK.

3. Transcript. See note 25, Chapter 7.

4. See Robert Jervis, "Hypothesis on Misperception," *World Politics*, April, 1968.

5. LBJ/DHK.

6. *Ibid.* Johnson often repeated this remark in slightly varied forms.

7. See James Thomson, "How Could Vietnam Happen? An Autopsy," *op. cit.*

8. LBJ/DHK.

9. Memo to the President from McGeorge Bundy, January 25, 1965, as printed in Neil Sheehan *et al.*, *The Pentagon Papers; As Published by the New York Times; Based on Investigative Reporting by Neil Sheehan*, New York, Bantam, 1971.

10. Lyndon Johnson, *The Vantage Point*, p. 123.

11. *Ibid.*, p. 125.

12. Report from McGeorge Bundy to the President, February 7, 1965, as printed in *The Pentagon Papers*.

13. For a description of the dissenters, see David Halberstam, *The Best and the Brightest*, New York, Random House, 1972, pp. 492–499.

14. This point is argued by Leslie Gelb, "Vietnam: Some Hypotheses about Why and How," paper delivered at meeting of the American Political Science Association, September, 1970.

15. LBJ/DHK.

16. For a similar phenomenon during World War I, see Randolph Bourne, *War and the Intellectuals: Essays 1915–1919*, edited by Carl Resek, New York, Harper & Row, 1964, Chapter 1.

17. John Mueller, *War, Presidents and Public Opinion*, New York, Wiley, 1973, p. 115.

18. LBJ/DHK.

19. Louis Hartz, *The Founding of New Societies*, New York, Harcourt, Brace & World, 1964, p. 118.

20. This point is made by Frances FitzGerald, *Fire in the Lake: The Vietnamese and the Americans in Vietnam*, Boston, Little, Brown, 1972, p. 15.

21. *Ibid.*, p. 17.

22. Quoted in Eric Goldman, *op. cit.*, p. 404.

23. Lyndon Johnson, "Address at Johns Hopkins," April 7, 1965, *Public Papers, 1965*.

24. Speech before AFL-CIO, March 22, 1966.

25. Air War Study Group, Cornell University, *The Air War in Indochina*, edited by Raphael Littauer and Norman Uphoff, Boston, Beacon Press, 1972, pp. 60–63.

26. Quoted by Frances FitzGerald from the declaration following the Honolulu Conference in 1966, *Fire in the Lake*, p. 233.

27. Frances FitzGerald, *ibid.*

28. Lyndon Johnson, "Address at Johns Hopkins," *op. cit.*

29. Frances FitzGerald, *op. cit.*, pp. 23, 9, 10. See also Stanley Hoffmann, *Gulliver's Troubles.*

30. Robert Jervis, *op. cit.*, p. 455.

31. LBJ/DHK.

32. Air War Study Group, *op. cit.*, pp. 23-26, 153, 158.

33. Jonathan Schell, *The Military Half: An Account of Destruction in Quang Ngai and Quongtin*, New York, Knopf, 1968, p. 172.

34. Air War Study Group, *op. cit.*, pp. 153-155.

35. Randolph Bourne, *op. cit.*, Chapter 1.

36. David Halberstam, *op. cit.*

37. Frances FitzGerald, *op. cit.*, p. 357.

38. This point was made by Professor Martin Shapiro, Harvard University, in an introductory course on American politics, 1973.

39. Frances FitzGerald, *op. cit.*, p. 357.

40. David Halberstam, *op. cit.*, p. 508.

41. See Bernard Bailyn, *The Ideological Origins of the American Revolution*, Cambridge, Harvard University Press, 1967.

42. Louis Koenig, *The Chief Executive*, Chapters 9-10, pp. 209-264.

43. James Polk, "War with Mexico," letter to Congress on invasion and commencement of hostilities, Doc. No. 196.

44. See Merlo Pusey, *The Way We Go to War*, Boston, Houghton Mifflin, 1969.

45. Quoted in Arthur M. Schlesinger, Jr., *The Imperial Presidency*, Boston, Houghton Mifflin, 1973, p. 59.

46. See Francis Wilcox, *Congress, the Executive and Foreign Policy*, published for the Council on Foreign Relations, New York, Harper & Row, 1971, Chapter 4, pp. 68-95.

47. This point is made by Richard Fenno, "The Internal Distribution of Influence: The House," in David Truman, ed., *Congress and America's Future*, Englewood Cliffs, N.J., Prentice-Hall, 1973, p. 61.

48. Arthur M. Schlesinger, *The Imperial Presidency*, p. 331.

49. Francis Wilcox, *op. cit.*, p. 70.

50. Memo to the President from Robert McNamara, July 20, 1965, as reprinted in Lyndon Johnson, *The Vantage Point*, p. 145.

51. *Ibid.*, p. 149.

52. This point was made to me by William Bundy in a seminar at the Lehrman Institute, New York, 1973.

53. LBJ/DHK.

Chapter 10/Things Go Wrong

1. LBJ/DHK.

2. *Ibid.*

3. *Ibid.*

4. *Ibid.*

5. The official name was the "Commission on Governmental Reorganization," chaired by Ben Heineman.

6. Conversation with Professor Richard Neustadt, Harvard University.

7. Letter from Donald Stone to Richard Neustadt.

8. The implications of this point are developed by Herbert

Kaufman in *Administrative Feedback: Monitoring Subordinates' Behavior*, with Michael Couzens, Washington, Brookings Institution, 1973.

9. Johnson showed me a transcript of this conversation, which took place in 1964.

10. LBJ/DHK.

11. *Ibid.*

12. These figures are taken from the introduction to the special issue on "The Great Society" in *The Public Interest*, Winter, 1974, p. 9.

13. Interview with Charles Schultze, December, 1969.

14. LBJ/DHK.

15. For further discussion of this theme, see Lance Liebman, "Social Intervention in a Democracy," *The Public Interest*, Winter, 1974, pp. 14–29.

16. LBJ/DHK.

17. The reference here is to the statements made by Senators Mansfield and Muskie in 1966 calling for congressional attention to the administrative problems of the Great Society.

18. For a discussion of the growing anger toward Johnson in the Congress, see Evans and Novak, *op. cit.*

19. This memo, as will be the case for most of the material on the tax struggle, was gathered in the LBJ files when I worked on a chapter for his memoirs called "Bite the Bullet" and should now be on file in the LBJ Library.

20. *Ibid.*

21. LBJ/DHK.

22. Niccolò Machiavelli, *The Prince*, p. 35.

23. The analysis in this section is drawn from Richard Neustadt, *Presidential Power*, Chapter 5.

24. Conversation with Joseph Califano, July, 1971.

25. LBJ/DHK.

26. *Ibid.*

27. These figures were reported in a memo to LBJ from Hayes Redman in December, 1967.

Chapter 11/Under Siege in the White House

1. LBJ/DHK.

2. Hannah Arendt, "Lying in Politics," in *Crises of the Republic: Lying in Politics, Civil Disobedience, On Violence, Thoughts on Politics and Revolution*, New York, Harcourt Brace Jovanovich, 1972, p. 34.

3. These figures are drawn from John Mueller, *War, Presidents and Public Opinion*, Table 2.2, p. 28, and Figure 2.1, p. 36.

4. Johnson showed me typed notes of this conversation, which were then filed in the LBJ Library under "Fulbright."

5. LBJ/DHK.

6. *Ibid.*

7. *Ibid.*

8. *Ibid.* Monologues like this one, which I heard in 1971, are said by Bill Moyers and Richard Goodwin to have taken place as early as 1965 and to have continued with increasing frequency as the years went by.

9. These concepts are more fully developed in Albert Hirschman,

Exit, Voice and Loyalty: Responses to Decline in Firms, Organizations, and States, Cambridge, Harvard University Press, 1970.

10. Richard Neustadt, *Presidential Power,* Chapter 3, pp. 33–57.

11. Alexander George, "The Case for Multiple Advocacy in Making Foreign Policy," *American Political Science Review,* September, 1972, Vol. 66, pp. 751–785.

12. For a discussion of the importance of action channels, see Graham Allison, *Essence of Decision: The Cuban Missile Crisis,* Boston, Little, Brown, 1971, pp. 148–149.

13. The concepts of voice and exit are borrowed from Albert Hirschman, *op. cit.*

14. For a fuller discussion of why the dissenters remained, see Albert Hirschman, *op. cit.*; James Thomson, "How Could Vietnam Happen?," *Atlantic Monthly,* pp. 47–53; and James Thomson, "Getting Out and Speaking Out," *Foreign Policy,* Winter, 1973–74, pp. 49–69.

15. LBJ/DHK.

16. For a description of the increasing isolation in the White House, see David Halberstam in *The Best and the Brightest,* p. 637.

17. LBJ/DHK.

18. These weaknesses are discussed in Henry Graff, *The Tuesday Cabinet: Deliberation and Decision on Peace and War under Lyndon B. Johnson,* Englewood Cliffs, N.J., Prentice-Hall, 1970.

19. See Halberstam on Dean Rusk in David Halberstam, *op. cit.,* pp. 308–346.

20. *Ibid.,* p. 459.

21. Francis Bator, Professor of Economics at Harvard, has described this process in other contexts as well.

22. For a description of the vacuum phenomenon in totalitarian societies, see Carl Friedrich and Zbigniew Brzezinski, *Totalitarian Dictatorship and Autocracy,* Cambridge, Harvard University Press, 1965.

23. Memo to the President, October 15, 1967.

24. Memo to the President, July 19, 1967.

25. Chester Cooper, *The Lost Crusade: America in Vietnam,* New York, Dodd, Mead, 1970.

26. This phenomenon is described in psychoanalytic literature. See Karen Horney, *The Neurotic Personality of Our Time.*

27. George Reedy, *The Twilight of the Presidency,* New York, World, 1970, p. 18.

28. *Ibid.*

29. *CR,* March 2, 1967, p. H2066.

30. This is described by Ira Zaleznik, "Structure and Influence in the U.S. Congress: Voting Patterns on the Vietnam Conflict," Senior Thesis at Harvard University, March, 1974.

31. Francis Wilcox, *op. cit.*

32. Ira Zaleznik, *op. cit.*

33. LBJ/DHK.

34. *Ibid.*

35. *Ibid.*

36. Erik Erikson, *Identity: Youth in Crisis,* New York, Norton, 1968.

37. For an excellent discussion of the youth culture, see Philip Slater, *The Pursuit of Loneliness: American Culture at the Breaking Point,* Boston, Beacon Press, 1970.

38. LBJ/DHK.

39. This analysis of public opinion is drawn from Milton Rosenberg, Sidney Verba, and Philip Converse, *Vietnam and the Silent Majority: The Dove's Guide,* New York, Harper & Row, 1970, pp. 42–48.

Chapter 12/The Withdrawal

1. Halberstam, *op. cit.,* p. 647.

2. This is reported in Townsend Hoopes, *The Limits of Intervention: An Inside Account of How the Johnson Policy of Escalation Was Reversed,* New York, McKay, 1969, pp. 208–209.

3. These figures are taken from the "Gallup Opinion Index," December, 1968.

4. Philip Converse and Warren Miller, "Continuity and Change in American Politics: Parties and Issues in the 1968 Election," *American Political Science Review,* December, 1969.

5. Taken from the total population figures, 1968, published by the Survey Research Center, Ann Arbor, Michigan.

6. Fred Greenstein, "What the President Means to Americans: Presidential Choice Between Elections," in James D. Barber, ed., *Choosing the President,* Englewood Cliffs, N.J., Prentice-Hall, 1974, p. 146.

7. Told to me by Richard Goodwin.

8. Philip Converse and Warren Miller, *op. cit.*

9. Rowe's comment was reported later in the *New York Times,* April 15, 1968.

10. Excerpts from both speeches are found in Townsend Hoopes, *op. cit.,* pp. 205–206.

11. See Harry McPherson, *A Political Education,* Boston, Little, Brown, 1972, pp. 430–431.

12. LBJ/DHK.

13. These observations were gathered from interviews with members of the White House staff.

14. LBJ/DHK.

15. Lyndon Johnson, *The Vantage Point,* pp. 427–431.

16. LBJ/DHK.

17. *Ibid.*

18. Johnson discusses his reasoning in *The Vantage Point,* pp. 426, 427.

19. Quoted in Harry McPherson, *op. cit.,* pp. 433–435.

20. Paper prepared for me by research assistant Tom Karas.

21. Lyndon Johnson, *The Vantage Point,* pp. 451–452.

22. Speech on TV, March 31, 1968.

23. LBJ/DHK.

24. *Ibid.*

25. *Ibid.*

26. *Ibid.*

27. *Ibid.*

28. *Ibid.*

Epilogue

1. Lyndon Johnson, *The Vantage Point,* p. 566.

2. LBJ/DHK. All the quotations from Johnson that follow are from this same source.

Index

About the Author

Doris Kearns was born in Rockville Centre, New York. She graduated from Colby College in 1964 and received her Ph.D. in Government from Harvard University in 1968. In 1967 she was a White House Fellow, assigned first to Secretary of Labor Willard Wirtz and then to the White House. She is now a professor in the Government Department at Harvard University.

She lives in Concord, Massachusetts with her husband and two sons.

More Big Bestsellers from SIGNET

☐ **THE SURVIVOR** by James Herbert. (#E7393—$1.75)

☐ **RIVER RISING** by Jessica North. (#E7391—$1.75)

☐ **THE HIGH VALLEY** by Jessica North. (#W5929—$1.50)

☐ **WHITE FIRES BURNING** by Catherine Dillon.
(#E7351—$1.75)

☐ **CONSTANTINE CAY** by Catherine Dillon.
(#W6892—$1.50)

☐ **FOREVER AMBER** by Kathleen Winsor.
(#J7360—$1.95)

☐ **SMOULDERING FIRES** by Anya Seton.
(#J7276—$1.95)

☐ **HARVEST OF DESIRE** by Rochelle Larkin.
(#J7277—$1.95)

☐ **THE PERSIAN PRICE** by Evelyn Anthony.
(#J7254—$1.95)

☐ **EARTHSOUND** by Arthur Herzog. (#E7255—$1.75)

☐ **THE DEVIL'S OWN** by Christopher Nicole.
(#J7256—$1.95)

☐ **THE GREEK TREASURE** by Irving Stone.
(#E7211—$2.25)

☐ **THE GATES OF HELL** by Harrison Salisbury.
(#E7213—$2.25)

☐ **TERMS OF ENDEARMENT** by Larry McMurtry.
(#J7173—$1.95)

☐ **THE KITCHEN SINK PAPERS** by Mike McGrady.
(#J7212—$1.95)

THE NEW AMERICAN LIBRARY, INC.,
P.O. Box 999, Bergenfield, New Jersey 07621

Please send me the SIGNET BOOKS I have checked above. I am
enclosing $_____(check or money order—no currency
or C.O.D.'s). Please include the list price plus 35¢ a copy to cover
handling and mailing costs. (Prices and numbers are subject to
change without notice.)

Name_____

Address_____

City_____State_____Zip Code_____

Allow at least 4 weeks for delivery

SIGNET Books of Interest

☐ **THE ROCKEFELLERS: An American Dynasty by Peter Collier and David Horowitz.** The story of the most powerful family in America—the myths, the rumors, the scandals, and, above all, the endlessly enthralling, often shocking truth as it has emerged from heretofore secret family sources. A Main Selection of the Book-of-the-Month Club. (#E7451—$2.75)

☐ **ELEANOR AND FRANKLIN by Joseph P. Lash.** Foreword by Arthur M. Schlesinger, Jr. Introduction by Franklin D. Roosevelt, Jr. A number 1 bestseller and winner of the Pulitzer Prize and the National Book Award, this is the intimate chronicle of Eleanor Roosevelt, with its painful secrets and public triumphs. "An exceptionally candid, exhaustive . . . heartrending book."—The New Yorker   (#E7419—$2.50)

☐ **ELEANOR: THE YEARS ALONE by Joseph P. Lash; Foreword by Franklin D. Roosevelt, Jr.** Complete with 16 pages of photographs this is the best-selling companion volume to the prize-winning ELEANOR AND FRANKLIN. "Everyone who read ELEANOR AND FRANKLIN will want to know the end of the story."—Life. "The story Eleanor thought was over when her husband died. . . . It is her capacity for love which shines through these pages."—Los Angeles Times
(#J5627—$1.95)

☐ **MEMOIRS BY HARRY S. TRUMAN: VOL. I, Year of Decisions.** Truman's own story of the crucial first year of his Presidency—the year that marked the end of World War II and the beginning of the Atomic Age. (#J6183—$1.95)

☐ **MEMOIRS BY HARRY S. TRUMAN: VOL. II, Years of Trial and Hope.** Truman discusses his most controversial decisions in this volume covering his administration during the first critical years of the cold war. (#J6184—$1.95)

THE NEW AMERICAN LIBRARY, INC.,
P.O. Box 999, Bergenfield, New Jersey 07621

Please send me the SIGNET BOOKS I have checked above. I am enclosing $_____(check or money order—no currency or C.O.D.'s). Please include the list price plus 35¢ a copy to cover handling and mailing costs. (Prices and numbers are subject to change without notice.)

Name_____

Address_____

City_____State_____Zip Code_____
Allow at least 4 weeks for delivery